Kurt Schumacher

SOURCES OF PHOTOGRAPHS. Frontispiece
and Nos. 2, 3, 4, 7, 8, 9, 11, 15 courtesy S.P.D.,
Bonn. Nos. 1, 5, 6 from private collections. No.
10 courtesy Eugene Kammerman, *Saturday Evening Post,* © 1947 by The Curtis Publishing
Company. Nos. 12, 13 courtesy Arno Scholz.
No. 14 United Press International Photo. No.
16 courtesy Schafgans, Bonn.

Stanford University Press, Stanford, California
London: Oxford University Press
© 1965 by Lewis J. Edinger
Printed by Stanford University Press
Stanford, California, U.S.A.
L.C. 65-12731

Acknowledgments

For providing me with information based on personal recollections and personal papers, I am deeply indebted to all the informants named at the end of the Bibliography, as well as to John J. McCloy, Lucius D. Clay, Willi Eichler, Wilhelm Kromphardt, and Franz Olah.

For assistance in gaining access to informants and source material, I wish to thank Annemarie Renger, Hermann Schmitt-Vockenhausen, Maria Seibert, Dorothea Kollmorgen, Arno Scholz and Margot Schwager of *Der Telegraf* (Berlin), and Herbert Kosok and Rudolf Rothe of the S.P.D. Parteiarchiv (Bonn); Archivinspektor Bartelman of the Stadtarchiv, Esslingen am Neckar; Regierungsrat Dr. Zwoch, Leiter des Benutzungsdienstes der Bibliothek des Deutschen Bundestages (Bonn); Alfred Faust of the Pressestelle des Senats der Freien Hansestadt Bremen; Fritz Ohlig, Bezirkssekretär of the S.P.D. in Stuttgart; and the librarians of the Bibliothek des Deutschen Bundestages, Würrtembergische Landesbibliothek, Princeton University, Michigan State University, Stanford University, and the Hoover Institution on War, Revolution, and Peace.

For advice and criticism, I wish to thank Drs. Richard Bates, David Hamburg, and Jean and Walter Poznanski, as well as staff members of the Neuro-Psychiatric Clinic, Ford Hospital, Detroit; also Robert Lane, Harold Guetzkow, Milton Rokeach, Herbert McClosky, Gabriel A. Almond, and Sigmund Neumann, as well as my students at Michigan State University and Washington University.

For research, editorial, and clerical assistance, I would like to thank Hilda Jaffee, Hanne and Peter Pollmann, Dieter Piel, Alvin Magid, Gerhart Schneider, Hanni Edinger, Larry Gillingham, Ruth G. Zimmerman, David P. Demarest, Jr., Theodore Fiedler, Roger Benjamin, and Pauline Wickham, as well as members of the clerical staff of Michigan State University and the Social Science Institute of Washington University.

I am indebted to the United States Educational Commission in the Federal

Republic of Germany for the award of a senior research fellowship, to the Social Science Research Council for a faculty research grant, to the All-University Research Fund of Michigan State University and the Graduate School of Arts and Sciences, Washington University, for additional financial assistance, to Professor Otto Stammer and his colleagues of the Institute für Politische Wissenschaft an der Freien Universität Berlin for their hospitality during the year 1959–60, and to Michigan State University for released time from regular teaching duties in the fall quarter of 1962.

Finally, I owe a special intellectual debt to Harold D. Lasswell, Alexander and Juliette George, Karl W. Deutsch, Erik H. Erikson, Talcott Parsons, Neal Gross, Ward S. Mason, Alexander W. McEachern, John Wahlke, and Heinz Eulau, who directly or indirectly helped me to formulate many of the thoughts that went into this study.

Washington University, St. Louis
February 1965   LEWIS J. EDINGER

Contents

Kurt Schumacher

Do not forget you are a German socialist, and should and must work for Germany.

FERDINAND LASSALLE
in a letter to KARL MARX

Everything depended on the initiative of the right leader.

KURT SCHUMACHER'S
doctoral dissertation

Introduction

At the end of World War II a prominent American political scientist declared that the political reconstruction of post-Nazi Germany should be placed in the care of native Germans "on whose backs in concentration camps the lash has written the new gospel in blood and tears."[1] This was the view of many people. Even before the war had ended, government and opinion leaders in the victor countries were saying that postwar Germany should be led by men who represented a complete break with the past and gave promise of guiding their people in a direction diametrically opposite that taken by the fallen regime.

Kurt Schumacher, postwar leader of the German Social Democratic Party (S.P.D.) until his death in 1952, seemed just such a man. He could claim a record of consistent, courageous, and uncompromising opposition to the Nazis; his personal qualities were likely to assure him respect and support at home and abroad; and his proclaimed aim was to establish a new, democratic Germany that would never again threaten world peace and stability. For seven years he was undoubtedly the most prominent German politician; only during the last years of his life did his great adversary, Konrad Adenauer, begin to rival him inside and outside Germany.

But when he died in August 1952, the sighs of relief upon his passing easily exceeded the tears that were shed for him. As the *Manchester Guardian* correspondent noted at his death, "No postwar figure on the German political stage aroused feelings of fiercer animosity or more devoted partisanship."[2] Some said that his service in trying to establish a democratic system in postwar Germany had been immense; others felt that he had obstructed political reconstruction by his fanatical nationalism, hysterical demagoguery, and authoritarian party leadership. Even before his death, this controversial figure had been something of a myth, surrounded by numerous legends assiduously fostered by friend and foe alike. Since then, the passage of time has obscured his motives and actions still further.

One purpose of this study is to separate the man from the myth, and to explain behavior that in so many ways seems contradictory and even self-defeating. I have not sought to write a definitive biography in the conventional sense; instead, I have focused on those aspects of the man's life that bear on his postwar political behavior. A reader interested in a detailed account of Schumacher's life will not find it here. I have tried neither to improve upon two highly favorable biographies published soon after his death,[3] nor to join the ranks of his many critics. My aim is to explain—rather than to defend or attack—the behavior of a political actor in various settings and situations.

My second major purpose lies in the realm of theory and method. This book is intended to be a case history illustrating an approach to the study of political leadership. By focusing on the interaction between Schumacher's personality and the setting in which he operated, we may gain a better understanding not only of his behavior, but, hopefully, of the behavior of other actors seeking political leadership. Here let me pause to review the present state of biography among political scientists, and to set down briefly my own methods. We can then return to Kurt Schumacher, whom we shall be able to see, from this special perspective, as "a case study."

American political scientists take a paradoxical, if understandable, attitude toward biography: we assert that the study of individual leadership is basic to the theoretical study of politics in general, yet we prefer to leave it to others to write about the individual political leader. We tend, in fact, to look with some disdain at the most recurrent modes of political biography: the "descriptive," which assumes that the facts *per se* are enlightening; the "literary," which depends primarily on imaginative empathy; and even the "historical," which attempts a combination of the first two modes. The result has been a widening gap between self-professed humanists and social scientists, at the expense of advances in the analysis of individual political leadership.

Reasons can be found for this attitude.[4] One may be the process of political socialization in America, which has led American scholars to emphasize the group. They allow the importance of an individual leader, but they usually consider the "hero-leader" (who continues to fascinate European scholars) an aberrant. This bias may be compounded in the older generation of American social scientists by personal involvement in the left-of-center political views of the 1930's, views that attribute decisive political influence to social and economic factors rather than to individual leaders.

But clearly the main reasons for the political scientist's ambivalence about biography are to be found in his conception of the discipline of political science itself. More and more the profession has embraced the so-called behavioral approach, which is characterized by a conscious striving for a "science of politics." This involves "a theoretical search for stable units of analysis" that can be subjected to explicit, testable propositions in order to establish empirically and logically acceptable generalizations.[5] In general, the "attempt to make the empirical component of the discipline more scientific"[6] has involved (1) a preference for quantitative analysis of objectively selected data, (2) insistence on an explicit conceptual framework, (3) a demand for a research design that permits replication, and (4) an emphasis on research and analysis specifically focused on the development and elaboration of theories of political behavior.

Narrowly conceived, such an approach seems well-nigh irreconcilable with the study of individual political leadership. Consider the problem of data: the political scientist may turn up little empirical information in an area in which private communication between individuals can be so important (and can be rendered more private by such modern inventions as the telephone), and in a situation in which a man's followers may be unaware of why, how, or even where they are being led. The behaviorally oriented political scientist cannot simply assume that a leader leads, or that the measure of his influence on men and events can be inferred from their reactions; he demands empirical proof of an explicit cause-and-effect relationship. The problem is compounded by the complexity of a leader's motivations, the difficulty of discovering, identifying, and attributing motives; again in this regard it is practically impossible to satisfy the requirements of the behavioral approach.* Further, the conceptual models most used by political scientists are not readily adaptable to the study of individual leadership. Both the rational-behavior model, for which political scientists are largely indebted to economists, and the group-behavior model, derived from social psychology, sociology, and social anthropology, de-emphasize the specific and unique aspects of leadership. In both models, a given leader's specific personality characteristics tend to be factored out as irrelevant or more or less unimportant.

Where does this leave us? Does it mean that the present-day "behavioral mood" in American political science is irreconcilable with insistent demands for applied research on the behavior of individual leaders? Do the rules of the game disqualify political scientists from applying their skills to a subject which, according to their informal comments, they regard as important? Must we forfeit the rights of analysis to people we consider inadequate for the task? Or do we have a public as well as a scholarly obligation to participate ourselves?

We can, it seems to me, strive to have the best of both worlds—that of the humanist and that of the social scientist. By bringing to bear some of the findings and methods of the behavioral approach, we should be able to achieve a more sophisticated and objective understanding of individual political leadership than is present in much of the popular literature. At the same time, we must go beyond collecting and collating available data, and make judicious

* Admittedly, it is exceedingly difficult to study the behavior of political leaders objectively and accurately, given our frequent personal involvement and the problem of procuring reliable data. As Robert McIver has pointed out (p. 209), the outsider can "read motives only through their manifestations"; Freud (p. 208), like many historians, recognized that even the best analytical techniques and the most abundant data can provide only a possible, not a certain, explanation of why a given leader behaved as he did and took one action rather than another.

use of imaginative thinking to capture the mood of a man and his times. In short, I propose that for the analysis of individual political leaders we employ conceptual models and quantitative analysis in conjunction with a frank but disciplined use of empathy and other forms of imaginative speculation.

If we are to understand the workings of the individual political leader, we must start by defining our terms. The most familiar and objective definitions of leadership are the "positional-ascriptive," which speaks of formal, institutionalized roles, and the "behaviorally descriptive," which examines the performance, the actual ways and means, of the leader. These are safe approaches, but they will not lead us to the particularities of individual personality. If we are truly to catch the conscience of the king, we must deal with the nature of the central actor himself; our definition must be cognitive and attitudinal. Who or what a leader is can be established—over and beyond the familiar perspectives just mentioned—in terms of the man's subjective perception. That is, leadership can be seen as an attitudinal phenomenon in the mind of an actor, who ascribes it to others, to himself, or to both, and responds accordingly to his social environment. He may aspire to lead because he considers himself a leader; he may follow or want to follow others or delegate authority to them because he attributes leadership qualities to them. In this sense, leadership is subjective orientation to a situation, not actual behavior, and its functionality can be evaluated in terms of the individual actor's personality needs, such as ego satisfaction and tension reduction—even though this satisfaction of conscious or unconscious personal goals may not correspond to rationally posited or group-oriented goals and norms.

This does not imply that we should focus on the actor's personality to the exclusion of situational variables; such a method would be no more to the point than its opposite extreme—simply tabulating situational data.* The appropriate way to study leadership is to examine the interaction of the actor's personality and the situation. What concerns us here, of course, is political leadership, as distinguished from leadership in general.† We have already been speaking of our subject as the *central actor,* and we shall discover other

* The skepticism of American political scientists about the possibility of arriving at a useful conception of the impact of personality on politics seems to derive from an uncertainty about whether the leader's personality or the situation in which he operates is more important (as Harold D. Lasswell noted in Christie and Jahoda, eds., p. 203). For purposes of analysis, this is a misleading and unnecessarily confusing pseudo-problem. Neither individual character structure nor the contextual configuration can by itself explain a leader's behavior; but careful analysis of their interaction, in as many instances as possible, may reveal certain patterns and facilitate understanding.

† Political leadership focuses on what David Easton has called the authoritative allocation of values in a community, and involves both the attempted exercise, and the actual exercise, of the power to make policy choices between alternative courses of action affecting the distribution of values. The study of political leadership thus calls for analysis of the interaction between the decision-makers and those who are subject to the decisions, as well as the struggle of individuals and groups for direct or indirect influence over these decisions as a means to realizing certain of their values and interests. In other words, it deals not only with relations between leaders and followers, but with

useful terms by pausing for a moment on that time-honored comparison of politics and the theater.[7] The principal actor, center stage, occupies the *focal position*; interacting with him are various *counter-players*, who make their entrances and exits as the setting changes. We the audience, nonparticipants, see the whole stage—the total situation, the dynamic interaction of all the roles, the composite tableau of given, interlocking roles that we may call a *role-set*. The objective environment, i.e. the stage as we see it, must be kept explicitly distinct at all times from the subjective perceptions of the actors, i.e. their psychological environment.* And if empathy is unavoidably one of our tools, we must not project our own standards into the minds of the actors.

Insofar as the roles we have been visualizing constitute "the individual's attempt to structure his social reality, to define his place within it, and to guide his search for meaning and gratification," as a social psychologist has expressed it, they constitute "an ego achievement."[8] That is, the actor strives to satisfy personality needs through the assumption and performance of certain roles. Thus, a political actor's orientation to a situation, his opinions, and his style of role behavior are shaped by the interplay of personality characteristics and the perceived demands of his political environment. This applies in particular to how he perceives and reacts to sanctions, the primary significance of which is gratificational-deprivational in terms of expectations and behavior.[9] Consciously or unconsciously, the actor chooses, performs, and reacts to certain roles in order to gratify some needs or to avoid denial of their satisfaction. How closely he conforms to "legitimate" role expectations will depend on whether he is prepared to accept or reject internal sanctions (i.e., sanctions that he applies to himself) and external sanctions (i.e., those that someone else appears in a position to apply to him), and on how willing he is to postpone

the interaction between different leaders, between the leaders of one political group and the members of another, between potential leaders and potential followers, and between actual leaders and aspiring leaders. See Easton, pp. 130ff. See also Gabriel A. Almond in Almond and Coleman, eds., pp. 5–58; Lester Seligmann in Eulau, Eldersveld, and Janowitz, eds., pp. 181–82.

* The cognitive approach to role analysis uses the concept of role to interpret interpersonal behavior in terms of phenomena that are assumed or inferred to take place in the minds of the actors in a system of social relationships, and that are seen as mediating between situational stimuli and behavioral responses. In this sense, *role* means a set of expectations applied to the incumbent of a position in a social relationship, *expectations* means an evaluative standard applied to the incumbent, and *role behavior* is the perceived performance of the incumbent, which can be referred to an expectation for an incumbent of such a position. Such expectations may relate to attributes, behavior, or both.

An actor may hold such expectations about the incumbent of a particular perceived position, against which he will evaluate what he sees as the actual behavior and qualities of the incumbent. He may himself occupy the perceived position, in which case comparison of expected and actual attributes and/or performance takes the form of self-evaluation, or he may evaluate the incumbents of other positions in terms of his expectations. He may also hold expectations and make evaluations about how other actors should and do perceive him. In short, the attributes and behavior of the incumbent of any particular perceived position in a social relationship are evaluated by the participant observer in terms of conformity with, or departure from, the expectations he holds about such a position.

gratification to further his goals (i.e., perceived and desired future states of affairs). A number of roles are thus available to the aspirant for political leadership. Which of these he chooses to play and how he chooses to play them depends at bottom on his personality characteristics.

In this actor-centered model we have been describing, the test of successful and effective political leadership will be the apparent congruence of the aspiring or actual leader's role perception with the perceptions of his counterplayers in a given role-set. Such a person may be sustained in his role behavior in a particular role-set if his counter-players more or less share the legitimacy expectations he brings to his position, as in the case of the party bureaucrat sustained by organizational norms or the prime minister who is seen as acting in the public interest. He may successfully perform in accordance with his expectations because the other actors believe he is realizing group goals or reconciling apparently conflicting subgroup and individual interests. Lack of congruence between his role perception and the perceptions of the others may be skillfully concealed—for a time at least—if the actor can persuade other relevant actors that he shares their goals (when in fact he does not), that he is performing a sanctioned role in a legitimate fashion, or that the king can do no wrong. Despite actual incongruence, the exercise of leadership at this point is still functional in terms of the incumbent's efforts to direct the collective behavior of the group. In the case of a persistent incongruence perceived by the other actors and unmeliorated by changes in the situation, the leader's role performance, or both, the central actor will face political overthrow.

Within this broad framework, however, it is abundantly clear that we must concern ourselves intensively with the personality of our leading actor—especially with those variables that relate to his political motivations, attitudes, and responses.* No one personality model will be adequate for our purpose; we must be eclectic and holistic. In examining the development of his personality, we must consider antecedent as well as contemporaneous events, psychic as well as somatic factors, the "inner man" as well as sociopolitical "outside" variables. With the data available and—where they are inadequate—imaginative theorizing, we must trace the growth of the biological organism and its degree of maturation at various stages in the actor's political career, as well as any somatic factors that may have influenced his role and performance. In considering the psychological development of our subject, we must examine not only his formative childhood experiences, but also the experiences of his

---

* In the actor-centered personality model, "the self" is the intervening variable between situational stimuli and the individual actor's response in role choice and role behavior. Role analysts, insofar as they deal with personality variables, tend to be rather ambiguous in distinguishing between the self and other elements of personality. It is usually posited that the self is only a part of personality, some writers identifying it with the socially oriented aspects of personality, and others with the dynamic organization of attitudes and feelings as distinguished from a more permanent component called "the ego." Because the distinction strikes me as rather vague, I shall take the liberty of using the terms "self" and "personality" interchangeably.

adolescence and adulthood, especially traumatic events or personality crises that may have significantly influenced his subsequent behavior. Nor must we neglect the impact of socialization on personality development, the continuous process by which the individual adjusts and responds to his social and political environment.

Throughout our study we must keep in mind the larger meaning of biography for the political scientist. If it tells us not only what our chief actor did in certain situations but why, a political biography is also a case history, which, when taken in conjunction with similar investigations of other men, should move us toward comparative generalizations about the success or failure of similar men in different situations and different men in similar situations. In studying one person, we strive to identify salient personality and situational variables that may allow us to classify political actors by personality types, behavior, and the context in which they operate. For example, compulsive persons may make effective crisis leaders because the "abnormal" man fits "abnormal" times, whereas the "well-adjusted" person may make a good caucus chairman but an ineffectual revolutionary. Moreover, such case studies may have a predictive value: they may enable us to predict to some extent the future behavior of a given actor, or the behavior of a class of actors with similar characteristics in similar situations, or the type of person most likely to achieve positions of leadership in various situations. For these purposes, political success is irrelevant to the choice of a subject for investigation, for failure can teach us as much as success about the interaction of men and the political situation in which they operate.

To a certain extent, this sort of analysis gives an unbalanced and even distorted picture of the person being studied. Because we are interested only in those factors that seem relevant to his political behavior, we are likely to slight aspects of the "real man" that would interest the descriptive or creative biographer. We seek explanations at a different level and in a different form from the humanistically oriented biographer. By committing ourselves to explicit constructs or models, we sacrifice *a priori* some of the concrete and unique aspects of our subject, and slant our investigation toward those aspects that can be isolated for comparative purposes. This bias seems as unavoidable as it is justifiable. Our concern is not the whole man, but the political actor and the factors bearing upon him as such. The political scientist writing political biography is not trying to displace the humanistic biographer; he merely wants to bring his particular interests and skills to bear upon those aspects of a man's life that will illuminate his political behavior, and through it that of others like or unlike him.

The organization of this study is in part chronological, part topical. Chapters 2–4 trace Schumacher's personality development up to the time of his emergence as a leading figure in postwar German politics. In considering these formative years, we shall try to identify those attitudinal and behavioral characteristics that seem relevant to his subsequent political actions, and to delineate personality patterns that apparently were more or less shaped prior to 1945. Chapter 5 seeks to describe and assess the general perceptions of reality, roles, and goals that appear to have guided Schumacher's behavior in specific situations and relationships in the postwar era. This is followed by three chapters detailing Schumacher's perceptions and behavior in various political settings. Chapter 6 examines Schumacher's relationship with members of his own party and considers the reasons for his success in the position of S.P.D. chairman. Chapter 7 concentrates on his relationship with prominent non-German counter-players in occupied Germany—especially the leaders and officials of the four occupation powers—and considers the reasons for the friction that characterized this relationship. Chapter 8 deals with Schumacher's relationship with his domestic counter-players in the fight for political leadership in West Germany, particularly his conflict with Konrad Adenauer. Finally, in Chapters 9 and 10, I attempt to summarize and interpret Schumacher's postwar political activities in terms of the interaction between personality, role behavior, and political setting.

As I pointed out earlier, in studies of this sort we depend to a considerable extent on inferential analysis in seeking out motives and relating them to behavior. In the case of Schumacher and those who were associated with him as his counter-players, the paucity of available data forced me to go further in this direction than I wished. I have relied mainly on three types of sources: (1) published material, notably Schumacher's writings and speeches and various biographies, memoirs, newspaper reports, and secondary accounts relating to his political activities (see the Bibliography); (2) intensive interviews with about a hundred informants, including many former associates and intimates of his, his physicians, and a number of political opponents and former Allied officials (see the Bibliography, p. 370); and (3) unpublished material, notably Schumacher's papers and letters, his appointment diary for the years 1945–52, and personal written communications to me from persons who either were unavailable for interviews or were interviewed as well.

If the book is not as smooth and readable as I could have wished, this is in part due to the nature of my subject, in part to the nature of my purpose. Schumacher was a dramatic figure and anyone writing about him is tempted to treat him as such. However, it was not my purpose to reinvoke his moments of high drama and thus to make him "live" again. Rather, I have sought to understand him and explain to others what he did and why he did it. And in the process I had to learn that a case history, if it is to be accurate and useful, demands that its author shun the constant temptation to elaborate beyond the limits set by his creative but disciplined imagination, his data, and his analytical framework.

TWO

The Marriage to Politics

Character Development in Childhood and Adolescence

October 13, 1895, was a day of jubilation in the family of Carl and Gertrud Schumacher. Carl, proud and delighted that after five daughters—two of them dead in infancy—he now had a son, placed gold coins and good-luck charms in the crib. Gertrud and the three girls showered affection on the baby. Kurt grew up under comfortable circumstances.* His father, like his father before him, was a well-to-do small businessman in Kulm on the Vistula, a town of about 10,000 inhabitants, in which he and his wife had lived all their lives. Kurt was not a particularly robust child and was inclined to be tense and nervous. Apart from this, though, he was a normal little boy, a bit cheeky and quite frequently involved in scraps with schoolmates. As he grew older, he liked to swim, but was otherwise not interested in athletics or any organized activities. He read a great deal and did well at school, though his record was not outstanding.

Carl Schumacher seems to have played a relatively minor role in his son's development. He had to travel a good deal in connection with his business, and his children always welcomed the temporary respite from his stern rule that such trips afforded them. Kurt, who came in for even stricter treatment than his sisters, would later often refer to his father as "the Russian Government," more facetiously than in awe. Carl occasionally punished the boy for breaches of domestic discipline such as coming home late for dinner, but such measures do not appear to have been particularly effective. Kurt seems to have respected his father, and to have admired him for his moral righteousness, but the relationship was apparently never very intimate. In later years he would remark on his father's passivity, particularly with regard to his intellectual development and future plans. "My father never made the least attempt to win me toward a particular profession or point of view," Schumacher recalled decades later, shortly before his death. "He always told me it was my life and

---

* Schumacher's first name was originally spelled Curt. In 1920, however, at the beginning of his political career, he changed it to Kurt to avoid confusion, he claimed, with his father, who was also C. Schumacher.

it was up to me to make the decisions affecting it."[1] After World War I, Carl lost his entire property and became dependent on his son for support. Evidently discomfited by this altered relationship, Kurt expressed his dismay to a friend shortly before the old man died in 1928. "The Russian Government" had long since fallen from whatever authority it once exercised.

Schumacher inherited his father's tall and slim figure, but in other respects he was more like his mother. Gertrud was an attractive, vivacious, and intelligent woman—"She always hit the nail on the head," said one of her daughters—but was troubled by "nervous ailments" and various other physical complaints, particularly after Kurt had left home for good. All her children adored her as they never did their father, but her relationship with her youngest was especially close. As a child Kurt would seek her protection when in trouble with his father, and she would readily plead his case. She remained "my Trude" for him all his life. On his infrequent visits to her as a grown man, his attitude was as easy and affectionate as it had always been.* As his letters show, he worried about "the sweet old lady" even while he languished in a Nazi concentration camp, feeling that her devoted efforts to ease his lot and gain his freedom remained her sole purpose in life. When she died at seventy-two without having seen him released, her last thoughts were of "my poor boy."

Schumacher's three attractive sisters, all many years older than he, shared their mother's solicitude and affection for "the baby." Lotte, the middle sister, was particularly close to him. Seven years his senior, she married one of Kurt's teachers, when Kurt was still a boy, but remained childless. She was to look after him during two of the most critical periods of his life: just after he lost his arm in 1914, and again after he was released, a physical wreck, from the concentration camp in 1943.

Our information on Schumacher's childhood and adolescence is too scanty to do more than indicate what seems a significant aspect of his immediate family environment: the importance of women, particularly his mother, in his life. They smothered him with affection, they admired him, and his mother shielded him against his father's attempts at punishment. Neither his father nor any other male—teacher, relative, or friend—appears to have had any significant influence on his early character formation.

These feminine influences, particularly his relationship with his mother, may have had two important effects on the boy. First, they may have given him an exaggerated sense of his own importance, since he had few if any male intimates to counterbalance this tendency. Second, he may have developed an increasing disposition to rebel against all this female attention, at the same time that he continued to accept it, by asserting his masculinity and indepen-

---

* One of the sisters recalled how on these visits to Hannover in the 1920's Schumacher would hand his mother an orange to peel, with the plea-command both of them remembered so well from his childhood, "Altchen, krall!" (roughly, "Little old woman, claw!").

dence in spheres he conceived to be outside the feminine realm. As a boy he was involved in occasional fights, and as an adolescent he began to develop political and intellectual interests beyond the comprehension of his mother and sisters. His sisters recalled that he impressed them at this time with his intellectual achievements and his independence of mind.

Early Political Socialization

Schumacher, like all young people, went through a process of political social-ization during which he acquired certain values, images, and expectations concerning the society he grew up in.[2] His home town, Kulm, was close to the eastern borders of the German Empire in what was then the province of West Prussia. Under the name of Chelmno it had been Polish until 1772, as it was again after 1918. A small manufacturing town and trading center for agricultural and horticultural products, it was also a military center for the defense of the eastern frontier against the Slavs, dating back to the days of the Teutonic Knights. Its population of some 10,000, like that of the surrounding countryside, consisted mostly of Roman Catholic Poles, who outnumbered the Lutheran Germans about eleven to one.[3] Most of Kurt's fellow students at the gymnasium were Poles, and when he took his graduating examination in 1914, seventeen Poles and only three other Germans were being examined with him.[4]

The Schumachers belonged to the liberal German bourgeoisie, which, in these West Prussian towns, attempted to mediate between the Lutheran East Elbian landed nobility on the one hand and the Catholic Polish peasants and workers on the other. Schumacher was to recall that the relationship between Germans and Poles in Kulm was a good one; his father, he remembered, was for many years chairman of the city council, thanks to the support of Polish as well as German votes. Nonetheless, latent, and sometimes overt, ethno-religious friction between Germans and Poles certainly existed, and the boy could not escape intimate exposure to it quite early in his life. There were no Poles among his friends, and his family's contacts with them were limited mostly to his father's political and business activities. Schumacher claimed later that his dislike for both the reactionary Polish clergy and the equally reactionary Prussian military turned him toward socialism, and according to a frequently repeated story, living between a Roman Catholic convent and an army barracks left him with no alternative but to become a socialist.

Another element in the socio-religious structure of Kulm that influenced Schumacher's early attitudes was the Jewish community. In Kulm, as in other West Prussian towns, there was little anti-Semitism among the urban German bourgeoisie.* Members of the Jewish community were vehemently anti-Polish

---

* In 1900 an attempt by agitators from Berlin to arouse anti-Semitic feeling by means of a ritual murder trial in Konitz, not far from Kulm, provoked an enormous counter-protest movement among German liberals in general, and the local bourgeoisie in particular.

German patriots, and were joined to the German Lutheran middle class by common economic, political, and cultural interests. The Schumacher children had Jewish friends, and Kurt undoubtedly acquired his pronounced liking for Jewish stories and jokes, Jewish expressions, and Jewish food from these contacts. Throughout his life he chose Jews as friends and associates—extending this preference even to landlords—and reacted with particular bitterness toward anti-Semites.

A third environmental influence in young Schumacher's political socialization was the proximity of the Russian border, only about twenty miles away. West Prussia's inhabitants traditionally thought of themselves as the defenders of Western civilization against ever-threatening Russian barbarism. Before World War I, German liberals and socialists in particular identified themselves with Western democratic and libertarian traditions, and looked upon West Prussia as the last outpost and bastion of the West. In young Schumacher the traditions of the "frontier German" (*Grenzdeutschtum*) and the anti-authoritarian values of the liberal German middle class and socialists probably fused to produce a lasting image of authoritarian, uncivilized Russia confronting Germany in the East. Against it he would readily volunteer to bear arms in August 1914, and against it he would wage his fight in the name of a prostrate German people after World War II.

The world beyond the confines of Kulm must have appeared quite stable and secure to the young Schumacher, who, apart from annual vacations with his parents on the Baltic coast, had no opportunity to get to know the world outside. He was growing up in what has been called "the Golden Age of Security."[5] His country was one of the leading world powers and had been at peace for decades. Its economy was booming; its army seemed unbeatable; German scholars and artists were attracting world-wide attention and admiration. A record of rapid industrial growth, scientific progress, and technological advances seemed to promise a continuing rise in the standard of living and the national product. Few Germans seriously feared the outbreak of a major war.

As we noted, Carl Schumacher—himself not a member of a party but in sympathy with the left-of-center Progressives—allowed Kurt to form his own political opinions. The boy began to show a definite interest in politics in his early teens, which was not unusual for a youngster of his background and intelligence. Many of his contemporaries were joining the various youth groups which, in one form or another, protested against what they saw as shortcomings of the Imperial state. Kurt, however, did not join any of these organizations, and remained apart from his closest friends in his political interests and views.

Young Schumacher seems to have been a lone wolf in his intellectual development in general and his political education in particular. There is no indication that anyone—father, teacher, friend—gave him specific guidance. The independence of his political views must have been noticed by his teachers, but in later years he could not recall that this ever brought him any difficulty or serious criticism from them. His family was made aware of his growing social consciousness when he began demanding better hours for the Schumacher maids—a cause for amusement more than concern. His mother jokingly called him a Social Democrat. He began to interest himself in local labor problems, and on one occasion derived great pleasure from being taken for one of the workers at a strike meeting of the local brewery. His father subscribed to the *Berliner Tageblatt,* a daily representing the viewpoint of the liberal democratic opposition in Prussia, and this was the boy's chief source of information about the world beyond Kulm. When he was seventeen, Kurt became a subscriber to *Der März,* a South German literary journal that had just started, and *Die Sozialistische Monatshefte,* a Social Democratic periodical. *Der März* was published by two well-known novelists, Ludwig Thoma and Hermann Hesse. *Die Sozialistische Monatshefte* was the organ of Eduard Bernstein, the Social Democratic critic of orthodox and revolutionary Marxism, whose Revisionism served as a theoretical underpinning for the reformist elements in his party who wanted "more for the better present and less for the better future." Schumacher evidently read the one journal to educate himself in the literary field, and the other to obtain political information.

Schumacher's own recollections indicate that before World War I his political views and values were still rather unformed.[6] Like many of his contemporaries in other parts of Germany, he found much to criticize in the prevailing social, economic, and political order. The situation in Kulm no doubt aroused his awareness of the problems of ethno-religious conflict in general and German-Polish differences in particular. Although he received no particular religious training, his family being quite casual about its membership in the Lutheran Church, he was shocked by the intolerance of the Roman Catholic Polish clergy on the one hand and the German Lutheran pastors on the other; he thus acquired early a lasting dislike for the clerical leadership of the established churches, though he was never to be anti-religious. The proximity of Russia and the image of that country and its government which he derived from his immediate environment, as well as from the liberal and socialist publications he read, may have influenced his later views toward the Soviet Union. He came to identify himself and his country with Western European civilization, but at the same time thought of himself as a German first and a European only afterwards.

Schumacher was unable to recall in later years whether the Social Democratic party was active in Kulm or was even represented there. He could remember no direct contacts with the party or any of its affiliates, such as its youth group.[7] It may have attracted him already at this point as a party of progress and opposition—in 1912 the S.P.D. won a smashing electoral victory to become the party with the largest representation in the Reichstag—but there is nothing to prove that before World War I he had contemplated the "marriage to politics" he was to enter at the end of the war.

The future must have looked rather pleasant for young Schumacher in 1914. He faced a year of military training following his graduation from the gymnasium in 1915, after which he intended to start his university studies. He was interested in journalism, law, and politics, but apparently had no definite ideas about his future career. For an intelligent and presentable young man of Schumacher's social background and education, the prosperous society of prewar Germany offered quite a few possibilities. Carl Schumacher accepted Kurt's plans and was ready to foot the bill for his university education. Apparently there was never any question of Kurt's becoming a businessman like his father and grandfather. Like many a bourgeois father at the time, Carl may have been rather pleased at the idea of his son's getting a doctorate and rising in the social hierarchy. His oldest daughter had become a teacher, and the two younger ones had married university-trained high school teachers (*Studienräte*) employed in neighboring towns. The Schumachers could hardly know that within six years they would be forced to leave their home in Kulm forever.

Thus Kurt's memories were of a secure and pleasant youth. Some thirty years later, he spoke of thinking "often and with great pleasure" of "das alte Nest an der Weichsel," and claimed that he would rather be living in Kulm than anywhere else in the world.[8] The expression "das alte Nest" conveys a meaning far beyond a sleepy hick town. The home on the Vistula had indeed been a "nest," the place in which Kurt spent the most secure and relaxed period of his life, and it was scarcely surprising that he looked back on it fondly and often.

The Cripple

The outbreak of war on August 4, 1914, was greeted with enthusiasm in all parts of Germany. The conflict was expected to be short and inspiring, and to end in a German victory. Max Weber spoke of "this great and glorious war," and regretted being too old to fight in it.[9] A fellow scholar wrote that Germany had become the defender of "constitutional legitimacy against Russian autocracy, of the Germanic race against the onslaught of the Slavs, a bulwark of European civilization against Asiatic barbarism."[10] Social Democrats, liberal democrats, and others formerly in opposition enthusiastically supported what they felt was primarily a war against Russian autocracy, hoping that Germany would emerge from the conflict not only stronger but more democratic.

Kurt Schumacher, not yet nineteen, rushed to volunteer his services—after taking an emergency graduating examination (*Notabitur*)—on August 3, 1914. He was undoubtedly seized by the patriotic fervor that gripped young men throughout the country, particularly in the border regions closest to Russia; he was decidedly not a pacifist, and Kulm was an obvious target for the Russian armies only a short distance away. But his eagerness to enlist may have been motivated, too, by a desire to break away from the predominantly feminine influences at home—in the most masculine way of all. After a few weeks of training in nearby Thorn, Kurt became worried when immediate German successes against the Russians seemed likely to bring an end to the war before he had had a chance to prove himself in action. Hoping to be moved to the front more quickly, he requested transfer from the artillery to the infantry—without letting his family know. The request was granted, and after five weeks of infantry training he was sent into action. On December 2, less than a month later, he was gravely wounded in an attack near Lodz across open ground without proper artillery cover. He was hit by shrapnel and machine-gun fire, and two bullets through his right arm shattered the bone. After many agonizing hours on the battlefield, he was finally taken to the rear, where doctors removed the entire arm up to the armpit. Barely nineteen, Schumacher had become a cripple for life."[11]

Exactly five years elapsed between the battle near Lodz and the formal start of Schumacher's political career with his arrival in Stuttgart to work on the *Tagwacht*. These years are probably of critical importance in the development of his personality, yet they are also the years about which the least is known. Schumacher refused to talk about them later, and did not keep up with any of the people he had known in this phase of his life. This was the period during which he grew into a man, and more particularly a political man, the period that culminated in what he described as his "marriage to politics."[12]

It took Schumacher almost a year to learn to function sufficiently without his right arm to be discharged from the army. The nature of the amputation made it impossible for him to wear an artificial arm, and for the rest of his life he was troubled by painful contractions of the "phantom limb." Never robust, his constitution was badly undermined by his injuries. Shrapnel fragments remaining in his body and a serious case of dysentery were to trouble him for many years to come. No doubt the need to learn to live with these physical discomforts was a considerable drain on his nervous energy, aggravating a condition of tension that had troubled him since childhood. Various observers later attributed his tenseness and aggressiveness exclusively to these physical causes, but though they certainly influenced his development, they are not in themselves sufficient to explain the transformation that his personality appears to have undergone after he was crippled.*

* Many German commentators appear to apply to Schumacher's case, implicitly or explicitly, Kretschmer's theory regarding the influence of bodily irritations on behavior. His appearance and behavior after 1945 seemed to many to mark him as the "asthenic type" *par excellence*: the lean and bitter agitator. This typology, however, attributes to the younger Schumacher personality characteristics based purely on his appearance and behavior when he was in his fifties.

Schumacher had to learn to live not only with pain, but with one arm. Such an adjustment is never easy, and it must have been particularly difficult for someone of his youth and temperament. Clinical observations indicate that the patient's somatically determined condition tends to exert a strong influence on his personality development as the effort to adjust physically is paralleled by an effort to adjust psychically. The crippled person must cope with the changed meaning his physique now holds for him and seems likely to hold for others, with changes in his self-image and in his expectations concerning the response of others, with what he believes he can and cannot do with his crippled body, and with the effect all this is likely to have on his future. The manner in which this psychic adaptation is attempted (whether or not it succeeds), and how it influences attitudes and behavior, depend on the total structure of the personality at the time of the trauma, its previous development, and its latent defense mechanisms.[13]

Recent studies of the somato-psychological problems following the amputation of a limb indicate that—at least in Western societies—the patient experiences a loss of self-esteem and feelings of helplessness and anxiety about the real or imagined consequences of the amputation. And, in many cases, his attitudes and behavior change as he invokes various defense mechanisms against these disturbing emotions.[14]

Kurt Schumacher was still in his teens when he lost his arm, an age beset with tensions in any case. Erik H. Erikson writes of an "identity crisis" during which a young person strives to find a stable image of himself and his relations to the social environment, to "forge for himself some central perspective and direction, some working unity, out of the effective remnants of his childhood and the hopes of his anticipated adulthood; ... some meaningful resemblance between what he has come to see in himself and what his sharpened awareness tells him others judge and expect him to be." In some young people this crisis may be slight; in others it "will be clearly marked off as a ... kind of 'second birth,' apt to be aggravated either by widespread neuroticisms or by pervasive ideological unrest."[15] Our examination of Schumacher's previous development points to the distinct possibility that he was entering upon such an "identity crisis," or was perhaps already in the midst of it, when he lost his arm. In this case, the experience must have been even more traumatic for him than it would have been for an older man.

The picture of Schumacher which emerges at this time is that of a young man, only a few months out of the security of his early adolescence, who is suddenly confronted by an extreme challenge to his self-esteem at a critical phase in his character development. He had left home to prove he was a man; now he would never be a "whole man." He wanted to be independent, but now it seemed that he would be forever requiring assistance. We must remember that this was but the beginning of the war, and that cripples were far more of a rarity than they were later on. In 1915, Schumacher may have seen himself as an oddity and a perennial outsider, set apart from normal men by his handicap.

After a lonely year of recuperation and physical therapy in various military hospitals, instead of going home he went to Halle, and soon after to Leipzig to begin his university studies. One of his pretty young girl cousins, who came to know him well during this period, recalled that he shut himself in his room and would see no one on the second anniversary of the loss of his arm. She had the distinct impression that he did not consider himself "a whole man" and went out of his way to assert his virility. He liked to tell ribald stories in mixed company, to play the protective male with his girl cousins, and to engage in heated man-to-man political arguments with their father. He became a chain-smoker on the day of his injury. It helped to control the pain and to stimulate his mind, he said. Also, nicotine is believed to increase self-esteem and reduce anxiety.[16]

Our evidence is admittedly limited and circumstantial, but, taken together with what we have concluded about Schumacher's earlier character development, it points to a severe personality crisis after the amputation. On the basis of similar clinical cases, we see Schumacher confronted by a situation to which he could react either by denying its reality, the psychotic "solution," or by facing and adapting to it. Unless he was to succumb to a full-fledged psychosis, he had to recover his self-esteem and overcome feelings of inferiority and weakness by achieving a new, satisfying self-image. He sought this new image, it seems, by finding a sphere of competence in which he could "prove" to himself and others that a one-armed, ailing cripple could be not only a man, but perhaps a better man than others. This special sphere was politics.

Various writers have noted that a striving for political power may be a compensatory reaction against a low estimate of the self, a device for repairing crushed self-esteem and relieving anxiety arising from feelings of hostility, weakness, humiliation, or inferiority.[17] Political behavior that appears to some as arrogant and aggressive, and to others as charismatic and militant, may in fact derive ultimately from the need for self-expression.[18] It is my contention that Schumacher chose a career in politics because it permitted him to satisfy his private needs in a socially and ethically acceptable manner.

As we have already noted, Schumacher's interest in the politics of reform began when he was quite young. Social democracy, in particular, attracted his attention as a means to correct what seemed to him political, social, and economic shortcomings in his environment. His personal experience and observations during the war years, as well as his university studies in law, economics, and political science (*Staatswissenschaften*), continued this earlier process of political socialization, and culminated in his joining the Social Democratic Party toward the end of the war.

The enthusiasm of August 1914 had quickly evaporated in Germany, and by the time Schumacher was discharged—decorated with an Iron Cross, Second Class—it was evident that the war was going to be long and bloody. Schumacher matriculated at the University of Halle for the winter semester 1915-16, then switched to the University of Leipzig for a year, and went to Berlin in the spring of 1917. He was thrown into an entirely new environment from which to view the disintegration of the increasingly authoritarian German Empire. We know little about his life at this time, but for a young man from the provinces both the intellectual climate at the universities and the political climate in all three cities must have been stimulating influences.*

The Halle-Leipzig area was a center of radical socialist activity against the war and the German ruling elites, particularly after the split of the Social Democratic Party in 1916. Schumacher, however, adopted the values of the "social-patriotic" leaders of the Majority Social Democrats. His cousin, who saw him almost daily in this period, recalled that he echoed their moderate criticism of the prevailing political and social system and the annexationist ambitions of the ruling groups, but could remember no expressions of pacifist or unpatriotic sentiments. Schumacher himself, when pressed some thirty-five years later to name the political leaders he admired at the time, refused to commit himself, claiming he was more interested in ideas than men.[19] However, his chief sponsor after he joined the S.P.D. was Konrad Haenisch, one of the principal extreme right-wing "social-patriotic" leaders, who vehemently proclaimed his loyalty to the nation and its war effort during the war.

We do not know what caused Schumacher to shift his university studies to Berlin in the spring of 1917, but it seems likely that political ambitions influenced the decision. It was becoming clear that major upheavals inside and outside Germany were in the offing, and that the future of the Majority Social Democratic Party would be affected. Although the split in the party ostensibly caused Schumacher to defer joining it,[20] his values and ambitions had probably matured sufficiently by this time to need only the catalytic developments of the following year to push him into membership. The collapse of the Czarist regime, Germany's declaration of unrestricted submarine warfare, the entry of the United States into the war, and the rapidly increasing war-weariness, starvation, and industrial unrest were all intimations of the changes to come. In April almost a quarter of the workers in Berlin struck in protest over alleged inequities in food rationing; in July a majority of the Reichstag called for immediate peace without annexations; in November

---

* In Berlin, Schumacher's closest friend was another disabled veteran, Walter Kromphardt, who also studied law and political science. Kromphardt, however, did not join the S.P.D., but became affiliated with the Deutsche Volkspartei, the party of the big industrial interests, as a political editor. His certainly was not an influence likely to have drawn Schumacher to the S.P.D. Letters from Friedrich W. Kromphardt, August 20, 1961, and Professor Wilhelm Kromphardt, May 3, 1960.

came the Bolshevik Revolution; in January 1918, 180,000 armament workers struck in Berlin.

For Schumacher this must have been an exciting, even intoxicating, period, and one wonders how much time he found for his university studies. Berlin had probably always been the center of his political universe, even when he was in Kulm; it was certainly to be that from now on. Schumacher spent only a few years of his life in the capital, but it became his new home town, the birthplace of the political man and the focal point of his interests, both political and intellectual. As he told the Württemberg Diet in 1928, Berlin was the place where "questions affecting the future of the German Reich are decided."[21] He even developed some of the characteristics generally associated with native Berliners, particularly their quick-wittedness and sarcasm. The turmoil of this wartime capital must have suited his mood perfectly. Here he could indulge the propensity to frantic activity that was to characterize the whole of his political career. On January 9, 1918—aged twenty-two —he joined the Social Democratic Party.

The Marriage to Politics Is Consummated

Kurt Schumacher had just turned twenty-three when the Revolution of November 1918 signaled the ignominious end of the Imperial regime. The complete collapse of the old order, the attitude of the Emperor and the Allied Powers, and fear of Bolshevism, civil war, and utter chaos forced the leaders of the Majority Social Democrats to proclaim and take charge of a Republic that neither they nor the German people were prepared for, or even wanted. Ebert, Scheidemann, Noske, and other "social-patriotic" leaders considered themselves Germans, democrats, and socialists, in that order. Upon assuming control, they considered it their principal duty to keep the state on its feet until a democratically chosen assembly could select a permanent government. With the example of the Bolshevik Revolution before them, they felt that the government by Workers' and Soldiers' Councils that was demanded by the more radical Independent Social Democrats would be a prelude to dictatorship, Allied intervention, and civil war. They believed that their party's duty was to end the war, prevent civil strife, and revive as quickly as possible the paralyzed organs of state and society. The state was not to be overthrown, but to be saved from further disintegration; if it was to become socialist, let the decision be made by a majority vote of the entire adult population, not by a proletarian dictatorship of a minority. They did not hesitate to use the forces of the military high command to crush the social revolutionaries; they considered themselves morally bound to permit a democratic vote to settle the future of Germany. They kept immediate reforms of the political and economic structure to a minimum, not wishing to encroach upon the rights of a properly constituted majority government.

The formation of a government posed a problem. The election of the Constituent Assembly in 1919 gave the Majority Social Democrats only 38 per cent of the vote, and a coalition with the radical Independents proved impossible; the Majority Social Democrats were therefore obliged to form the so-called Weimar Coalition with the liberal middle-class Democrats and the Roman Catholic Center Party. This completed the S.P.D.'s forced shift to the right; in only a few months the party had been constrained to accept a new position in German political life. Its reformist leaders were considered responsible for the conclusion of the armistice, the suppression of the radicals, and the proclamation of the Republic, whose founding fathers they had thus become. Their prewar opposition to the state had to be abandoned, since the state's welfare and security now rested primarily upon their shoulders.

The Revolution of 1918 was the start of Schumacher's political career. As a representative of the Association of Disabled War Veterans, he participated in the Soldiers' and Sailors' Council of Greater Berlin and began to speak in public in support of the Majority Social Democratic leadership. In 1919 he managed to find time to take the first of the two state examinations required for admission to the legal profession, although by now he was clearly planning a political career. His university studies in Berlin, however, were cut short by his inability to find a professor to sponsor a dissertation on the development of German socialist ideology and by financial difficulties at home. By the Treaty of Versailles Kulm became Polish, and the Schumacher family, including the girls and their husbands, felt compelled to leave their native soil. Carl Schumacher lost his entire property; not only could he no longer finance his son's education, but he needed money himself. Kurt had to find a job.

Schumacher worked six months in the Ministry of Labor, where he was introduced to Erich Rossmann, a leader of the Association of Disabled War Veterans and also a leading figure in the Social Democratic organization of the state of Württemberg in southwestern Germany. Apparently at the recommendation of the Majority S.P.D. leaders in Berlin, Schumacher was engaged as political editor of the *Schwäbische Tagwacht,* the daily organ of the Württemberg S.P.D. At about the same time, Konrad Haenisch, now the Prussian Minister of Culture, found a sponsor for Schumacher's doctoral dissertation—Professor Johann Plenge of the Wilhelms University of Münster, Westphalia. After studying briefly under Plenge, Schumacher took his preliminary oral examinations in 1920 or 1921, but he did not complete his dissertation until 1926, when he received his doctorate *magna cum laude*.[22] At the beginning of December 1920, he arrived in Stuttgart to start his new job.

Schumacher's "marriage to politics" had begun. The days in Kulm were but a fond memory, the bonds with parents and sisters almost severed. He contributed a sizable portion of his modest income to support his parents, who were living with his sister Lotte and her husband in Hannover, but he saw his family very rarely. His father, a broken man, died in 1928. The friends of his youth had been killed in the war or lost sight of. Kulm became Chelmno, and Kurt was never to see it again.*

In another sense also, there was no returning home. Schumacher had completed the transition to a new existence, a life almost exclusively taken up with the pursuit of political power. He was never to marry. He had entered into a union that was indissoluble because it was indispensable for his psychological well-being.

* Not so another native of Kulm, General Heinz Guderian, who was to return twenty years later at the head of Hitler's armored columns.

THREE

The Socialist Militant

The Setting

In retrospect, the Weimar Republic seemed to have been no more than an interlude between the autocratic Empire and the totalitarian Third Reich, at least so it struck many people, including Kurt Schumacher. The First German Republic was the product of a military defeat that took most Germans completely by surprise, and as a result the legend that Jews, socialists, and other traitors had "stabbed" the unbeaten armies in the back found ready believers from the start. The new democratic and republican political system, more the creature of accident than revolutionary intent, could never claim affective support, since most Germans associated it with the acceptance and fulfillment of a universally unpopular peace treaty that had been signed by its founding fathers. The Weimar Republic was to be remembered as a political system never far from the brink of collapse, caught up in several major economic crises, and unable to satisfy or reconcile the conflicting demands of bitterly antagonistic interest groups. Its governments seemed incapable of dealing with the demands of the growing number of economic, military, and bureaucratic elites, who subtly undermined the democratic system they disliked and distrusted.

The leaders of the S.P.D., the largest party for all but one of the fourteen years of the Republic, had achieved their positions by long and loyal service to party or trade union. The more flamboyant and self-conscious patriotism of men like Scheidemann, Noske, and Haenisch gave way after the Revolution to the capable and honest administration of men like Hermann Müller, Gustav Bauer, Otto Wels, Robert Schmidt, Otto Braun, Karl Severing, and Paul Löbe. Most of them came from the working class, and many had started out as radical or orthodox Marxists, but later turned to a reformist socialism while still retaining an almost religious belief in evolutionary determinism. From Marxism and Positivism they derived their optimistic faith in progress through science and the development of man's reason; from Utopian socialism and Kantian philosophy they culled ethical socialist and liberal humanist beliefs that they substituted for the "irrational" creeds of the churches.

The electoral successes of their party before the war they attributed to its rational appeal; years of experience in party and trade union offices had convinced them that industrialization had created in Germany a mature and disciplined proletariat, which would be joined by the lower middle class and the farmers in building a truly socialist society, once these two groups had been properly enlightened. They willingly attributed to others their own strong sense of duty, fair play, and unemotional "realism," and patterned their political conduct accordingly.

Within the party, the leadership considered skillful and levelheaded negotiators, parliamentarians, and loyal subordinate functionaries to be of greater value than men with charismatic qualities. Such men were accordingly cultivated. Their centralized control of a highly bureaucratized party organization and their unwavering loyalty to party goals served to curb intraparty criticism. The principal party posts did not change hands throughout fourteen years.

For almost the entire life of the Weimar Republic the leaders of the S.P.D. felt obliged to cooperate with nonsocialist parties and governments in order to defend the democratic republic against its enemies. The desire to safeguard the republican foundations of democratic socialism led them to tolerate actions that they knew to be inimical to their immediate partisan interests, and to abandon a position that they realized had been politically more convenient: namely, their absolute opposition to the social and economic order prevailing before 1918. In domestic as in foreign affairs, the need to defend the state they had helped to create forced them to work in coalitions they could not dominate and to tolerate governments they dared not overthrow.

The Independent Social Democratic Party disintegrated soon after the war, but its mass following was inherited by the new Communist Party, which fought bitterly against the Social Democrats throughout the life of the Republic. The Communists' increasingly successful competition caused the S.P.D. leaders to cling to Marxist slogans that were belied by their reformist practices but offered ready targets for the extremists of the right. The S.P.D. sought on the one hand the allegiance of the "class-conscious" workers by offering Marxist programs and slogans, and on the other the support of the middle classes by presenting itself as the *staatserhaltende* party, the principal defender of the "bourgeois" state. Its pleas for international understanding and friendship with the Western powers earned it the undying hatred of all extreme nationalists. Its insistence that Social Democracy defend the national interests was met with derision. While the Communists described the S.P.D. leaders as the "social fascist stooges" of the ruling bourgeoisie, the radicals of the right denounced them as "internationalist Marxist traitors." The S.P.D.

leaders responded by calling the extremists irresponsible, and by seeking ambiguous compromises in their theory and practice between the ideology of the class struggle and the liberalism of the Weimar Constitution, between the eschatological doctrines of Marx and Engels and the reformist "realism" of the thousands of Social Democratic functionaries active in national, state, and municipal affairs.[1]

Stuttgart must have afforded Schumacher a striking contrast to both Kulm and Berlin when he began his political apprenticeship there in December 1920. A predominantly Protestant industrial city in a state with a predominantly Roman Catholic population of small independent farmers, Stuttgart was known throughout Germany for the mildness of its political climate. Not far from France and Switzerland, it had been exposed to political influences that had helped make Württemberg, whose capital it was, perhaps the most liberal state in Germany. In 1848 Stuttgart had offered refuge to the members of the German National Assembly fleeing from the forces of reaction, and in March 1920, just a few months before Schumacher's arrival, it had sheltered the Reich Government and Constituent Assembly when reactionary military elements occupied Berlin in an unsuccessful effort to overthrow the newborn Republic during the Kapp putsch.

An old and beautiful city, Stuttgart was well equipped with theatres, concert halls, and libraries, and had a highly active cultural life. Pleasant hills, covered with vineyards and orchards, rose above the town. Three-quarters of its population of some 340,000 was Protestant, and most of its workers were connected with its many industries, like the Daimler-Benz automobile works, which made Stuttgart the largest industrial center in the state and one of the most important in all southern Germany. With over 73 per cent of the working population engaged in industry, trade, or commerce, and only 2 per cent in agriculture, Stuttgart, along with some smaller Protestant industrial cities, was a stronghold of the left-wing parties and the liberal Democrats, while the Roman Catholic Center and the right-wing parties drew their support primarily from the rural areas and small towns.[2]

The political situation in Württemberg as a whole was rather unfavorable for the Social Democrats when Schumacher arrived on the scene. During the war the city had been one of the centers of radical left-wing strength. However, the Kaiser's abdication in 1918 so alarmed the Majority Social Democratic leaders of Württemberg that they quickly formed a coalition, patterned after the national Weimar Coalition, with the liberal Democrats and the Catholic Center to keep in check any Independent Social Democrat or Communist attempts to establish a radical Soviet government in Stuttgart. Just before Schumacher's arrival, this coalition had come to an end as a result of the combined elections of a national and state legislature in June 1920. The Majority Social Democrats had suffered a staggering defeat at the hands of the dissident

Independents, whose voting strength showed an enormous gain in comparison with the Constituent Assembly elections in January 1919. On the national and state levels, the Majority Social Democrats just managed to outpoll their rivals, but in Greater Stuttgart their votes dropped from 72,208 to 27,927, while the Independents' went up from 13,512 to 34,138, and the Communists' from nothing to 9,915.[3] The Center and the Democratic Party, with 23 and 15 representatives in the new 101-member Parliament, were apparently prepared to continue coalition with the 17 Social Democrats in the chamber, but a majority of the Social Democratic state leaders thought it better to go into opposition.[4] The Social Democrats were not to assume governmental responsibility in Württemberg again—except for a very brief period—until Hitler abolished the state government in 1933.

Role Choice and Role Behavior

The Social Democratic leader who brought Kurt Schumacher to Stuttgart in 1920 was Wilhelm Keil, a leading member of both the German Reichstag and the Württemberg Landtag (state parliament), as well as editor-in-chief of the *Tagwacht* and *de facto* boss of the state organization. Now in his fifties, Keil—who himself had started his political career at Schumacher's age by working on the *Tagwacht*—had hired Schumacher as political editor in the expectation that the young disabled veteran would gradually take over the management of the paper. In engaging a university graduate to play what was conceived to be basically an intellectual rather than a political role, Keil was following a common pattern in the S.P.D. However, since he himself was of humble working-class background and had only a primary education, he was somewhat wary of having an "intellectual" in his employment—particularly in view of his bitter opposition to the largely intellectual leadership of the radical Independent Socialists. But the recommendations that Schumacher's right-wing sponsors in Berlin had given him and the need for a skilled journalist overcame Keil's scruples. "Things did not turn out exactly as expected," Keil later recalled.[5]

Schumacher started off satisfactorily enough, it would seem. He worked hard on the *Tagwacht*, attacking his employers' radical opponents of the Right and Left with considerable skill, particularly in his special column on state politics. Only Keil was allowed to sign his contributions to the paper, but a livelier spirit in both news features and editorials bore witness to the authorship or inspiration of the man who was very soon referred to as the paper's "editor." Schumacher also did his expected duty as the young intellectual the party had imported from Berlin by giving frequent lectures to the faithful in Stuttgart and surrounding areas on such topics as the socialist view of recent German history, the economic injustices of the Treaty of Versailles, and the Communist world revolution. According to reports in the *Tagwacht*, "Dr.

Schumacher"—as he was called from the start though he earned his degree only several years later—quickly became one of the local organization's most popular speakers and lecturers.[6]

It soon became apparent that Schumacher had his own ideas about the nature and possibilities of his position. The disorganized and demoralized local party organization, the challenge of a strong Communist organization in Stuttgart, and the absence of any able younger leaders among the Social Democrats encouraged him to interpret his mandate in a manner that accorded more with the needs of his personality than with Keil's image of the task. Rather than becoming Keil's loyal lieutenant and editorial assistant, he interpreted the situation as a challenge and an opportunity to prove himself in the field he had chosen as his special competence—politics. The post of political editor on the *Tagwacht* was made to serve his drive for the acquisition of political power.

Schumacher's popularity as a speaker, his untiring and single-minded dedication to political work, and his aggressiveness caught the attention of Karl Oster, district (*Kreis*) secretary of the S.P.D. in Stuttgart and an opponent of Keil. Though there were great differences in the two men's ages and backgrounds, Oster saw in young Schumacher a man who would be able to reorganize and rejuvenate his hard-pressed organization. Oster—rather than Keil—became Schumacher's sponsor and gave him his real start in politics. Less than a year after his arrival, Schumacher was chosen to represent the Stuttgart organization at the national convention of the S.P.D. at Görlitz, and on November 9, 1921, he was Stuttgart's chief speaker for the celebration of the third anniversary of the November Revolution.[7] Before long it became evident to Keil and his associates, as well as to younger and less important party members, that Schumacher was not going to be content to bury himself in the editorial offices of the *Tagwacht*.[8]

Schumacher's associates of those days felt later that he had appeared on the scene at a propitious moment, from the point of view of the local organization as well as his own ambitions. There was strong dissatisfaction with the old-guard state leadership in the Stuttgart organization, above all among the members of the Social Democratic Youth Organization, the Arbeiterjugend, who had no direct say in party affairs. The Arbeiterjugend had lost many members to the youth organization of the new Communist Party—in the key working-class district of Bodnang, its entire membership—and its local leaders were chafing under the heavy hand of the traditionalist party leaders, whom they accused of lethargy, political arteriosclerosis, anachronistic tactics, and oligarchical control. The old guard, for their part, looked upon the auxiliary youth organizations as the traditional instrument for molding future party members and functionaries in their own image and in accordance with their own values, many of which the postwar generation had rejected.[9]

In Schumacher these elements found a young leader who was able to direct their somewhat vague but nonetheless real dissatisfaction. Providing intellectual guidance as well as emotional inspiration, he gave them the sort of leadership they craved. He readily stepped into the role of heroic leader, becoming for them a symbol of uncompromising militancy and fearless dedication. They worshiped and admired him, as some of them were to recall, because he had the willpower and vitality to meet the blatant challenge of left- and right-wing radicalism, qualities that the older party leaders lacked.

Schumacher had a definitely charismatic effect upon his youthful followers. Even decades later, those who had been in his entourage could recall with animation the emotional impact of watching and listening to him. They spoke of the magnetic effect of his piercing eyes, the seemingly inexhaustible vitality of the lean cripple, the empty right sleeve tossed about by the vigorous movements of his gesticulating left arm. He was said to have perspired heavily as he poured his energy into his speeches because he was in almost constant pain from his war wounds.

What had seemed a handicap in the pre-political phase now proved an advantage—the advantage of the crippled veteran, whose extraordinary vigor awed as well as shamed the able-bodied who had neither fought nor been injured in the war. The effect of one's physical appearance on others has a definite impact on one's personality development,[10] and there seems little question that the bonds of Schumacher's "marriage to politics" were strengthened by his conscious or subconscious awareness of the magnetic effect of his physical appearance. In his chosen field of competence, to be crippled was proving to be an asset. In a sense, he was unassailable.

Another component of Schumacher's success with his young followers was his intellect. He awed them with displays of learning, even if they could not follow everything he said. In a world of frightening complexity, "Der Doktor" always had an answer. For these working-class youths, keenly conscious of their own limited education and eager to learn, Schumacher became teacher as well as political leader. They eagerly accepted his intellectual guidance, for he, unlike so many of the older party leaders and Marxist theorists, seemed to take them and their problems seriously, and did not simply put them off with admonitions to mature.

Finally, it should be noted that Schumacher's relationship with his immediate followers was one between superior and inferior, based more on affect than on the institutional norms of the party organization. Very few of them addressed him with the familiar *Du*, as was customary among party associates. Almost all of them were not only younger than he, but decidedly his intellectual juniors as well. They looked up to him as their superior in intellect, political ability, and general *savoir faire*; he accepted their homage readily, but never took them into his confidence. He would lead the group in discussing common political goals, but kept his personal goals to himself; he encouraged his followers to look to him to solve problems facing the party, but did not discuss his own problems with them.

It seems that this relationship was based on a strong congruence of role perceptions, equally satisfying to both parties. Schumacher's followers found in him a hero image and a means of self-identification, and he found in them a source of self-gratification. Their admiration seems to have served to reinforce his perception of himself as a superior individual in his chosen field. The cripple appears to have found in the superior-inferior relationship with physically "whole men" proof of his psychological eligibility for the role of political leader. Their response to his appearance and behavior apparently strengthened his inclination to embrace behavior patterns that would satisfy his inner need to prove his superiority by wielding power over theirs. Accordingly, his role as a militant and determined leader was functional not only in terms of the inner man, but in terms of the needs of the party and the democratic order.

Schumacher's life in Stuttgart was entirely dominated by his political aspirations. Photographs of him in those years show a determined if not particularly distinguished-looking young man. His eyes and mouth had lost the soft and troubled expression that we find in a picture taken after his amputation in 1915. His bearing was erect, but hardly military—he did not cut a particularly impressive figure in his Reichsbanner uniform.* His health, apart from nervous tension and occasional pains in the phantom arm, was in fact much better than many of his admirers realized. His consumption of cigarettes was enormous. He was known as a hard worker, full of nervous energy, who spared neither himself nor those who worked with him. He was among the first to arrive at the offices of the *Tagwacht* in the morning, and restlessly remained on the move until late at night, often managing with only two hours of sleep. His outside interests were rather limited. His nonpolitical reading consisted largely of detective stories; his musical taste was in light opera. Sports did not interest him and he traveled very little, rarely taking a vacation. Once or twice he spent a few days in neighboring countries, but that is the known extent of his travel abroad.

Though his political life was always dominant, Schumacher did not submerge his existence in the Social Democratic movement as did some party members, who grew up in its youth organizations, married fellow socialists, hiked with the *Naturfreunde*, exercised with the *Arbeitersportler*, and were ultimately buried by socialist cremation societies. On the contrary, he carefully guarded the limited private sector of his life—to the point of practically concealing it from even his closest political associates. Few of them were ever asked to his comfortable rooms or allowed to join him at the high-class res-

---

* The Reichsbanner was a national paramilitary organization consisting mostly of Social Democrats. Its purpose was to defend the democratic Republic against domestic foes.

taurants and coffeehouses at which he liked to mingle with local artists and intellectuals and "shake the proletarian dust off his feet," as one of these acquaintances later put it.

What was known in the party about the young bachelor's private life—and even more what was not known—earned him a reputation as a Bohemian *bon vivant,* fond of wine, women, and song. Schumacher seems to have enjoyed encouraging this image among the morally upstanding party stalwarts—perhaps because in his own mind it accentuated his break with the philistine pattern of the life in Kulm; perhaps also because it emphasized his virility to his associates.* In fact, however, this reputation was largely undeserved. He did not have to prove his masculinity by playing the Don Juan—he was "married to politics." He apparently had a few casual liaisons, and from 1925 on he maintained a steady relationship with a pretty young soprano employed by the local radio station. This attachment appears to have served his psychological needs only incidentally, rather than being the focal point for his compensatory devices—as is the case of some physically defectives in their sexual relationships. He actually had little in common with the girl. She was a devout Roman Catholic, he an atheist; she came from the mild Swabian region, he from the harsh borderlands of West Prussia; she was a singer who hardly cared about politics, he a politician who knew little about music. But Schumacher did not try to change her, to wean her from her church or interest her in politics. He never discussed his political problems or goals with her, or took her to a political meeting. He wanted her to remain as she was, he told her, uncontaminated by what he called the gutter life of politics. Few of his political associates ever met her.

This attachment, so carefully concealed from public view, afforded Schumacher temporary escape from his political tasks without forcing him to assume the responsibilities of married life or yield to feminine demands. That the girl was pretty and an artist no doubt attracted him to her. But, perhaps more important, she was maternal, she wanted to take care of him, urged him to smoke less and to relax. With her as with his mother, he could be childlike and humorous—without being sarcastic—a boy as well as a man, a son as well as a lover, and yet remain free to pursue his primary goals. It was apparently a stable and happy relationship for both, terminated after many years by Schumacher's arrest in 1933. Yet Schumacher never proposed marriage; in fact, he refused it, once again asserting his independence from maternal-feminine influences. In his lonely quest for political power there was no room for competing loyalties and encumbering attachments, particularly to women. Ultimately, his self-chosen political role was the be-all and end-all of his life, the

---

* The memory of the period in Stuttgart was a source of delight to Schumacher all his life. Years later he still liked to recall how this Bohemian existence (*Budenleben*) had rubbed many a respectable party functionary the wrong way. Kaufmann Int.

role to which his role as son and lover was strictly subordinate, as he was to make quite clear after his imprisonment in a Nazi concentration camp.*

The very qualities that endeared Schumacher to his supporters aroused bitter animosity in his opponents. If his relationship with the former rested on a clear acceptance of his superiority, that with the latter was based on his inability to recognize equals or superiors, and his determination to prove his superiority. Schumacher, recalled many of his former associates, seemed to thrive on political sparring, and to enjoy battle to the point of deliberately provoking it. He seemed to go out of his way to challenge and insult actual or presumed competitors for political power. Provocation he held to be a first principle of political tactics, and he applied it with skill and ruthlessness. An angry opponent, he claimed, was a weak opponent; an aggressive fighter an effective one.[11] Politics, he told his girl friend once, was not for gentlemen; its victories were won by conflict not compromise, militancy not tolerance. In some people's view, Schumacher found it difficult to control his aggressiveness, to moderate his attacks, to apologize, to admit he had been wrong. What his admirers considered his unselfish dedication, uncompromising militancy, and self-assurance seemed to many of his opponents, inside and outside the party, unbridled ambition, aggressive arrogance, and dogmatic intolerance.

Schumacher fought with the traditional weapons of the European intellectual: sarcasm, ridicule, irony. These qualities, alien to the easygoing Swabians, he had probably learned from his Jewish friends in Kulm, from reading Voltaire, Heine, Heinrich Mann, and the *Simplicissimus*'s devastating satires of life in Imperial Germany, and from the workers and intellectuals he had met in Berlin.† They were the weapons that radical writers like Tucholsky and Brecht were employing with such skill to criticize the society and institutions of Weimar Germany.

Schumacher's speeches and writings were characterized by the same biting sarcasm and ribald witticisms that spiked his private conversations.[12] He was always on the watch for new and sharper barbs to hurl against his opponents. According to a close friend of this period, he wrote his speeches around nasty personal cracks that delighted his supporters and infuriated his victims.

Conflict with the Old Guard

Once Schumacher had decided on his role in the party, a very different one from that intended for him by the men who had brought him to Stuttgart, the pattern of his future relationship with those men was set. Wilhelm Keil, effective boss of the state organization, was far too strong a personality to accept

---

* Schumacher did not care to discuss the affair in later years, and avoided questions on the subject. His biographers have next to nothing to say about it.
† The *Simplicissimus* was a well-known German satirical paper.

Schumacher's claim to prominence in the party. Schumacher, for his part, would not accept Keil's image of the proper relationship between a young beginner in the party organization and its seasoned leaders. As a result, the battle between them was joined early, and was waged with such bitterness that neither ever forgave the other.[13]

Wilhelm Keil and his principal associates in the leadership of the state organization were lifelong Social Democrats who had risen to their positions by faithful service to the party and expected their potential successors to do the same.* They were in a particularly strong position, since the war and the secession of the radicals had eliminated most of the younger men who might otherwise have challenged their leadership; and they sincerely believed it their duty to retain firm control of the party so that socialism and democracy might flourish in state and nation. Challenges against them from within the party— from whatever quarter—were felt to be disloyal and radical. They had long worked together, and they shared the same values. Most important, they could depend upon each other; and dependability, as Keil stresses in his biography, is a virtue that is required of subordinates and equals alike.[14]

From ten to thirty years older than Schumacher, and by at least as many years senior to him in service to the organization, the older party functionaries viewed the newcomer with suspicion from the start. His youth, his intellect, his bourgeois origin, and the fact that he came from a part of Germany totally alien to them were all points against him. They were willing to give him a chance, but he did his best to spoil it. He hardly tried to disguise his contempt for men to whom he felt in every respect superior. Everything he was and did seemed a direct challenge to them, above all to Keil himself. He flaunted his superior intelligence, education, and manner of living in the faces of men who had painfully and slowly acquired the rudiments of an education, and who adhered loyally to the style of life of the workingmen they had once been and with whom they still identified themselves. Many years later, Schumacher still relished the memory of his conflicts with these old-timers: "When once in a while I gave one of those old bosses a piece of my mind, in a discussion or the like, one of them would say, 'Just listen to this college kid.' They would glare at me. . . . That was because of my entire behavior and my entire style of life."[15]

To Keil, who typified the S.P.D. leadership during the Weimar Republic, Schumacher must have seemed an ungrateful young upstart. Mostly self-taught and by no means brilliant, he no doubt resented Schumacher's constant displays of intellectual superiority in speeches and articles, as well as in private

* In addition to Keil, the principal leaders during the Weimar Republic were Erich Rossmann, the state chairman; Otto Steinmayer, the state secretary; Karl Hildenbrand and Alexander Schlicke, Reichstag deputies; and Albert Pflunger and Karl Ruggaber, Landtag deputies.

encounters. Twenty-five years older than Schumacher, Keil could not understand Schumacher's identification with the young party rebels in the "conflict of the generations." Believing unemotional "realism" to be the best and only manner for dealing with the political problems, Keil was alarmed by what he regarded as Schumacher's irresponsible radicalism. He doubly resented Schumacher's assertions of moral superiority, most of which took the form of charging the party leaders with opportunism and lack of militancy, when it became clear that Schumacher was using these charges to advance his career.*

Until Schumacher had succeeded in establishing a solid power base in the Stuttgart organization of the S.P.D., he was no real threat to the older party leaders. Keil and the other state leaders quickly withdrew from sponsoring his political career, and for some years the ascent was steep and slow. After having been a delegate to the national S.P.D. congress at Görlitz in 1921, he did not attend another national congress until 1929. He was not among the twelve candidates on the Social Democratic list for the Reichstag elections of May and December 1924, though men no older than he were nominated. However, the Stuttgart organization did place his name second on its list of five candidates for the state legislature in the election of May 1924. He was elected, but the Communists managed to outpoll the Social Democrats by 10 per cent in Stuttgart. In the light of far smaller relative Communist gains in the rest of the state and nation, the outcome constituted a severe defeat for the local party organization.[16]

The thirteen Social Democrats in the state legislature were headed and dominated by Wilhelm Keil, who occupied a seat in the Reichstag as well. Keil would appear in the state parliament to make the speeches for major decisions, but relied on his subordinates to attend to everyday affairs. Schumacher, for the first years at least, was definitely a second-string player. But since, apparently, he was the only academically trained member of the group, it fell to him to deal with some of the more complex legislative issues, such as the administration of justice and budgetary problems, and he made the most of this situation. He spoke infrequently—on the average he made about three major speeches a year during his seven years as a state legislator—but his far-ranging, aggressive, and skillful presentations soon became high spots in the otherwise rather tedious debates, and filled the galleries.[17]

All this time, Schumacher was consolidating his position in the Stuttgart organization as the leader of the younger and more militant elements. In 1924 he became local leader of the Reichsbanner, the S.P.D.'s paramilitary organi-

---

* Wesemann (p. 25) relates an apocryphal story according to which Keil once showed Schumacher the title page of a pamphlet he had written, and asked him if he knew what was meant by the letters "MdL" and "MdR" under his name. Instead of answering correctly "Mitglied des Landtag" and "Mitglied des Reichstag," Schumacher is said to have replied "Mitglied der Linken und Mitglied der Rechten" (Member of the Left and Member of the Right), in an obvious reference to what he held to be Keil's political ambivalence.

zation, and in 1925 his supporters Erwin Schoettle and Frieder Wurm took control of the state Socialist Youth organization. Simultaneous attempts, however, to get Schoettle into the party's state executive committee proved premature; Keil and his associates still held the reins. By 1928 Schumacher and his Stuttgart following were strong enough to elect Schoettle to the state executive committee over the opposition of the old leaders, and to force them to change their candidate list for the forthcoming Reichstag election: Schumacher was moved into fifth place, with a chance, though not an assurance, of election.[18]

The results of the combined Reichstag and Landtag election of 1928 were a personal triumph for Schumacher. The Social Democratic vote in Stuttgart increased 81 per cent over 1924, as against an increase of 13 per cent in the state and 15 per cent in the country as a whole. As the *Tagwacht* proudly proclaimed, over 80 per cent of the entire state-wide increase came from Stuttgart (see Table 1). By a quirk of the electoral system, Schumacher failed to win election to the Reichstag despite the increase in the S.P.D. vote, but he triumphantly returned to the Landtag at the head of the local list. No doubt he would have had a strong claim to a ministerial post in the state government had his party succeeded in its efforts to form a coalition government in Württemberg, as it now did in the Reich. One wonders what effect such a post of responsibility would have had on the political behavior of a man who was to spend all his political life in opposition.

Schumacher was now strong enough to challenge Keil's leadership openly. The opportunity came soon after the election over an issue that stirred the party to its depths. In August 1928, Keil undertook to defend a decision made by the Social Democratic members of the newly formed *Reich* coalition government to vote with their nonsocialist colleagues in approving funds for the construction of a pocket battleship. The S.P.D. had consistently fought all such appropriations during its many years as an opposition party, and the appropriations for the new "Battlecruiser A" had been a major issue in the electoral

TABLE 1

SOCIAL DEMOCRATIC VOTES IN REICHSTAG ELECTIONS, 1920–30
(In thousands)

	June 1920	May 1924	Dec. 1924	May 1928	Sept. 1930
STUTTGART	27.9	32.0	31.7	57.6	55.6
% gain or loss	—	+14.7	−0.9	+81.0	−2.6
WÜRTTEMBERG	179.3	191.2	240.8	272.8	283.3
% gain or loss	—	+6.6	+25.9	+13.3	+3.8
GERMANY	5,614.5	6,243.9	7,979.9	9,171.3	8,577.7
% gain or loss	—	+11.2	+27.8	+14.9	−6.5

campaign just past. Keil took the position of the S.P.D. ministers in the government that it was "realistic" to break their campaign promise and vote for the appropriations, rather than risk the collapse of the newly formed government and bring about new elections that might send the party back to the wilderness of opposition. Accordingly, before going on his summer vacation, Keil sought to set the local party line for the inevitable debate on the issue by a lead editorial in the *Tagwacht* defending the ministers' decision.[19]

Schumacher had been one of the earliest opponents of the battlecruiser program, long before the election in which it had featured so prominently and in which he had scored a personal success.[20] Local socialist left-wingers, Communists, and pacifists were certain to pounce upon the issue to attack him and his party. But here, too, was the perfect issue on which to focus his aggressive opposition to what he called the opportunistic willingness of state and national S.P.D. leaders to tolerate government decisions not in the interest of democratic socialism.* Thus, while the editor-in-chief was enjoying his vacation under the illusion that he had established the local party line, the political editor of the *Tagwacht* was launching a bitter attack on the Social Democratic ministers and, by implication, on Keil.

The Social Democratic ministers' action on the battlecruiser appropriation aroused such a storm in the party that in the end the S.P.D. deputies in the Reichstag—including these ministers—voted against the appropriations. Keil, who found himself almost alone in defending the cabinet decision, felt that Schumacher had not only violated party discipline but betrayed him personally. He never got over his resentment of what he considered disloyalty, if not insubordination, on Schumacher's part. Years later he still alluded to Schumacher's behavior as that of an unrealistic, irresponsible radical. For Schumacher, however, the dispute proved a turning point. Not only did it consolidate his position locally,[21] but his outspoken demand for greater militancy and intra-party democracy brought him national prominence in the S.P.D. A few months later he spoke for the first time before a national party audience at the Magdeburg Congress of 1929.

Measured by the old guard's standards, Schumacher was still extremely young and inexperienced when, in July 1930, he was elected chairman of the Stuttgart party organization at the age of thirty-four.[22] The Stuttgart organization now demanded that he be assured of election in the forthcoming Reichstag election, and succeeded in placing him fourth on the list of the state party's candidates by forcing the retirement of one of Keil's rather incompetent old friends. At the same time, Keil resigned as editor-in-chief of the *Tagwacht*.[23]

---

* Schumacher had long objected to party policy on this point. He claimed that the S.P.D.'s tolerant attitude would merely encourage the "bourgeois" parties to sacrifice "proletarian interest" still further. See, for example, his speeches in *Protokoll, Landtag,* June 1 and Dec. 16, 1926.

After a vigorous campaign against the Communists and National Socialists, Schumacher was elected to the Reichstag in the fateful election of September 1930 that brought Hitler's first major electoral victory. Württemberg was one of the districts in which the Social Democrats managed to increase their vote and capture even the fifth Reichstag seat that had eluded Schumacher two years earlier (see Table 2).

As one of the youngest members of a very large Social Democratic Reichstag, Schumacher remained a relatively obscure backbencher for the last hectic years of the Republic's national parliament. He made no formal speeches, and the protocol records only one brief and extemporaneous attack on Goebbels, which the presiding Social Democrat, Paul Löbe, sought to silence. Neither Löbe nor most of the other older leaders particularly cared for Schumacher, who struck them as the complete opposite of their ideal of a junior colleague, daring, reckless, and lacking in respect.[24] With Carlo Mierendorff, a young Hessian deputy, as his chief ally, Schumacher sought to rally the comparatively few younger Social Democratic deputies to a more militant policy toward the Nazis and the "bourgeois" parties. However, even among the men who shared his views, Schumacher seems to have made few friends. In August 1932, in the wake of a slight rejuvenation of the Social Democratic faction in the Reichstag, he was elected to its executive committee with 45 out of 143 possible votes as a spokesman for "youth."* Although this may have raised his status in the party hierarchy, he had little opportunity to profit from it. The Reichstag had only a few more months to go before Hitler put an end to its deliberations.

Back in Württemberg, Schumacher's battle against the older leaders was close to victory when Hitler came to power. Keil felt the authority he had wielded for so long slipping from his hands. He had a difficult time defending the party's toleration of the unpopular Brüning government as a stopgap measure against Hitler, a policy that was opposed by both the left and the right in the state organization.[25] Schumacher, since 1930 a member of the state executive committee, reluctantly supported this policy in the Reichstag in compliance with party discipline, but had to face severe criticism from left-wing members of his own organization in Stuttgart, who accused him of having sold out to the enemy.† However, he managed to keep such criticism to a minimum and prevent any significant number of desertions to the Communists and left-wing splinter groups—as had happened in several other cities—"by the sheer

---

* The votes were reported by Keil in a letter to his wife. He commented on Schumacher's small popularity, and pointed out that by contrast he, Keil, was re-elected with 116 votes despite his expressed wish to retire. See *Erlebnisse,* II, 456.

† Schumacher's critics were particularly outraged by his refusal to join nine dissident Social Democrats who in March 1931 voted with the Communists against appropriations for a second battlecruiser rather than accept the decision of the party leaders to abstain.

TABLE 2

SOCIAL DEMOCRATIC, COMMUNIST, AND NAZI VOTES IN STUTTGART, WÜRTTEMBERG, AND GERMANY, 1928–33
(In thousands)

	Dec. 1924 Reichstag	May 1928 Landtag-Reichstag	Sept. 1930 Reichstag	Apr. 1932 Landtag	July 1932 Reichstag	Nov. 1932 Reichstag	Mar. 1933 Reichstag
STUTTGART							
S.P.D.	31.7	57.6	55.6	56.8	61.9	52.5	59.4
% gain or loss	—	+81.0	-2.6	+2.1	+8.97	-15.1	+13.1
K.P.D.	28.1	27.3	36.1	33.4	36.9	47.7	37.2
% gain or loss	—	-2.9	+32.2	-7.5	+10.5	+29.3	-22.0
N.S.D.A.P.	5.3	4.4	21.4	51.7	60.2	53.9	84.5
% gain or loss	—	-17.0	+386.4	+141.5	+16.4	-10.5	+56.7
WÜRTTEMBERG							
S.P.D.	240.8	272.8	283.3	206.6	247.2	200.1	231.9
% gain or loss	—	+13.3	+3.8	-27.1	+19.7	-19.1	+15.9
K.P.D.	96.2	82.5	130.0	116.6	155.4	190.8	144.3
% gain or loss	—	-14.5	+57.6	-10.3	+33.3	+22.8	-24.4
N.S.D.A.P.	25.3	20.3	128.7	328.2	425.6	344.8	662.4
% gain or loss	—	-19.8	+534.0	+155.0	+29.7	-19.0	+92.1
GERMANY							
S.P.D.	7,979.9	9,171.3	9,577.7	—	7,959.7	7,248.0	7,181.6
% gain or loss	—	+15.0	+4.4	—	-16.9	-8.9	-0.9
K.P.D.	2,709.1	3,262.9	4,592.1	—	5,282.6	5,970.8	4,845.4
% gain or loss	—	+20.5	+40.7	—	+15.0	+13.0	-2.1
N.S.D.A.P.	910.6	809.7	6,401.2	—	13,745.8	11,705.3	17,265.8
% gain or loss	—	-11.1	+690.5	—	+114.8	-14.8	+47.5

force of his personality," as a former leader of one such dissident group recalled. The Stuttgart S.P.D., firmly controlled by Schumacher and his young associates, managed to hold its own better than the state organization, despite Nazi and Communist gains in the numerous elections that preceded the final collapse of the Weimar Republic.[26]

During the last months of the Republic, Schumacher progressed rapidly toward the leadership of the state organization that he had sought for so long. For the Reichstag election of July 1932, he moved from fourth to third place on the party's list of candidates, and for the last free election in Württemberg in November 1932, to second place—thanks to Keil's withdrawal. In a debate with Schumacher in the state executive committee over party policy, Keil found in the fall of 1932 that he no longer enjoyed the support of the state leadership and yielded to Schumacher. Though he was only sixty-two, he recalls, he gathered that he was "looked upon as 'the old man,' for whom the time had come to make room for younger men."[27] The *Tagwacht* reported that "Comrade Wilhelm Keil . . . voluntarily surrendered his position in order to contribute to the rejuvenation of the party and enable it to attack new political tasks with youthful vigor."[28] Schumacher had triumphed at last—but too late to profit from the victory.

The Education of an Opposition Leader

Whereas Schumacher's attacks on his own party's leaders were relatively restrained and were screened from the public eye, his clashes with opponents outside the S.P.D. were conspicuously and openly belligerent. The political setting was particularly suitable for the militant role that he sought to play. His party was the principal opposition to the so-called "blue-black" coalition of conservative and Roman Catholic parties that ruled Württemberg from 1924 to 1933. He entered the Reichstag in 1930, after the last national government in which his party participated had fallen, and after the battle against Nazism had begun.

As a member of the opposition party in Württemberg, Schumacher could find a legitimate outlet for his belligerence. He was an oppositionist *par excellence*, recalled a fellow socialist who observed his behavior in both state and national parliaments. Schumacher took his seat in the state parliament in 1924, with a number of court cases pending against him for insulting deputies, judges, and police officials, as well as "the honor of the armed forces," in his *Tagwacht* articles.[29] Right from the start, his speeches were aggressive and designed to score polemical points off his opponents. He never admitted an error or modified his attacks, and ignored or ridiculed evidence contrary to his arguments. To the delight of his admirers, the discomfiture of more decorous deputies, and the fury of his victims, he brashly asserted his moral and intellectual superiority over older opponents with scornful ridicule, particularly in replies to interruptions from the floor.* He would engage in reasoned argument only with opponents he judged worthy of it, such as the longtime Minister of Justice, Joseph Beyerle.

Until the rise of Hitler and his own entry into national politics, the principal target of Schumacher's attacks was the leader of the arch-conservative and nationalist elements in Württemberg. Wilhelm Bazille, the outspokenly re-actionary leader of the Bürgerpartei and Reichstag deputy of the German Nationalist Party, was perhaps the most striking and controversial figure in Württemberg politics. The son of a naturalized Frenchman, he was extreme in his nationalism; exempt from wartime military service for medical reasons, he was aggressive in support of the traditional military elite and its values. Brilliant, temperamental, arrogant, and a first-class orator, he was in political orientation Schumacher's antithesis, in political behavior, however, closely akin. As spokesman of agrarian and industrial interests, he was bitterly op-posed to everything the Social Democrats favored, and like Schumacher he enjoyed deliberately provoking his opponents; he, too, was considered "a born oppositionist."[30]

For Schumacher, Bazille was an ideal antagonist: he not only challenged Schumacher's determination to prove his superiority in political battle, but allowed this personal drive to express itself in a manner sanctioned by the party. Whereas attacks on the party leaders were subject to stricture, attacks on Bazille could meet only with approval—from Social Democrats of every stripe. Even before the issue between the two men was clearly joined, when Bazille became head of the "blue-black" coalition government in the state and Schumacher entered the diet as a member of the opposition in 1924, the latter had earned himself a three-month jail sentence for "continuing libelous at-tacks" against Bazille in the *Tagwacht*.† And from 1924 to 1930, Schumacher dedicated most of his energy, in the Landtag and out, to attacking Bazille and the values and interests with which he was identified. In response to Bazille's attacks on the patriotism of the S.P.D., Schumacher repeatedly questioned the loyalty of "Monsieur Bazille," calling him, in effect, a stooge of Poincaré, a

---

* It was quite customary for Schumacher to tell a "knucklehead" or "lout" to stop his "bleating" or "twaddle." Once when he was asked to break off the very long and technical speech he was making on financial problems because fellow deputies were getting restless, he replied that he "did not expect attention from those to whom I have not conceded the intellectual ability to understand me in the first place." ("Ich kann von niemand verlangen, dass er zuhört, wenn ich ihm von vorneherein nicht die geistige Begabung zubillige, dass er mich versteht.") To a mild protest he replied that "even in interruptions there is a minimum level of intelligence below which one ought to find it difficult to fall." ("Es gibt auch in den Zwischenrufen einen Grenze der Minusintelli-genz, die man nicht gut unterschreiten dürfte.") See *Protokoll, Landtag*, Jan. 17, 1928.

† The S.P.D. claimed that the sentence was a tendentious political judgment. Though the Landtag refused to grant Schumacher immunity from prosecution for articles written before his election, he apparently never served his sentence, and may have won a reversal in appeal. See "Der beleidigte Bazille," *Esslinger Volkszeitung*, May 7, 1925.

name that was anathema in Germany on account of the Frenchman's punitive policies.[31] Bazille's leading role in a coalition with the Center Party gave Schumacher occasion to accuse him of making common cause with the particularist enemies of a united Germany. Bazille's rather vague, but still emphatic, support of corporatist theories led Schumacher to attack and ridicule what he termed the pseudo-philosophical intellectual pretensions of a political expressionist.*

The senior member in the "blue-black" coalition, the Roman Catholic Center Party, drew Schumacher's fire almost as much as Bazille's Bürgerpartei. The largest party in the state, it dissolved a brief partnership with the S.P.D. shortly before Schumacher arrived in Stuttgart; thereafter it consistently rejected Social Democratic overtures to follow the example of its affiliates in other states—particularly in Prussia—and re-form a so-called "Weimar Coalition," preferring to remain loyal to the "anti-Marxist" coalition with the Protestant, urban Bürgerpartei and the agrarian Bauernbund.

The trend in the Württemberg Center Party—and in the predominantly agrarian coalition government in general—was increasingly toward a Bavarian-type particularism. This trend coupled traditional anti-Prussian and anti-unitary tendencies with anti-democratic and anti-parliamentarian opposition to the social and economic policies of the socialist-led "Weimar Coalitions" in Berlin.† In Württemberg it was the Social Democratic Party—if we ignore a single Nazi deputy—that stood alone, until 1932, for a strongly unitary, centralized Reich, and for a German rather than a local patriotism. The governing "blue-black" coalition was thus separated from the Social Democratic opposition by deep political, economic, and social differences.

It was in this setting that the postwar opposition leader received his political education. The Württemberg S.P.D., both by its commitment to a strongly unitary democratic state and by its opponents' distrust of socialist religious, economic, and social policies, was forced into permanent opposition. Its representatives saw themselves, and were looked upon, as the spokesmen for policies identified with Berlin rather than Stuttgart, with the Reich rather than Württemberg. No problem, Schumacher asserted in his maiden speech in the Landtag, was more important than "the unity of the Reich."[32] He accepted, and amplified upon, the division between "bourgeois particularism" and "so-

---

* *Protokoll, Landtag,* Jan. 28, 1928. However, twenty years later Schumacher was to remember Bazille as a "very learned and well-informed man" though "utterly reactionary" in his political views. Letter to Calhoun Ancrum, Sept. 8, 1950 (Pers. Archiv, S.P.D., P.V.). Bazille became a decided opponent of the Nazis after their electoral victory in 1930, and broke with his party when it moved toward an alliance with Hitler. He committed suicide in 1933 after Hitler came to power. His son joined the S.P.D. after the war, and was elected to the Bundestag with Schumacher's blessing and support.

† The Weimar Coalitions governed Prussia from 1920 to 1932, and for part of that time the whole of Germany.

cialist centralism," calling the one reactionary and the other progressive. Federalism, he claimed time and again, was a weapon of the propertied interests and of the capitalist victor powers of 1918 against the political and social progress of the German nation. Centralism, by contrast, he represented as the only way to strengthen and advance the national welfare. The Republic, he claimed, was but a way station on the road toward a stronger unitary and socialist state upon which Bismarck had started the German nation in 1870. And like Bismarck, a fellow Prussian Protestant, he viewed with suspicion and anger the support that the Roman Catholic Church and its state-paid spokesmen "in clerical robes," the party secretaries of the Center Party, allegedly gave to the particularists in Württemberg and Bavaria.[33]

With the election of September 1930, Schumacher moved into the field of national politics. Despite stormy clashes with extremists of the right and left in the preceding campaign, neither he nor other S.P.D. leaders had anticipated the dramatic increase in Communist and, above all, Nazi votes in the election.[34] Over the next two and a half years, the new Reichstag deputy was caught up in a steadily deteriorating economic and political situation, in which the rapidly declining power of the Social Democrats was met by the rising strength of the extremist parties (see Table 3).

Schumacher had vigorously opposed both Communists and Nazis from the beginning. Before 1930, the former were of greater concern to him because of their far greater electoral strength and their rivalry with the S.P.D. for the support of the workers and young leftists; their influence was particularly strong among the important metalworkers. Schumacher attributed their success partly to Communist propaganda, partly to inferior Social Democratic organizational activities, and successfully countered both factors as his influence in the organization grew.[35] His task was eased by disputes and purges within the local K.P.D., which, in Stuttgart, never undermined the position of the S.P.D. to the same extent that it did in other German industrial centers. However, beginning in 1930, the K.P.D. grew in strength not only in Stuttgart, but throughout the state.

Schumacher's behavior toward the Communists was characterized by the same mixture of provocation and contempt that marked his behavior toward other political opponents. He categorically rejected the Leninist theories and tactics as a mixture of lies, cunning, and stupidity, and proclaimed that he saw little difference between the right- and the left-wing enemies of Social Democracy and the democratic order. Communist charges that the Social Democrats had betrayed the working class in 1918 he described as the Communist version of the "stab-in-the-back" legend launched against the S.P.D. by the extreme right.[36] The Communists, in his opinion, were "nothing but twin editions of the National Socialists, varnished with red [*rotlakierte Doppelausgaben der Nationalsozialisten*]," since both parties were characterized

TABLE 3

PROPORTION OF VALID VOTES RECEIVED BY THE S.P.D., K.P.D., AND N.S.D.A.P.
IN STUTTGART, WÜRTTEMBERG, AND GERMANY, 1928–33

	Dec. 1924 Reichstag	May 1928 Reichstag	Sept. 1930 Reichstag	July 1932 Reichstag	Nov. 1932 Reichstag	Mar. 1933 Reichstag
S.P.D.						
Stuttgart	17.9	30.5	26.5	27.8	22.5	23.7
Württemberg	20.8	23.6	20.1	17.6	15.2	14.7
Germany	26.4	29.8	24.5	21.6	20.4	18.3
K.P.D.						
Stuttgart	15.9	14.5	17.2	16.6	20.4	14.8
Württemberg	8.3	7.2	9.4	11.0	14.5	9.2
Germany	8.9	10.6	13.1	14.3	16.9	12.3
N.S.D.A.P.						
Stuttgart	3.0	2.5	10.2	27.1	23.1	33.7
Württemberg	2.2	1.9	9.4	30.3	26.2	42.0
Germany	3.0	3.5	18.3	37.3	33.1	43.9

by a hatred of democracy and a preference for brute force.[37] They and not the Social Democrats, he asserted with increasing vehemence during the last months of the Weimar Republic, were the betrayers of the German workers, tools of "neo-Russian Imperialism, Stalinist version," undermining Social Democratic attempts to defend the democratic system and deliberately instigating right-wing attacks on the S.P.D.[38] He was never to forgive the Communist leadership in Berlin and Moscow for the part it had played, in his view, in bringing about the victory of Hitler.

Although the Nazis showed considerably less strength in Württemberg than in many other parts of Germany, Schumacher opposed them from the very start of his political career. He attacked the Hitler movement long before it became a major force in national politics, on the characteristic principle that the best defense against the enemies of the Republic and Social Democracy was to take the offense while the opponent was still weak.[39] His reputation as a militant and aggressive leader rested to a large extent on his record as the organizer of extra-parliamentary action against the Nazis. As early as 1921 he led anti-Nazi demonstrations, and he attacked and exposed the activities of the Nazis even before the abortive Hitler putsch of 1923. He organized a semi-covert paramilitary organization of young socialists to provide him with intelligence on Nazi subversive activities, which he then exposed in the *Tagwacht* and in public speeches.[40]

In 1924, he was responsible for establishing the local unit of the newly founded Reichsbanner, and as leader of the unit, he used the organization to fight the Communists, and in particular the Nazis, with some of their own methods. To arouse support for democratic socialism and the republican form of government, and to demonstrate the determination of the younger socialists to fight for their cause, he led uniformed Reichsbanner and socialist youth groups with drum, fife, and bugle through the streets of Stuttgart and neighboring towns and villages.[41] A special group of young toughs accompanied him to his meetings, and dealt summarily with the Nazi outbursts that inevitably followed his deliberate provocations. The thrashings they got they fully deserved, he proclaimed afterwards, literally adding insult to injury.[42]

Schumacher reserved his most vituperative and scathing language for the Nazi leaders. On several occasions he called Christian Mergenthaler, sole Nazi representative in the Landtag during Schumacher's tenure, an ignorant lout who represented a party based on a tissue of lies.[43] Time and again he charged that Nazism was nothing but an "appeal to the swine in man [*ein Appell an den inneren Schweinehund*]," a description that became famous when he used it in 1932 in the Reichstag in a clash with Goebbels—whom he called a "presumptive dwarf" too big for his breeches.[44] "We won't say that every National Socialist is a scoundrel," he declared at a mass rally shortly before Hitler came to power, "but we know that today every scoundrel is a National Socialist." Characterizing the Hitler movement as the rebellion of the most incompetent, bankrupt, and insolent elements in the nation, he told wildly applauding listeners that the Social Democrats, once victorious, would send the Nazi leaders not to the gallows, but to the padded cells where they belonged.[45]

As the political situation became more critical, Schumacher became increasingly vituperative and belligerent. His savage ridicule, combined with arrogant contempt, provoked violent reactions from the local Nazi leaders. Clashes between Schumacher's militant followers and Nazi storm troopers were frequent, and became more so once it was apparent that the police and the courts either were indifferent or openly favored the Nazis.[46] However dangerous, these actions appeared to Schumacher morally and politically sound. Moreover, they proved that the one-armed politician was an opponent to be reckoned with.

Political Behavior and Political Values

Schumacher's behavior in his drive against the S.P.D.'s old-guard leadership was subsequently to create a good deal of confusion about his political orientation during the Stuttgart period. Whereas to the old reformist functionaries of the party his views seemed very radical, to the left-wing extremists inside and outside the S.P.D. he appeared to be an ultra right-winger. Some later recalled that he had been a categorical pacifist, others that he had worked to create in Social Democracy a more positive attitude toward the military establishment. Some claimed that he had been a radical Marxist, others that he belonged to the orthodox, moderate "Marxist Center," while still others held that he had been all but an anti-Marxist. Whereas his admirers likened his political philosophy to the militant creed of a Protestant reformer, his critics, particularly among the older party leaders, thought it an almost fanatical anarchism, bare of constructive values.

In later years Schumacher maintained that he had been a political pragmatist. "I never attempted to determine my political behavior on the basis of a preconceived ideology," he informed an interviewer in 1952.[47] His Stuttgart associates remember him as a man of strong convictions, but extremely pragmatic in seeking his political goals. What Keil recalled as Schumacher's "independent radicalism" seems to have been political behavior rooted in personality needs.[48] More often than not, his need was to prove his superiority. His behavior when he was pressed to make a formal break with the Evangelical Church is typical: he refused categorically, not on religious grounds, but because he felt unable to accept what he believed to be the authoritative claims of those whose superiority he could not recognize. He would not, he was to recall, "cower before the bigoted priests of latitudinarianism" any more than he would "cower before anyone else."[49]

Neither his speeches nor his exclusively journalistic writings show him to have been a very profound socialist thinker, and this at a time when German left-wing politics were heavily interlarded with theoretical debates. His doctoral dissertation, written in 1926, strikes the reader as rather a slipshod and superficial piece of work. Perhaps when he wrote it, he had neither the time nor the interest to do more than meet the minimum requirements for the long-deferred degree.[50] Nonetheless, the dissertation and Schumacher's other writings and speeches in this period provide a number of clues concerning his political values during the Weimar Republic.

The subject of the dissertation was the crucial question of the role of a workers' party in a bourgeois state—anything but a theoretical problem at that time. Schumacher was by no means the only one to concern himself with it. The subject had long been debated by German Social Democrats, who were divided into two camps: the radical followers of Marx, who insisted that the bourgeois state had to be overthrown before one could begin to introduce a socialist order of society, and the disciples of Ferdinand Lassalle, who advocated a sort of fusion between Fichte's and Hegel's idealization of the German state and the idealist-ethical socialism of such "Utopians" as Blanc and Weitling. When Schumacher joined the S.P.D., the dispute was raging with renewed intensity inside and outside the party.[51] Schumacher's first political sponsor, Konrad Haenisch, and his academic sponsor, Johann Plenge, are only two examples of those who were searching for a new theoretical foundation for a socialist movement that in 1918 had become the chief upholder of the new regime.

After the wartime split of the German socialists, it seemed for a few years that the Majority Social Democrats would hereafter follow Lassalle more than Marx. At the first national S.P.D. congress that Schumacher attended, a new party program was adopted in 1921, in which the S.P.D. was envisaged as an evolutionary socialist reform party striving for a "free people's state" within the framework of the new democratic Weimar Republic. The leaders of a party that had become the principal supporter of the existing political order found it temporarily expedient to treat its Marxist heritage as a socio-economic analytical scheme rather than a precept for political action. However, the rise of the Communist Party, and the return of many orthodox and radical Marxists to the reunited S.P.D., caused S.P.D. leaders to revert within a few years to the ambivalent compromise between Marx and Lassalle, between radicalism and reformism, that had characterized the party before the war—before Schumacher entered it.[52]

Emotionally, as well as intellectually, Schumacher was apparently strongly attracted by the figure of Lassalle. It seemed later to his closest friend in this period that Schumacher, whether consciously or not, modeled his behavior on that of the dashing, charismatic founder of the German socialist movement, who had been a rebel, a patriot, a dynamic leader, and in his personal life a highly unconventional man.* Intellectually, Lassalle's strongly positive attitude toward the state seems to have appealed to Schumacher far more than either the determinism of the orthodox Marxists or the radicalism of the revolutionary Marxists. In word and deed Schumacher took the position that it was the foremost duty of the German worker to love and defend the Weimar state.[53] He readily acknowledged the primacy of the national interest and *raisons d'état* over the interests of individual or class, but also asserted that the nation had an obligation to provide for the social and economic needs of its members.[54] Like Lassalle he rejected the liberal conception of the *laissez-faire* state that had found expression in the Weimar Constitution. Like Lassalle he favored a strong state whose economic activities were regulated in the interests of society as a whole, rather than in those of a "capitalist" minority.†

Schumacher's positive attitude toward the Weimar state was reflected in his emphatic patriotism. Like Lassalle, he considered himself first and foremost a *German* socialist, and would yield to no one in his devotion to the Fatherland. Replying to the charges of Württemberg states' righters that he was not

* Lassalle was killed in a duel over a woman in 1864, only a year after he became the autocratic leader of the German Workingmen's Association.

† Perhaps even more important than his attitude to Lassalle, at least in terms of his role conception, was his sympathy for Jean Baptiste von Schweitzer, Lassalle's successor in the leadership of the Workingmen's Association. Von Schweitzer, who was a bitter enemy of Marx and his German supporters, was traditionally viewed in the S.P.D. as an autocrat and a stooge of Bismarck because he had supported the Prussian cause in the unification of Germany. Schumacher, however, saw him as a man who was not an original thinker like Marx, but who still showed a far greater understanding of the political needs of the German socialist movement; for he gave it strong leadership at a time when "everything depended on the initiative of the right leader." Dissertation, p. 32.

a native of the state, he said proudly, "I can claim the great 'excuse' that I am a German."[55] He was equally concerned about what he considered the pseudo-patriotism of the right-wing extremists and the anti-patriotism of the Communists and considerable elements in his own party.

The one-time volunteer in the Kaiser's armies was infuriated by right-wing accusations that the Social Democrats had betrayed the Fatherland in a war that had cost him his arm and his home. The so-called patriotism of the German Nationalists and National Socialists, Schumacher insisted, was a subterfuge of the property-owning classes, a pseudo-patriotism that expressed itself in anti-democratic and anti-Semitic outbursts, but showed an unlimited respect for the wallets of the privileged orders. No wonder, he exclaimed more than once in bitter debates with right-wing opponents, less privileged Germans found it difficult, if not impossible, to identify with their fatherland. They had been, and continued to be, exploited by ruthless "capitalists" masquerading as great patriots, men who were in fact enemies of the German nation.[56]

At the same time, Schumacher sought to create loyalty toward the new Weimar state among workers indoctrinated for decades with Marxist ideas about the need to overthrow the "bourgeois" state, as well as among younger Germans who viewed the Weimar Republic with distrust, if not hatred, as a corrupt and anemic offspring of a lost war. "A large number of our people lack the spirit of dedication and devotion toward the republican and democratic state that is essential for its welfare," he wrote seven years after the Revolution of 1918. If the new democratic republic were to survive, the people had to learn to "love" it as a state dedicated to their welfare, to pass beyond an evaluative respect for the legal forms of the Weimar Republic to an acceptance of it as the Fatherland, a matter not of the mind but of the heart.[57] Such patriotism was not the worship of "intoxicating illusions of power and glory," but "love for a nation and a fatherland" that demanded service and sacrifice from its people. Anyone could love a country that could distribute largess; true patriotism was devotion to a poor and defeated fatherland that not only had nothing to give, but had to demand sacrifices from the entire nation.[58]

Schumacher fully shared his party's resentment over the punitive provisions of the Treaty of Versailles and the efforts of the French to enforce them. His political activities gave him only limited opportunities to comment on international affairs, but his occasional observations indicate a rather parochial outlook.[59] He made obeisance to the Socialist ideal of international cooperation —particularly cooperation among member parties of the Labor and Socialist International (the Second International)—but at the same time expressed the hope that German statesmen would achieve increasing independence of action in foreign policy. "The other nations must give the Republic the opportunity to establish a peaceful, satisfactory, and promising relationship with the rest of the world," he wrote in 1924. "The present dependence of our policies on con-

ditions abroad must not cause us to sit on our hands. In the last analysis, the
deciding factor will be how we ourselves manage our fate and that of our
state."[60]

Peace, commerce, and honest friendship with all nations, entangling alliances with none—Thomas Jefferson's advice to Americans in 1801—sums up
well Schumacher's rather rudimentary ideas of foreign policy in these years.
He held the Western powers accountable for preserving the capitalist system
in Germany after the 1918 Revolution, and for saddling the young democracy
with a punitive peace treaty and vindictive French harassment. He especially
resented—and was never to forgive—the efforts of the French to dismember
the Reich by supporting separatist movements in the Rhineland during the
1920's. But generally he favored "cooperation" with the Western powers, and
condemned suggestions that Germany use force to try to obtain a revision of
the peace terms. He was particularly opposed to "chauvinistic" threats against
Poland, which he said showed a lack of comprehension of a people he himself
knew only too well.[61] As for the Soviet Union, he categorically rejected its
political system and its German supporters, but he was quite prepared to maintain normal diplomatic relations, and in 1922 defended the Rapallo Treaty as
a realistic measure. Arguing for German aloofness and neutrality at the S.P.D.
national congress at Magdeburg in 1929, he stated: "By joining any alliance
system . . . we would be playing our trump card—freedom from alliances
and responsibilities [toward other nations]—without having properly exploited it."[62]

At the same congress, Schumacher gave clear evidence that he was by no
means a categorical pacifist, even if he had but recently attacked the party
leadership for supporting the battlecruiser appropriations. In the great debate
over the relationship between Social Democrats and Reichswehr, he affirmed
the need for a defense establishment, in opposition to the uncompromising
pacifists and left-wingers in the S.P.D. He wanted the Republic's armed forces,
like the judiciary and the bureaucracy, to be "democratized" instead of serving
the "interests of reaction." He also wanted to make certain that should a world
war start in Europe—presumably between the Soviet Union and the Western
powers—Germany would not become involved. Germany, he claimed, was not
obliged to become the "foil" of the European powers.[63]

Schumacher's unabashed appeal to patriotic emotions was probably an expression of personal sentiments rooted in his background, but it was also part
of the role he had chosen to play in Stuttgart as the spokesman of militant
Social Democracy. His was the Jacobin "national socialism" of Lassalle as well
as of Jean Jaurès, the French socialist leader whose name Schumacher liked
to invoke. It was a revolutionary reformism that stood for the aggressive advancement of social and economic democracy within the framework of the
democratic Weimar Republic—conservative with regard to the extremism of

right- and left-wingers who wanted to overthrow the Weimar state, and radical with regard to the evolutionary reformism of the dominant S.P.D. leadership. It was, even then, what one observer later labeled "a militant social democratic nationalism."[64]

Marxist theories, by contrast, served Schumacher as an analytical framework within which he could justify his political behavior, rather than as a definitive and prescriptive doctrine for action.[65] He used Marxist concepts and slogans in his articles and speeches as a means of attacking the "economically powerful classes" who were resisting Social Democratic efforts to advance economic democracy. The concept of the class struggle served as an intellectual underpinning for his criticism of many kinds of wrongs: discrimination against "the less privileged" in the administration of justice, "feudalistic chauvinism" in the armed forces, resistance by a "reactionary bureaucracy" to progressive legislation, and, generally, what he called the opposition of "big capital" to the advance of political and industrial democracy in Weimar Germany. Finally, Marxist analysis led him to declare that Nazism and Fascism were but temporary devices in the battle of the "big capitalists" against the poorer classes, a connection made by many Social Democrats.[66]

Such ritualistic employment of Marxist concepts and slogans was standard political procedure in Weimar Social Democracy, but Schumacher may have found in it a personally satisfying vehicle for his belligerent assertions of superiority over political opponents.[67] However, there is no evidence to sustain the assertion of some writers that he was a dedicated Marxist at this time.[68] On the contrary, he was highly critical of both orthodox and radical variations of Marxist thought. In his dissertation he took the "neo-Marxist" radicals to task for refusing to face political reality, particularly for clinging to the illusion of international working-class solidarity, and he categorically rejected Leninism as a Russian perversion of Marxism. He had little patience with what he conceived to be a lack of realism among the orthodox Marxists in his own party, whom he held largely responsible for the persistent and paralyzing conflict between the theory and practice of German Social Democracy. Thus, in the debate over a Social Democratic military program at the Magdeburg Congress of 1929, he attacked "the fathers of the Marxist Church" for their preposterous "exegesis" of a problem that was primarily of practical importance.[69] He firmly rejected the doctrine of Marxist determinism that was formally embraced in his party's program.[70] The German people, he insisted, were the masters of their fate, and it was up to them to decide how they would use the opportunities for social and economic improvement that the Revolution of 1918 had given them. "History . . . does not ask whether something can be explained or excused," he wrote; "it asks only whether or not a political idea, a militant class, can master its own fate."[71]

Schumacher has often been described as belonging to the small group of

Social Democrats known as the "Young Turks," who sought in vain to rejuvenate the leadership, theory, and practice of their party in the last years of the Weimar Republic. Superficially, there was a considerable similarity of background and political behavior among members of this small group, who sought a position between the dominant majority in the party, on the one hand, and the radical Marxist left-wing opposition to the leadership, on the other.[72] They consisted mainly of university graduates, journalists, and war veterans, who were relatively recent recruits to the party, politically aggressive and ambitious, and attracted more by the Lassallean "national socialist" tradition of the party than by its Marxist legacy. The most prominent oppositionists, Schumacher, Carlo Mierendorff, Theodor Haubach, and Julius Leber, were all close enough in age to sympathize with the thousands of young German war veterans and university students who vaguely longed for a "collectivist" but not "Marxist" cure for what they believed to be a sick society. Moreover, to a certain extent they shared the rebellious mood of a generation that rejected as anachronistic and anemic the philosophical outlook of the founders of the Weimar Republic, and that ultimately played a considerable role in the growth of the anti-democratic extremist movements. They, too, were impatient with the old leaders and their methods, and desired to fight right- and left-wing extremists with their own weapons.

Such were the similarities of the younger S.P.D. leaders. However, it would be going too far to speak of a common ideological orientation among such diverse, strong personalities as Schumacher, Mierendorff, and Leber.[73] It is often overlooked that they disagreed on such important issues as their party's relations to the armed forces, and that they cooperated only for the last brief year or two of the Republic in seeking a more militant strategy. Leber, in particular, seems to have had little liking for Schumacher. And in all probability there would have been serious clashes among these men, in their competition for power, had not Hitler's victory suddenly ended their brief association.

Frustration: Hitler's Victory

Many of Schumacher's admirers ascribed to him in retrospect more prescience about the Nazi dictatorship than appears justified. According to persons close to him in the period immediately before and after Hitler's accession to the chancellorship in January 1933, Schumacher shared the belief of most Social Democratic leaders that if the Nazis came to power at all, they would not rule for long. This belief was shaken once or twice when he was under the pressure of Nazi attacks, but for most of the time he refused to concede that Hitler's mass support was anything but a temporary phenomenon. He expected it to disappear with economic recovery, and believed that a regime resting merely on bayonets would soon disintegrate.[74]

The decline in Nazi votes in the November 1932 election gave Schumacher

—like so many Social Democratic leaders—new hope that the tide was about to turn. There was a strong feeling that if Hitler failed to gain power now, his chances would be gone for good. Furthermore, Schumacher's own political future probably looked rather promising to him, after his victory over Keil in the fall of 1932, if the political situation in Germany could improve. The older S.P.D. leaders appeared to be giving way to the younger militant elements that he represented, and a decline in Nazi and Communist strength promised to advance their fortunes not only in the party but in German politics in general. Perhaps the wish was father to the thought, as it was to be more than once in Schumacher's career.

As we noted earlier, Schumacher had become increasingly vocal in opposing the Social Democratic strategy that "tolerated" the conservative Brüning government from 1930 to 1932 as "the lesser evil," and accepted policies that appeared to many party members inopportune, if not a rank betrayal of the economic and political goals of Social Democracy. Brüning's dismissal in May 1932 by President Paul von Hindenburg, the old Imperial field marshal, must have been a relief, particularly since the S.P.D. leaders had just felt compelled to support Brüning's campaign for the re-election of Hindenburg against Hitler and the Communist Ernst Thälmann. The appointment of arch-conservative Chancellor Franz von Papen and his "Cabinet of Barons" ended this period of toleration of nonsocialist governments, and gave Schumacher the opportunity to give full vent to his longing for political warfare against the conservative and extreme right.

In December 1931, Schumacher and some other young S.P.D. leaders had been instrumental in forming the so-called Iron Front, which aligned the S.P.D. with the Reichsbanner, trade unions, and socialist athletic organizations, and was designed to mobilize the supporters of the democratic republic for physical combat, if necessary, against the anti-republican forces of the right. Though many of the old Social Democratic and trade union functionaries viewed the organization with considerable distaste, its leaders managed to acquire arms and to stage some impressive demonstrations.[75] Schumacher was in his element, and used the demonstrations to make rousing speeches throughout Germany against the "reactionary" von Papen government and its financial and military backers as well as the Nazis.

On July 30, 1932, the Social Democratic and trade union leaders submitted without a struggle to von Papen's seizure of the government of Prussia, only two days after Schumacher had announced in Stuttgart "We have no intention of submitting."[76] "The taste for bloody adventures was completely alien to them," one of these leaders was to explain later; "Social Democracy had for decades been a party that believed in peaceful evolution, rational judgment, and nonviolent compromise."[77] The failure of the S.P.D. and trade union leaders to give the long-promised signal for resistance in just such an event was bitterly resented by the militants, who believed some show of resistance would have been possible. The relationship between them and the party and trade union leaders became increasingly tense, though a traditional sense of discipline prevented an open rupture. While members of the Reichsbanner and socialist youth groups clamored for action, the party leaders viewed with suspicion and distaste attempts to fight Hitler with his own weapons, and clung to more moderate tactics in the hope that the tide would turn.

Whatever Schumacher's private sentiments, in public he faithfully echoed the party line that "premature" resistance would be useless, and that the democratic forces must husband their resources for extra-parliamentary counteraction until the situation was "right." Also in line with Social Democratic strategy, he bitterly denounced the Communists, and called upon the workers to follow only the S.P.D. in the class struggle for a socialist Germany. Von Papen and his successor as Chancellor, General Kurt von Schleicher, he denounced as crypto-fascists, saying that he saw little difference between "the blue aristocratic fascism of the barons and big industrialists, and the brown petty-bourgeois fascism of Hitler."[78]

This is not the place to recount the collapse of German Social Democracy after Hitler came to power on January 30, 1933.[79] It is sufficient to note that the party and trade union leadership once again failed to give the promised signal for resistance. Even while the Nazi terror got under way, mass demonstrations of the Iron Front and scattered preparations by the Reichsbanner preserved the illusion that the signal would still come. In Stuttgart, intensive preparations for open resistance continued right up to the election of March 5, 1933, in which the Social Democrats in general, and Schumacher's bailiwick in particular, did far better than anticipated (see Tables 2 and 3 above).

The party leaders, including Schumacher, hardly knew what to expect next. Schumacher's associates later recalled that he was relatively optimistic and did not think Hitler would rule for long, though he did not share the extreme illusions of some party leaders who expected the Nazi regime to collapse within months. Like many people, he seems to have counted on pressure from abroad to force a return to a more conservative government, such as that of von Papen or von Schleicher. He knew the Nazis well enough not to underestimate how violent their regime was likely to be, but he apparently did underestimate its stability and duration.

About his own immediate fate Schumacher had few illusions. He knew that he could expect no mercy from men he had done his best to provoke and insult. The local Nazi boss, his old enemy Gauleiter Wilhelm Murr, had already told a Nazi victory demonstration in Stuttgart on the March 5 election night that heads would roll and bones be broken.[80] Already hundreds of anti-Nazis were being beaten, imprisoned, and murdered by Nazi leaders determined to settle old scores and stifle any possibility of opposition. Capitulation, flight, suicide, or resistance were the options that lay open to anti-Nazis. Wilhelm Keil chose to capitulate, Wilhelm Bazille committed suicide, and many others fled abroad. Schumacher characteristically chose to defy his enemies.

Only the certainty of a bloodbath persuaded Schumacher to call off the mobilization of his militants on election night and cancel a counterdemonstration of the S.P.D. On March 23 he appeared in the Reichstag to vote with the other remaining S.P.D. deputies against giving Hitler dictatorial powers. During the brief conflict that followed the passage of this law, in which a majority of the national S.P.D. leadership sought to appease the Nazis and a minority advocated resistance, Schumacher strongly argued for resistance. He opposed the final ignominious appearance of the Social Democrats in the Reichstag on May 17, and to the last vainly urged the remaining party leaders to disband the official organization before it was outlawed by the Nazis, and thus make it possible for the party to continue the fight illegally.[81]

Although for himself Schumacher categorically rejected the road to exile urged on him by his anxious friends, he defended those of the S.P.D. who did leave against the bitter attacks of those who stayed behind and sought some sort of accommodation with the Nazis. However, he never forgave those who not only capitulated but collaborated, such as his old chief Wilhelm Keil. Keil, assured by the Nazis that they respected him as an honorable patriot, and considering opposition useless, called upon Social Democrats "to support the reorganization of Germany in the spirit of the National Revolution" of 1933.[82] While Schumacher and others suffered in concentration camps, Keil and a number of other once-prominent S.P.D. leaders lived comfortably on a pension from the Nazi state. Schumacher never forgot.

Schumacher worked frantically in the weeks of freedom remaining to him. He held secret meetings with his closest associates, making plans that were to prove far too optimistic and entirely inadequate for resistance to the Hitler dictatorship. Although he knew that a warrant was out for his arrest, he appeared at a meeting of S.P.D. leaders in the Prussian parliament building in Berlin to voice his opposition to the appeasement course that ended three days later with the prohibition of the S.P.D.* He managed to escape arrest for almost three more weeks, during which time he worked with a number of other young Social Democrats in Berlin, trying to establish a nationwide underground organization and drawing up a revolutionary manifesto calling upon the German workers to rise against Hitler.[83]

On July 8, Schumacher was to meet his cousin in Berlin. "I am pretty certain to be free," he had written her, perhaps deliberately giving his words a

---

* The warrant for Schumacher's arrest, a copy of which is in the possession of Frau Annemarie Renger in Bonn, was issued on June 13, six days before the meeting of the S.P.D. leaders. In a postcard to his cousin, Dorothea Kollmorgen, he mentioned having learned of it on a trip to southern Germany.

double meaning. But he had to apologize soon after for missing the meeting, on the grounds that "higher powers had interfered." At five o'clock in the morning of July 6 Schumacher had been taken into "protective custody."

Schumacher's letters from the police prisons in Berlin and Stuttgart immediately following his arrest indicate that once again he was conscious of ending a phase in his life. He wrote to his girl friend that he did not know what would become of him, but he hardly expected his Nazi friends in Stuttgart to suppress their desire for revenge and set him free. Indeed, the local Nazi press proclaimed the arrest of "one of the most shameless Social Democratic agitators in Germany," and expressed "the desire of the broadest public" that he be given the "special treatment" he deserved:

With a criminal hatred bordering on hysteria, he spit upon and libeled the National Socialist leaders and movement. No citizen of Württemberg will ever forget this top Red's aggressive attacks in public meetings and in the *Schwabische Tagwacht*. His malicious accusations ... were so abysmally vulgar that Dr. Schumacher cannot expect to be treated as a political opponent but only as a criminal.

He was one of those who could not find big enough words with which to demand from the deluded workers the complete destruction and eradication of National Socialism. He called for violence at every opportunity, and threatened the brutal annihilation of all National Socialists by force of arms.[84]

Schumacher was sent to the concentration camp at Heuberg, not to be free again for ten years. Like some other young militant Social Democrats, Mierendorff and Haubach for example, he had refused to save himself by flight in the belief that his "calling" demanded sacrifice. Did he realize what was in store for him? Probably not, for how could he even guess at the conditions he would face in the concentration camps or anticipate the length of his imprisonment? He felt he had to stay, his friends recalled, because it was his duty as a beaten opposition leader to do so. It seems that once again he had to prove himself. Frustrated in the performance of his role as an aggressive political leader by the sudden transformation of the political context, he had to find a new role that would suit the needs both of his personality and of the situation now facing him. This was the role of the concentration camp prisoner.

FOUR

The Prisoner

The Universe of the Concentration Camp

Kurt Schumacher spent practically the entire Nazi era in what David Rousset has called "the universe of the concentration camp."[1] Many observers were later to consider this experience of decisive importance for his postwar behavior; it was said that it left him a changed man. However, any effort to assess its impact on Schumacher's personality development faces two obstacles: first, lack of information about the experience itself, a lack largely due to Schumacher's subsequent reticence, which even his biographers were unable to overcome;[2] and, second, limited knowledge of his character before this period. Nevertheless, the most important aspects of the experience can be roughly reconstructed on the strength of available evidence, circumstantial as well as direct. Some excellent studies of the German concentration camps furnish material for a general description of the setting and the characteristics of long-term inmates like Schumacher, while letters he wrote and the testimony of a number of his former associates in the camp permit some inferences about his particular adjustment to camp conditions in the light of his previous personality development.[3]

The German concentration camps were self-contained communities with their own particular institutions, laws, norms, and symbols—even their own historical traditions. There were very definite patterns of interaction among the strongly interdependent inmates, and between them and their S.S. guards. There was a distinct system of social stratification among the prisoners, and in each camp the community was further divided into subgroups based on political and religious values, national or geographic origins, work activities, and sleeping quarters in the camp. No inmate could avoid involvement in the life of this community, though the degree of involvement could vary a good deal according to his personality and situation. As Hans Gerth and C. Wright Mills have pointed out, the chances of survival in an extreme situation such as that of the concentration camp are greater for the person who involves himself closely in group activities than for the person who attempts to remain aloof.[4]

The camp at Dachau in Bavaria, not far from Munich, where Schumacher was imprisoned for most of the ten years, was one of the first large camps. After such "extermination" camps as Mauthausen and Auschwitz were established, Dachau seemed comparatively mild; officially it was categorized as a Class I camp with somewhat better living conditions and food rations than other camps.[5] However, to the inmates such differences of degree were meaningless; conditions at all times were bad enough, and they deteriorated greatly over the years Schumacher was there.[6]

As in most camps, the prisoner compound at Dachau was surrounded by an electrically charged barbed-wire fence, which was punctuated by watchtowers equipped with searchlights and machine guns. This fence completely sealed off the compound from the living quarters of the guards and the world beyond, and had only one gate. Within the compound were the prisoners' barracks, hospital, kitchen, orderly room, latrines, and washrooms. A large open space, the so-called roll-call area, served for the assembly of the prisoners in the morning and at night, as well as for special events such as floggings.

The prisoners wore striped uniforms and small caps. Most had their heads shaved, but the specially privileged, according to Schumacher, were allowed to write a few more letters and let their hair grow a bit longer.[7] The prisoners slept on wooden bunks, usually arranged in tiers of three or more, and in Class I camps like Dachau they were given some bedding. It was a deliberate policy of the Dachau camp administration to require the shapeless pallets and bolsters to be arranged each morning, in record time, as neat and flat as the boards that supported them. Sometimes an entire barrack would be penalized for a wrinkle on one prisoner's bedding.

All prisoners were badly undernourished. The official minimum per head was 2,000 calories a day, but after war broke out, it was usually far less than that. In the early years, prisoners at Dachau could supplement their meager rations with small purchases from the prison canteen, but this practice was apparently stopped when war broke out. The daily rations consisted of about a pound of dark bread, a pint of ersatz coffee, a bowl of a foul soup, and minute amounts of margarine, sugar, and sometimes jam. The prisoners were always hungry, and were subject to the severe physical and emotional reactions of constant malnutrition. They resorted, often ruthlessly, to any means to satisfy their hunger. Those who could not procure additional food fell victim to the physical and psychological effects of starvation and eventually died.*

---

* Harry S. Sullivan has noted that "if for a long time one has had an adequate diet, and then this diet becomes seriously inadequate and continues so, there are likely to appear certain disturbances

The prisoner's day began with screaming sirens, which woke him between four and five o'clock in the summer, six and seven in the winter. He had half an hour to attend to his personal hygiene, bedmaking (or "bed-building" in such camps as Dachau), and breakfast. Then came the dreadful morning roll call—rain or shine, winter or summer—in the open area designated for this purpose. Each man had to be accounted for, and if the count did not tally with the lists, the prisoners had to remain standing until the error or the missing prisoner, dead or alive, was discovered. This could take hours, sometimes twenty-four or more. After roll call, each prisoner either went to a regularly assigned place of work or was picked for a labor detail; the workday was ten to twelve hours. Most prisoners had to work almost continuously at a frantic pace, usually outdoors, at extremely hard tasks. Before wartime needs brought about a more "productive" use of their labor, most of them were given economically senseless tasks, which were designed exclusively to humiliate, torture, or break them in body and spirit. Work assignments inside the compound, and particularly indoors, such as in the kitchen, hospital, clothing-supply depot, or offices, were far more desirable than outside details, and could mean the difference between life and death for a physically weak prisoner. Evening roll call, after work, could again last many hours and might cut into the precious hour or two of "free" time before lights out, when prisoners could converse, mend their clothing, and attend to other needs for which the daily routine allowed no opportunity.

In the course of their day, the prisoners were subjected to constant physical and mental abuse from the guards, and often from fellow prisoners as well. The sadistic horrors perpetrated in the camps are well enough known to obviate their description here. It is sufficient to say that the prisoners were at the mercy of men who were free to abuse, torture, or murder them. The sole defense was passivity: to avoid such encounters, as far as possible, by inconspicuous behavior.

The original camps were designed to help the Nazi regime consolidate its position in Germany by taking into "protective custody" prominent political figures, trade unionists, writers, and journalists, thereby leaving their followers too terrorized and disorganized even to think of opposition. The camps also served to satisfy the desire of individual Nazis to be revenged on political enemies and to settle personal scores. Without having to resort to regular judicial procedures, the Nazi leaders could simply send known or suspected enemies to the secluded concentration camps, to be dealt with by the peasant boys and psychopaths who wore the uniform of the Nazi storm troops and

---

of the vital biochemistry of the body which seem to leave one peculiarly unable to 'pull one's self together' after unpleasant events, and therefore ready prey to demoralization." In Stanton and Perry, eds., p. 81.

elite guards. Intellectuals and professional men were treated with particular brutality, since their persecutors took pleasure in humiliating men who in regular life were regarded as their superiors.

The original population of the camps consisted largely of former Communist and Social Democratic functionaries; they were soon joined by actual or alleged members of left-wing underground resistance groups. Most of these early inmates were of working-class background; intellectuals of middle-class antecedents like Schumacher were relatively few at first, but the social background of the prisoners gradually became more heterogeneous. In 1936, members of religious groups of lower middle-class background, such as Jehovah's Witnesses, began to arrive. Jewish professional men, businessmen, and shopkeepers were sent to the camps in increasing numbers. At the same time, the Nazi regime decided on a policy of "re-education" through hard labor— "Work Redeems [*Arbeit macht frei*]" was written over the gates of most camps—and hardened convicts who had served their regular terms, along with pickpockets, vagrants, gamblers, alcoholics, and homosexuals, poured into the camps. In 1938 and 1939 the conquest of Austria and Czechoslovakia brought an influx of Austrian and Czechoslovakian prisoners, who were followed after the outbreak of war by large numbers of Poles, Russians, Czechs, Frenchmen, and other non-Germans from conquered countries. In the last years, more Germans, suspected of anything from hoarding to outright sabotage during wartime, joined the procession to the camps.

The result of the influx was twofold. First, the camps became vastly overcrowded. Living and sanitary conditions deteriorated correspondingly, and far more deaths were caused by hunger and disease than by the brutalities of the guards. Second, the prison population came to include more and more persons of middle-class background, particularly with the influx of Jews and intellectual leaders from conquered countries. German political prisoners— surviving old-timers or "concentrationnaires," to use Eugen Kogon's expression—were easily in the minority.

A prisoner's social background had no bearing on his status in the society that evolved within the universe of the concentration camps. The S.S. camp administrations sought to impose a rough stratification by classifying prisoners according to the reasons for their imprisonment.* However, because they found it convenient to have the prisoners themselves assume responsibility for executing S.S. commands and work quotas, they capriciously awarded positions of authority to individual prisoners and whole groups of prisoners, and as capriciously withdrew them, thus establishing a stratification based upon positions of influence within the camp society. So far as the prisoners were concerned, social status was evaluated according to the extent to which

---

* Prisoners wore insignia of different colors, which indicated whether they were political, religious, or racial enemies of the Nazi state, or criminals, homosexuals, or "asocials" such as vagrants.

a prisoner's position permitted him, if he wished, to help his fellows improve their lot—improvements that ranged from procuring them food, clothing, medicines, and other supplies to placing them in better quarters, keeping them from being put on bad work details, and preventing them from being sent to worse camps or extermination camps. Thus the prisoners' interpretation of camp positions hardly tallied with that of the S.S. administrators, a conflict that presented the incumbents of these positions with a difficult choice.

The camp aristocracy—the "prominents" in the camp lingo—were the prisoners who held the most influential positions. The S.S. appointed ex-convicts whenever it could, since it felt that they were the most likely to interpret the job according to S.S. standards. The political prisoners, among whom Communists were most numerous, fought mortal battles with the convicts for control of these positions. Whereas the convicts tended to exercise the role according to S.S. norms, the politicals played it according to the norms of the inmates. The Senior Camp Prisoner represented the community in its formal relationship with the camp administration. The job, as Kogon has pointed out, was considered crucial and dangerous; an incumbent who shared the values of the community could do a great deal for the inmates, whereas "the wrong man" in this spot could do enormous harm.[8] Similar considerations applied to lesser positions, such as the job of Senior Block Prisoner, Senior Barracks Prisoner, and Block Clerk.

Camp trusties, called "Capos," headed up all work details, and the S.S. usually filled these positions not on the basis of skill, but for the incumbent's ability to work his men to the point of exhaustion and death. Ex-convicts and former freebooters, who sought to outdo the guards in abusing the prisoners, were favored. However, Capo positions that demanded a certain amount of skill and intelligence could not be filled in this manner. Since many of the camp administrators were incompetent, they needed help in operating the machinery of oppression, and they were forced to permit political and other nonconvict prisoners to fill clerical or similar positions in offices, hospitals, shops, and so forth. The incumbents had the power of life or death over a prisoner by their opportunity to alter personnel files, make work assignments, assign quarters, and prepare lists for transfer to other camps. Capos in the hospitals could often save sick prisoners from medical experiments, or hide healthy ones in isolation wards; those in the kitchens, food stores, clothing depots, tool shops, and laundries could provide fellow prisoners with food, clothing, or barter items necessary for survival.*

The holders of these influential positions in turn appointed the members

---

* Occasionally a special skill won a prisoner a position in the aristocracy. A barber, a musician, or a good painter might find sufficient favor with key S.S. personnel to influence them for the community's benefit. One of Schumacher's associates in Dachau, who was a painter and amateur poet, claims to have literally "bought" lives with his pictures and verses.

of the second estate, so to speak, clerks, barracks and hospital orderlies, and minor work overseers. The willingness of a "prominent" to make such an appointment—the S.S. rarely interfered—depended on friendship, factional ties, or bribes. To be elevated into this middle position, a prisoner had to have the right connections, and in this way, the "prominents" were able to establish small feudal domains within the camp community. They sought to create as many such secondary positions as they could within their own domain; featherbedding was a regular procedure.

The great mass of prisoners belonged to the lowest stratum in this social pyramid. They got the least food, the worst jobs, and the poorest quarters. In their case, the internally evolved social structure and the externally imposed stratification of the S.S. overlapped to a certain extent. In camps containing both Jews and "Aryan" prisoners, the former hardly ever rose above the lowest stratum. Those on this level who lacked the means and energy to procure extra food and clothing tended to become what were known as "Moslems," inmates who no longer cared whether they lived or died. Prisoners to whom the S.S. assigned the grim task of making up the lists for the extermination camps and death transports usually filled the required slots with Moslems, who were considered virtually dead anyway.[9]

Challenge and Response:
Schumacher in the Concentration Camp

There is considerable disagreement among analysts of the German concentration camps about how much a prisoner's personality had to change before he could adapt to the extreme situations prevailing in the camps.[10] However, most observers agree that it was previous character development even more than physical stamina that determined how successfully a prisoner could adjust—from his first exposure to the situation to his maturation into a seasoned veteran. How he sustained the continuous assault on his personality during the adaptive process, and how much it caused fundamental changes in his personality, appear to have depended in the last analysis on his emotional resilience.[11]

Severe shock was the initial reaction of most prisoners to the conditions that distinguished even the very first concentration camps from ordinary prisons. Denied satisfaction of the most basic needs, and subjected to or forced to witness abominable cruelties, the new inmate might succumb then and there. If he had the inner strength to withstand this first assault on his personality, he usually passed into a state of reactive depression and demoralization which, too, could be fatal to his mind and body.* The prisoners who

---

* A study of 30,000 American prisoners captured in 1942 by the Japanese in the Philippines found that "emotional shock and reactive depression played great parts in individual ability to cope with physical symptoms and disease and undoubtedly contributed to the massive death rate . . . during

overcame these initial experiences most successfully were those whose ego defense mechanisms were such that they could maintain strongly held political, religious, or ethical values in the face of extreme pressure to adopt others with an apparently higher survival worth. Those who lacked such values, who sought only to adjust to the new universe and concerned themselves "merely with the day-to-day camp life, food, work, releases and transports, gossip and rumors," either underwent a basic personality change in order to regain their emotional equilibrium, or went into a rapid decline ending with death.[12]

The men who sent Schumacher to the Heuberg concentration camp in August 1933 obviously intended to break him. His closest friend from the Stuttgart period witnessed his arrival in the camp, and later recounted the "welcome" he got from a double row of guards, who beat him as he passed between them. He was given senseless and exhausting work to do, such as collecting small pebbles in a bucket, emptying it, and starting all over again. A former leader of the S.P.D. in Württemberg observed the one-armed man rushing about the camp grounds occupied in this fashion, but was not allowed to come near him.[13] For not meeting his "work quota," Schumacher had his already meager food rations reduced to the lowest category, and was not permitted to receive food parcels. The former chain smoker was not allowed to smoke. He could have no visitors, and his only regular contact with the world outside was an exchange of censored letters every three weeks with a single person—first his girl friend and later his oldest sister. Books they sent him were taken away again as punishment for "uncooperative behavior." He never complained in his letters, but indicated between the lines that his health was failing rapidly.

Schumacher's letters from the concentration camps at Heuberg and Kuhberg during the first two years of his "protective custody" indicate that he prepared himself from the start for a long imprisonment. A friend who shared his barracks said Schumacher told him soon after arrival that he expected to be imprisoned for ten years—until the Nazi system collapsed.* For the other prisoners the mere idea of remaining in the concentration camp for more than a few weeks or months was unendurable; they would have committed suicide had they thought they would be imprisoned longer, this friend recalled. Schumacher accepted a fate that he repeatedly declared he had delib-

the first months of imprisonment." As in the case of the concentration camp inmates, the feeling of being deserted and abandoned to a hostile people, the severe deprivation of food, clothing, and living comfort, and the exposure to constant physical and psychological abuse and intimidation caused the psychic collapse of a large number of American prisoners. See Nardini, in *American Journal of Psychiatry*; also Harry S. Sullivan, in Stanton and Perry, eds., p. 49.

* As this informant pointed out to me in an interview, Schumacher's attitude regarding his own fate was inconsistent with his intellectual analysis of the duration of the Nazi regime. He was unwilling to concede his Nazi opponents the strength to rule long, but at the same time he was girding himself psychologically for the personal trials of an extended imprisonment.

erately brought upon himself by his past political activities, by his failure to emigrate, and now by his refusal to surrender in the camp. When his correspondents on the outside expressed the hope that he would soon be released, he replied that he had no such optimistic illusions. He indicated in his letters that he did not expect to see his loved ones again for a long time, and wrote that it was premature, to say the least, to worry about what would happen to him when he was released. His girl friend had lost her job after his arrest, and he urged her with increasing insistence to emigrate to the United States. After her departure, he told her emphatically that she should devote herself to starting a new life abroad and stop worrying about his most uncertain future.

Schumacher's biographers report that when he first arrived in the concentration camp, a guard advised him to hang himself right then and there, but he replied that he would not relieve his jailers of this task.[14] This response, and his response to the concentration camp in general, seems entirely consistent with his previous personality. His self-esteem was apparently enhanced by the retribution that he believed he had invited by his militant anti-Nazi activities, and this appears to have strengthened his determination not to submit. He refused to surrender to men who seemed afraid to let him go free and whom he had long despised as an inferior breed.[15] He defiantly challenged them either to destroy him or to keep him imprisoned; either course would again prove that the one-armed cripple was superior to his political opponents. To submit would have meant not only political surrender, but total frustration of the compensatory drive which, according to our theory, was vital to the maintenance of his ego. For Schumacher, a *pro forma* act of submission such as signing some document conceding defeat was as much out of the question as an open surrender. His nature would not allow him to buy freedom in this manner, even if such a concession were to enable him to take up the fight against the regime outside the camp or save himself for future tasks. By denying himself this opportunity, which reportedly was offered him several times, he asserted his superiority over men who in his eyes would be conceding defeat if they killed him or released him unconditionally. Thus the fact that they continued to keep him imprisoned as a dangerous political adversary confirmed the high estimate he put on his competence in his chosen field.

Bettelheim has said that to survive as a man in the concentration camp, debased and degraded but still a man, an inmate had to be constantly aware of the point of no return, the point beyond which he could never, under any circumstances, give in to his oppressor.[16] What we might describe as Schumacher's threshold experience occurred in the spring of 1935, after almost two years of abuse, humiliation, and starvation. He reached the limit of what he would take, and confronted the Nazis with a categorical choice by going on a twenty-eight-day hunger strike. For reasons that are not entirely clear, he was not allowed to die. Whether the Nazis were impressed, or whether they feared adverse publicity if the crippled war veteran should die (both reasons have been suggested), they yielded in the face of Schumacher's continuing defiance. He was sent to Dachau, where the conditions of his imprisonment were a good deal better.

Schumacher's action, however, had its adverse side. Not only did he ruin his digestive system and gravely weaken his constitution, but he made his continued imprisonment a certainty. He had successfully impressed his unalterable opposition upon the Nazi rulers, and made it quite clear that he would join the active anti-Nazi opposition as soon as he should be freed. Though other former Social Democratic militants were released, repeated efforts by Schumacher's mother and sister to obtain his freedom failed. When in 1937 his girl friend in Chicago petitioned the German government to free her "fiancé," a secret directive from Hitler's chancery informed the Foreign Office that there could be no question of Schumacher's release. His "radical, Marxist attitude" was said to constitute "a direct danger to the public safety," since upon his liberation he could be expected to join the anti-Nazi movement at once. The regime had to protect itself by keeping him in its custody.[17]

In Dachau, where Schumacher was sent in the summer of 1935, he became a veteran of the concentration camp, a concentrationnaire. He learned to adapt himself to the universe of the camp without sacrificing his personal integrity, and to face with equanimity the uncertainty of indefinite imprisonment and the unlikely chance of survival. With the marriage of his girl friend in the United States and the death of his mother in 1937, his personal ties with the world outside were practically severed, so that his dedication to his chosen role of political martyr became complete. From this time onward private attachments and pleasures played no part in his life. He had become a political man pure and simple, his political task was all-encompassing, and political considerations and values his sole criteria of conduct.

Schumacher was never given a position of responsibility during his imprisonment, but enjoyed relatively gentle treatment in these later years. He was given a job in the camp library, where he spent practically all his waking hours. This circumstance may have saved his life. Not only did he have an indoor job with a limited demand on his dwindling physical energy, but with a modicum of caution he could find plenty of time for reading, since the S.S. guards rarely visited the library. He was allowed to correspond once a month with his sister Lotte, who assumed responsibility for him after the death of his mother, and to receive from her occasional packages and a small monthly allowance that enabled him to buy some extra food and a few cigars.

Nonetheless, the chances of Schumacher's survival diminished with the length of his imprisonment. He was not exempt from the grueling camp routines, such as the long roll calls in all kinds of weather. He suffered from painful stomach ulcers, and a weakened digestive system made it difficult for him to retain camp food that was steadily deteriorating in quality and quantity. Cold, malnutrition, and reduced resistance further undermined his constitution and probably accelerated the onset of the circulatory disorders that were later to cost him a leg, and eventually his life. Coffee, which his sister sent him occasionally, and cigars and cigarettes, which he was now allowed in limited quantities, probably aggravated this condition. His vision became seriously impaired, most likely from a Vitamin A deficiency, and he would probably have lost his sight had it not been for an operation performed in a Munich hospital in 1940.[18] The authorization of the operation constituted a most unusual concession on the part of the camp administration, and must be attributed to the persuasive arguments of friends of Schumacher's who were working in the camp hospital. Some time later, a medical commission from Berlin came to Dachau to select economically useless and ailing prisoners for transportation to the extermination camp at Mauthausen. Schumacher was apparently saved from joining several hundred prisoners in the gas chambers only by his own wariness and the assistance of his friends.[19]

Schumacher's behavior in the concentration camp community made him one of those exceptional prisoners who exercised a certain amount of influence without holding a key position. More than one former inmate literally worshiped beyond the grave a man who seems to have had a charismatic impact even under the extreme conditions prevailing in the camp. Twenty years later, men who had been imprisoned with him still recalled the strong impression his appearance and behavior had made upon them. One, who was neither a friend nor a political associate, recalled vividly the striking impact of the lean, erect, ascetic figure of a man apparently unaffected by his environment and psychologically quite self-sufficient.[20] He was considered a good comrade, but aloof, impersonal, and uncommunicative, a man who attracted others because he seemed able to surmount his environment by sheer force of personality.

Most of the seasoned veterans were tough, coarse, sly, and often ruthless in their relations with other prisoners. They felt they could not afford pity or compassion, and usually lived according to values that bore little relation to those they had held before their imprisonment. Theft, dishonesty, and selfishness were "normal" in a situation that constantly tempted men to betray their principles and their comrades in order to survive. Schumacher's courage, intellect, and incorruptibility commanded respect and admiration in a community in which these qualities were in short supply. He was known to go out of his way to assist prisoners who were starving, ill, or headed for the extermination camps. He gave advice and encouragement to new arrivals, which helped ease them over the first critical period in the camp, and sought out "non-Aryan" prisoners despite a rigid camp rule prohibiting such contacts.* In a

* Former prisoners recalled seemingly small gestures on Schumacher's part that meant a great deal to them at the time. For example, a supreme court justice recalled twenty-five years later how

highly competitive social system, he was believed to seek no special advantages for himself. His unyielding opposition to the Nazi system, and his courageous behavior toward the S.S. and visiting Nazi dignitaries (who sought him out to gloat over his fate), were widely known and admired.* In short, he seemed to his fellow prisoners not only to have maintained his dignity and mental balance, but to have the strength of character to adhere rigidly to his ethical and political principles under conditions that to some extent had corrupted most of the inmates of the camps.

At Dachau the camp aristocracy was composed of political prisoners, mostly Communists but also some Social Democrats. Schumacher had a certain amount of influence over the latter, since many of them were impressed by his martyrdom to a cause that other Social Democrats had deserted. It was well known that other S.P.D. leaders had somehow made their peace with the Nazi system, or had gone abroad; in the isolated universe of the concentration camp, martyrdom seemed rather senseless—but admirable.

Most of the Social Democrats who held key or middle positions in the camp society were men of simple background and limited education, who came to Schumacher for advice. He cautiously sought to use his influence with them to prevent factional disputes that might be exploited by the S.S., or by the convicts, who wanted the influential positions for themselves. He also sought to persuade these aristocrats to assist other prisoners and avoid the ever-present danger of becoming tools of the camp administrations. Though he tried to remain aloof from the intrigues of camp politics, he apparently found it hard at times to maintain this position. Not only was he the object of constant efforts to involve him in factional intrigues, but he was intensely aware of the harm that could be done by the wrong man in a position of authority, and the ease with which a weak man could be corrupted by the S.S., or even a strong man persuaded to execute criminal orders in the hope of preventing worse.

After the war, Schumacher was repeatedly accused by Russian and German Communists of having directly or indirectly caused the maltreatment and death of fellow prisoners at Dachau. In particular, he was charged with collusion with a Senior Camp Prisoner named Kapp, who was later tried in the Soviet Zone of Occupation for collaborating with the S.S. in the murder of prisoners. Schumacher had no difficulty in disposing of these accusations; nu-

---

Schumacher had eased the first shock for a group of new arrivals by offering them cigars. Benedict Kautsky remembered how he, the "non-Aryan" Austrian Social Democrat, was sought out by Schumacher when he arrived in Dachau, and advised to forget all thoughts about early liberation and accustom himself—as Schumacher had done—to the prospect of a long imprisonment. Kautsky said that this proved to be a great psychological boost, which helped him to make the all-important adjustment to camp life. A letter to Schumacher after the war from a former fellow inmate at the Neuengamme camp thanked him for lending him money.

* Thus Schumacher's old enemy the Gauleiter of Württemberg, Wilhelm Murr, had Schumacher brought before him on an inspection trip to Dachau to ridicule and taunt him. Schumacher's provocative replies may well have helped to extend the term of his imprisonment—at least Schumacher himself and other inmates believed that they had.

merous ex-prisoners volunteered statements testifying to his unimpeachable personal conduct. But he did not deny having tried on several occasions to warn Kapp and other prisoners in positions of authority that their collaboration with the S.S. was bound to have catastrophic consequences, not only for the other prisoners but eventually for themselves. As he wrote a political associate, he had felt it his duty to do so. He claimed that though these men at various times assured him that they would resist S.S. pressure to collaborate, they capitulated when such pressure was seriously applied. He had no intention of defending them now, he said, but he did wish to point out that it was all too easy to be corrupted when disobedience would certainly mean loss of status and privileges, and probably severe punishment.[21]

We have already noted that Schumacher belonged to that rare breed of concentration camp prisoner who eschewed the social contacts most inmates found essential for their psychic survival. Lone wolves such as he seldom survived under the extreme conditions that made men closely dependent upon each other, physically and psychologically. The men with whom for many years he worked in the library all day, and those who shared his barracks, found him taciturn and withdrawn. His closest associates were a handful of men with whom he felt an intellectual kinship, regardless of political background. With them he would walk through the camp streets in the evening, discussing political problems and developments about which he managed to be unusually well informed, thanks to his position in the library and his interest in new arrivals at the camp. Purely private and personal matters he rarely, if ever, discussed with anyone.

Schumacher owed his survival to the help of men whom, it appears, he accepted as neither equals nor intimates. They, in turn, admired and respected him as a kind of symbol. To survive as a human being in the face of deliberate efforts to murder the moral person in man, to use Hannah Arendt's expression, one "had to find some life experience that mattered, over which one was still in command."[22] For some of these men, helping Schumacher may have been a way of retaining a hold on certain human values—ethical, moral, political— that threatened to vanish under the brutalizing impact of camp life. For some he may have embodied the unbroken spirit of Social Democracy and anti-Nazism, for others courage, decency, and unyielding conviction. Fellow prisoners who helped him make his bed, keep his clothes clean, and keep up with the rigorous camp routine probably derived considerable moral satisfaction from performing these services.

Schumacher felt a great moral debt to the Capo in charge of the library, whose solicitude for him was described by another of the librarians as almost maternal. After the war Schumacher went to great lengths to help this man. But above all he owed his life to men who worked in the prison hospital as Capos and orderlies. To be ill in a concentration camp was a very serious matter, particularly during the war, for not only was disease rampant and medical care totally inadequate, but a sick prisoner was in constant danger of being given a fatal injection or being sent to the gas chambers. The men in the hospital provided Schumacher with food that his ailing digestive system could absorb and with drugs to ease his pain; they probably saved his sight when they persuaded the S.S. physician to send him to Munich for the operation on his eyes; and, finally, he owed them at least one narrow escape from transportation to an extermination camp.

When Schumacher's cousin from Leipzig met him shortly after his release from Dachau in 1943, she was shocked and frightened by his appearance. The damage he had suffered was purely physiological, he assured her; he was not the sort of man whose spirit could be broken even under the worst conditions. "Those ten years did not leave a very deep impression," he said later. "I do not depend solely on the material things in life."[23] This was not an empty boast—Schumacher's personality does seem to have been singularly suited for survival in the camp—but it would be going too far to maintain that his character development was entirely unaffected by the experience.

Various authors have stressed the great importance of ego maintenance for the concentration camp prisoners in view of the constant threats to which their personalities were being exposed. Feeling forgotten and abandoned by an outside world that was seemingly ignorant of conditions in the camp and the fate of its inmates, even those with the strongest personalities found it difficult not to succumb to despair. Extreme sacrifice for a secular political cause was far more difficult to accept and sustain when it seemed doubtful that anyone on the outside knew that the sacrifice was being made, or would ever know. According to Benedict Kautsky, "Precisely those [prisoners] who expected the regime to last a long time and deliberately accepted the prospect of a long imprisonment realized how insignificant the propagandistic impact of their behavior would be." Lacking support from outside, political prisoners in particular were entirely dependent for ego maintenance upon whether they could adhere to their principles, and it was essential for the survival of most of them that this loyalty find recognition from at least a few other inmates.[24] For Schumacher, there were very few inmates whose belief in him and his martyrdom could satisfy this need for self-reaffirmation.

If our basic hypothesis is correct that Schumacher had sought to compensate for a low self-estimate by asserting his superiority in his chosen field of politics, then the need to compensate was probably even stronger at this stage of his life than before. Not only was a deliberate attempt made to degrade him personally during the first phase of his imprisonment, but the entire system was designed to degrade all inmates, to make them feel inferior, helpless, abandoned. Schumacher, one of his fellow librarians at Dachau recalled, was deeply upset by the taunts of his oppressors. Others remembered that he was exceedingly sensitive about his dependence on other prisoners, including political opponents, for even minor services such as making his bed. Such help emphasized once again that he was a cripple, who could not take care of himself. Camp life brutally threatened his defense mechanism against inferiority feelings.

In trying to maintain his self-esteem and emotional equilibrium, Schumacher could not compensate for feelings of inferiority in the overt and aggressive manner that had characterized the pre-1933 phase. He was keenly conscious of one of the most important rules in the camp, the need to be inconspicuous, because it applied to him even more than to most inmates. The Bavarian peasant boys, whom he later declared to have been too stupid to merit his hatred, nonetheless had the power to abuse him; moreover, they had a marked predilection for tormenting intellectuals. On the one hand he defied the S.S. and held his jailers in contempt, but on the other he had to watch his step in order to survive. On one level of consciousness he was aware of the need to maintain his self-control, no matter what the provocation, and to obey the camp rules rigidly; on a deeper level he risked self-betrayal by antagonizing the S.S. and Nazi visitors in order to assert his defiance. Bruno Bettelheim recalls deliberately provoking an S.S. officer in the camp "in order not to collapse. I had to prove to myself that I had some power to influence my environment. I knew I could not do so positively, so I did it negatively."[25]

Schumacher must have lived in a constant state of tension during those years. In addition to the mounting psychological pressure of his precarious existence, he could not satisfy in the accustomed manner an increased need to compensate for his feeling of inferiority.[26] This psychological deprivation probably aggravated his physical complaints, particularly those of the digestive system, leading in turn to even more intense somatic-psychological reactions as he sought to overcome his physiological complaints by sheer strength of will. It was this iron determination to survive that saw him through, according to the testimony of a number of people who observed him closely; and to maintain it he required an extreme, self-assertive power drive focused on the future.

We have noted already that Schumacher deliberately chose to play the role of political martyr and sustained it throughout the Nazi era. What gave him the physical and emotional strength to do so appears to have been an absolutely unshakable belief that his voluntary martyrdom would find its justification when the Nazi system collapsed and he could assume a leading role in the reorganization of German society that was certain to follow. The conviction that political martyrdom would some day prove justified involved in the first place a strong sense of exclusiveness and superiority, of belonging to a counter-elite feared and hated by the Nazis. "I never altered my behavior while in protective custody," he proudly and truthfully asserted immediately after the collapse of the Third Reich, "nor my political attitude toward the S.S. in the camp or Nazi policies in general."[27] Not only did he despise his oppressors, but he felt superior to other former political figures who had come to terms with the new political system, including members of his own party.

In the second place, Schumacher's martyrdom appears to have been based on a strongly self-righteous and critical attitude. We know nothing specific about his opinions during these years, but fellow prisoners recalled that in conversation he spoke with great bitterness of the shortcomings of the Weimar Republic and its supporters. He appears to have shared the belief expressed by many people after the catastrophe of 1933 that the old Social Democratic leaders had been too tolerant, too ready to compromise, too uninterested in acquiring power, and too indifferent to the longing of the German masses for strong charismatic leadership.[28] He was particularly bitter about the part that the Communist leadership had played in destroying the Weimar Republic, a matter that he considered beyond dispute. Since most of the Communist prisoners were equally categorical in defense of their past policies and leaders, he avoided all political discussions with them, and consistently rejected all suggestions for a united front between Social Democratic and Communist prisoners such as took place in many other concentration camps.

Schumacher claimed later that he already held in camp the political beliefs he expressed immediately after the war.[29] Fellow prisoners with whom he discussed political problems recalled few specific topics of conversation, but remembered that in general he took a very assertive position and became easily impatient with those of his listeners who were unable to follow his arguments. He was relatively well informed about political developments outside the camp, but apparently interpreted them quite dogmatically.

Former prisoners agree that the most depressing part of concentration camp life was not knowing how long it would last. Victor Frankl, one of the most astute participant observers of the camps, puts it this way: in time, "it was the limitlessness of the term of imprisonment which was most acutely felt; in space, in the narrow limits of the prison." The world outside seemed remote and unreal, "almost as it might have to a dead man who looked at the world from another planet."[30] Daydreaming became a common defense mechanism under these circumstances. Many a prisoner sought to escape the uncertain and horrible present by dreaming of a past that by contrast seemed very attractive. This form of escape weakened his ability to adapt to the present and usually meant that he did not survive long, for life simply lost its meaning. However, a prisoner whose value system included a future beyond the term of his imprisonment, whether in heaven or on earth, possessed a time perspective, which gave him a reason to adapt himself to the present rather than try to escape it. His belief in his future gave meaning to a miserable life, and his aspiration toward future goals was a strong reason for surviving a provisional existence that thus acquired a definite limit. As Frankl points out, Nietzsche's words

"He who has a why to live for can bear with almost any how" could be called the guiding motto for all such efforts to fight the camp's psychopathological influences.[31]

In discussing the importance of such goals in the prisoner's conscious or unconscious efforts to survive the psychopathological influences of the camp, Frankl has stressed the particular importance of a feeling of personal indispensability. A prisoner who was convinced that no one could take his place at some all-important future task—particularly if it seemed to him an altruistic goal, such as caring for loved ones or executing an important project—felt the responsibility to survive especially strongly.[32] All the available evidence indicates that Schumacher projected his claim to distinction into the future, and believed that he must survive because it was his mission to play a leading role in post-Nazi Germany. Moreover, he sought to encourage other prisoners by telling them, too, that martyrdom would entitle them to a leading role after the fall of the Nazi system. He merely regretted that more Social Democrats had not qualified.[33] Among long-term prisoners of various political complexions and nationalities, the belief that they were "called" to assume leading roles in a post-Nazi world was quite prevalent. This mystique of a concentrationnaire elite sustained many political prisoners through the long night of their captivity.*

Coupled with this projection into the future of a sense of uniqueness was a firm conviction that the present existence would not last forever. Schumacher had known from the start that his imprisonment would be long, but according to his own statement he had felt equally sure that Hitler's policies would lead to war, and "no power on earth" would be able to prevent the loss of such a war and the collapse of Germany.[34] Such psychotherapeutic certainty seems to have emerged from a far more rigid and dogmatic adherence to Marxist determinism than had been typical of Schumacher before his imprisonment. The onetime pragmatic politician appears to have derived from Marxist theory psychological support and assurance of ultimate victory. His conversations and discussions both in camp and afterward indicated that much of his time in prison was devoted to re-examining the past and analyzing the present and future in terms of economic determinism.

"The way in which a man accepts his fate and all the suffering it entails, the way in which he takes his cross, gives him ample opportunity ... to add a deeper meaning to his life," Frankl has written. "He may remain brave, dignified, and unselfish. Or in the bitter fight for self-preservation he may forget his human dignity." Only a few prisoners succeeded in defending themselves against the camp's "degenerating influences" on mind and body.[35] Kurt Schu-

---

* Bettelheim considered such "messianic hopes" a form of escape from the unpleasant reality of the camp; in such cases as Schumacher's, however, these wishful projections into an uncertain future did not deny reality, and therefore did not prevent the prisoner from adapting to camp life.

macher was particularly well equipped to do so. The course of his character development was little affected, it appears, since his personality required no fundamental adjustment to accept this new phase in his life. In general, the ten years of imprisonment seem to have reinforced traits that were already central to his character when he entered the camp.

Schumacher's responses became more rigid as a result of his camp experiences. Far more than in the days before 1933, his style of life became routinized, his habits highly ordered, and the pattern of his relationships inflexible. Always a cynic about his fellow men, for the rest of his life he trusted few and was suspicious of most. Always a stubborn man, there was now no moving him when he had set his mind on something. Never notable for tolerance, he was now far more dogmatic and self-righteous.* Perhaps most important of all, the camp experience confirmed his single-minded drive for political power. Nothing else mattered any more. He had lost his taste for wine, women, and song, as he put it himself. The compulsions of this compensatory drive now monopolized every aspect of his life and thoughts.

A Period in Limbo

Schumacher was released from Dachau in March 1943, in the custody of his sister Lotte and her husband, Leo Trinkwalter.† The Trinkwalters lived in Hannover, where Schumacher was a complete stranger, and the Gestapo apparently had no fears that he would become involved in anti-Nazi activities there, despite his defiant assurances that he was still categorically opposed to the regime. Besides, he appeared physically incapable of causing any more trouble; indeed it seemed unlikely that he would live for long.‡ He was ordered to report daily to the police and given a minor clerical job in a local factory.

For the next two years he lived a life almost as precarious as his existence in the concentration camp, with apparently only one thought in mind, to survive a regime that he felt was doomed. The German Sixth Army had capitulated at Stalingrad just before his release, and in May 1943 the Axis forces surrendered

---

* It can of course be argued that all men become confirmed in their ways; these developments in Schumacher's character, however, were too pronounced to be regarded as no more than part of the natural process of aging.

† Trinkwalter was a civil servant and a member of the Nazi party (which he had joined in the hope that it might help Schumacher). His pleas and his guarantee for his brother-in-law's good conduct were apparently instrumental in effecting Schumacher's release. Schumacher appreciated these efforts on his behalf though he did not approve of them, and in all likelihood they influenced his compassionate attitude toward "little Nazis" in later years. There appears to be no substance to the story (*Turm.*, I, 37) that plans had been made by friends to smuggle Schumacher out of Germany after his release and that he refused to go. His sister, the only person notified of his impending release, categorically denied the story when I interviewed her.

‡ With bureaucratic thoroughness, the local draft board summoned Schumacher for a physical examination after his release, but they dismissed him as entirely unfit for military duty. They almost took him, Schumacher wrote with typical sarcasm to his cousin, for it was found that he had had military training thirty years earlier and that his remaining arm was in fine shape.

in North Africa. Hannover, like other large industrial centers, was beginning to feel the full weight of the Allied strategic air offensive. The city had "a rather impressive visitor from the United States," he reported to his cousin in July 1943, "and since then, one alarm follows another."

Schumacher must have reacted to these developments with mixed feelings. The collapse of Germany could not come soon enough for him, but at the same time he could not be certain that he would survive the holocaust. In October 1943, he and his relatives were bombed out in a raid that destroyed most of Hannover. Schumacher's first reaction, his sister recalled, was to give voice to his fear that all his sufferings in the concentration camp would have been in vain if now, at the last moment, he should fall victim to an Allied bomb. His fear was not unreasonable. Although Schumacher did not know it, Carlo Mierendorff, his onetime associate in the leadership of the Iron Front, was killed in just such an air raid at about this time, after spending six years in a concentration camp and subsequently becoming deeply involved in the plot that culminated in the July 1944 attempt on Hitler's life.

Schumacher's letters to his cousin between his first release and his re-arrest reflect a certain fatalism. He had learned by bitter experience to take life as it came, he wrote her repeatedly, and he would give way neither to despair nor to optimistic illusions. His future must have seemed less certain and predictable to him than it had been in the concentration camp, and his life even more subject to influences over which he had no control. His physical condition did not improve with his release, though he now received some regular medical attention. Rationing made it impossible to get the kind of food his stomach ulcer could tolerate; he was close to starvation and hardly equal to the demands of his job. His supervisor at the factory recalled how he would arrive at work gasping for breath after a one-hour trek from the little attic to which he had moved after his relatives had been bombed out and left the town. He did the best he could during his eight-hour workday, but if it had not been for the kindness of this supervisor and the directors of the factory, he would probably have collapsed at the job.

Schumacher was exceedingly careful to comply with all the rules of his probation. He concealed his past and his academic training from his fellow employees and avoided all political contacts. He rejected absolutely some tentative approaches from former Social Democrats in Hannover, and suspiciously avoided any social contacts outside the factory. His only friend in this intensely lonely period was his supervisor, who managed to break through his guard, and frequently took him home with him. Schumacher knew nothing of the July 1944 conspiracy to kill Hitler and overthrow the Nazi system, though a number of his former fellow militants in the S.P.D. were directly involved. Nonetheless, he was picked up in the mass wave of arrests that followed, a so-called screening action (*Gitteraktion*), and was sent to the notorious concentration camp at Neuengamme in August 1944.

Schumacher was imprisoned at Neuengamme only a few weeks, but it was long enough to make the contacts he had previously so carefully avoided. He met a number of former Social Democrats from Hannover and the surrounding area, who were greatly impressed by his personality and behavior. These connections were to prove of immense value to him in the ensuing months. After his release, he felt secure enough in the chaos that preceded the final collapse of the Third Reich to hold surreptitious meetings with a number of his new acquaintances, from which emerged the underground nucleus of a new Social Democratic organization. As the Allied troops approached Hannover, Schumacher thought it wise to disappear, and was hidden by the factory supervisor who had befriended him. Later it was reported that orders had indeed gone out a couple of days before the occupation of the city to shoot a number of anti-Nazis, including Schumacher.[36]

Hannover fell to American troops on April 7, 1945. Schumacher was ready. Even before Hitler's suicide on April 30 had signaled the end of the regime, Schumacher had taken the initiative in reorganizing a local party organization. Once more he entered upon a radically new phase in his life, a phase which, gravely ill as he was, he expected to be the terminal phase and wanted to be the crowning one. He had found his identity in a marriage with politics; to maintain this self-image he had accepted severe deprivations and experienced extreme tensions. Now, at last, the time had come to obtain ultimate confirmation of his superiority as a political man, the time to prove himself in open battle and to justify the long wait, the suffering, the frustrations.

FIVE

Perspectives of a
Post-Totalitarian Leader

The Setting: Germany, 1945–52

Kurt Schumacher lived to play a leading role in his party and his country for only seven years after the end of the war, but for most of that period he was undoubtedly the most prominent German political leader. Not until 1948 did his great adversary, Konrad Adenauer, begin to rival him both inside and outside Germany. During the entire period, German leaders were compelled to operate under limitations imposed upon them by the Allied powers.

With the unconditional surrender of the Nazis in 1945, Germany was divided into four zones of occupation. Supreme authority was formally assumed by a four-power Allied Control Council, which consisted of the commanders-in-chief of the United States, the Soviet Union, Britain, and France. Whereas the commanders acted as independent administrators in their respective zones, in their capacity as members of the Control Council they were to serve as a sort of interim central government for a Germany federated into these four zones. A fifth area, east of a line corresponding roughly to that of the Oder and Neisse rivers, was to remain partly under Polish and partly under Russian administration until a peace treaty between a new all-German government and the Allied powers could be concluded. In the west, the Saar was placed under French administration, and it, too, was to remain outside Allied authority. Berlin, the seat of the Control Council, was under the jurisdiction of an inter-Allied military government for the entire city.

At the Potsdam Conference of August 1945, to which France was not invited, Russia, the United States, and Britain agreed to cooperate in the administration and political reconstruction of Germany. Joint control, however, proved to be impossible owing to conflicting conceptions of the purpose of the occupation and the future of the country. There was formal agreement that Nazis should be punished, anti-Nazis encouraged, and radical changes effected in Germany's socio-economic and political structure, so that a democratic regime could develop under Allied tutelage. The economic power of Germany was to be drastically reduced, heavy reparations in kind—capital and consumer goods—were to be paid to nations victimized by Nazi aggression, and German military power was to be eliminated entirely for an indefinite period. The difference between the Western conceptions and those of the Soviet Union turned out to be irreconcilable, whereas those among the three Western powers were eventually overcome.

The leadership of the Soviet Union apparently conceived the occupation as an opportunity to eliminate Germany as a potential threat, to render it harmless either by including it in the satellite empire, or, failing that, by delaying (if not actually preventing) the recovery of a united Germany as Europe's largest power. The Russians' efforts in this direction varied according to the opportunities they saw in a given situation. At first they tried to strip Germany of as much economic potential as possible, and at the same time to elevate Communists into positions from which they might influence the political complexion of a future German government. Later, they concentrated on building up the Russian zone of occupation into a Communist stronghold that could serve both as a power base for influencing the future of all Germany, and as an economic and military component of the evolving Soviet satellite empire in Eastern Europe.

The leaders of the Western democracies were initially agreed that Germany must not become a major power again, and they therefore took action in their respective zones to limit economic recovery, eliminate German war-making capacity, and create conditions for a very gradual evolution of a democratic and peaceful Germany under their tutelage. The measures taken in each of the three Western zones varied a good deal, according to the interpretation given to them by the different governments. The British Labour government, which controlled most of the industrial resources of Germany, fluctuated between a punitive policy of exacting reparations in kind for itself and other victims of Nazi attacks, and efforts to democratize German society by means of economic reforms in its own zone, such as the socialization of basic industries. The American democratization efforts placed chief emphasis on formal and legal measures, such as constitutional engineering, denazification proceedings, and the deconcentration of political and economic power. The French leaders, particularly while de Gaulle headed the government from 1945 to 1947, were concerned less with making reforms in their own zone than with bringing about the permanent destruction of Germany as a major power by dismemberment, far-reaching governmental decentralization, and international control of major industrial centers. The growing disagreement between the three Western powers on the one hand, and the Soviet Union on the other, gradually compelled the former to reconcile their differences and abandon most of their initial objectives.

After about two years of fruitless efforts to maintain four-power control and work toward the re-establishment of a united Germany, the Soviet Union and the Western powers abandoned all attempts at a cooperative occupation. As a result of the growing tensions between East and West throughout the world and in Germany in particular, the Western zones were amalgamated between 1947 and 1948 under American leadership, while the Soviet zone evolved into a full-fledged satellite of Russia. In September 1949, the three Western powers sponsored the creation of the Federal Republic of Germany in their amalgamated zones, while the Soviet Union simultaneously established the German Democratic Republic in its zone. Each side began to build up its "Germany" as a bulwark against the other, and to restore limited sovereignty to the governments of the two states. Parallel developments took place in Berlin, while Poland and Russia annexed the areas east of the Oder-Neisse line outright.

In addition to factors originating mainly outside the German political system, a number of internal factors impinged upon the activities of an aspirant for post-totalitarian leadership. These arose primarily out of the socio-economic situation of the immediate postwar years. The total defeat of Germany was accompanied by the virtual collapse of its economic and social structure. Chaotic conditions arising from the destruction of practically every city and a considerable proportion of the industrial plant, as well as the enormous number killed or crippled in the most productive age groups, formed the background for political action at this time. Allied bombing alone had destroyed or heavily damaged approximately 20 per cent of all dwelling units in the nation, mostly in the larger cities. Forty-nine of the larger cities had 39 per cent of their dwelling units destroyed or seriously damaged, and many had lost their entire central and business districts. About four million soldiers and between three and four hundred thousand German civilians had been killed in the war, about two million had been orphaned, and at least a million and a half had been crippled more or less seriously.[1] Communications were only slowly restored owing to a lack of rolling stock, fuel, and material for repairs. The dismantling of remaining industrial and transportation facilities for reparations handicapped economic recovery, particularly in the Soviet and British zones, in which German industrial capacity was concentrated. In general, the population of the urban centers in the British zone—Schumacher's main area of activity for the first four and a half years—suffered most from the aftereffects of heavy bombing, such as large-scale unemployment and housing and food shortages. The population of rural areas and small towns in the American and French zones was probably least affected.

The Allied conference at Potsdam had agreed that the German standard of living was not to rise above the average for any of the other European countries, many of them ravaged by war. However, according to the report ex-President Hoover submitted to the U.S. government in February 1947, the situation in West Germany had become far worse than that in any other part of Europe. The housing shortage, aggravated by the influx of at least six million refugees from Eastern Europe, was described as desperate, and the food situation as being at near-famine level. The report said the official target ration of 1,550 calories a day was wholly inadequate for health, and even that was rarely attained.[2] The British and American zones, moreover, were deprived of staple products that formerly had been shipped to West Germany from the Soviet zone, and a particularly severe food crisis developed in the British zone in 1946, which at one period forced official food rations down to the near-starvation level of 1,000 calories a day.[3]

The collapse of the economy was accompanied by a collapse of the prevailing social structure. Those who had held positions of authority under the Nazis were subject to the denazification program of the occupation powers. Not only Nazi leaders, but civil and military officials, business and industrial leaders, journalists, and educators were, at least temporarily, removed from office, and many were jailed, fined, or denied employment in any but menial positions. In the Soviet zone the purge was extended to include the landed aristocracy and other large property owners, regardless of the nature of their association with the Nazi regime. Thus in one form or another, all of the former elites were deprived of their status, with the sole exception of the religious elite of the Roman Catholic and Evangelical (Protestant) Churches.

The urban middle class of small businessmen, professional men, civil servants, artisans, and pensioners had suffered severe financial losses during the war; in the postwar chaos, many used up what money they had left, and many were hit by the currency reform of 1948, which practically wiped out remaining savings and investments in other than real property. Those who had been minor functionaries under the Nazis tended to be purged sooner and more severely than those who had held elite positions. They were usually fined, and particularly in the case of civil servants, forced to find new jobs. It has been estimated that immediately after the war about two-thirds of the previous middle class was "proletarized" economically.[4] Social leveling was increased by the flight or expulsion of about eight million Germans from Eastern and Southeastern Europe. Most of these refugees landed in West Germany, notably in Schleswig-Holstein and Lower Saxony in the British zone, and Bavaria in the American zone. Concentrated in rural areas, where employment was scarce and friction with the native population severe, they became for the greater part déclassé bourgeois, who had lost both their property and their social status.

The gradual restoration of economic order, the abolition of Allied restrictions on German industrial production, a drastic currency reform, and generous United States financial assistance eventually improved the situation in West Germany. Beginning in 1949, the national income began to rise rapidly, but the middle and lower economic strata were not to benefit at once. On the contrary, the immediate effect of recovery was a continuing polarization of the socio-economic strata in West Germany, with a new propertied elite rapidly emerging at the top and a broad stratum of workers and déclassé bourgeois at the bottom.[5]

The mood of despair that prevailed in Germany during the first postwar years both united and divided its people. The young novelist Heinrich Böll conveyed it particularly well in his depressing novel *Und sagte kein einziges Wort*. Millions of refugees and discharged soldiers crowded into the ruined cities in the hope of finding work and a place to live. Privacy, food, and warmth seemed all-important in this period of starvation and widespread poverty. Women who had lost their husbands, youngsters without parents, unemployed ex-officers, professional men, and artists sought desperately to find some basis for a new existence, or drifted apathetically from one makeshift job to another. City dwellers hated farmers, who seemed to be relatively well-off, whereas the rural population resented the evacuees and refugees who crowded their villages and were unable to leave for want of work and housing elsewhere. Families in inadequate and filthy quarters quarreled bitterly over petty matters. Self-pity and selfishness were prevalent, natural enough qualities in men and women preoccupied with satisfying the most elemental needs.

Ideological issues and political action were of little interest to most people at this time. A series of opinion surveys in the American zone of occupation indicated indifference or even hostility toward political action, parties, and leaders. In March 1946, one-third of those polled declared they were no longer interested in politics and considered it safer to stay out of them; over three-fourths said they had no intention of joining any political party. In October 1947, 70 per cent said they would refuse to assume a responsible political office, and over one-third thought that the "people" had no influence on political parties and leaders anyhow.

A survey just after the first general election of September 1949 showed that interest in politics in West Germany had not increased since the end of the war, and that public apathy and ignorance continued. A majority of those questioned said that political parties and their spokesmen in parliament were concerned far more with satisfying their own selfish interests than with doing anything for the voters or the country.[6] A survey a month before this same election had shown that more than 50 per cent of a cross-section of West Germans were thoroughly dissatisfied with the democratic parties and what they had accomplished since the end of the war.[7] At the same time, anti-democratic attitudes persisted. Between 50 and 60 per cent of the respondents in various surveys between November 1945 and October 1948 had expressed the belief that Nazism had been a good idea poorly executed.[8] In particular, many of the young West Germans born between 1919 and 1928, about one-fifth of the population, felt indifferent, cynical, or hostile toward postwar politics. They had been the most intensely involved of the West Germans in the Nazi system, and now that they were deprived of their former faith and ideals, they suffered most from the social and economic dislocation.

Though Germans were overwhelmingly apolitical in these years, they felt that the government should take action to provide economic and social security for the people. Something had to be done by someone, it was generally said, and in Germany this someone was traditionally the state. Far from reacting against the regimentation of the Nazi era, most West Germans preferred a political system that offered "economic security" over one that offered free elections, freedom of speech, and freedom of the press and of religion.[9] For a time there was a strong sentiment in favor of some form of socialization, particularly of heavy industry. Almost one-half of the respondents in a November 1947 survey in the U.S. zone favored socializing heavy industry, while less than one-quarter opposed it. Socialization was found to be particularly popular among former Nazis, civil servants, and skilled workers.[10] Although in subsequent years this specific demand declined, a more generalized sentiment for "socialism" and social welfare measures by the state, and an opposition to "capitalist ideas," remained strong.[11]

The setting for the actions of a man aspiring to become the leader of post-Nazi Germany was thus a political system subject to two major sets of determinants. One set consisted of the highly dynamic interventionist activities of the four occupation powers, each of whom pursued policies in accordance with its own images and expectations of a desirable future German state. In each of the occupation powers, these images, expectations, and resulting policies changed in response to interaction with the other powers, to changes in the attitude of the decision-makers, and, increasingly, to feedback reactions from within the German political system itself. The second set of determinants consisted of internal factors that derived from the political attitudes and behavior of the Germans. In this set, the actors comprised the population of the Soviet zone (in Schumacher's lifetime still one of the domestic factors) and the potentially and actually politically active West Germans, who ranged from the masses of eligible voters, letter writers, and demonstrators to the incumbents of domestic elite positions.

Schumacher's Interpretation of the Setting

Schumacher's interpretation of the postwar setting was manifestly based on historical memories set in a Marxist though ethnocentric frame of reference. Widely read but rather limited in his contacts before 1933, for the next ten years he had been isolated from developments outside the world of the concentration camp. Such information as he got had come to him through the totalitarian mass media, other prisoners, and the rumor mill. He had no personal knowledge of the countries that now occupied Germany, and had met very few non-Germans except fellow socialists and prisoners in the concentration camp, who were a special breed. He knew little or nothing about developments in the social sciences since 1933, such as the advances in the study of individual and group behavior. Thrown immediately into intense political activity, he had no time to catch up and reorient himself with the help of new information and new analytical tools. Lack of both opportunity and inclination led him to rely almost entirely on information and analytical tools which he had acquired before Hitler came to power, and upon which he had based his intensive, solitary speculations on the future of his country, his party, and himself while he was in the concentration camp. Thus he perceived and interpreted the context for his political activities after the collapse of Nazi Germany primarily in terms of learned and experienced history as seen through the prism of Marxist theory.

As we have seen, Schumacher had not been an orthodox Marxist before 1933, but the testimony of his former associates and many of his observations indicate that he relied heavily on Marxist analytical methods to interpret the postwar setting. He was far too intelligent and independent in his thinking to follow any dogma slavishly, but his perception of the political environment as fundamentally challenging was clearly Marxian. "A truly educated person," he told a group of intellectuals in 1946, "must be a universalist, must try to achieve a broad perspective of developmental patterns. If he cannot find a *Weltanschauung,* he must at the very least possess a theory of history."[12] Schumacher's theory of historical development, if not his view of world affairs, was explicitly based on dialectical materialism.

Marxism for Schumacher was "an indispensable analytical method in the fight for the liberation of the workers."[13] And the "two most important aspects of Marxism, the economic interpretation of history and the class struggle," seemed to him as valid in postwar Germany as they had ever been. A German labor movement not based on Marxist methods of socio-economic analysis he declared to be impossible. "The class struggle will end only when all men have equal rights and responsibilities," he informed the first postwar congress of the Social Democratic Party in May 1946.[14] He insisted that he used Marxism purely as a descriptive analytical tool and rejected it as a prescriptive dogma. He was certainly not "orthodox" in his interpretations, and refused to commit himself to a programmatic "party line." But it seemed to his closest associates that the economic interpretation of history and the concept of the class struggle determined his postwar assumptions and behavior far more than he would ever admit. Although he was more outspoken in his public application of Marxist analysis during the first years of economic and social dislocation than later on, there does not appear to have been any fundamental change in his outlook. His apparent ambivalence during the last years of his life seems to have been due to political prudence and tactical considerations.

In his first public appearance just after the occupation of Hannover (still before the formal surrender of Germany), Schumacher presented to a group of Social Democrats his perception of political developments, based on twelve years of intense reflection.[15] Looking beyond the immediate issues of defeat and occupation by foreign powers, he depicted German society as entering upon a new phase in the historical class struggle between the formerly dominant class of big property owners and the mass of the German people. The owners of the great banks and industrial empires, in alliance with large landowners and militarists, he said, had used the toil and blood of the masses for their profit-seeking, imperialist ambitions. Hitler and his Nazis, he claimed, had been brought to power by this unholy alliance. That the Nazis had failed to live up to the expectations of the capitalists, and had pushed them aside in order to indulge more freely their natural propensity to rob and kill, had been an unfortunate miscalculation on part of the ruling class—and a catastrophe for the rest of Germany. In no way, however, did this absolve the big capitalists of full responsibility for the Nazi system and its inevitable consequence, a catastrophic world war.

For at least a year or two, Kurt Schumacher believed Germany to be in a state of latent "proletarian revolution," which was kept in check only by the presence of the occupation powers. It seemed to him that the vast majority of Germans were either already economically proletarians or about to become such.[16] What he termed "the classic discrepancy" between capitalists and the proletariat seemed to him to have reached an unprecedentedly advanced stage in Germany. He told the Second Congress of the S.P.D. in 1947 that the polarization process was being rapidly accelerated as the poor became poorer and the rich richer.[17] While he publicly warned his fellow Social Democrats that it would be folly to ascribe "proletarian class-consciousness" to people who had lost their property but not their bourgeois outlook, he felt at the same time that a hopelessly impoverished majority in Germany had become anti-capitalist because of its economic proletarization.[18]

Why, then, did he view the political environment as hostile and challenging? Why didn't he feel that economic determinism would make the proletarian revolution inevitable? For that, it seems, Schumacher's Marxism was too unorthodox and voluntaristic. He could no more believe now in the certain defeat of the German capitalists than he had been able to believe in 1933 in the inevitable victory of Hitler and his "capitalist backers." On the basis of his analysis of past developments in Germany, he deeply feared that the large industrial and banking interests might manage to make a comeback.

Although Schumacher regarded the "feudal and capitalist elements" as ultimately to blame for Germany's misfortunes, he was not content to let the laws of economic determinism dispose of the foe. He maintained that it would take the utmost efforts of anti-capitalist Germans and the support of the occupation powers to frustrate the efforts of the big industrialists, bankers, and landowners to regain their former estate. In his first speech after his release in 1945, he warned that those who had turned German blood to profit in two world wars would not hestiate now to profit from the ruins of Germany in order to recover power and influence. Five years later he believed his prediction had come true: the same groups were once again seeking dominance in West Germany, this time with approval from abroad.

Thus, while Schumacher explicitly rejected Marxism as a prescriptive theory of political action, he implicitly made class warfare and the theory of the polarization of the classes the basis of his postwar strategy in the struggle for power in Germany. As one of his associates put it, he held a "grand view" of political developments and subordinated tactics to a strategy based on his Marxist assumptions. He tended to systematize and analyze political events in terms of the perceived dialectics of the situation, and tried to anticipate the next "logical" moves of his counter-players and plan his own moves accordingly. The class struggle against the reactionaries and capitalists was not only an analytical but an operational concept, with built-in images of the roles of other players in the system, whose behavior and motives could thus be readily explained. Similarly, with the nature of the capitalist enemy clearly understood, proposals for weakening, if not eliminating, the economic basis of his actual or potential power could be devised, for the problem was not new. Only rarely did Schumacher find it difficult to fit developments into this theoretical Marxist framework, or to decide between a tactical move that seemed momentarily opportune and the requirements of his grand strategy. Time and again he was to insist upon political moves that seemed inopportune to others in his party because to him they appeared to be dictated by the dialectics of socio-economic development. Purely economic or administrative questions did not exist, he insisted. However unimportant and purely technical an administrative act might seem, he said, in the last analysis it was a political act, subject to political considerations.[19]

On a more specific level, Schumacher's interpretation of the post-totalitarian setting was decisively influenced by what he perceived as parallels with earlier events in German history, particularly with events in the Weimar era. Although in the immediate postwar period he maintained that socio-economic and political conditions were completely different from those in the past and called for an entirely new political approach, in later years, especially after the creation of the Federal Republic in 1949, he referred increasingly to what he saw as analogous past situations. He professed to distrust historical parallels, but was perceptive enough to recognize that such professions were largely theoretical.[20] His own long preoccupation with the lessons of the past, and his phenomenal memory for relevant details such as election figures, no doubt caused such parallels to occur more readily to him than to other people.

A subject that he apparently regarded as particularly relevant to the postwar setting was the past behavior of the German masses and elites, notably in connection with the defeat suffered by the Social Democrats and Schumacher himself in 1933. He hated the "capitalist" and "reactionary" ruling elites, whom he held responsible for the war that had cost him his arm and for the destruction of the Weimar Republic; and he now saw them trying to get back into power. He believed them incapable of genuine democratic or patriotic attitudes or a sincere change of heart. He also deeply distrusted the hierarchy of a Roman Catholic Church, which he had come to identify with Polish reactionary nationalism when he was a boy, and with anti-socialism, separatism, and suspicion of democracy when he was a young politician. On the basis of past experience, he expected these groups to do their utmost to manipulate the masses once again under the guise of democratic practices and patriotic sentiments.

One of Schumacher's closest friends once observed that Schumacher loved the German people in the abstract, but had little confidence in the political sense of the individual German. Schumacher wrote to another old friend in October 1946 that the servile and unthinking attitude of the average German often made him wonder whether his countrymen were worth all his efforts to help them. Most of them, he felt, were distressed more by the fact that the war had been lost and their country occupied by foreign troops than by their own culpability in allowing themselves to be led like sheep to slaughter. All too many of them, he thought, were accustomed to being regimented and liked it. Corrupted by immoral and irresponsible teachers and reactionary Nazi propaganda, many of them had been taught to worship power and despise personal freedom. Might they not again fall victim to the irrational, emotional appeals with which militarists, nationalists, and Nazis had so often seduced them? Might they not revert to old habits of blind obedience to leaders who promised the sky but were bent only on exploiting them? Might they not succumb to the seductive propaganda of a radical right covertly financed by big business? They had done so in the Weimar era, and now, in their impoverished condition, the danger was greater. Might not desperate, unemployed veterans and workers once more rally in large numbers to Communism, as they were already doing in Italy and France?

Schumacher saw many signs in the postwar situation that indicated to him developments similar to those that had doomed the Weimar Republic. Once again democracy was the child of defeat, imposed by Germany's conquerors upon a reluctant or apathetic people instead of being the indigenous product of a genuine revolution supported by the masses. Once again separatism, sponsored by outside powers, seemed to threaten civil war and the unity of Germany. During the socio-economic chaos of the first postwar years, Schumacher believed the country to be in a state of latent revolution, and warned that the members of an impoverished lower middle class—hapless refugees and jobless veterans, and youngsters who had never known democracy— might fall prey to a new totalitarian movement. Rabid nationalist agitation, in his opinion, was likely to result from the heavy punitive measures he expected the Allies to impose. Right-wing radicals financed by the big capitalists and Soviet-sponsored Communists seemed to him once again the two mill-stones between which democracy and its supporters might be crushed. "We saw this same game being played in Germany before 1933" by "authoritarian capitalism ... and nationalist Communism," he reminded his fellow Social Democrats in 1947.[21]

"Once again" were words that cropped up with increasing frequency in Schumacher's speeches, as big business and conservative political groups recovered along with the economy. The currency reform of 1948 reminded him of the inflation of 1921–23 and the radicalization of an impoverished lower middle class that had followed. American Marshall Plan aid prompted him to recall that United States assistance had also helped German big business in the 1920's, only to be suddenly withdrawn when it was desperately needed in the Depression years of the early thirties. The result, he said, had been eco-nomic chaos, the growth of the Nazi movement, and eventually Hitler's vic-tory. He professed to see the German capitalist elite resorting to the same methods it had found useful in the past; it was already backing allegedly "democratic" right-wing parties, and it would soon be supporting clearly anti-democratic ones.

Insofar as these assessments were made for public consumption, they un-doubtedly contained symbolic warnings designed to mobilize anti-Nazis and opponents of "reaction." But in private conversations, too, Schumacher ex-pressed this same belief that conditions in West Germany were becoming increasingly like those preceding the crisis years of the Weimar Republic. Along with most of his economic advisors, he distrusted the evidence of economic recovery. On the basis of Marxist economics and memories of the past, he was inclined to believe that it could not last and would certainly fail to benefit the large mass of Germans.

Schumacher's interpretation of the postwar setting could not and did not fail to take into account the actions and apparent motives of the occupation authorities and their governments. The realization that all his public utter-ances, as well as some of his private remarks, came to the attention of the representatives of the occupation powers possibly led him to soften or leave unsaid what he may at times have thought. Though he was outspoken, he was usually aware of the need for discretion. However, in general, it seems that the motives and actions of non-Germans were important to him only so far as they appeared to affect his self-chosen roles in post-totalitarian Ger-many.

Goal and Role Perceptions

When the Nazi system collapsed, Kurt Schumacher publicly dedicated him-self to fight for "the indivisible trinity of peace, freedom, and socialism" in Germany.[22] The objective he was to set himself in the years that followed was the spiritual and political regeneration of the German people, which he hoped to achieve by liberating them from the domination and exploitation of big business and its henchmen. He and his followers, he said, sought to lead post-Nazi Germany toward the establishment of a democratic and socialist commonwealth; their goal was not power for its own sake, but power for the salvation of Germany and the world from the consequences of rampant German capitalist imperialism.

The available evidence indicates that Schumacher firmly and sincerely believed in what was to him a highly moral and unselfish goal, a goal to which he dedicated literally every ounce of his waning strength during the last seven years of his life. The establishment of a democratic socialist state was to him an ethical imperative supported by Marxist dialectic; he saw no contradiction between the moral goal and its scientific foundations. A democratic socialist system, he declared, would not only provide permanent economic security and social justice for the German people, but—even more important—it would give each German the freedom to develop his spiritual and moral resources to the full. And he was willing to wage uncompromising battle against all enemies of this goal, whether German or foreign.

Schumacher's dedication to the liberation of the German people from capitalist oppression allowed him to identify his personal drive for power with an ethically commendable, task-oriented social purpose. What he was doing was not for himself, but for his beloved, long-deluded, and exploited German people. He apparently perceived the more mundane and immediate problems of economic and political reconstruction in terms of his image of the German public interest in the struggle against capitalist oppression. If he tended to be rather ambivalent and vague about the organization of the state of the future, the ethical goal was no less useful to him in giving his political activities an acceptable moral purpose.

A strong moral fervor characterized all Schumacher's utterances about the imperative need for a socialist democracy in Germany. Along with the dialectic image of political reality went a moral-immoral dichotomy in his perception of what his country's goal should be. He spoke of this goal in terms of categorical absolutes. Either Germany would become a genuine democracy, or it would cease to be at all; either German democracy would be a socialist democracy, or it would not be a democracy; either socialism was democratic, or it was not socialism; there was no dictatorship of the proletariat, only a dictatorship over the proletariat; either the German people would find the road to their salvation, or they would once and for all be enslaved by one form of totalitarian dictatorship or the other, Communist or capitalist.

I shall not discuss critically or in detail Schumacher's elaboration of his categorical demand for "a new Germany, not a reconstruction of the old." Suffice it to say that he rejected every form of totalitarianism as inherently evil, corrupt, and destructive—the very opposite of socialism. He held that "bitter experience" had shown that large capitalist enterprises were incompatible with democracy, at least in Germany. The socialization of key industries—if not all the means of production—and other large properties was not merely an economic necessity but a political one. As long as immense economic power remained at the disposal of politically irresponsible groups, any formal democratic system was sooner or later doomed; it was doomed not only because such interests used their power to destroy or subvert majority rule, but because the uncontrolled pursuit of private profits by trusts and cartels was bound to lead to economic chaos and the surrender of power to a totalitarian dictatorship. Socialization and a planned economy for the benefit of all was a political, social, and economic necessity in the light of past experience and prevailing conditions. The more the masses participated in the political process and the greater their enjoyment of the benefits of the economy, the stronger the support for democracy; the smaller their participation, the greater the possibility of mass exploitation, misery, dictatorship, and war.[23]

The note of categorical moralism was even stronger in Schumacher's demand for a change in popular political mores. To break Germans of their habits of unquestioning obedience and political passivity, he sought to awaken a new sense of responsibility among them. He flatly rejected the Allies' theory of the collective guilt of all Germans for Nazi crimes, but he asked that Germans recognize and accept collective responsibility for the Nazi regime and its actions. The distinction seemed to him both morally and legally important. While he demanded severe punishment for all who were clearly guilty of Nazi crimes—whether Nazi leaders, industrialists, or military men—he wanted those who had been active or passive supporters of the regime to recognize their responsibility in permitting the Nazis to gain and maintain power, and to commit vast outrages. It seemed to him that the majority of Germans belonged in this category, for only a few had actively resisted the Nazi system. Frank admission of such responsibility was for Schumacher the first essential step away from the immoral power worship of the past toward a new political morality and sense of individual responsibility. He was ready to accept the sincere conversion of former Nazis, Nazi sympathizers, and camp followers. But he demanded more than lip service to new slogans and new masters, more than a mere reorientation toward new foci of power in accordance with the old values. He wanted each German to examine his past attitudes and behavior, and grope his way toward a new value system, toward a new appreciation of individual rights and liberty. Only then, he felt, would Germans be prepared to fight for these values.*

---

* Restitution to Nazi victims, particularly Jews, seemed to Schumacher perhaps the most immediate and effective way in which Germans who had supported Hitler could freely acknowledge their responsibility. Restitution (as distinguished from reparations to victor powers) was a moral act of atonement, however inadequate, because it was made voluntarily by an impoverished people, not for reasons of political expediency but out of a sense of moral obligation.

There was thus, in Schumacher's view, potential mass support for a genuine, i.e. socialist, democracy in Germany. But, he told the first postwar congress of the S.P.D. in 1946, he could at present see few real German democrats outside the Social Democratic Party. "All the others needed the persuasive power of the war potential and the superiority of the Anglo-Saxon weapons to discover their love for democracy. We [Social Democrats] did not need that; we would be democrats today even if the British and Americans were fascists."[24] According to Schumacher, only the Social Democrats, who had fought and suffered for convictions that events had proved to be true, had the historical and moral right to succeed the Nazis in the leadership of the country. They were the counter-elite, whose turn it now was to assume power. They alone had remained undeviatingly faithful to peace and democracy; they alone had been the true "counter-players of the Nazis," diametrically opposed to everything the Nazis had stood for; they alone had earned the right to lead.

According to Willy Brandt, one of Schumacher's close associates at this time, Schumacher was obsessed by the idea that the S.P.D. *alone* was qualified to become the governing party of post-totalitarian Germany, that it alone could "become the party of national deliverance and assume leadership ... to blot out the mistakes of the past."[25] He felt that in view of what he saw as the self-evident bankruptcy of German capitalism and the collapse of the old order, it was the legitimate right and duty of the Social Democrats to lead the German people out of chaos into a new era. The logic of history, and the moral and political imperative to establish a socialist democracy, made this clear. The Nazi dictatorship had been the culmination of the rule of monopoly capitalism in the class struggle against the German proletariat and its political representatives; now it was the mission of the Social Democrats, the counter-elite, to give political actuality to historical developments, and to create for the proletarized masses a democratic state.

To Schumacher only Social Democrats were intellectually and morally equipped for the task of leadership. Only they could claim as a group to speak for the anti-Nazis on behalf of the nation. They had fought Hitler in the name of peace and democracy even before he came to power. Their sacrifices had proved to the world "that not all Germans were Nazis, and that there was another Germany besides Nazi Germany."[26] And, finally, they had remained uncontaminated not only by Nazi totalitarianism, but also by Communist totalitarianism.

Schumacher did not deny that there had been other Germans who fought against Hitler, and Social Democrats who succumbed to totalitarian pressure. He appealed to the former to make common cause with the only major anti-Nazi movement, and he treated the latter with contempt. It was for Social Democracy as a movement, the movement of the active anti-Nazis, that he claimed the mission to lead Germany out of chaos. The existence of a strong

Social Democratic Party in postwar Germany was not just a partisan matter, "but a question of survival for the entire German nation and for Europe."[27]
In short, he claimed for Social Democrats an exclusive historical, moral, and
intellectual mandate to save Germany and the world by teaching the German
people political responsibility and giving them a new self-confidence.

Despite Schumacher's explicit professions to the contrary, his conception of
those qualified to become Germany's post-totalitarian leaders was clearly
elitist. There were certain similarities between Lenin's conception of the vanguard party as the "subjective factor" that gives history a "push" in the right
direction and Schumacher's voluntaristic interpretation of Marxist theory.
Though such a thesis cannot be proved, there is some reason to believe that
Schumacher, like other socialists during the Nazi era, made some of Lenin's
organizational concepts his own. However, the notion of the party as an
organizational vanguard of the proletarian movement was apparently not
central to his conception of the role of party leader. Rather, the elite position
he ascribed to the Social Democrats as a group served to substantiate his picture of their leader's task. His image of his own position as a post-totalitarian
leader rested on his complete identification with the Social Democratic elite
and its group goals, and at the same time set him apart from all other party
members and anti-Nazis.

Schumacher was absolutely convinced that the re-education of the German
people and the struggle for a socialist democracy would require exceptionally
strong and able leadership. In the fight for these goals, the obstacles that he
had anticipated, as well as those that developed unexpectedly, confirmed this
conviction. Moreover, he was sure that he was the only person inside or outside the Social Democratic Party who could direct the task at hand. Without
ever making the assertion explicit, he never left anyone in doubt that he believed himself called to lead the nation.

Schumacher seems to have regarded his entire political life up to this point,
particularly his voluntary martyrdom in the concentration camp, as a period
of apprenticeship for his postwar mission. What he asserted about the moral
and political rights of a Social Democratic counter-elite seemed to apply
most directly to himself. Had he not been preeminent among the young militant socialists who had fought the rising Nazi movement while the older
S.P.D. leaders remained largely passive? Could he not add to this record an
even more impressive claim to leadership based on his long and severe imprisonment for the cause? He brought to the image of post-totalitarian leader
the mystique of the concentrationnaire elite, the cream of the anti-Nazis,
whose fate, voluntarily incurred, stood in sharp moral contrast in Schumacher's
mind to that of men who had either profited under the Nazi system, or at
the least not suffered any great discomfort. Even underground fighters and
exiles could not claim to have made so great a sacrifice. He had "sat behind

barbed wire" and could therefore speak in the name of "my former comrades in the concentration camps, penitentiaries, and other institutions of penal servitude of the Third Reich."[28]

Schumacher's perception of his role as leader had the same high moral content as his perception of the goals he and his party should aim for. What remained of his life was now dedicated to the task of leading the crusade for the new Germany. He always avoided the first person singular in his speeches, and spoke in the plural for his party and those he believed it represented. His postwar letters substantiate the impression of his associates that he saw himself called to lead a sacred cause. He knew it was a "miracle" that he had survived the Hitler era, he wrote to an old friend in 1946, but "someone" had had to remain alive to help the German people onto their feet again. In exceedingly poor health even before the amputation of his left leg in 1948, and driving himself to the point of exhaustion, he felt that he was bearing the heavy cross because it was his moral duty, not a personal preference. As he wrote in a private letter in September 1946:

The situation in Germany is so unpleasant and the position of my party so very difficult that I have no idea where it will all lead,—not for me, either. Personally I have little desire to assume responsibility for conditions for which I feel in no way responsible. What keeps me going in my position as party chairman is simply a sense of duty toward Social Democracy and the German people. As far as I am personally concerned, I would much rather lead an entirely private life in as minor a position as possible. . . . One slowly uses up one's remaining physical strength. The desperate struggle for something that must be and will be achieved, though presumably too late, is slowly but surely completing the job of destruction that the concentration camp left unfinished.

But if in moments of depression he wondered whether there was any sense to it all, he also reminded himself and others that the "long years behind the barbed wire" had taught him never to capitulate, not even under the most severe strain. In a revealing letter written to a blind veteran in 1950, he said that the true test of the political man was the extent to which he was able to detach himself from personal misfortunes. Even if at times, he continued, the temptation to yield to a feeling of resignation was strong, the knowledge "that others have a claim to insights based on the experience of persons no matter how outwardly handicapped" sustained him. The important thing was to accept this duty willingly and without any sense of distinction.[29] And when in an interview a few weeks before his death he was asked to define the "democratic way of life," he spoke of it as "a willingness to work for causes that goes beyond the pursuit of mere personal advantages and interests."[30]

Schumacher's picture of himself reflects that curious mixture of modesty and arrogance which so often marks a dedicated man. He evidently saw himself in a dual role of both moral and political leader in a time of extreme crisis. In his capacity as a moral leader, he sought to set the highest possible standard for German politics, calling for absolute honesty, decency, and loyalty.* In his capacity as a crisis leader, an even more important function in his eyes, he saw himself as protecting the German people from a repetition of the situation that had led to Hitler's victory in 1933. "Those who have lived through 1933 and have seen the reactions of professors, students, the middle class, and even the workers know that there is something in our people which believes in the great leader," the German philosopher Karl Jaspers said after the war.[31] "Great leaders almost always emerge in a period of chaos," Julius Leber wrote after his arrest in 1933. "Therefore extraordinary times that see old walls and foundations being destroyed to make room for a new future to emerge out of the chaos usually witness the appearance of great leaders as well. These men and their goals give ultimate expression to the full force of their era."[32] Like Leber, Schumacher seems to have concluded from Hitler's success in mobilizing mass support that chaotic times, particularly in Germany, demand the strong leader who can personify as well as direct the longing of the bewildered masses for salvation.

Schumacher's interpretation of the postwar political context and the behavior it demanded of his party and its leader was an entirely subjective one. He turned a deaf ear to demands from within the party for a new *Grundsatzprogramm,* a reformulation of basic principles like that of the Heidelberg Program of 1925. "*Primus vivere deinde philosophari*: first survive, then philosophize," was his reply.[33] He refused to permit Social Democratic strategy and tactics to be codified or predetermined in any manner that might restrict his freedom to determine them himself. The facts of political life and the actions they required could not be determined by dogma, but only by a "realistic" appraisal of the situation, he maintained. He interpreted and prescribed strategy and tactics for the struggle for power, but he never submitted or approved a program for a Social Democratic government of Germany once power had been obtained.

First, Schumacher said, a democratic mass party such as the Social Democrats, committed to nothing less than the transformation of the entire world, could have only one strategic objective, the acquisition of decisive control in the state. In a newly emerging political system like that of post-totalitarian Germany, this drive for complete power had to be the touchstone of all Social Democratic activities. Until the strategic objective had been obtained, the party had to remain unswervingly on the offensive against any and all ob-

---

* "Es gibt eben keine Politik verschiedener Graduierungen, es gibt Dinge der politischen Moral und des Rechts, die kann man nicht beschneiden und die kann man nicht zum verschiedenen Gebrauch in verschiedenen Preislagen führen. Ein Prinzip der Politik ist nicht die Agitation des Gemischtwarenladens und des Warenhauses. Prinzipien sind unvertauschbar und unauswechselbar." *Turm.,* II, 246.

stacles. It had to avoid the lure of personal or factional opportunism and the danger of "excessive" compromise. It must refuse to take responsibility for decisions over which it had no control, and agree to cooperate with other groups only if it was in a position to command. Such were the lessons of the past. If Social Democrats could not obtain the key posts in the nation's life, it was better to refuse responsibility altogether and pursue a consistent opposition policy against those in power, rather than fritter away the party's strength in ineffectual positions. In this sense, attitudes and behavior that seemed negative today would prove to have been positive and constructive on the morrow.

Second, the fight for power required a strongly led, disciplined, and militant party that could attract overwhelming mass support and mobilize mass opinion behind its leaders and their goals. If "we Social Democrats have learned anything, or should have learned anything, from the experiences of the last decades," Schumacher said in Berlin in January 1950, "it is that one cannot simply depend blindly on evolution and progress." The S.P.D. could have won power fifty years ago, he maintained, "if we had managed to carry our ideas to the masses on a broader front and in greater depth."[34] More recently, Hitler had demonstrated all too successfully the uses and abuses of irrational appeals to a seemingly incongruous mixture of anti-capitalist, anti-socialist, and patriotic sentiments to mobilize mass support among a frightened and desperate people. The Weimar Republic, according to Schumacher, had been destroyed not because it was a democracy, but because its defenders had lacked adequate support. The younger generation, in particular, "was unable to realize how much had been achieved under the Weimar Republic," and had "staggered into the Hitler movement," lured by its pseudo national socialism, without knowing what they were doing.[35]

The lesson of these mistakes of omission seemed clear to Schumacher. To gain mass support now, the Social Democrats had to turn such sentiments to their own, and consequently to the German people's, advantage. It was essential to reorient traditional attitudes, but if the drive for power by democratic means was to succeed rapidly against the opposition of the surviving forces of reaction, it required the immediate support of most of the people, and above all of the young people, who had been educated mostly or entirely by the Nazis. The masses had to be not only enlightened, a duty that Social Democrats had always recognized, but inspired by appeals to the emotions which, for better or for worse, Schumacher perceived as a dominant element in men, particularly in times of crisis.

To mobilize mass support, Schumacher sought to go far beyond the traditional labor and trade union sources of Social Democratic strength. He was acutely aware of the need to attract members of the old middle class, and again and again he proclaimed that in postwar Germany socialism was no longer of concern merely to "the working class in the traditional restrictive sense of the word," but to all whose interests conflicted with those of the exploiting capitalist class.[36] There was room for all of them in the ranks of the Social Democrats so long as they supported the ideals of liberty, justice, and tolerance. Schumacher asked every German to join the fight, no matter what his ethical, political, religious, or philosophical beliefs—whether he followed Christ's Sermon on the Mount or the teaching of Marx—just as long as he was not an unreconstructed Nazi or a capitalist exploiter. Although the attempt to gain support from farmers was rather halfhearted (as had always been true of a party oriented toward urban groups), every effort was made to win over the old urban middle class and the new refugees. Schumacher believed that these classes had been "objectively" proletarized by the war and its aftermath, but that subjectively they were still captive to traditional anti-democratic and anti-socialist attitudes.

As we have noted, Schumacher was particularly anxious for the support of young veterans and former members of the Hitler youth organization. His public position toward former Nazis was a self-assured mixture of moral compassion, a strong sense of justice, and political realism, a stand that seemed hypocritical to some of his critics and opportunistic to others. Punishment of the guilty according to the degree of their crimes, yes, but permanent discrimination against former Nazis, no. At the S.P.D. congress in Hamburg in 1950, he warned fellow party members against the easy and smug temptation to recruit new members and potential leaders from the ranks of those who already supported Social Democracy, and pointed out that it was undemocratic to discriminate permanently between two types of Germans. Although "it is our duty to deal with the guilty, with those who benefited and profited from the Nazi system, it is also incumbent upon us to help the misguided, particularly those of the younger generation," he maintained amid loud applause (but doubtless to the discomforture of some party members).[37] It was necessary not only to protect former members of Nazi youth organizations against the alleged excesses of Allied denazification procedures, but also to see that their idealistic, if misguided, support for the Third Reich was not held permanently against them. So long as they were repentant and anxious to make their contribution to the building of a new Germany, no Social Democrat or any other German had the right to deny them a part in it.

Justice and morality, however, were not Schumacher's only considerations. The problem of these "little Nazis" struck him as a major political issue. They constituted, to his way of thinking, a vast reservoir of *deracinés,* who might some day support a new radical anti-democratic movement. Alternatively, they might be drawn as rapidly as possible into the fight for a socialist democracy. It was apparently this belief that led him in 1951 to swing his party's support behind the so-called "131 Law," which provided for the restoration of the pension rights, or reinstatement in office, of most officials of the Nazi regime, including military officers, teachers, judges, and policemen.[38]

Schumacher made a particular effort in the last years of his life to obtain the support of the younger ex-Nazis. He talked to former leaders of the Hitler Youths and ex-members of the Waffen S.S., the military branch of Hitler's elite corps.[39] In these conversations, a onetime Hitler Youth leader recalled, he sought more to win support for his general goals than to recruit new members for his party. In answering criticism of his behavior, Schumacher held to his position that collective condemnation of all participants in the Nazi regime—particularly those who were too young to have voted for it—was immoral, unjust, and politically unwise. It was in the nature of a totalitarian system, he wrote to a Jewish socialist in Switzerland, to do its utmost to implicate all its subjects in the crimes of the ruling elite, and it would be both unfair and unwise to perpetuate this principle of guilt by association. As a victim of the Nazi system, he claimed for himself the right to decide the moral and political propriety of his behavior on this issue.*

Schumacher was particularly anxious that "German youth should not come to feel that democracy and national decline go hand in hand."[40] He was aware that the younger generation had but recently been introduced to democratic ideas and practices, frequently not under the most happy circumstances by Allied "re-educators," and that their newfound faith, such as it was, still had tender roots. Victory for Social Democracy, in his view, depended ultimately upon this coming generation of German voters and political leaders, not on the relics of the Weimar era and the foreign military governors who temporarily dominated political life. Only the leaders and the party that could demonstrate that democracy need not mean national humiliation, only those who could show that they had the true patriotic interests of Germany at heart, could hope to gain the allegiance of the young.

Patriotism was for Schumacher the common denominator that could unify the diverse elements among the German people behind his campaign for a socialist democracy. This emphasis on national rather than international goals, on German rather than world problems, seemed to many of his critics inconsistent with his socialist professions, irresponsible in the light of world conditions, and utterly immoral in view of the past excesses of German nationalism. Schumacher's endeavors to distinguish between the patriotism of a defeated and occupied people and a chauvinistic nationalism—not only that of Hitler, but that of some of the victor powers as well—seemed hypocritical and arrogant to many observers. However, it seems that his expression of patriotic sentiments was more than a manipulative technique for mobilizing mass

* Schumacher's attitude toward "naïve idealist admirers" of Hitler was undoubtedly influenced by conversations with his nephew after his release from Dachau in 1943 and 1944. The nephew had joined the Nazi party as a young student before 1933, but, according to Schumacher's letters, had become thoroughly disillusioned with the party even before the Nazi system collapsed. He seems to have symbolized for Schumacher the idealistic faith of the younger generation in Hitler's National Socialism, just as Leo Trinkwalter, Schumacher's brother-in-law, had influenced his attitude toward "little Nazis."

opinion behind his leadership. It appears to have been a complex and subtle mixture of strategic considerations, based upon his perception of political developments in his occupied country, and intensely felt personal sentiments.

Schumacher loved his country and was deeply grieved by the fate that had befallen it. "This sad beggar's role in which we find our people," as he expressed it in a letter to an old friend in 1946, hurt the pride he had always had in being a German. We had occasion to note earlier, in connection with Schumacher's militant democratic socialist patriotism in the pre-1933 period, that his unabashed appeal to patriotic emotions appeared to be largely an expression of the sentiments of an expatriate from West Prussia and a fervent Jacobin "national socialist." Now, as then, he identified his own patriotic socialism with that of Ferdinand Lassalle and Jean Jaurès, and professed to see nothing contradictory about an adherence to Marxist and internationalist values and a love for Germany and its people. He evidently believed sincerely that a cynical, militaristic, and imperialist nationalism was diametrically opposed to his own moral patriotism. He saw the former as destructive and intolerant, the latter as constructive and tolerant. Not only was national self-determination a natural corollary to democratic self-government, but the recovery of German independence and self-respect was the sole means by which European unity and international cooperation could develop.

These personal sentiments strengthened, and were strengthened by, Schumacher's belief that the lessons of the past and the political situation of the present required the Social Democrats to identify themselves explicitly and emphatically with the defense of German interests. Personal inclination no doubt contributed to his willingness to assume the role of the militantly patriotic leader, but the fear that a new cynical perversion of patriotic sentiments might forever doom German democracy, Germany, and its people was evidently sincere. Like most contemporary observers, both German and non-German, he expected an upsurge of nationalist sentiment among a beaten and economically destitute people who were being occupied and ruled by foreign armies. He hoped not merely to contain this sentiment, but to harness it to Social Democratic purposes.

Schumacher stressed the identity of German and Social Democratic interests on international as well as national issues. In fact, he considered that the occupation and division of Germany and the apparent proletarization of most of its people made the distinction meaningless, since it was no longer possible to concentrate on purely domestic questions as the Social Democratic leaders had done in the past. He sought to identify the Social Democratic movement with the struggle of the German masses for socio-economic and political recovery, and depicted his opponents as tools of international capitalism or Catholicism or the competing national interests of foreign powers. Just as he felt German patriotism had been and still was being grossly misused by selfish interest groups indifferent to the country's needs, so he also saw internationalism being perverted by the enemies of the German people under the guise of European unity and international working-class solidarity. The Social Democrats alone, he said, were indebted to no interest group, foreign or domestic, nor were they the tool of any foreign power; they alone, therefore, were worthy of the trust and support of all German patriots in the fight for a free and democratic Germany.

Such were the goals and roles that Kurt Schumacher conceived for himself, his party, and his people. Moral right, historical justice, and the laws of economic determinism seemed to favor his cause, but the road to power was not without obstacles.

First there were the victors who occupied Germany, and who between them appeared to control its fate. Schumacher believed it was necessary to minimize their intervention in the socio-economic and political reconstruction of the nation, in the hope that they could be prevented from prejudicing future developments in Germany. Above all, this applied to the question of German reunification, for, as Schumacher once said to an associate, "You can't take effective political action in a pocket handkerchief Germany."[41] As he saw it, only the reunification of all four occupation zones would make the transformation of German society a possibility. His attitude and behavior toward the occupying powers, which we shall examine later, were governed by the principle of cooperation as far as necessary, independent action as far as possible.

This principle could not be said to apply to Schumacher's attitude toward the second major obstacle he saw on the road to power, his German competitors for post-totalitarian leadership. Characteristically, he regarded these rivals as unalterably and categorically opposed to everything he stood for. He saw himself and his cause threatened on the one hand by the Scylla of German Communism and on the other by the Charybdis of reactionary capitalism. Time and again he saw these two seemingly opposed groups allied in their hostility to democracy and socialism, just as they had been in the Weimar Republic. Cooperation with either seemed to him impossible for reasons of morality, ideology, and practical politics. His perception of his goals demanded the defeat of both—in bitter warfare if necessary—if the German people were to achieve a secure future by means of a Social Democratic commonwealth.

SIX

The Party Leader

The Fight for the Leadership

The keystone of Kurt Schumacher's aspirations as a post-totalitarian leader was his belief in the need for a disciplined and militant Social Democratic movement. The S.P.D. was the chosen instrument in the fight to establish a socialist democracy in Germany, and Schumacher's perception of the internal and external setting shaped his concept of the leader's role. To adapt the instrument to the requirements of the situation demanded a strong leader who could surmount internal and external obstacles, unite heterogeneous elements, and overcome centrifugal tendencies, thus evolving a disciplined party for the struggle for power. Beyond this, the leader would determine the strategy and tactics of the party in its battle against a hostile political environment. The party's leaders, functionaries, officeholders, and members were expected to subordinate other values and goals to the higher purpose of establishing a Social Democratic commonwealth, this being the mission history had assigned to the party.

This conception of the S.P.D. and its members was to pattern Schumacher's intraparty behavior from his battle for the leadership in 1945 to his death in 1952. Since its foundation in 1863 by Ferdinand Lassalle, the Social Democratic movement had known two types of leaders. One type, represented notably by Lassalle himself but also by August Bebel, party chairman from 1875 to 1913, was the monocratic leader. The other, far more prevalent in the movement, was the leader who believed that he was the creature rather than the molder of events. The monocratic and innovating leader had been a rare phenomenon in a movement strongly oriented toward Marxist determinism and anti-authoritarian democracy. During the twenty years between Bebel's death and Hitler's accession, corporate guidance by a practically anonymous national executive committee was thought to accord more closely with the party's democratic and Marxist values than monocratic or even charismatic leadership. The national party chairman was only first among equals in a committee that was regarded by most members and party functionaries as the instrument of historical determinism and the spokesman for the collective interests of the German proletariat. Schumacher's interpretation of the national chairman's role was strongly at variance with this tradition, and was much closer to the interpretation that Lassalle and Bebel had given it.

The intraparty context for Schumacher's interpretation of his role was probably decisively influenced by the events that preceded his elevation to the chairmanship in May 1946. The interpersonal and institutional patterns that subsequently governed his relationship with the party's public officeholders, functionaries, and ordinary members were then laid down. These relationships may have changed somewhat during the following years, but basically they remained unaltered. Before considering these structural patterns, however, we must examine the development that had a great deal to do with determining them: Schumacher's initial fight for the leadership of the S.P.D.

Retrospective testimony of Schumacher's associates, as well as some of his initial postwar statements, indicates that he expected to wage his fight for leadership primarily against the surviving leaders of the Communist Party (K.P.D.) and of various small socialist groups who had been prominent in organizing the left-wing resistance movement and political life of the concentration camps. The old functionaries of the Weimar S.P.D. he evidently considered too old or discredited to offer serious competition, or, for that matter, to play any influential part in the re-establishment of the German labor movement. After the occupation of Hannover he had to modify these expectations considerably, it seems, as he gradually established contact with scattered centers of reviving political activity.

In the Western occupation zones, a blanket ban on all political activities quickly put an end to an initial bid for succession leadership by the so-called Anti-Fascist Committees that had been formed in a number of cities. Controlled largely by Communist and socialist survivors of Nazi prisons and concentration camps and left-wing underground cells, most of these committees had proclaimed radical revolutionary goals and tended to exclude from membership political leaders from the Weimar era who had no militant anti-Nazi record. Western Allied policy was a carefully regulated, very gradual development of German political life. The self-constituted Anti-Fascist Committees were outlawed, and Germans believed to be politically reliable were appointed to various advisory and administrative posts. The criteria of selection tended to favor the return of the more conservative of the surviving political leaders of the Weimar era whose names and records were known to the military governments, and who were considered better equipped to maintain public services and more likely to use democratic methods than the obscure radicals of the Anti-Fascist Committees.*

* The Western military authorities possessed lists of local personages rated politically reliable for appointment to administrative office. The lists were based largely on information from anti-Nazi exile sources and records of the Weimar Republic, and hence the bias in favor of men who had served in the Weimar era.

Many old Social Democratic functionaries were able to achieve positions of some local and regional prominence in the early days of the occupation of the Western zones, and used them to place old friends and associates in positions that promised to be of political importance, such as administrative offices and editorial positions in the licensed German newspapers. In the British zone, for example, Carl Severing, perhaps the most prominent surviving leader of the Weimar S.P.D., became what he himself termed "a sort of personnel manager" for the military government. Finding that "younger men familiar with the principles and organization of the Social Democratic party [were] in short supply," he recommended for appointment friends who had held important positions in the party before 1933.[1] In Württemberg, Schumacher's old adversary Wilhelm Keil, who, like Severing, had quietly lived on a government pension during the twelve preceding years, sought to play a similar role for the American military authorities. Though now in his seventies, Keil believed that his services were once again needed, and re-entered political life. So did another of Schumacher's foes from the Stuttgart days, the former state chairman of the S.P.D. in Württemberg, Erich Rossmann, who had operated a successful real estate business during the Nazi era.[2]

Schumacher strongly opposed the return of leaders he considered discredited or compromised. In June 1945 he wrote to one of his old associates in Stuttgart, who was active in reorganizing the party there, that those who had "selfishly capitulated" in 1933 should not now be allowed a voice in the staffing of governmental and party offices. It was his hope that "truly uncompromised Social Democrats could be found to fill these positions, particularly younger men who had fought against Hitler in the socialist youth groups and the resistance movement.[3] However, there were few such men. Twelve years of Nazi persecution and terror had left a vacuum; a whole generation of Social Democrats was missing. Some had been seized in 1933 and never reappeared; resistance work, for which most of the older party members had been neither physically nor psychologically equipped, had further depleted the ranks; and many had been killed in the war. Some of the most promising young militants who had worked with Schumacher in the pre-1933 Iron Front had died shortly before the regime collapsed—men like Carlo Mierendorff, who was killed by an Allied bomb, and Julius Leber, who was hanged by the Nazis. Still others, who had gone into exile, had long given up all thought of returning and were settled in new lives abroad.

The leadership vacuum was therefore filled mostly by the old-guard functionaries, who had either remained passive under the Nazi regime or escaped abroad to await the day they could return to political life. Not only the occupation authorities, but their friends and fellow party members from the old days, welcomed them back as trusted leaders. They had the contacts and the organizational know-how to resuscitate the party, and they were initiating semi-covert Social Democratic groups in the Western zones months before the military governments formally authorized such activities. First locally and then regionally, they began to establish themselves in positions of political prominence. They were, in the words of a former British occupation official, "practical men . . . prepared to accept political and governmental responsibility." Moreover, they were willing to form working alliances with the "bourgeois" politicians in their communities, which, in view of the multitude of administrative tasks that needed immediate attention, was a considerable point in their favor. The occupation authorities, who were seeking "men of action rather than theorists" to carry out their instructions, were more than glad that there were few intellectuals among them.[4]

While the mass of the population remained politically inert, the old Social Democratic rank-and-file responded readily to the summons of their former leaders. The men and women who came to the reorganization meetings were mostly loyal Social Democrats in their fifties and sixties, eager to reaffiliate with a party to which most of them had belonged for many years before 1933.*

Thus in the Western occupation zones, where the reorganization of the Social Democratic party was to proceed slowly from the bottom up, key positions were mostly in the hands of old-timers. Their views on the re-establishment of a nationwide Social Democratic movement were conditioned on the one hand by affective loyalties toward the traditional organization and its values, and on the other by highly pragmatic power considerations relating to local and regional problems of political and economic reconstruction. They were strongly attached to the traditional values of their party, but they were also keenly sensitive to contemporary issues arising out of relations with the military governments, the Churches, and incipient new political groups.

According to reports that reached Schumacher from Berlin and other former centers of the S.P.D. in the Soviet zone of occupation during the early summer of 1945, the Soviet authorities, unlike their Western counterparts, had encouraged surviving members of the left-wing parties and resistance groups to resume political activities. Thus they had given almost immediate permission for the establishment of a zonal organization of the S.P.D., as well as for the K.P.D. and two "bourgeois" anti-Fascist parties, the Christian Democratic Union and the Liberal Democratic party. A Central Committee (*Zentralausschuss*) of the S.P.D. had been established in Berlin under the leadership of a former Reichstag deputy, Otto Grotewohl. Provided with offices, funds,

---

* Some of these old-timers reportedly appeared with their old membership books to pay the dues that had been outstanding since 1933. It has been estimated that less than 20 per cent of the membership of these local S.P.D. organizations was under forty, and that at least an equal proportion was over sixty. Perhaps 40 per cent had also been trade unionists before 1933. I am indebted to Dr. Albrecht Kaden for this and other information on the reorganization of the S.P.D., treated in invaluable detail in his dissertation, "Die Wiedergründung der S.P.D."

and a newspaper by the occupation authorities, it was proceeding with the reorganization of the party from the top downward. By the fall of 1945, when the Americans and British (though not yet the French) finally gave formal permission for the establishment of political parties, the S.P.D. in the Soviet zone already had between three and four hundred thousand members. In mid-June the Central Committee in Berlin had issued a "Manifesto of the German Social Democratic Party," which called for early fusion with the K.P.D. A joint Working Committee was accordingly formed with the K.P.D. Central Committee, and in mid-July an "anti-fascist bloc" with the two "bourgeois" parties.

Otto Grotewohl, the leader of this self-constituted Central Committee of former Social Democratic deputies and functionaries in Berlin, impressed his associates as a dynamic yet conciliatory personality and a skillful tactician. A year older than Schumacher, he, too, had been a young S.P.D. Reichstag deputy when Hitler came to power; he, too, had remained in Germany and been imprisoned, if only briefly, and had apparently participated in anti-Nazi resistance work. He and his associates in the Central Committee were encouraged by the initially friendly attitude of the Soviet authorities and by the great popularity of the resurrected S.P.D. in the Soviet zone to believe that they had nothing to lose and a great deal to gain by close cooperation with the K.P.D. They hoped, it seems, that the S.P.D. would emerge far stronger than the K.P.D., not only in the Soviet zone but throughout Germany, and that therefore its leaders would dominate any united front or merger of the two parties. Moreover, like quite a number of Social Democrats, they believed that a united working-class movement could have prevented Hitler from coming to power. Their reading of the "lessons of the past," the situation of the present, and their hopes for a socialist commonwealth in Germany made them think that cooperation with the Communists and the "socialist" Soviet Union was in the best interest of the German proletariat. They evidently thought, too—for a time at least—that the Soviet leadership endorsed their efforts.

The Central Committee's Manifesto confirmed the expectations of Social Democrats throughout Germany that the initiative for the nationwide reorganization of their party would come from the traditional seat of the party headquarters. In the summer of 1945, Berlin was still regarded by both the Germans and their conquerors as the nation's effective capital. When the Big Three met in suburban Potsdam in early August, they decided that the old capital should remain the center of occupied Germany. The Allied Control Council, as well as central German administrative institutions for all four zones of occupation, were to be established there. For all practical purposes, Berlin was once more "the focal point of the news, the center of public attention, the base of principal government activity."[5]

The Central Committee had a considerable headstart over any other bidder for the party leadership. In Berlin itself, S.P.D. membership quickly reached 70,000, and in other Social Democratic strongholds in the Soviet zone—cities like Leipzig, Chemnitz, Magdeburg, and Halle—the work of reorganization made similar progress. Old party members by the tens of thousands flocked to the party offices to renew their membership. To them and their officers the Central Committee in Berlin was the obvious focus for the national reorganization, since they had no news about party organization in the Western zones other than what came to them by way of the Committee and the Soviet-controlled press. Moreover, in most respects the Committee's proclaimed aspirations corresponded to the social revolutionary goals that many left-wing anti-Nazis had envisaged for the "new" Social Democratic movement while they were in prison, concentration camps, and exile: the destruction of German "monopoly capitalism" and the establishment of a social democratic order.

In one respect, however, the group in Berlin did deviate from these rather general aspirations. This was on the question of cooperation with the K.P.D. Grotewohl proposed intimate collaboration and ultimate amalgamation with the Communists, whereas other Social Democrats were at best prepared for only limited cooperation. They still distrusted Communist and Soviet intentions, whereas Grotewohl insisted that the Communists had lost their old antagonism toward the S.P.D. and were no longer merely the tools of Soviet policy. His view was shared by a number of Social Democrats in the first weeks after the collapse of the Nazi regime, particularly by members of anti-Nazi resistance groups and survivors of Nazi concentration camps and prisons (the segment of society that in the Western zones had formed the Anti-Fascist Committees). To them the obvious lesson of the "suicidal fraternal conflicts" of the past was "unity of action," if not amalgamation, between the S.P.D. and the K.P.D.

Here was a grave threat to Schumacher's aspirations at the very start of his postwar career. Not only were Grotewohl and his associates rival bidders for the leadership of the re-emerging S.P.D., but they appeared to be aiming at its eventual amalgamation with the Communist movement. Both contingencies were diametrically opposed to Schumacher's goals. He quickly identified Grotewohl as his principal antagonist and proceeded to give battle. He categorically rejected amalgamation with the Communists, and insisted that the Social Democrats and Communists differed not in degree, but in kind. The Communists' political values, and above all their subservience to Soviet control, ruled out amalgamation. A unity party, he insisted, would become the instrument of Soviet policy in Germany.

It seems entirely in character that Schumacher should not only initiate the conflict, but do so under relatively unfavorable circumstances. Grotewohl's position initially seemed much the stronger; at first he was able to dismiss Schumacher's aspirations as the petty ambitions of a provincial party functionary manipulated by the Western "capitalists," according to one of his associates at the time. In the ensuing conflict he tried to avoid a head-on clash, whereas Schumacher insisted on accentuating the differences between them. In the end, however, in the face of Schumacher's inflexible antagonism, his conciliatory gestures proved quite in vain.

That Schumacher made good his claim to lead the postwar Social Democratic movement, despite apparent early disadvantages, is attributable to three main factors. First, he was able to exploit the anti-Communist sentiment that was developing throughout Germany to mobilize support among the Social Democratic functionaries in the Western zones. Grotewohl and his group, by contrast, were prevented from exploiting their initial advantages both by inadequate contacts with the grass-roots organization in the West, and by mounting Soviet pressure that undermined their claim to be independent political actors. Although the S.P.D. rank-and-file in the West retained considerable sentiment for "working-class unity," the Western party leaders soon came to agree with Schumacher's argument that Grotewohl's course would ultimately destroy the Social Democratic movement and lead to a Soviet dictatorship in Germany.*

Second, Schumacher was helped by the attitude of the British and American occupation authorities. During the first few months they were more or less indifferent toward the fight to control a political movement that officially they did not even recognize. Schumacher and other anti-Communist opponents of "working-class unity" bitterly resented this policy, which seemed to favor the proponents of collaboration, if only by default. However, as the unification drive from Berlin increasingly assumed the appearance of a Soviet bid for power, the two military governments—though not the French—began to encourage Schumacher's efforts. Formal restrictions on political organizations and activities were interpreted with considerable latitude, in the British zone in particular, and Schumacher was given help in establishing and maintaining direct contact with Social Democratic leaders in other parts of the two Western zones. In February 1946 he was flown by a British military aircraft to Berlin for his final confrontation with Grotewohl.

Third and last, it was undoubtedly Schumacher's unwavering determination that placed him at the head of the S.P.D. and established him as the most prominent politician in post-Nazi Germany in less than a year's time. From

---

* The extent of pro-unity sentiment among rank-and-file Social Democrats even outside the Soviet zone has often been overlooked. Thus, in March 1946, after months of intensive agitation against collaboration with the Communists, one out of three supporters of the S.P.D. in the American zone was prepared to support the "unity party" proposed by Grotewohl if it should indeed take the place of the Social Democratic and Communist parties. See O.M.G.U.S., *Opinion Survey Reports*, Series I, No. 3, March 15, 1946, p. 1. In the West Berlin plebiscite of March 31, 1946, in which S.P.D. members rejected immediate amalgamation, 62 per cent at the same time expressed their support for "unity of action" between the K.P.D. and the S.P.D. Kaden, p. 225.

his unchallenged assumption of leadership in the Hannover organization in May 1945 to his uncontested election as chairman of the national party a year later, it was above all his personal contacts and influence, his organizational and tactical skill, and his undeviating determination to achieve his goal that brought him success.

Schumacher's thorough familiarity with the old party organization and its leaders, and his wide circle of acquaintances from Weimar days and the concentration camps, were of inestimable value in establishing his "Büro Dr. Schumacher" as a coordinating center for scattered Social Democratic groups in the Western zones and in exile. Despite formal restrictions on political activities and poor communications, he quickly established contact with these groups and gained acceptance for Hannover as a rival center to Berlin in the reorganization of a national party organization. Neither the party leaders in exile nor any Social Democrat in the Western zones seriously challenged his bid.* In August 1945, fourteen of the nineteen district (*Bezirk*) organizations in the Western zones authorized him to summon a meeting of party leaders.† He immediately used this authorization to dispatch, along with the invitations, a pamphlet outlining the general principles that should guide local party leaders in their relations with other political elements.[6] Probably the first major Social Democratic publication of the postwar era, this pamphlet was in fact a program for coordinating action toward occupation authorities and other German political organizations, particularly the Communists, and was apparently accepted as such by most of the local leaders who received it. Schumacher further identified himself as the focus of Social Democratic activities in the Western zones by demanding and receiving—at least in the British zone—information from the district leaders concerning their activities, membership, and financial resources. It was he who personally invited the Berlin Central Committee, the exiled executive committee in London, and remnants of various socialist splinter groups and resistance organizations to send representatives to the Hannover meeting.

The meeting was held at Wennigsen, near Hannover, early in October 1945, and delegates from all four occupation zones as well as from exile groups

* Armed with a mandate from the party executive committee, a group of Social Democratic leaders had gone abroad in May 1933 and established a leadership in exile in London. By the end of the war, only two of the members of the group, along with a small staff, were left. The chairman, Hans Vogel, died in early October 1945, without having been able to return the "mandate" of the exiled executive committee to the new party leaders in Germany as he had wished. See Edinger, *German Exile Politics*, pp. 239f and *passim*.

† In none of the three Western zones were such district organizations as yet licensed by military government. The Americans sanctioned the establishment of local party groups in mid-August, and the British four weeks later; by then regional and even state (Länder) S.P.D. organizations were in fact already well established. In the French zone, party activity was inhibited for some time by the rigorous enforcement of prohibitions on political activity that were not lifted until the spring of 1946.

were present. At it Schumacher scored his first major victory. Grotewohl, heading the delegation from the Berlin Central Committee, tried in vain to persuade the Western Social Democrats either to call a national congress immediately so that a new and legitimate party leadership could be chosen, or to expand the Central Committee into a provisional national leadership. Schumacher, operating on his home ground, had matters well in hand. He argued successfully that either move would be illegal as long as the party was not allowed to organize nationally by the four Allied powers. Grotewohl found himself forced to accept an arrangement proposed by Schumacher that authorized the Central Committee to represent Social Democracy provisionally in the Soviet zone, while the "Büro Dr. Schumacher" represented it in the three Western zones. Until the four occupation powers made it possible for a national congress to re-establish the S.P.D. formally and elect a leadership for the entire party, Grotewohl and his Central Committee were to take no further action that would commit Social Democrats to cooperation with the Communists.

Schumacher subsequently claimed that his categorical "No" to the leadership bid of the Grotewohl Central Committee had prevented the creation of a Communist-controlled "unity party" in the Western zones and the destruction of an independent democratic socialist labor movement. Some of his admirers went further and asserted that he had stopped the advance of Soviet imperialism into West Germany. In any case, Schumacher's jurisdictional arrangement with Grotewohl probably helped seal the fate of the Social Democrats in the Soviet zone. He was determined to eliminate Grotewohl as a rival and to bar the members of the Central Committee from the leadership of the Social Democratic movement. He apparently never trusted Grotewohl, and he may have felt that the situation of the Social Democratic organization in the Soviet zone was hopeless in any case, and that it was better to risk destroying the Central Committee by quarantining it than to permit it to pursue its bid for national leadership. Compromise might indeed have been a serious error, but in any case he was not the man to make a compromise arrangement.

Soon after the meeting at Hannover, the Soviet authorities began to press Grotewohl and his Central Committee for an amalgamation of the two parties. While the Central Committee sought to delay, arguing that only a national convention of the S.P.D. could decide the question, Schumacher made no move to come to its rescue. Rigidly adhering to the letter of the jurisdictional agreement, he let the Soviet-zone Social Democrats shift for themselves. He insisted that Grotewohl stay out of his bailiwick and waged a bitter campaign against amalgamation in the Western zones. When in the winter of 1945–46 the party in the Soviet zone moved rapidly toward a merger with the Communists, he made no effort to intervene. Perhaps he could not have done anything, but the effort was apparently never made except in West Berlin, and there very late in the game. When, under Soviet pressure, Grotewohl began to negotiate with the Communists, Schumacher accused him of violating the October agreement; and when the merger appeared inevitable—no matter what the Central Committee did—Schumacher advised Grotewohl to dissolve the party in the Soviet zone. As presumably Schumacher had anticipated, Grotewohl refused and took his place at the head of the merger movement, thus removing himself and the other members of the Central Committee once and for all from the leadership race. In April 1946 Grotewohl became cochairman of the new Socialist Unity party and the symbol of opportunist collaborationism for Western Social Democrats.*

Schumacher's effective appointment at the Hannover meeting as the representative of the S.P.D. for the Western zones legitimized his efforts to weld the remaining Social Democratic organizations into an interzonal movement under his leadership. His campaign against amalgamation with the Communists became not only the principal vehicle for his drive for power in the S.P.D., but his opening bid for the leadership of the nation.

Driving himself relentlessly, Schumacher spent the first postwar winter almost constantly on the road, exhorting Social Democrats in the American and British zones to repudiate the Central Committee in Berlin and support his battle for an independent German Social Democratic party. He traded on their traditionalistic and formalistic conviction that only a national congress of the S.P.D. could legitimately decide a question that Grotewohl and his group seemed by their actions to be trying to prejudge. Besides, the Social Democratic leaders in the West were keenly sensitive to prevailing anti-Soviet and anti-Communist public sentiment, and were by no means anxious to endanger their political power by association with the Communists. Increasingly suspicious of Communist intentions and recalling the savagery of Communist attacks against Social Democracy before 1933, the old party officials readily joined Schumacher's campaign against amalgamation in general and against Grotewohl—whom he depicted as either a fool or a pawn of the Soviets—in particular.

Starting out as a little-known local leader, in the course of this campaign Schumacher created the leadership image that was to govern his relationship with the party's officials in the years to come. His anti-Nazi record, his intellect, his verbal skill, and his passionate dedication to an independent Social Democratic party and its ultimate control of a united Germany appeared unrivaled. Party members were impressed by his breadth of vision, awed by his courage, and overwhelmed by his determination to realize his aspirations in the face of his physical handicaps.

In January 1946 the Social Democratic leaders in the British and American

* In 1949 Grotewohl became prime minister of the newly founded German Democratic People's Republic (D.D.R.), but all other former leaders of the S.P.D. Central Committee sooner or later either fled to the West or were purged.

zones formally voted to support Schumacher in his opposition to Grotewohl and his amalgamation proposals. In February the last encounter between the two men took place in the Central Committee offices in the Soviet sector of Berlin. Schumacher denounced Grotewohl's collaboration with the Communists and threw his support behind the anti-amalgamation forces in Berlin. These dealt the Central Committee a moral defeat in the plebiscite of March 1946, in which a majority of the city's Social Democrats repudiated Grotewohl's merger agreement. Schumacher's actions served to focus national and international attention not only on the struggle against fusion with the Communists in Berlin, but also on Kurt Schumacher as the champion of militant resistance to Soviet efforts to dominate all Germany.

Even before formal election confirmed his leadership of the S.P.D. in the Western zones, Schumacher had become internationally known as the most dynamic politician in post-Nazi Germany. His anti-amalgamation campaign and his flawless record against the Nazis made his name a symbol of resistance to totalitarianism. As a post-totalitarian leader, he appeared to have no rival either inside or outside his party. He stood at the head of the only party with an effective interzonal organization, staffed by experienced and loyal officials; moreover, when the first postwar national S.P.D. congress elected him party chairman in May 1946, it was supported by 600,000 devoted members.

Although the S.P.D. was the strongest party in West Germany, it had suffered heavy losses at the outset of its return to political life. It had lost half its membership and untold millions of potential voters as a result of the forced amalgamation with the Communist party in the Soviet zone, where it was then outlawed and its Western leaders excluded.[7] Schumacher called it "an enormous tragedy" that the Social Democrats had to start their fight for power without their traditional sources of support in predominantly Protestant East Germany.[8] As the leader of a party that even in its best days had received the support of no more than 38 per cent of the nation's votes, he was now compelled to fight for power in areas that were traditionally hostile to the S.P.D.

If the Soviet-sponsored amalgamation drive had helped to gain Schumacher the leadership of a rump party in a rump Germany, it had at the same time created a tremendous obstacle to his larger aspirations for leadership over a united Germany. He blamed the Soviet Union and its German supporters for creating this obstacle. He never ceased to demand the reunification of Germany and to insist that the Social Democratic movement was essential for the establishment of a democratic socialist commonwealth. But such reunification could come about only with the consent of the Soviet Union. Schumacher wanted it, but not at the price of repudiating his fight against Grotewohl, Communism, and amalgamation. Having taken a strong stand, he refused to reverse himself or even to compromise. If reunification meant accepting the unity party and its dominant position in East Germany, it was a price he would not pay.

The Intraparty Setting, 1946–52

Without committing ourselves to a rigid deterministic approach, we may say that the pattern of relationships between Schumacher and other members of his party was strongly influenced by two factors that were already well established when he became party chairman. He was able to modify these to some extent, but not to make decisive changes. One factor was the party's organizational structure, which was characterized on the one hand by the unprecedented power of the constituent district organizations and their leading officials, and on the other by the important part that Social Democrats played in public office in postwar Germany. The other was the predisposition of the postwar Social Democrats toward particular intraparty role assignments.

Schumacher's dynamic personality and the traditional public image of the Social Democratic organization tended to obscure the strength of the constituent party units and their leaders in the postwar S.P.D. Though strongly organized and centralized in comparison with other major parties, it was by no means the unitary organization that Schumacher had known before 1933. The nineteen constituent district organizations enjoyed unprecedented independence from and control over the party leadership, particularly during the first four years of Schumacher's chairmanship. In a party in which formal procedures and adherence to intraparty democracy were taken very seriously, it proved a source of considerable weakness for the national leadership that it lacked the formal power to determine the structure of the constituent units and the activities of their officials. Whereas before Hitler the key functionary in the party, the district secretary, was a salaried official of the national executive committee, he was now selected and paid by the district organizations. Whereas formerly the national leadership had in many cases controlled the nomination of candidates for public office, now the district leaders had the decisive voice.

Financially, the national leadership was almost entirely dependent upon dues collected by the districts, and until 1950 set by them as well. Allied regulations had "neutralized" the trade unions, which had made substantial contributions to the S.P.D. before 1933, and also deprived the party of income formerly received from its vast newspaper empire. Unlike other parties, the S.P.D. did not receive much financial support from outside sources. Even after the national leadership acquired authority in 1950 to determine the amount of the membership dues jointly with representatives of the district organizations, the actual amount allotted to the party headquarters and its activities still depended upon the local organizations. For although the national headquarters received a fixed proportion of the amount collected, dues collection and payment and the recruitment of new members were entirely in the hands of the local officials and party members.

Lastly, the officials in the districts were, in effect, the gatekeepers controlling the flow of communications between party headquarters and the ordinary party member. On the one hand, it was next to impossible for a member to bypass established channels of intraparty communications to gain access to the national leadership; on the other, in the downward flow of communications the local officials acted usually as both transmitters and filters. During the Weimar Republic, some two hundred Social Democratic dailies had constantly explained to party members the decisions and intentions of the national leaders. The S.P.D. executive committee itself had operated a daily newspaper, *Vorwärts,* as well as a wire service that supplied the regional party papers with news items and articles expressing the position of the national leadership.* But after 1945 these media were no longer available, and downward communications became both less extensive and less intensive. Owing to Allied regulations, the party neither owned nor controlled a single daily, and its national leaders had to compete for space in regional public or privately owned media with other political leaders, with no assurance that their messages would be transmitted. They could and did provide the lower echelons with material for the publications of the local and district organizations, and with pamphlets and broadsides for distribution among the membership, but in each case actual publication or distribution depended upon the cooperation of the local functionaries. Mass meetings with party members provided the only direct means of contact available to the party chairman, but this opportunity for bypassing normal intraparty communication channels had very limited advantages and did not constitute a satisfactory alternative to indirect communications.

In effect, the party chairman could make no major move without the support of the district organizations and their leading officials. These key functionaries were mostly the old-timers who had played so large a part in reorganizing the party in 1945, whose support had enabled Schumacher to gain the chairmanship in 1946, and who remained solidly entrenched in their positions in subsequent years. Some of the most prominent of them, men like Severing, Keil, and Löbe, retired from active political life, but other old officials who had long been faithful party workhorses continued to run the district and local organizations. Relatively few newcomers became party secretaries during Schumacher's chairmanship. Qualified personnel was believed to be unavailable, and in many cases local party officials held several key positions at once, often in conjunction with some public office such as mayor or deputy. The increased organizational needs of the party, and the fact that the Nazi era had deprived it of a trained corps of younger leaders, tended to support this trend toward multiple officeholding.

The old-time functionaries, as already noted, were supported by a member-

* Since after the war the Communists preempted the name of the S.P.D. journal for one of their own publications, the S.P.D. organ changed its name in the first postwar years to *Der Neue Vorwärts.* Subsequently, however, the old name was readopted.

ship also largely composed of old-timers. When Schumacher became party chairman in 1946, approximately two-thirds of the members had belonged to the S.P.D. before 1933. This proportion changed little up to the time of his death in 1952.[9] Relatively few newcomers replaced old-timers who died or withdrew from the party. Party membership declined from 875,479 in December 1947 to 627,817 in December 1952, at which time only 32 per cent were under forty-five years of age, and 42 per cent were over fifty-five.[10] Schumacher headed a party consisting predominantly of men and women who had been members of the party or its affiliates before 1933—95 per cent according to one estimate.[11] These people had experienced the destruction of the S.P.D. as adults; they were or had been manual workers and trade unionists, and were led, at least locally, mostly by the old party officials. In social structure and composition, it was still in effect the Weimar S.P.D. (see Table 4).

TABLE 4

OCCUPATIONAL STRUCTURE OF THE S.P.D., 1930 AND 1952

(Figures in rounded-off percentages)

Category of worker	1930	1952
Total membership	1,002,000	627,817
Manual workers	60%	45%
Salaried employees	10%	17%
Self-employed, pensioners, farmers, and housewives...	31%	38%

SOURCE: S.P.D., *Jahrbuch, 1930,* and *Protokoll, Parteitag,* 1952, p. 170.

The unprecedented number of Social Democratic public officeholders in state and local governments was another important element of the intraparty setting during Schumacher's chairmanship. After their initial appointment by the Allied military governments, most locally prominent Social Democrats were confirmed in office by the elections that followed. At first in all, and later in most, of the states of West Germany, as well as in West Berlin, Social Democrats either led or were prominent participants in coalition governments with Christian Democrats and other parties throughout the entire period (see Appendix B, p. 324). In most cases these surviving officials of the Weimar party, in their new positions as ministers, deputies, and mayors, were concerned first and foremost with local and regional problems of reconstruction in the war-damaged, impoverished, and divided country—an emphasis that Schumacher did not share. They held that these problems required cooperation between the major moderate democratic parties, with a minimum of competitive politics between them. Particularly in the American and French zones, but also in the major urban centers of the British zone in the north of Germany, they tried to work in close cooperation both with the leaders of other parties and with the occupation powers in providing food, clothing, and shelter for the people within their immediate jurisdiction. Even after the gradual emergence of a common government and the beginnings of economic recovery, they remained strongly oriented toward regional and local tasks.

One of the major sources of these public officeholders' power was the patronage they dispensed. Particularly at the beginning, before former civil servants cleared by the Allies of Nazi taint had been reinstated and an interzonal civil service developed, fellow party members believed to be deserving and trustworthy were installed in state and local offices.* The national party leadership was in no position to use the power of patronage directly, to reward or to punish, during Schumacher's chairmanship of the S.P.D. It was forced to rely upon the voluntary cooperation of Social Democrats in state and local governments, just as it needed the agreement of local party functionaries to further the political careers of persons it sought to sponsor. In these, as in most instances bearing upon the relationship between party chairman and lesser party leaders, the extent of the chairman's influence depended more on personal affect than on the formal powers of his office.

A word should be added at this point about the new relationship between party and trade union leaders. Before 1933, probably the most important source of the power of the national S.P.D. leadership had been the financial and electoral support of the General Confederation of Labor, whose membership was about five million. Almost all its leaders had been members of the S.P.D., and the most important of them had exercised great influence in the party. No important decision was taken without consulting them. In 1945 the reestablished trade unions had been "neutralized" by the Western occupation powers, and although many of the leaders were veterans of the old General Confederation, they now tended to pursue their goals in comparative independence of the party. Many of the union leaders still belonged to the S.P.D., even to its elite, but others joined the Christian Democratic party. The top leaders of the new Confederation, founded in 1949, took care to maintain unity through relative neutrality toward the S.P.D. The party leaders were no longer encumbered by the direct dependence that had often hampered them in the past, particularly just before Hitler came to power; but at the same time they were unable to employ the trade union movement as an instrument to further their own goals. Postwar cooperation between union and party leaders was based largely on informal relationships and ad hoc arrangements dictated by pragmatic, rather than ideological, considerations. Both groups followed their own aspirations, which sometimes brought them to-

* According to a British military government official, "The . . . old professional politicians refused . . . to trust anyone who was not known to them or was not fully committed to their own party programme. They thus usually insisted . . . on being given control of an appropriate portion of the senior full-time appointments. . . . At one time the work done at most party headquarters resembled that of an employment exchange rather than a political party." Ebsworth, pp. 47f.

gether in a common effort and at other times led them to go their separate
ways—once or twice even in opposite directions.

The climate of opinion in the party was characterized by both a general
desire for reform and a clinging to tradition. Recalling the party's failure
under the Weimar Republic, most party members agreed that changes were
necessary if the mistakes of the past were not to be repeated. In general, there
was little disagreement over the need to avoid excessive factionalism, to rejuvenate the party with an infusion of new blood, and to make a more militant
bid for the positions of power in postwar Germany. Speakers and writers
called for more dynamic leadership and a more determined effort to win mass
support beyond the traditional working-class base of the party. But there was
also a widespread sentiment that the S.P.D. should remain true to its traditional values, which were believed to have been confirmed by uncompromising opposition to Nazis and the party's subsequent resurrection.

More than any other major political group in West Germany, the S.P.D.
was rooted in the past. It was not a new party in either name or membership,
but was explicitly re-established on hallowed principles that had sustained
loyal adherents through twelve years of Nazi oppression. Whether they had
been imprisoned or exiled, or had simply quietly survived the Hitler era, postwar members were generally united by a strong in-group feeling that was
rooted in the traditional goals and sentiments of socialist solidarity, as well as
in memories of shared experiences in the highly integrated party of Weimar
days. It was a feeling based less on specific common aspirations than on an
emotional sense of community, a feeling that the party united in camaraderie
the best and most decent Germans, a feeling that was reaffirmed daily by the
symbolic use of the familiar *Du* and the appellation *Genosse* ("Comrade")
among most party members.[12]

Translated into specific attitudes, these traditionalist and in-group sentiments muted, if they did not entirely still, the desire for concrete reforms
among the old-timers who controlled the party's grass-roots organizations.
A certain amount of enthusiasm for a "new beginning" in theory and tactics
had been generated in the reorganization phase, but this soon died down.
Immersed in inumerable managerial tasks voluntarily assumed or thrust upon
them, party officials were inclined to fall back upon familiar methods of
organization and agitation rather than add to their burdens by adopting new
ways. The strength of their in-group feeling manifested itself in two ways.
First, position and sinecures were given to old comrades or their children,
whose loyalty and merit were assumed to be known quantities. Second, newcomers were usually treated with suspicion, especially if they were young,
critical, and ambitious for office. The old-timers were particularly wary of former members of the Nazi or Communist parties or their youth organizations.

Proponents of party reform were to be found notably among the small, but vocal, intellectual elite of the S.P.D. A rather heterogeneous group, it consisted of former members of the Social Democratic youth organization, ex-Communists, and former members of various small left-wing dissident groups, as well as newcomers to the party from the ranks of the Protestant clergy and liberal anti-clericals. Some of these people had suffered long years of imprisonment under the Nazis, some had been active in the resistance, and quite a few had been exiles, mostly in the countries of Western and Northern Europe and in the United States.

Especially during the first three or four years after the re-establishment of the S.P.D., proponents of reform raised their voices at party meetings and in various small, fugitive journals, such as *Das Sozialistische Jahrhundert* in West Berlin. Liberated at last from the frustrating debates of powerless émigré factions, finally free to give full voice to ideas that had either germinated silently under the dictatorship or been discussed surreptitiously in concentration camps, prisons, and resistance groups, they burst forth with proposals for the "new" Social Democratic movement. Some insisted that, above all, the party needed a new definitive theoretical-ideological program to give meaning and direction to its new tasks. Others argued for a purely pragmatic revision of Social Democratic strategy and tactics. Some conceived the party as a dedicated elite, others wanted it to be a mass movement. Marxists of various coloration stressed the proletarian nature of the movement and the importance of its part in the international class struggle against "imperialist capitalism," and were opposed by those who believed that the party had to become a patriotic popular reform movement in order to come to power in postwar Germany. Christian socialists wanted greater emphasis on religious socialism and advocated co-operation with the churches, while the anti-clericals lumped the churches with the forces of reaction. Proponents of "working-class unity" were by no means silenced by the enforced merger in the Soviet zone, and were bitterly denounced by anti-Communists, or anti-Stalinists, who conceived the S.P.D. as the vanguard in the democratic socialist battle against Soviet totalitarian imperialism. But no matter how much these reformers disagreed amongst themselves, they were agreed in their criticism of the old-timers and the force of tradition they represented.

Sources for serious friction were abundant in the postwar S.P.D.; unity behind Schumacher's leadership could not be taken for granted. Yet while differences arose, many of them involving the party chairman himself, they were neither as intense nor as far-reaching in their consequences as the bitter factionalism that had characterized party life before 1933. Although pragmatists and idealists, traditionalists and reformers, old-timers and newcomers, did clash in and out of party congresses, they apparently lacked not only the power but, more significant, the will to destroy the broad intraparty consensus on strategy and tactics that had developed. It was this consensus, it would seem, that both sustained and derived from Schumacher's leadership.

The party's almost unprecedented unity in the face of considerable organizational and ideological diversity may have been due to several factors: a conscious determination to avoid the divisive disputes of the past; unifying pressures present in the political setting outside the party, such as the threat from the Communists in East Germany on the one hand, and the "forces of reaction" in West Germany on the other; and the bonds of tradition and comradeship that united the old-timers forming the mass of the party membership. But many of these factors had been present also before 1933, if in a somewhat different form. It appears that the crucial new element underlying the party's unity was a generally accepted pattern of role relationships based primarily on emotional ties between Schumacher and the mass of his followers.

The Monocratic Leader

As chairman of the Social Democratic party, and after August 1949 of the S.P.D. parliamentary delegation in the Bundestag as well, Schumacher was subject to certain formal rules of election and intraparty conduct. The collective authority of the national executive committee (*Parteivorstand*) was weaker than it had been in the highly integrated and centralized party of the pre-Hitler era. The committee was elected by the delegates to the party congress, which met four times during the six years of Schumacher's leadership: in 1946, 1947, 1948, and 1950. It was headed by the party chairman, who with his deputy and three or four other salaried committee members formed the acting executive committee (*Geschäftsführende Vorstand*). The acting executive conducted the daily business of the national party organization and coordinated its activities throughout the country; it was thus charged with the formal task of representing the party in between the meetings of the full committee, which met relatively infrequently.* The other 22 to 24 members, called *Beisitzer,* were assigned strictly secondary positions by the organizational statutes and received no pay.

The national executive committee was formally accountable to the party congress, and more immediately to the so-called *Parteiausschuss,* which consisted of representatives of the regional district organizations. The executive committee was supposed to summon this group four times a year to discuss important party problems; and in addition the Control Commission (*Kontrollkommission*), elected by the party congress, was charged by the statutes with keeping a close eye on the executive's conduct of party affairs. All three groups met together periodically to consider important issues.

The authority of the party leadership was theoretically further curtailed when the establishment of the Federal Republic created two new national

---

* The full executive committee met only five times in 1946, six times in 1947, twelve times during the following two years, and eight times in 1951.

decision-making groups in the Social Democratic delegations in the upper and lower house of the new legislature. In theory, the Social Democrats in the Bundesrat, the upper house, represented the interests of their state governments rather than the national party, while those in the Bundestag, the lower house, were specifically charged by the constitution with representing their constituents, and voting according to conscience rather than in obedience to commands from party leaders outside parliament. The constitutional arrangements of the new Basic Law were supposed to free the parliamentary representatives from the sort of dominance by party leaders and committees that characterized the Weimar Republic.

Schumacher, however, was not hampered by formal rules. Until a stroke in December 1951 removed him from the scene eight months before his death, he dominated the leadership of his party both in and out of parliament. The Party executive committee, particularly the inner group of salaried members, and the party parliamentary body (Fraktion) were controlled by him. Not only did he head both bodies personally, but the key positions in the executive of the party as well as that of the Fraktion were held by devoted deputies— in many cases the same men. Whereas before the Federal Republic was established he used his authority in his capacity as party chairman, afterwards he operated principally in his capacity as leader of the chief opposition party in the Bundestag.

More than any other political leader in West Germany in these years Schumacher could speak and act with the assurance that whatever he said or did would be accepted by the overwhelming majority of his party. Nationally and internationally, he was the focus of attention whenever the activities of the S.P.D. were in the news, for he determined the party line. His admirers attributed his great authority to his personal qualities as a democratic leader in a democratic party, whereas his detractors attributed it to his ruthless dictatorship over a highly bureaucratized movement. The actual explanation is probably more complex than either of these theories, for Schumacher's monocratic leadership rested on traditional as well as charismatic factors, on organizational power as well as personal influence.

To a considerable extent, Schumacher's authority can be traced to organizational factors and his tactical skill in molding them into the shape he wanted. During the four years preceding the establishment of the Federal Republic, he deliberately avoided public office so that he could devote himself to molding a centralized party organization and eliminating its initial strongly centrifugal tendencies. Already in the summer of 1945 he had refused to return to Stuttgart to head up a provisional government because he felt that the organization of a unitary party was more important. In 1946 he briefly attended meetings of a provisional parliament in Hannover and an Advisory Council that was set up by the British and composed of German political leaders appointed by them. He said that the leaders of national parties needed this kind of experience as a preparation for the task ahead, their future duties in the national Reichstag.[13] But he soon stopped taking part in such deliberative bodies, and participated in neither the state parliaments nor the interzonal councils that were established in the following years. This may have been because of his physical condition, but whatever the reason, he clearly felt that his time and energy could be more effectively used in building up his authority in the party and exercising political influence indirectly through his representatives in state and interzonal institutions.

The nucleus of Schumacher's organizational staff was the ad hoc group of devoted assistants who, in the summer of 1945, had helped him to establish the "Büro Dr. Schumacher" in Hannover's Jacobstrasse, and to expand it subsequently into the party's informal headquarters in the Western zones. Early in 1946 this group had been joined by several former émigrés who had been associated with the exiled executive committee in London. Schumacher apparently welcomed them not only because they were experienced party workers, but because their presence on his staff probably seemed to him to strengthen his claim to stand at the center of the postwar Social Democratic movement. The last surviving member of the London executive committee, Erich Ollenhauer, became his chief deputy. Two other former London exiles, Fritz Heine and Hertz Gotthelf, together with three members of the Hannover contingent, Alfred Nau, Herbert Kriedemann, and Egon Franke, completed the experienced group who headed up his organizational staff. When the party executive committee was formally re-established in 1946, they became its inner nucleus of salaried members and Schumacher's chief support.

After being elected chairman in 1946, Schumacher moved vigorously on several fronts to establish his dominant position. He blocked any actions by former S.P.D. leaders that seemed to threaten his leadership. He considered Keil, Severing, Rossman, and others discredited, including some old leaders returning from exile; they were ruthlessly shunted aside wherever possible. Most of them he kept out of positions of prominence; others he managed to force out without particular consideration for their feelings or those of the old-timers in the party who still revered them. Thus in 1947 Paul Löbe, the former Social Democratic President of the Weimar Reichstag, was publicly censured by the party leadership, and forced to resign as chairman of the S.P.D. foreign affairs committee, because Schumacher claimed he had acted against the interests of the party in supporting the appeal of the Socialist Unity party for a "national representation" from all zones of Germany to deal with the occupation powers.

When it came to old-time party officials of unquestioned anti-Nazi record and considerable local or regional power, Schumacher could not always proceed with the same ruthlessness, at least not in the early years. Some voluntarily refrained from playing a part in the national party leadership because they were content to devote their energies to district or local matters, or because age or poor health limited their activities. Some were eased out of the national leadership when their local power declined. Thus in 1946 Wilhelm Knothe, a party official of long standing, was elected to the first postwar national executive committee as perhaps the most prominent Social Democratic leader in the American zone; four years later he failed in his bid for re-election. Others maintained their local strength and even increased it, but placed their power at Schumacher's disposal in return for relative autonomy in matters that Schumacher did not consider of national importance. Schumacher for his part saw no need to go out of his way to arouse the opposition of men who were prepared to serve him loyally; he therefore vetoed the suggestion of some of his lieutenants that the district secretaries should be paid by the national party headquarters, a procedure that had been used before 1933, and that made the district officials dependent on the central agency. Finally, there were the local and regional leaders who served Schumacher out of personal devotion or opportunism. They included old associates from the Weimar years, the concentration camp, and the early days in Hannover, as well as former exiles and others who fell under his spell or found they could serve themselves best by serving him.

The results of the elections to the party executive committee between 1946 and 1950 reflected these developments (see Table 5 below, and Appendix A, Sec. 5). Schumacher's lieutenants and officials were chosen by the party congress on the basis of their readiness to follow him, and Social Democrats who disagreed with him or had otherwise incurred his disfavor were bypassed. Very soon, the executive committee became a ratifying rather than a decision-making body, and the delegates to the party congresses in 1947, 1948, and 1950 in turn confirmed what the executive had approved. Some feeble efforts at the

TABLE 5

TRENDS IN MEMBERSHIP OF S.P.D. EXECUTIVE COMMITTEE, 1946–52

Executive committee	Percentage new members	Percentage re-elected by party congress				
		1947	1948	1950	1952	1958
1946 (22 members)	100	88	72	48	44	20
1947 (29 members)	24	–	87	66	55	28
1948 (30 members)	17	–	–	77	66	34
1950 (30 members)	17	–	–	–	84	43
1952 (30 members)	17	–	–	–	–	40

SOURCE: S.P.D., *Protokoll, Parteitag*, 1946, 1947, 1948, 1950, 1952, 1958.

1950 Dortmund Congress to weaken the power of the national leadership were overwhelmingly voted down. Instead, a new statute added to its strength, particularly to the strength of the inner group consisting of the party chairman and his lieutenants.

With the help of such regional party leaders as his old friend Erwin Schoettle in Württemberg, Franz Neumann in Berlin, Egon Franke in Hannover, Waldemar von Knoeringen in Bavaria, and Franz Bögler in the Palatinate, Schumacher sought to keep the party organization under his control. Formally through the party executive committee (especially its headquarters staff in Hannover's Odeonstrasse), and informally through constant personal or telephone contact with trusted officials throughout the country, he and his lieutenants between 1946 and 1950 created an efficient party organization despite the political and administrative decentralization prevailing in West Germany. The efficiency of the organization overcame to a considerable extent the party's centrifugal tendencies, but at the cost of increased bureaucratization. Schumacher's larger aspirations, the pressure of political developments, and the rapid deterioration of his health made him increasingly dependent on the bureaucracy he professed to despise. Thus in 1948, when his left leg was amputated, he was for several months entirely dependent upon the trusted officials to carry out his instructions—and this at a crucial stage in political developments. His aims to reform the party and recruit new blood for its leadership had to be subordinated to his need for an efficient organization. Political developments were such that he was apparently unwilling or unable to risk damaging the smoothly functioning instrument he had set up.

Schumacher's choice of associates reflected his single-minded dedication to his role as leader and the manner in which he sought to play it. He surrounded himself with men who were first and foremost political associates, and his relations with them were determined almost entirely by political considerations. Gone were the women friends and coffee-house associates of the formative years and the social contacts with members of other parties. With one exception the inner circle of postwar lieutenants contained no old associates either from Stuttgart or from the concentration camp. And the exception, Erwin Schoettle, who had been one of Schumacher's lieutenants in Stuttgart, probably owed his place more to his political skill and influence in Württemberg than to past ties of friendship.

The group around Schumacher was roughly divided between organization men and expert advisers on special areas (law, economics, foreign affairs, etc.), though in a number of cases both functions were performed by the same person (see Appendix A, Sec. 1). The organization men were headed by the trio of Ollenhauer, Heine, and Nau—known as the "Skat Club" after the card game they liked to play—and included leading members of the headquarters staff, notably Herta Gotthelf, Sigmund Neumann, and Stefan Thomas.

The experts included parliamentary aides such as Walter Menzel, Herbert Wehner, Wilhelm Mellies, Gerhard Lütkens, and Adolf Arndt, as well as economic advisers such as Viktor Agartz, Fritz Baade, and Eric Nölting. Somewhat more difficult to classify were a few men like Carlo Schmid who were political advisers to Schumacher as well as prominent political figures in their own right. Then there were the regional chieftains, such as Waldemar von Knoeringen, Franz Neumann, Erwin Schoettle, and August Zinn. And finally, in a category all by themselves, Arno Scholz, a Berlin newspaper publisher and close confidant, and Annemarie Renger, who as Schumacher's secretary and nurse guarded access to him, particularly during the long months of illness in 1948 and 1952, and was believed by many to have had a strong influence on him.

According to the testimony of observers, as well as the evidence of his appointments calendar, these were the people who supported Schumacher's interpretation of his role most readily, whom he consulted most frequently, and to whom he entrusted the carrying out of his instructions (see Appendix A, Secs. 1, 2, and 3). From the time of his grave illness and subsequent leg amputation in 1948 to his death in 1952, physical limitations and the pressure of political events outside the party made him lean heavily on these trusted key associates as his sources of information, his agents, and his principle links with other party leaders and members. As his direct contact within the party became more limited, his image of intraparty affairs was increasingly shaped by information supplied by his lieutenants; as his ability to attend to organizational problems diminished, he increasingly relied on his organizational men to operate the instrument efficiently. When he suffered his first stroke in December 1951, they ran the party in his name, and in effect continued to do so for some time after his death.

None of Schumacher's close associates could match his combination of intellectual power and training, political experience, and record of suffering under Hitler (see Appendix A, Sec. 1). Almost all of them were younger than he, many had been exiles, and only a few had suffered serious imprisonment. True, Fritz Henssler, the Lord Mayor of Dortmund, was his senior in age, had been a member of the Reichstag, and had suffered ten years' imprisonment under Hitler. But he lacked Schumacher's education and intellect, and though Schumacher respected Henssler's political record, he did not consider him his intellectual equal nor did Henssler aspire to be. Conversely Carlo Schmid, who was a university professor and whom Schumacher respected for his intellect, had neither his political experience nor his anti-Nazi record.

A number of observers have noted that Schumacher seemed inconsistent in his selection of associates and his attitude toward them. He could ruthlessly expel a member of the inner circle for disagreeing with him, yet complain of the lack of intellectual independence and initiative among those about him.

He professed to despise mere yes-men and personally drew into the inner circle men who gave promise of independence of mind, but he also sought out and promoted men who agreed with everything he said and did. He seemed to ask advice and consult his closest associates frequently, but he insisted on having his way if their opinions differed from his. This was made abundantly clear to those who in the 1947–49 period represented the S.P.D. in the Bizonal Economic Council and the Parliamentary Council, and who differed with him on several important points of party strategy, and again later to those who disagreed with him about strategy in the Federal Republic. Firmly convinced of his role and the proper course for the party, he invariably insisted on having the last word, whether by demanding a formal vote in the executive committee or some other party body (the outcome of which was rarely in doubt because he made it a vote of confidence in his leadership), or whether by an arbitrary act in his capacity as party leader.

There was later absolutely no doubt in the minds of Schumacher's closest associates that he made every major decision affecting the national policy of his party between 1946 and 1952. There was hardly an instance, it seems, in which he was overruled or outvoted, and many in which his wishes proved decisive. He delegated tasks, but jealously guarded his formal powers as party leader and interpreted them broadly. He refused to share his authority, even when he was gravely ill. He consulted others when he thought it advisable, and ignored advice he did not like. He complained at times about the servility of his associates, yet he drew to him, and usually got along best with, men who accepted his assignments without question. He seems to have had few real confidants. He expected his lieutenants to accept his judgment and guidance in matters of political strategy, to share his aspirations for party and country, and to do their utmost to help him realize his goals.

Whereas Schumacher had little doubt of his competence to decide matters of political strategy, he frequently sought advice on economic matters. As we noted, his postwar political activities were based on assumptions derived from Marxist economic theory. His economic advisers shared these assumptions, and supplied him with interpretations of the economic situation that invariably confirmed his own assessment. In later years, many of Schumacher's political advisers blamed economists like Victor Agartz and Eric Nölting for bad council that had led to political errors. However, there are strong indications that Schumacher deliberately sought and followed their advice because it provided expert buttressing for his own preconceptions. There is no indication that he ever significantly altered his political attitudes or behavior as a result of any advice, economic or political.

One of Schumacher's chief problems in building up a strong central organization was the comparative independence of the Social Democratic public officeholders. The S.P.D. participated in and frequently controlled numerous state and local governments in West Germany during Schumacher's drive for national power (see Appendix B, p. 324), and the officers involved generally acted in accordance with regulations that the occupation governments had laid down in an effort to restrict the centralization of political power in Germany. In Schumacher's view, Social Democrats who held ministerial positions in the Länder (states), or were mayors, legislators, or administrators in the Länder, should conduct their public duties in accordance with policy laid down by the elected leaders of their party. Chafing under the restrictions that the Allies had imposed upon the centralization of political power, Schumacher and his supporters thought it intolerable that such public officials should follow any course of action opposed by the official leadership.[14] They felt that Social Democrats in state and local governments were usually far too preoccupied with bread-and-butter issues to have the political and socio-economic perspective that the overall situation of the German people required. To avoid the "mistakes" of the Weimar era, when, they believed, short–sighted opportunism and well-intentioned but foolhardy welfare measures had deprived Social Democracy of the opportunity to control the institutions of government in Germany, they considered it necessary that all Social Democratic forces in the states and cities of West Germany be placed under strong, centralized direction. Accordingly, they sought to compel reluctant party members in important public offices, particularly the Social Democratic Länder chiefs or "minister-presidents" as they were usually called, to accept the party chairman's strategy and role perceptions.

Most of these chief executives were Schumacher's seniors in age as well as party service, and many were powerful and popular enough in their own bailiwicks to balk at the more extreme demands of the party's organizational leadership. As a result, the relation between party chairmen and Social Democratic chiefs in the Länder was never close, sometimes strained, and occasionally openly hostile. With one or two exceptions, they rarely conferred with the party chairman (see Appendix A, Sec. 4); the relationship was at best a *modus vivendi*. Schumacher, with the organization backing him, won the right to direct national S.P.D. affairs, while they achieved a certain amount of tactical autonomy—how much depended on their personality and local influence—in such matters as their relations with other parties and the occupation powers. Still, friction was unavoidable, since under the conditions prevailing in postwar Germany there could be no clear and mutually satisfactory separation between local and national issues, between domestic and foreign affairs, between tactical and strategic questions, or between party roles and public office.

The economic merger of the British and American zones in early 1947 aided Schumacher's efforts to obtain control over the state chieftains. His earlier efforts had been considerably handicapped by the occupation authorities, particularly the French and American, and there was a tendency for the state ministers to slight the new party leadership.* It now became quite clear where the center of authority lay. The national organization sought control of the economic ministries in the various state governments, and had succeeded in most states when it also laid claim to the post of economic director in the new Bizonal Economic Council. When this was refused by the Christian Democrats and the Free Democrats, the Social Democratic members of the Council would not collaborate further with the two "bourgeois" parties, and went into opposition in obedience to the wishes of their party leader in Hannover. Schumacher had decided that categorical opposition to the bourgeois bloc was the best strategy in the fight for control of Germany, and for the rest of his life he led the S.P.D. against a dominant anti-socialist coalition. There was some opposition to this action among Social Democratic public officials, whereupon the executive committee admonished party members at its next meeting that such "unfortunate disagreements" with the party leadership could not be permitted. When the minister-presidents of the West German states met a year later to lay plans for the constitution of the Federal Republic, the Social Democratic minister-presidents took their instructions from Hannover, and in September 1948 the S.P.D. national congress at Düsseldorf voted unanimously that party members holding public office in the various states were to heed the national leadership.

During the drafting of the Basic Law for the new West German Federal Republic between September 1948 and May 1949, the Social Democratic delegates to the Parliamentary Council in Bonn, though ostensibly representing their respective state governments, were in effect led by their party chairman. Schumacher, operating from his sickbed in Hannover after the amputation of his leg, insisted that no decision be taken without consulting him, and, despite objections from some Social Democratic Länder ministers, issued statements and directives that committed the party and its representatives in Bonn to his strategy. Then, at the last moment, in April 1949 he threatened to withhold Social Democratic approval for the new constitution unless the Allies agreed to his demands for a more centralized state; when party members from some of the Länder protested, he reminded them that it was their duty to obey the will of the majority (which supported him). The warning proved effective and the dissenting minority submitted.

The bitter campaign for power in the new state, and the duel between Schu-

---

* Thus, when Schumacher and the S.P.D. executive committee had called upon Social Democratic ministers in September 1946 to withdraw from coalition governments unless certain demands of the party leadership were met by the occupation authorities, this injunction was in effect ignored by the ministers. Sometime later Schumacher took strong exception to a proposed meeting of minister-presidents from the states in both the Western and Soviet zones of Germany, but the S.P.D. chiefs refused to heed him.

macher and Adenauer that dominated domestic politics from 1949 to 1952, accentuated the position of the party leader as chief decision-maker in the S.P.D. As soon as Schumacher perceived that the election returns of August 1949 would not permit him to head the new federal government, he decided to cling to his strategy of categorical opposition and refuse participation in the government. The "lessons of Weimar," he told a caucus of leading Social Democrats, as well as economic developments, demanded that the S.P.D. stand aside and permit a "bourgeois" coalition full freedom to discredit itself before the German voters; the time was past for party members to nourish "illusions" about collaboration. Determined to forge the newly elected Social Democratic deputies into firm opposition behind his leadership, he insisted that both they and the representatives of the state diets to the Federal Assembly of September 1949 support his clearly hopeless candidacy for the federal presidency against Theodor Heuss. The vote in the caucus was close, but decisive.* Thereafter, Schumacher's authority in the party was never again seriously challenged.

As the leader of the principal opposition party in the Federal Republic and Chancellor Adenauer's potential successor, Schumacher achieved the pinnacle of his power in the S.P.D. He was no longer merely the principal functionary of the party organization, but the spokesman for the 136 Social Democratic deputies in the Bundestag and almost seven million voters. The distinction between his position as party chairman, accountable to the party members, and his position as leader of the Bundestagsfraktion, representing seven million Social Democratic voters, was obscure, and his words were as authoritative for the deputies as for the officials of the party organization. In his capacity as party chairman he exercised considerable influence over the deputies, hoping to be renominated by their local organization, and as leader of the parliamentary opposition he was free to bypass the party organization in his dealings with the Adenauer government, interest groups, and representatives of the occupation powers. Nationally and internationally his words and actions were accepted as authoritative for the party, and Social Democrats who disagreed

* According to one source, 112 members of the Social Democratic caucus preceding the balloting for the presidency opposed Schumacher's candidacy, several abstained, and only 134 supported it after Schumacher had reportedly threatened resignation. Some of the old Social Democratic leaders present, such as Carl Severing, liked Heuss and wanted him to be the unanimous choice of the Federal Assembly as a nonpartisan president. Others argued that a less controversial Social Democratic candidate like the former Reichstag president Paul Löbe, or the Lord Mayor of Hamburg, Wilhelm Kaisen, might gain sufficient support to win the presidency. Schumacher, however, not only wanted the "bourgeois coalition" to have its chosen president so that the battle lines of the future would be clearly drawn from the outset, but was determined to prevent a more acceptable Social Democrat from chancing election. The fate of Friedrich Ebert, the Social Democratic first president of the Weimar Republic, proved, he asserted, that it would be far better to be defeated than to obscure the division between government and opposition by voting either for the candidate of the "bourgeois coalition" or for a Social Democrat who might be forced to support an anti-Socialist government and its actions.

with him could not risk opposing him for fear of undermining their party's position.

In short, Schumacher's control of key positions in both the party and the parliamentary organization of the S.P.D., as well as his dual office of opposition leader and party chairman, enabled him to exercise his monocratic leadership with maximum effectiveness. Disagreements within the Bundestagsfraktion or dissatisfaction with some of his actions among the minister-presidents were almost invariably settled as he wished. He, for his part, did not hesitate to interfere in state and local politics if he considered interference to be warranted, either by the strategic needs of his campaign of categorical opposition to the Adenauer government* or by considerations affecting other party objectives at home or abroad.†

Psychological Aspects of the Leader-Follower Relationship

The altogether extraordinary influence that Kurt Schumacher exercised in the party is not to be explained simply in terms of his ruthless employment of the organizational "apparatus," as many of his critics alleged. His admirers asserted that if he ruled rather than reigned in the party, it was by the free consent of the governed. To support their contention that his authority rested on a democratic base, they pointed to his unopposed election and re-elections as party chairman by almost unanimous votes at party congresses (see Appendix A, Sec. 5), and to the overwhelming endorsement that he customarily received in the S.P.D. councils. Prestige, rather than organizational coercion and manipulation, was said to explain his influence. Schumacher himself, whose habit of using the first person plural in statements and speeches has already been noted, wryly commented that it seemed to be his "particular misfortune" to have his views invariably supported by a majority in the supreme party councils.[15]

Schumacher's influence in the S.P.D. derived its legitimation from a power base that contained ingredients of all three of Max Weber's categories, legal-rational, traditional, and charismatic. Party members accepted his interpreta-

---

* For example, in an effort to obtain control of the Bundesrat in 1951, he intervened in negotiations on the formation of a coalition government in Schleswig-Holstein.

† An interesting, if minor, case in point was Schumacher's attempt to persuade Social Democratic state officials to satisfy claims for restitution brought by Jewish organizations. Following a visit of a Jewish delegation, Schumacher wrote Minister-President Kopf that the political consequences of Jewish dissatisfaction with the restitution policies of his Lower Saxony government would seriously harm the party's efforts to create a favorable public image abroad. "I consider it essential that we avoid anything that might interfere with this development," he told Kopf. "I am of . . . the opinion that the funds needed for this highly important political purpose must be raised by the state of Lower Saxony," for failure to provide them might do the S.P.D. greater harm than a financial deficit in the state treasury. Letter to Minister-President Hinrich Kopf, Hannover, Feb. 19, 1951, "Betr: Ansprüche jüdischer Personen auf Grund des niedersächsischen Personenschaden -und Haftentschädigungsgesetzes," Pers. Archiv, S.P.D.

tion of his role as their leader with varying degrees of enthusiasm, ranging from reluctant acquiescence to eager endorsement, but none questioned the legitimacy of his position. As we have noted, the postwar setting imposed severe limitations upon any attempts by the party leader to compel compliance with his wishes through organizational means alone. But since the legitimacy of the decisions of a majority in the party and of its elected representatives in the supreme councils of the S.P.D. was accepted, opponents of the "Schumacher course" submitted to the party leader's will. Because Schumacher saw the importance of a legitimate power base within the party, he fought with great skill and determination for the chairmanship of the party. The S.P.D. during his leadership was at bottom still a *Weltanschauungspartei,* an ideological movement whose members were united by more or less consciously perceived common ideals as authoritatively interpreted by their legitimate leaders.

Acceptance of Schumacher's interpretation of his role was based in part on the strong belief of the old-timers that loyalty to the party demanded solid support for its elected leaders. This led them to support Schumacher's role performance even when they disagreed with his role conception. The desire to affirm and reaffirm the in-group sentiments that bound together most party members apparently induced even Schumacher's bitterest foes to confine their criticism almost entirely to intraparty channels of communication, and outwardly to support the chairman and the policies endorsed by a majority of the party. Even if they did not care for the incumbent, they respected the authority of his office. Thus, voluntary self-constraint rather than fear of external sanctions or coercion tended to curb the critics' tongues. In instances in which opposition to Schumacher and his policies was carried beyond the confines of the party or persisted after a formal decision of the party leaders, the wrath of the rank and file turned against the errant members, who were believed guilty of violating party discipline and solidarity.

Sentiments of loyalty and solidarity, however, do not suffice to explain how Schumacher came to exercise an influence far greater than either his predecessors in the Weimar party or his successor as leader of the S.P.D. Schumacher himself, as we noted, adopted the argument that the party followed him because his way was the way of a majority of its members; and, in point of fact, his was no longer a deviant view, as it had been before 1933. His conception of the role of the S.P.D. in post-Nazi Germany, his anti-Nazi sentiments, and his determination to place the party in a position to transform the country into a democratic socialist commonwealth probably reflected the sentiments of most Social Democrats in these years. Apparently Schumacher, to a greater extent than any other leader, had the intellectual and verbal skill to give voice to sentiments that others found difficult to define and express. In this sense, he became the symbol as well as the spokesman of a militant Social Democracy that had survived oppression to lay claim now to the post-totalitarian leadership of Germany. He embodied for a majority of the party the legitimacy myth of the principal anti-Nazi resistance movement, a myth that was the basis of all Social Democratic demands for power, since it represented Social Democrats as the rightful successors to the totalitarian elite.

Thus most Social Democrats apparently found Schumacher's role assignments, inside as well as outside the party, more or less consonant with their own values and expectations. This goes far to explain the extraordinary intraparty acceptance of his monocratic leadership. In-group norms, reinforced by general acceptance of Schumacher's claim to have no other ambition than to promote Social Democratic interests, sustained the legitimacy of the party chairman's authority. But there were other factors that for many party members were perhaps even more important in determining their relationship to the party leader.

Quite a few Social Democratic activists, particularly among the younger intellectuals and the former émigrés, accepted the relationship deliberately because they felt that strong monocratic leadership was needed for the tasks confronting the party and the country. Reflecting upon past mistakes and future promise, they arrived at much the same task-orientated perception of the leader-follower relationship as Schumacher. Despite frequent reservations about some of his personal characteristics and specific tactics, they believed that here was the man with the record, the drive, the intellect, and the mass appeal to provide party and country with the leadership that was needed. Some thought that he was the man to infuse new life into an antiquated, colorless political movement, that he might have the strength to transform Social Democracy from a class movement into a popular mass reform movement. Those who thought of him as primarily an agitator believed that Hitler had shown this to be a necessary attribute for political success in Germany. They reasoned that the German labor movement needed a strong hand at the helm to prevent its conquest by the Communists or a repetition of the factionalism that was believed to have crippled it in the past, that a man like Schumacher was needed to lead a militant socialist movement to power against strong opposition from domestic and foreign foes. Particularly to many younger men, he seemed the best equipped in the party to rally the masses behind the Social Democratic drive for power, and at the same time to overcome the deadweight of party bureaucratism and sterile dogmatism. They accepted his monocratic leadership because the party's future and their personal aspirations seemed to call for a man of his qualities, and no one else seemed available.

Most difficult to analyze, and also perhaps the most important aspect of Schumacher's extraordinary influence, was the affective relationship between him and many party members. The positive emotions he evoked among his supporters were as strong as the negative emotions he induced in his opponents. "One had to experience Schumacher to understand him," one woman employee at the S.P.D. headquarters told me. Sober functionaries grew animated when they recalled the fascination of the Schumacher image, the "sparkle" emanating from his "great, almost blind eyes," his "peculiar" face, his jerky gestures, and his emaciated and pain-wracked crippled body. "When he entered a room—during his last years one could not speak of walking, a mutilated form, leaning on his secretary and a crutch—everyone fell silent," observed an Austrian socialist. "He immediately became the center of all attention—his tortured body and indomitable spirit inspiring admiration, and the dynamic force of his personality inspiring awe."[16] The extraordinary qualities that already in Stuttgart and Dachau had exercised a magnetic attraction upon many, particularly relatively unsophisticated persons, appear to have been amplified by his appearance and behavior against the background of the emotional climate of opinion in the post-totalitarian party. The image of the austere, uncompromising, and dedicated wreck of a man apparently evoked feelings of guilt and fright as well as fervent devotion among his fellow party members. Some felt inspired and literally "glowed" in his presence, whereas others were discomfited by his appearance and behavior. But few who "experienced" Schumacher remained emotionally unaffected.

The evidence gathered in the course of this study strongly suggests that the personal emotional needs of many party members induced them to accept Schumacher's role assignments more or less readily. When Social Democrats recalled his leadership qualities (*Führungspersönlichkeit*), they generally mentioned a mixture of fear and admiration that his self-assertive behavior seems to have inspired. Few thought of him as a warm or affectionate person; most remembered him as austere and forbidding, set apart from his fellows not only by his physical condition but by his personality. His ravaged body and fierce temperament, his intellectual and oratorical feats, his authoritative leadership, all provoked fear as well as admiration. As in Stuttgart, few of his associates employed the familiar *Du,* the customary form of address among party comrades, and many addressed him as "Dr. Schumacher." Indeed he was not seen as a "comrade" in the traditional sense, but as a man without equal. At all levels of the party organization, but especially among his staff at the S.P.D. headquarters, Social Democrats apparently perceived themselves in an inferior relationship with him, a relationship that seems to have been based on feelings of guilt and the need to identify with a figure whose conduct could not be questioned.[17]

According to studies on the subject, the authority of a leader over a group relates to the leader's ability to resolve, or at least assuage, anxiety feelings aroused by feelings of guilt among members of the group. In Schumacher's case, his great personal influence in the party appears to have owed a good deal to the widespread acceptance of his claim to moral superiority, an acceptance that brought with it the resolution of anxiety caused by feelings of guilt. "Who but he could stand up at a mass meeting and confront the audience with the long list of crimes committed between 1933 and 1945 without having to fear an embarrassing query about his personal record in this era?" wrote one young party member.[18] For many conscience-ridden Germans the concentration camp survivor stood as a constant reminder of their own culpability.[19] This sense of guilt was probably far more prevalent among Social Democrats than among the population in general or among members of parties less explicitly anti-Nazi. As one perceptive observer has noted, Schumacher's role in his party was "beyond rational explanation," not merely because he symbolized the party's suffering and survival, but because the all too evident effects of his un-yielding courage and martyrdom produced strong feelings of guilt in those who had fared better under Hitler because they had been more "prudent."[20] Old-timers who had survived the Third Reich without great suffering felt morally inferior to him. That his most devoted aides were frequently former anti-Nazi exiles seems to have been only partly due to a shortage of qualified younger officials. Former exiles were apparently particularly sensitive to Schu-macher's unspoken claim to moral superiority. Because they did not feel them-selves morally qualified to challenge his role conception and aspirations, they were inclined to defer to his judgment even when they questioned the wisdom of his decisions. The more keenly this moral superiority was perceived, the greater his psychological advantage in imposing his conception of the leader-follower relationship seems to have been. Former exiles and old-time leaders of the Weimar S.P.D. who had survived the Nazi era in relative comfort sub-mitted to imperious and even humiliating treatment from him. By accepting his monocratic leadership, it seems, they provided themselves with a means of relieving guilt anxieties.

An unprecedented need among many Social Democrats to identify with an authority figure appears to have been another reason for accepting Schu-macher's role perceptions. Identification with the party leader seems to have taken two main forms. For some he was evidently a conscience symbol, a super-ego figure. For them, submission to his views was a reconciliation of their role behavior with the dictates of a stern and uncompromising authority identified with imperatives imbedded in their conscience. Their relationship to the party leader resembles that of the devout believer to the priest who can give him absolution. Others seem to have identified Schumacher with an ego ideal to be emulated. Striving to be like him, they adopted for their own the admired leader's interpretations of proper role relationships and political be-havior.* Both forms of identification were particularly evident in the relation-

---

* It has been called to my attention by a number of persons that some of Schumacher's closest as-sociates seemed to imitate their leader's gestures and manner of speaking when they addressed large audiences. After his death they gradually appeared to shed this habit.

ship between Schumacher and his aides. Some of these men worshiped him with an almost religious fervor, and saw him as a "Christ-like figure," in the words of one of them. Even many years after his death, one of his closest and most sophisticated aides recalled that, like Moses, the party leader gave the impression of standing upon a mountaintop, from which he alone could see the "promised land." Close to a decade after Schumacher had died, party members who apparently had striven to identify with him still basked in the glory that they felt had been reflected upon them by loyal service to a man they had both loved and feared.

The testimony of Schumacher's former associates suggests that he may have provided some Social Democrats with a substitute focus of identification for a firm faith in the inevitable triumph of democratic socialism. In the past, adherence to the eschatology of Marxist determinism or neo-Kantian ethical idealism had given party members a firm sense of participation in a movement that seemed bound to be victorious sooner or later. The Nazi dictatorship had shaken, if not destroyed, such blind faith in progress for quite a few Social Democrats, and it seems that an unabated need to feel a sense of participation in a historical movement may have led some of the rather colorless officials in the Schumacher entourage to strive for a new transcendence by means of identification with a hero personality who represented militant socialism in its most uncompromising and vigorous form. The striving for transcendence, according to one view, involves empathy, "the stepping out of one's present self into an idealized alter-ego," and this search for transfiguration requires "the projection of the self into something believed much greater."[21] Before Hitler, most Social Democrats had identified the role of the party chairman with the general tasks of their party as the agent of historical determinism, or, more rarely, of ethical imperatives. After Hitler, many old-timers in the S.P.D. evidently retained this image of the chairman's role, but others, particularly in Schumacher's immediate entourage, seem to have identified it with a charismatic projection of the transcendent self. Schumacher for them was the charismatic hero who enabled them to experience a certain state of transcendence; by accepting his role assignments in the leader-follower relationship, they achieved a new identification with a revolutionary transformation of German society, this time through a charismatic living leader rather than remote teleological doctrines.

Intraparty Opposition: Hoegner, Kaisen, and Reuter

We noted earlier that although Schumacher complained of the servility he found among his associates, he was apparently best pleased when the men he worked with seemed willing to accept his interpretation and assignment of roles. The same applied to the larger context of the Social Democratic party. Schumacher repeatedly called for vigorous debate in party councils, yet seemed to find serious opposition and criticism hard to take, at times intolerable, par-

ticularly during the last two or three years of his life. He admitted in a letter
to a Social Democratic Bundestag deputy that dissent was to be expected in a
group of 136 representatives: "We must reconcile ourselves to the semi-con-
scious swaggering of a few comrades intoxicated by a sense of their own importance."[22] But in fact he could not reconcile himself to dissenting opinions,
and complained of a tendency among some ambitious elements in the party
to criticize the leadership in order to enhance their own prestige. When he
was a young socialist, he told an interviewer, he loyally obeyed the direction
of the party leadership; nowadays it seemed fashionable to seek popularity,
particularly outside the party, by claiming to have better judgment than the
leadership.[23] Once a dissenter himself, he now sought to crush disagreement
whenever it threatened to challenge his views of Social Democratic aspirations
and strategy.

In short, Schumacher was intolerant whenever he felt his self-assigned party
role questioned. One of his closest associates recalled that he was forever demanding formal votes in party councils, even though the outcome in his favor
was almost always a foregone conclusion. To all appearances supremely self-
confident, he nonetheless insisted on constant reaffirmation from the party's
leading members. He was quick to allege disloyalty toward himself, and therefore the party and its cause, and brooded at length over the identity and
motives of those who voted against him or abstained in secret balloting at party
meetings. It appears from the testimony of many of his aides and associates
that he took any criticism of the party leadership as an expression of personal
antagonism toward himself. More than one unhappy party member found
himself unexpectedly and savagely censured for words or actions that he had
not consciously aimed at Schumacher.*

It seemed even to some of Schumacher's closest advisers that he was sometimes not only unjust but unwise in his behavior toward men he suspected of
disagreeing with him. He appeared to go out of his way to pick a quarrel when,
in their view, it was neither necessary nor desirable. He provoked and exacerbated disputes over comparatively minor issues, usually with men who had
no desire for a fight.† As one of Schumacher's key deputies later observed, he
seemed unwilling to compromise his differences with those he believed had

---

* For example, when Schumacher's principal adviser on foreign policy, Gerhard Lütkens, in a
Bundestag speech inadvertently let slip a phrase that seemed to question or contradict Schumacher's
position, the unhappy deputy found himself promptly repudiated and publicly censured on the
floor of the chamber by Schumacher's principal deputy, acting on the instructions of the party
leader.

† A minor, but characteristic, case in point is a letter that Schumacher wrote in October 1949 to
the S.P.D. deputy, Hermann Brill, like himself a former concentration camp prisoner. Writing
in his capacity of party chairman, Schumacher notified Brill that the S.P.D. executive committee
had formally disapproved of certain of his political activities. In the typed copy of the letter, Brill's
actions were described as "incorrect," but apparently Schumacher found this wording too mild,
and substituted in his own hand that the party leadership had "explicitly disapproved of your activities." See letter to Hermann Brill, Oct. 24, 1949, Archiv Annemarie Renger.

challenged his authority, preferring to obtain a clear and undisputed victory over them. They were to submit voluntarily, or suffer formal censure by a vote of the party congress or executive committee. Only then would he forgive, and perhaps forget, acts he considered disloyal and in violation of party discipline, as in the case of Paul Löbe mentioned earlier. When a clear resolution proved impossible, his antagonism toward his supposed opponent apparently became boundless. Within the party, such sentiments seem to have influenced his attitude toward the Bavarian leader Wilhelm Hoegner and the lord mayors of Bremen and Berlin, Wilhelm Kaisen and Ernst Reuter. Outside the party, similar reactions appear to have played a large part in his violent antipathy toward Adenauer.

None of Schumacher's occasional critics in the postwar party was ever a serious rival, as Grotewohl had been. Their differences with him arose out of their apparent unwillingness to accept his strategy and role assignments unquestioningly. Thus Hoegner, like Kaisen and Reuter, was a prominent public official whose perception of his duties and functions as a Social Democratic officeholder was rather different from that of the party's national chairman.* His quarrel with Schumacher was at its height in the years 1945–47. First as minister-president and later as deputy minister-president of a Bavarian coalition government with autonomist leanings, he not only sought to cooperate closely with the American occupation authorities, but claimed that the nature of Bavarian political conditions demanded far-reaching autonomy for the Social Democratic state leaders in their relationship with non-socialist parties and other groups, such as the Roman Catholic Church. Opposed to Schumacher's plans for a centralized Social Democratic party and German state, he first fought against the re-establishment of a national organization, and then engaged Schumacher in a bitter fight for control of the Bavarian branch of the S.P.D.

Schumacher was infuriated by the challenge, and charged that Hoegner's position conflicted with the party's plans for the establishment of a democratic socialist society in Germany. It did Hoegner no good to paint Schumacher as an arrogant Prussian to his fellow Bavarians. The former exile could not match the prestige and influence that Schumacher's personality and outstanding anti-Nazi record commanded. In 1947 he had to yield his place at the head of the Bavarian S.P.D. to a devoted Schumacher supporter, and he was forced to leave his ministerial office when the party chairman decided to end the Bavarian coalition government.

---

* In May 1933, when both men were young Reichstag deputies, Hoegner had supported the last effort of some party leaders to save the party by voting for Hitler's foreign policy. Furthermore, whereas Schumacher refused to leave the country and chose martyrdom in a concentration camp, Hoegner escaped to Switzerland and remained there in comparative comfort until 1945, when he was appointed minister-president of Bavaria by the American occupation authorities.

Schumacher visited Bavaria repeatedly, but he apparently conferred only once with Hoegner and that was before he had become chairman of the party. Though Hoegner remained a power in Bavaria as leader of the Social Democrats in the state legislature, Schumacher made a great show of ignoring him. In 1950, however, the S.P.D. became the strongest party in Bavaria, and Hoegner triumphantly returned as deputy minister-president and interior minister in a coalition government with the Christian Socialists, the Bavarian branch of the ruling Christian Democrats whom Schumacher was fighting in national politics.

Hoegner was neither strong enough to defy Schumacher nor weak enough to be successfully purged by him. He was popular in Bavaria and an able politician. There is reason to believe that a more conciliatory attitude on Schumacher's part would have served his purpose better. In the case of Wilhelm Kaisen, Schumacher's inability to compromise differences for the sake of larger aspirations was even more clearly demonstrated.

The President of the Senate of the city-state of Bremen was, like Hoegner, a few years older than Schumacher. His background resembled that of Schumacher's old foe Wilhelm Keil. Of working-class origin and largely self-educated, he had joined the S.P.D. in 1905, and had given it a lifetime's devoted service. In many respects, Kaisen was typical of the pragmatically oriented party functionaries whom Schumacher had so often criticized in the Weimar days. Although he had been active in Bremen politics before 1933, he was left in peace by the Nazis, and allowed to till his small farm on the outskirts of the city. Like Severing, Keil, and other Weimar party leaders who, thanks to Nazi tolerance and their own prudence, had survived the Nazi era relatively unscathed, Kaisen returned to public life when the Hitler regime collapsed. Appointed to head a coalition government for Bremen by the occupation authorities, he remained in this position throughout Schumacher's postwar career and for many years afterwards. Unlike Hoegner, he did not quarrel with Schumacher during the re-establishment of the party, but supported his efforts to reorganize the S.P.D. He became a member of the new national executive committee in 1946, to be re-elected in 1947 and 1948 with majorities almost as large as those for the party chairman (see Appendix A, Sec. 5). Popular not only with the Bremen voters but with the American authorities and the leaders of the "bourgeois" parties in his coalition, he was highly successful in his efforts to rebuild one of Europe's largest ports.

Kaisen's belief that the cooperative Social Democratic policy that worked so well in Bremen might prove equally effective in national politics gradually brought him into opposition to the party chairman. To Schumacher, as to the attentive public, he became identified with a group that appeared to oppose the hard line of the party leader in favor of greater cooperation with the "bourgeois" parties and the Western powers. Kaisen, it was said, was one of the most

independent-minded of the Social Democratic leaders who resisted the abso-
lutist claims of the party's chairman. When Schumacher insisted on opposing
Heuss for the federal presidency in September 1949, Kaisen was prominently
mentioned as a compromise candidate. Once the new federal government had
been established, Kaisen maintained very cordial relations both with Heuss
and with Chancellor Adenauer—in sharp contrast to Schumacher's relationship with the two men.

Kaisen's behavior challenged Schumacher's perception of party roles and
party strategy. His popularity was undoubtedly an important asset for the
party and for its chairman's efforts to gain it mass support. In Bremen the
Social Democrats invariably gained large pluralities. But this did not keep
Schumacher from deliberately exacerbating the growing friction between himself and Kaisen. Shortly after the creation of the Adenauer government, Kaisen
sent a number of letters to the party headquarters indicating his unhappiness
with Schumacher's behavior and tactics, particularly with his bitter opposition
to the proposed West German association with the Council of Europe in Strasbourg. Frank but not at all vindicative in his criticism, Kaisen questioned the
wisdom of Schumacher's charge that Adenauer was betraying the national interest, and urged that Schumacher abandon his categorical denunciation of all
efforts toward the recovery of Germany by means of Western European political and economic cooperation. To Kaisen, Schumacher's militant opposition based on "national socialism" was utterly unrealistic and politically unwise. "In my opinion, we must pursue a policy that eases tensions, rather than
increasing them," he wrote to Schumacher on December 11, 1949. He strongly
objected to Schumacher's conception of the S.P.D. as primarily an instrument
in the struggle for power. If this stand were maintained, he warned, it would
force many party members holding public offices either to resign from their
positions or to assert their public responsibilities against the demands of the
party leadership. Kaisen sought to publish his criticism of what he termed
Schumacher's "all-or-nothing" course in the official party paper, the *Neue
Vorwärts,* but the editor refused on the grounds that his attitude was too
"negative" and lacked constructive ideas. Schumacher himself apparently
never replied.[24]

So Kaisen published his criticism in a Dutch socialist paper. The German
press immediately reported a severe crisis in the S.P.D. leadership. Schumacher summoned the party executive committee, which censured Kaisen
for his dissent and the manner in which he had chosen to make it public.
Kaisen contended that freedom of intraparty debate justified his action,
but the majority of the executive held that no party member had the right
to criticize the party chairman in this fashion. In May 1950 the national
party congress in Hamburg failed to re-elect Kaisen to the executive committee. Kaisen, however, continued to criticize Schumacher for opposing

Adenauer's policy of Western European integration. In March 1951, Kaisen's support of the Schuman Plan for a European Coal and Steel Community led Schumacher to accuse him publicly of sabotaging the Social Democratic cause, backed by new condemnations of Kaisen by the executive committee. However, he lacked the power to remove Kaisen from his position at the head of the coalition government in Bremen, and he could not prevent him from casting his vote in the upper house of parliament to help bring the Federal Republic into the European Coal and Steel Community, an institution that the party stood pledged to oppose.

In the Kaisen case, Schumacher's inability to accept determined opposition to his monocratic leadership was demonstrated in a manner that even some of his key advisers regarded as inopportune. In the conflict with Grotewohl his irreconcilable antagonism had proved to be functionally advantageous in the fight for power in the party; in the dispute with Hoegner it was of more questionable value: and in Kaisen's case it probably did him more harm than good in terms of his larger political ambitions. But it was in his relationship with Ernst Reuter that such dysfunctional intraparty behavior manifested itself in its most extreme form.

Schumacher's relationship with Berlin's lord mayor, it seems to me, must be seen in terms of the very special meaning that Berlin appears to have held for him. One might almost speak of a proprietary attitude toward the city that had been and apparently remained for Schumacher the center of his political world and aspirations. His dispute with Grotewohl for leadership of the S.P.D. had to a large extent been conditioned by this same perception of Berlin's dominant position in German politics, and though tactical exigencies had led him to deprecate the status of the city at the time, it is evident that it was and remained for him the capital of Germany. His insistence in subsequent years that what took place in Hannover, Frankfurt, and Bonn was but provisional action pending the reunification of Germany and the re-establishment of its government in Berlin seems to have been rooted in deeply felt sentiments that defied all rational political considerations. Berlin was "his" city to Schumacher in the same sense that he felt the leadership of post-totalitarian Germany was properly his, and that it was his mission to restructure German society. It was this attitude that seems to have strongly influenced his perception of the proper role behavior for the Social Democratic mayor of the city.

Reuter went to Berlin, somewhat reluctantly, in November 1946—apparently with Schumacher's blessing if not at his urging—to become Senator for Transport in the coalition that then still governed the entire city and included Social Democrats as well as members of the recently amalgamated Socialist Unity party.[25] The only prominent old-timer among the Social

Democrats in the city government, he was some six years older than Schumacher, and like him of middle-class antecedents and university-trained. He had joined the S.P.D. in 1912, and was wounded in World War I and captured by the Russians. He took part in the Bolshevist Revolution, and from 1918 to 1922 played a leading role in the German Communist party; he then returned to the S.P.D., however, as an expert in local administration. Elected to the Reichstag just before Hitler came to power, he had thought that some accommodation with the Nazis might be possible for the S.P.D., and like Hoegner had voted in May 1933 to support Hitler's foreign policy. After being imprisoned in a concentration camp, he chose exile in 1935, and spent the war years teaching at the University of Istanbul; he returned to Germany in 1946 to take part in his country's political and economic reconstruction.

Initially, Reuter did not strike Schumacher as a man likely to cause him trouble. Received rather coolly in Berlin by the veterans of the anti-Nazi resistance, and unpopular with left-wing groups who wanted amalgamation with the Communists, Reuter seems to have been drawn to Schumacher and his declared goals. The two men had a rather similar social and intellectual background, which separated them from the mass of party members of working-class origin and limited education, and they were agreed that the S.P.D. needed to become a broadly based reform party if the "mistakes" of Weimar were to be avoided.[26] At first Schumacher may have seen Reuter as one of his deputies in Berlin. The party chairman's authority there was a good deal weaker than in West Germany. By virtue of tradition as well as size of membership, the Berlin organization of the party enjoyed a special status, a preeminence reinforced by its practically independent fight against the fusion forces in the spring of 1946. Schumacher was respected and admired, but on his frequent visits to the city between February 1946 and November 1947 he was received more as the representative of the West German Social Democrats than as the authoritative leader of the entire party. His formal authority was severely limited by the four-power control arrangement in the city, and he depended even more than elsewhere on the voluntary cooperation of the local party officials. Most of these were relatively minor party officials, who had taken over the leadership of the state organization as a result of their successful fight against Grotewohl's efforts to merge the Berlin organization with the Communists.

The city-wide elections of 1946 had produced a plurality of almost 49 per cent for the S.P.D., and in June 1947 the party organization nominated Reuter for lord mayor. He was elected by an overwhelming majority in the city assembly, but was prevented from assuming office by a veto of the Soviet authorities. Until the city was split in 1948, he was lord mayor in name only, for the Social Democrats—encouraged by Schumacher—refused to back down, and the Soviets refused to withdraw their veto. As the elected but not acting chief of the city government, he was more a symbol of Social Democratic defiance to Soviet pressure than an effective leader. His political influence in his own party was not strong enough to elect him deputy chairman of the local party organization in the spring of 1948. Schumacher apparently liked Reuter well enough in this role, which fitted into his general perception of the Berlin situation as a side show to the larger struggle for the control of Germany. The Social Democrats in Berlin, particularly the public office holders, were playing important but strictly subordinate roles in the fight to establish a Social Democratic government for the entire country in the old German capital. On his frequent visits, Schumacher made it clear that Berlin remained for him the ultimate focus of German politics, and therefore of his own aspirations in the fight for political power. He conferred with Western Allied officials and party functionaries, and spoke at mass meetings about the re-establishment of a united Germany; of the elected lord mayor he saw comparatively little in the pre-blockade era.

The axial period in the Schumacher-Reuter relationship was the summer of 1948. While the Berlin blockade suddenly propelled the lord mayor into national and international prominence, the party leader was forced by his illness to disappear for an entire year from public view. When, soon after the start of the blockade, a seat for Reuter was sought on the national S.P.D. executive committee, Schumacher apparently had no strong objections, and the lord mayor was elected at the Düsseldorf Congress of September 1948 by a majority almost as large as Schumacher's own. At this point, however, it became clear to Schumacher, confined to his bed in Hannover, that Reuter was stepping out of the role assigned to him. Reports from trusted deputies in Berlin evidently fed these suspicions. Under the impact of the blockade, Reuter appeared to be redefining his role, and playing with mounting self-confidence the part of chief spokesman for millions of beleaguered Berliners.* No longer was he merely a symbol; he had become an independent actor who proclaimed the determination of "his people" to fight against Soviet pressure "as long as there is breath in us."[27] Once again Berlin had become the focus of world attention, but it was Reuter, not Schumacher, who occupied the center of the stage. When the city assembly elections of December 1948 gave the Social Democrats an unprecedented 64.5 per cent of the vote, it can hardly have escaped Schumacher's attention that the victory was hailed as a personal triumph for Reuter, who was promptly re-elected lord mayor by the new city assembly.

Schumacher was too ill to visit Berlin during the blockade, and his appoint-

* According to a public opinion interviewer, for the people of Berlin, Reuter's personality and name were "from a psychological point of view very well adapted to dispel any worries and manifestations of fear, or to redirect them into the 'fight for freedom.'" Cited in Davison, p. 138.

ments calendar does not note the name of Reuter during the year from April 1948 to April 1949. Reuter apparently claimed that he was too busy to visit Schumacher, and Schumacher interpreted his behavior as a deliberate slight. He apparently expected Reuter to consult with him regularly, and bitterly resented his failure to do so, particularly after Reuter's visits abroad. It seemed to him that by accepting invitations to Paris, London, and Washington, the "Prefect of Berlin," as he dubbed Reuter ironically, was undertaking to negotiate independently with the Allied governments though he lacked the necessary perspective and authority.

Once it was clear that Reuter claimed for himself the role of leader of West Berlin, his differences with Schumacher over the proper relationship between lord mayor and party chairman became irreconcilable. Although he formally disclaimed any ambitions for Schumacher's office, his words and actions conveyed the impression that he believed himself in many ways more competent than Schumacher to understand and deal with the problems of postwar Germany. His biographers relate that he admired Schumacher's courage and determination, but they also quote his implicit criticism of Schumacher: "The man who like an anchorite is sustained solely by political passion and lacks all contact with real life is not always the most suitable for political office."* A political leader, he held, should embody the qualities and aspirations of a "normal human being."[28] Although Reuter was careful to avoid an open break, he claimed the right not only to propose, but to conduct, a policy that was at odds with Schumacher's strategy and aspirations.

Reuter disagreed with Schumacher on two important principles: he did not believe that a bitter class struggle dominated postwar German politics, nor that Social Democratic strategy should be based on a conviction that economic conditions were inexorably deteriorating to the advantage of the party's struggle for power. In contrast to Schumacher's insistence on categorical militancy and opposition to "opportunist" compromises, Reuter favored a conciliatory and strictly pragmatic approach toward the "bourgeois" parties and the Western occupation authorities. Whereas Schumacher always spoke as a German to Germans (even when he was formally addressing a non-German audience), Reuter, who had lived for many years abroad and spoke several foreign languages fluently, was far more sensitive to the attitude and motivation not only of the Western leaders, but of the Soviet leaders as well. His experience as a Communist had given him an unusually intimate knowledge of Soviet attitudes, and his years of exile had taught him that the way to gain his ends with the Western leaders was by negotiation and compromise rather than belligerent demands.

---

* The German word *Säulenheiliger*, which I have translated "anchorite," literally means "stylite," a Christian ascetic living atop a pillar.

As the head of West Berlin's coalition government, Reuter worked in close cooperation not only with prominent members of the "bourgeois" parties opposed by Schumacher in West Germany, but with Western leaders who rarely consulted the S.P.D. chairman. This applied particularly to Reuter's relationship with the principal American representatives in Germany, General Lucius Clay and, later, High Commissioner John J. McCloy. In 1948 and 1949, while Schumacher was wrestling with the Western leaders over the structure of the future West German state, Reuter appeared to interpose himself time and again between the S.P.D. leadership and the occupation authorities. Whenever the opportunity presented itself, he seemed to assume the role of a German statesman not only in Berlin and Bonn, but in Paris, London, and Washington—to Schumacher's intense irritation. It was no doubt primarily Reuter whom Schumacher had in mind when he complained in 1952 of Social Democrats who sought to enhance their reputation at the expense of the party by claiming to have better judgment than the leadership. In Schumacher's eyes, he was clearly an ambitious rival, if not for the party leadership, then for the eventual leadership of Germany. His behavior appeared deliberately designed to sabotage Schumacher's strategy for the acquisition of power through uncompromising militancy. He seemed to be playing up to the Americans by posing as the chief anti-Communist crusader in Germany. It was Reuter who in April 1949 joined Kaisen and the Social Democratic minister-president of Schleswig-Holstein, Hermann Lüdemann, in an unsuccessful revolt against Schumacher's refusal to accept the American version of a Basic Law for the Federal Republic. After the federal election of 1949, Reuter was mentioned both as the head of a coalition government in Bonn, which he was known to favor in opposition to Schumacher, and as a compromise candidate for the federal presidency. And it was Reuter who joined Kaisen and a few other prominent Social Democrats in endorsing Adenauer's policy of cooperation with the Western powers, who led a minority of Berlin Social Democrats in voting against the Schumacher course on German membership in the Council of Europe at the S.P.D. national congress of 1950, and who subsequently defied the party's official position by espousing German participation in a European Coal and Steel Community. When in the fall of 1950 the magazine *Time* called him "one of the few really great men in Western Europe," the description reflected the general trend of attentive elite opinion in the West, whereas Schumacher at this time was extremely unpopular with the major powers.[29]

Reuter's increasingly irritating behavior led Schumacher to become involved in a bitter factional dispute within the Berlin state organization of the party. Determined to cut the lord mayor down to size, he lent his influence to the efforts of party functionaries in the city to force Reuter to submit to the discipline and guidance of the organization. When the end of the blockade had loosened the bonds of anti-Communist solidarity among party members, two of Reuter's opponents, Franz Neumann, the state chairman of the S.P.D., and Arno Scholz, editor-publisher of *Der Telegraf,* one of Berlin's large dailies, became Schumacher's principal contacts and advisers on matters affecting the city and its mayor.[30] Whereas Schumacher came to distrust the official representative of the party leadership in Berlin, Willy Brandt, and saw Reuter only rarely, he constantly consulted Neumann and Scholz, who were apparently only too eager to identify their cause with his. If Reuter slighted Schumacher at the time of his long illness during the blockade, Schumacher, to judge by his appointments diary, seems to have avoided meeting the lord mayor after his recovery, and to have preferred the company of Neumann and Scholz when he was in Berlin.

Schumacher's efforts to curb Reuter and gain acceptance of his own strategy in Berlin politics by reducing or eliminating Reuter's influence were unsuccessful; Reuter was re-elected to the S.P.D. national executive committee at the Hamburg Congress of 1950 (though only in sixteenth place) despite his opposition to Schumacher's foreign policy. After the party lost its absolute majority in the Berlin city assembly in December 1950, Reuter's opponents made several attempts to force him from office and break up his coalition with the parties supporting the Adenauer government in Bonn. All of them failed, though once or twice only by fairly narrow margins. Schumacher's notations in his appointments diary indicate that he encouraged these moves against Reuter, but realized that he lacked the power to proceed openly against him.

Schumacher's frustration at not being able to reduce Reuter's influence aggravated his antagonism toward a man he thought was undercutting his authority, and refusing to play the game according to his rules. He interpreted Reuter's failure to visit him or congratulate him on his birthday as a deliberate insult, reflecting the lord mayor's rejection of Schumacher's perception of their respective roles in party and country. Whether Schumacher also felt that Reuter was waiting for his death so that he might succeed him, as some of Schumacher's associates claimed in later years, can only be conjectured. At the Dortmund Congress immediately following Schumacher's death, Reuter emerged as one of the most popular party leaders, and jumped from sixteenth to second place in the election of the nonsalaried members of the executive committee. Had Reuter not himself died a year later, he might indeed have taken Schumacher's place.

Reviewing the Schumacher-Reuter relationship a decade later, friends and associates of both men felt that the dispute had done Schumacher more harm than good. In terms of his aspirations for personal popularity and for a strong and popular mass party, this may well have been true. Schumacher's differences with Reuter tended to identify his own role with the dogmatic and autocratic leadership of a tradition-bound, unimaginative party machine, an image not likely to attract the elements that he had proclaimed as essential to a new

Social Democratic party and the accomplishment of his goals. And yet it was Schumacher, not Reuter, who exacerbated the differences and was generally the aggressor. Some observers blamed his ill health; others blamed his aides and associates, who were said to have come between the two men. These factors may have contributed to his hostility, but they cannot have created it. Rather, it seems to me, Reuter became for Schumacher an object for aggression as soon as he appeared a potential obstacle to his drive for power. In this sense, though Schumacher's behavior toward Reuter may have been dysfunctional politically, it may have been highly functional in terms of the compensatory needs that we have seen in operation at various points in his career. Thus, actions that puzzled and distressed many of his admirers may have been rooted in the same behavioral characteristics that in other situations had proved highly successful for Schumacher.

Schumacher as Party Leader: An Assessment

What was the impact of Schumacher's role performance as party leader on the post-totalitarian Social Democratic party? According to his most ardent admirers, the party would have found it impossible to overcome the great obstacles to its re-establishment and postwar development without his energetic leadership. His critics, by contrast, have claimed that he stifled essential reforms in the party and committed the S.P.D. to a rigid, self-defeating strategy that ignored dynamic developments in a political environment that he did not comprehend. Both points of view attach a great deal of importance to Schumacher's performance as party leader; according to a third view, his activities were of comparatively minor significance for the postwar evolution of German Social Democracy. Intraparty developments would not have been very different, according to this interpretation, had he never headed the party; his leadership reflected, rather than determined, the postwar climate of opinion in the S.P.D. There appear to be elements of truth as well as exaggeration in each of these views.

It seems that as the leader of German Social Democracy, Schumacher was neither a great master builder nor a creature of forces beyond his control, but a catalytic agent. As a positive catalyst he accelerated certain developments in the post-totalitarian evolution of his party, and as a negative catalyst he delayed others. It is inevitable in a study such as this that we can do no more than speculate on what would have happened if the catalytic agent had not been present; but as the figure of Schumacher recedes into history, and the period of his leadership becomes an episode in the development of German Social Democracy, it seems likely that his role will emerge as a significant though not a decisive one.

In general, the postwar climate of opinion in the Social Democratic party favored both Schumacher's elevation to the party leadership and the performance of his role in this capacity. First, he symbolized and articulated more effectively than anyone else the Social Democratic succession myth according to which the resurrected S.P.D. was the only legitimate counter-elite to the leaders of the Third Reich. This belief had a large body of supporters. Second, his insistence that the party must rectify its past strategic and tactical errors and follow a militant course of action was widely accepted, notably by the younger survivors of the Social Democratic resistance and émigré groups, and by former inmates of Nazi concentration camps. These members shared Schumacher's belief in the need for a united and disciplined party, whose appeal should be aimed at a much wider section of society than had been true before 1933. Third, Schumacher's emphatic anti-Communism was shared by the vast majority of party members, particularly as Soviet actions in Germany appeared to conflict increasingly with Social Democratic objectives. Even those who had initially favored cooperation with the K.P.D. came to agree with the anti-Communist sentiments of older party members, who had never forgiven the Communists for their share in the party's defeat in 1933.

Schumacher's specific actions certainly did not always command as much support as demonstrative votes in party councils and congresses might indicate. Yet dissatisfaction was directed more often than not against Schumacher's deputies, rather than against him. Actions that seemed unfair or unwise were generally excused as the responses of an ailing and temperamental man who was operating in a political context of tension, frustration, and provocation. Besides, the postwar situation, many Social Democrats thought, required firm action both against recalcitrant party members and against political enemies on the right and left who were felt to be determined to frustrate the party's drive for power. Beyond such more or less rational considerations, emotional attachments to the party or to Schumacher himself supported his monocratic leadership.

Schumacher's most manifest and undisputed contribution to the development of the postwar S.P.D. preceded his formal elevation to the leadership. Largely owing to his efforts, attempts to associate, or even amalgamate, re-emerging Social Democratic groups with a Communist party directed from Moscow were frustrated in West Germany, and the S.P.D. was re-established as the first interzonal, centrally directed political movement. Schumacher's admirers have tended to exaggerate his part in blocking Grotewohl's endeavors to assume control of the Social Democratic movement, and later to gain support for its merger with the K.P.D. It is most unlikely that these efforts would have succeeded under political conditions prevailing in West Germany. Neither the occupation authorities nor most Social Democratic functionaries and public officeholders in the Western zones would have been likely to accept for very long a united front or merger with the Communists. However, Schumacher's determined counter-organizational drive was probably important in preventing the intraparty disputes and Western Allied intervention in party affairs that doubtless would have resulted had Grotewohl gained wider support.

Schumacher's success in uniting Social Democratic groups in the West against the Soviet-zone faction laid the groundwork for a separate party organization under his leadership. The rapid re-establishment of a united Social Democratic party in the Western zones, despite considerable opposition from not only Soviet but French and American occupation authorities, was primarily Schumacher's accomplishment. Without him, the reorganization of a central party organization would no doubt have been delayed, and Social Democratic influence in postwar political reconstruction might have been considerably weaker than it was. That Schumacher and his party could not take full advantage of their head start over other parties because of political conditions beyond their control, and that, as some have argued, rapid reorganization in the West unnecessarily deepened the differences with the new Socialist Unity party in the Soviet zone, does not detract from the importance of the achievement. Thanks to Schumacher, a year after the fall of the Nazi regime the S.P.D. was organizationally far better prepared than any other German political group to take over control of a new German government. Had the Allied powers permitted it, Schumacher and the S.P.D. might well have achieved their immediate goal by taking over the postwar government of Germany, at least of West Germany.

Schumacher's second important contribution to the development of the postwar S.P.D. was the speedy and successful assertion that the central party leadership should have preeminence in determining policy on matters affecting the political reconstruction of Germany. Against the wishes of the American and French occupation authorities as well as the inclinations of certain Social Democratic public officeholders, he managed to establish the supremacy of the central leadership over the Social Democratic delegates of the state governments to the Bizonal Economic Council in 1947, and to maintain it successfully thereafter. Although Schumacher and the Social Democrats failed to gain control of the new West German government in 1949, the central party leadership was strong enough to maintain its authority even without such governmental advantages as patronage. Again, Schumacher was the catalytic agent who, through personal dynamism and organizational skill, accelerated the movement toward a unitary party. By tradition and philosophy, German Social Democrats inclined toward centralism in party organization, but under postwar political conditions the re-establishment of a strong central leadership would in all likelihood have been delayed without Schumacher's intervention.

Third, Schumacher has been given credit for a substantial contribution to the transformation of the S.P.D. from a Marxist workers' party to a democratic

socialist reform movement; the extent of his contribution, however, is prob-
lematical. In the first enthusiasm following the re-establishment of the party,
there was much talk among a highly vocal minority of young intellectuals,
some of them newcomers to the S.P.D., of a basic transformation of the party,
its program, and its membership. Schumacher, who may have thought the
forces for reform were stronger than they were, initially sought to become their
principal spokesman. He denounced the forces of traditionalism, and admonished the old-timers to give way to youth. The party's future lay in the hands
of men under forty, he told older members who were trying to retain all important posts in the local party organizations. The S.P.D. had to pass through
an ideological and organizational crisis, he said at the 1947 party congress, to
be cleansed of the ideas and personalities representing the old order. It needed
a new face and a new spirit, not just a superficial application of "rouge and
powder," if it was to win the support of a majority of Germans, particularly
those under forty.[31] In the first two or three years after the war, he encouraged
intraparty discussion of new ideas in the apparent belief that it might help to
improve the S.P.D.'s popular image.* But he consistently opposed demands
for a new basic program from the more doctrinaire party members, evidently
preferring to pursue power with a minimum of visible ideological ballast.
His aim, it seems, was to preserve a flexible body of ideological opinion in the
party. In this respect, he may be said to have assisted the process of reorientation in German Social Democracy, a process that had begun well before he
became the party's leader, and that was to come to fruition a decade after
his death.[32] By holding in check and balancing off against each other various
ideological groupings, he assisted the trend away from a specific ideological
commitment.

As for more specific reforms concerning the composition and organization
of the postwar S.P.D., Schumacher's contribution was certainly not positive
and very likely negative. He needed an efficient and disciplined organization
to support his drive for power, and under prevailing political conditions he
was unable to reconcile this primary objective with his professed desire for a
rejuvenating "crisis" that would thoroughly shake up the party and its officers.
Because he preferred control to reform, he was compelled to come to terms
with the forces of traditionalism in his party, and to strengthen, however reluctantly, the power of the old-time officials in the organizational bureaucracy.
He criticized the "old fuddy-duddies" who lorded it over the local organizations, and called upon younger members to be more active in party affairs, but
he would not—and could not—give effective support to the dwindling elements

---

* For example, in 1947 Schumacher apparently encouraged a small group of young intellectuals
and Protestant clergymen in the party to propose that the S.P.D. modify its Marxist and anti-
clerical views in favor of certain religious and "idealist" values.

in the S.P.D. who wanted to rejuvenate Social Democracy and curb the bureaucracy. The less time and energy he found he could spare for party matters, the more he came to depend upon the old experienced officials to uphold his authority, while they, ironically, maintained and strengthened their power in the name of the party chairman. In the fight for power, the need was for efficiency; one could not afford to experiment with major organizational reforms and inexperienced youngsters.

After his first intensive contacts with party organizations throughout West Germany, Schumacher increasingly lost touch with the lower party echelons. The more he depended upon the intervening strata of party officials, the less aware he became of stagnant conditions in the local organizations and the failure of the party to attract new support. His failure to attend the 1948 party congress proved to be a symbolic if involuntary gesture. The immediate reason was the illness that forced the amputation of his leg, but his physical incapacity merely accentuated the shift of his attention from intraparty matters to the contest for leadership of the emerging West German state. He now largely took for granted the organizational instrument at which he had worked with such furious energy in the preceding three years, and left the details of its operation to others. Party organization, program, and reform were subordinated to the need for solidarity and discipline behind his fight for power in the nation. For the general public, Schumacher sought to de-emphasize his role as party leader, and to stress his image as a champion of the German people who was fighting for their interests against domestic and foreign adversaries.

From 1947 onward, the distance between Schumacher and the mass of Social Democrats increased, and direct interaction between party leader and party members diminished accordingly. This meant that whatever personal influence Schumacher exerted at lower party levels on behalf of organizational reforms had little effect, while the rigid traditionalism and in-group sentiments of the old-timers tended to repel newcomers to the party. Younger men who had been attracted to Social Democracy by the dynamic personality of its new leader and his promises of reform were disappointed, and frequently found the atmosphere of the local groups intolerable.* Those who wanted to transform the party into a militant democratic reform movement with a broad appeal found themselves blocked by old-timers who usually occupied several

---

* Thus one delegate to the 1952 S.P.D. congress complained that "whenever a younger comrade speaks on some matter in a manner that is thought to deviate from the party line, he immediately is told by any number of older party members that he is too young to understand such problems and needs to learn a great deal more before he can participate in a discussion." S.P.D., *Protokoll, Dortmund 1952*, p. 207. Delegates to the 1952 congress expressed their unhappiness with the stagnation in the local organizations, but could come up with no more than the suggestion that younger men be allowed to serve as apprentice assistants to the older functionaries. See *ibid.*, pp. 171–72, 219.

party offices at once, sometimes as many as ten, and who refused to give any of them up for anyone whom they considered less experienced and deserving than men with from twenty to fifty years of service in the party. Schumacher sought out and brought into the leadership a few men he valued personally, such as Herbert Wehner, Adolf Arndt, and Fritz Erler, but these were exceptions. Party membership in West Germany, which in the first years after the war had risen almost to the strength the party had had in all of Germany before Hitler, dropped from a high of nearly 900,000 in 1948 to 600,000 in 1953. Not only were there few new recruits to replace old-timers who died, but the S.P.D. failed to retain members who had joined in the first postwar years, particularly young members and reform-minded intellectuals. At the time of Schumacher's death, the S.P.D. was essentially the same organization it had been when he was elected chairman, a party of traditionalist, elderly workers who had belonged to the S.P.D. before Hitler and remained faithful to their entrenched functionaries.[88]

Schumacher's preoccupation with developments outside his party, as well as his poor state of health, may have caused him to put off measures that he had earlier declared absolutely necessary in order to revitalize the party and win the support of young people and other potential new members. He may have felt that he could resume these efforts later. His failure to win the chancellorship in 1949, and therefore the control of the government, made it even more difficult than before to force reforms in the party. Had he won, he might have used the chancellor's powers to free himself from dependency on the old party officials. But he might just as easily have relied on them to operate the government. Although the political context for a Schumacher chancellorship would have been entirely different from what it was for Adenauer, Schumacher's earlier activities as party leader indicate that, unlike Adenauer, he intended to use the party as his principal instrument of government. In this case, the pressure of events might have further delayed party reforms.

Finally, there seems considerable truth in the assertion that Schumacher's monocratic leadership committed the S.P.D. to a strategy that lacked the flexibility demanded by the postwar situation. The strength of this commitment became evident after his death. There was no succession crisis, no drastic break. The party made a smooth transition to a collegial leadership by Schumacher's lieutenants, headed by Erich Ollenhauer. They proved faithful executors of the dead leader's legacy, and for almost a decade held the party to the rigid opposition course that he had set in 1947. It took two severe defeats in the national elections of 1953 and 1957 to move the party in a new direction, a direction that was marked by the Godesberg Program of 1959 and the emergence of a new generation of more pragmatic leaders.

Under Schumacher's leadership, the S.P.D. followed a reactive strategy based on anachronistic perspectives. Schumacher's obsession with the mistakes of the past led him to try to make Social Democracy play the part he believed it should have played in the Weimar Republic. This perspective was reinforced by a determinist view of postwar political developments derived from Marxist theory. As a result, he committed the party to a policy that restricted its movements at every level of political action. It is impossible to guess what would have happened in different circumstances. However, it seems fair to conclude that a more flexible outlook and strategy would have made the S.P.D. much more successful in combating the forces that opposed its acquisition of power. Schumacher's behavior in the larger political context, and that of his submissive followers, proved to be dysfunctional in terms of the party's leader's proclaimed goals.

SEVEN

The Patriotic Leader

"The Man in the Way"

Shortly after the establishment of the West German Federal Republic in September 1949, the American Secretary of State, Dean Acheson, visited Bonn to meet the leaders of the new German state. He was received by the new Federal Chancellor, Konrad Adenauer. "Here was a man, I thought," Acheson related, "whose mind...could travel the road along which all our measures for the recovery and security of Europe had been moving." After lunching "in a small private room in a very Victorian Bonn hotel, where we drank the delicious white wines of the Rhineland and made formal speeches," Acheson was taken to meet the leader of the opposition. He found a cripple of frightening appearance and demeanor, who immediately launched into an "unrestrained and bitter attack against Adenauer...on the strange ground that Adenauer was working smoothly with the...occupation authorities." He seemed to the American entirely deaf to reason. "Breaking off this futile interview as soon as politeness permitted," Acheson concludes, "I went on to a reception which the Chancellor was giving for me."[1]

Nothing could better illustrate the contrast between Adenauer and Schumacher in the eyes of the Western leaders. Schumacher was respected for his anti-Nazi record, and his physical condition frequently evoked pity; but the strongest impression was that of an autocratic, arrogant, and inflexible rabble-rouser, whose "nationalist utterances" evoked memories of Hitler's outbursts. Sir Ivon Kirkpatrick, who in 1949 became the British High Commissioner in the German Federal Republic, considered Adenauer a "charming" and always "rational" man, who argued "on the plane of reason, courtesy, humour, and understanding." It was because of these qualities of Adenauer's "that all the points of Anglo-German friction...were resolved." In contrast not only to the Chancellor but to such Social Democratic leaders as Reuter, Brauer, and Kaisen, Kirkpatrick found Kurt Schumacher a man with whom it was impossible to "establish relations of confidence and friendship." He was "so touchy that he was apt to take offense at the slightest pretext," and relations between the two men ultimately reached the point at which "we were barely on speaking terms."[2]

In addition to such personal friction, Schumacher's attitude and behavior suggested that his idea of what constituted proper political action in postwar Germany was in direct conflict with the views of the occupation powers. Shortly before he died, the American magazine *Time,* writing for the mass public, described him as "one of the most important men in Europe"; but, it added, "on the course the West has chosen, Kurt Schumacher is the Man in the Way."[3] His image in the Soviet bloc was similar. Divided on practically every other matter affecting Germany, Western and Soviet leaders were united in their negative view of Schumacher. For example, in 1947 a Polish paper called him "an imperialist like Hitler," and in 1951 *Pravda* called him "an eager warmonger," and Tass an "unscrupulous demagogue" and a "fascist" enemy who was seeking to subjugate the German people to the Americans and wanted another war against the Soviet Union.[4]

In short, in terms of the political context within which he sought to gain power for himself and his party, Schumacher's behavior caused both Western and Soviet leaders to see him in an extremely unfavorable light. Why he chose to play a role that brought him into bitter conflict with his counter-players within the occupation powers, and thus in effect put up an obstacle to his ambitions, will be the subject of this chapter.

During the first phase of the occupation, the period of absolute control, the occupation authorities saw their role as givers of commands, and the role of the Germans, including their political leaders, as followers of these commands. It was a period of authoritarian military government, in which public policy was determined mainly on the basis of the interests of non-German decision-makers. Contemporary German opinion—elite and mass—was of no great importance. On the one hand the victors' decisions were based on a punitive policy toward the Germans, and on the other they reflected a tutelary "enlightened despotism" aimed at preventing future German aggression. War-crime trials, demilitarization, denazification proceedings, dismantling of factories, restrictions on industrial production, reparations payments, and carefully controlled political reconstruction were the means used by the occupation powers to implement their policies. United States leaders placed primary emphasis on the political reconstruction of Germany, which was to be based on the American model of a capitalist economy and a federally organized, democratic political system; French and Soviet leaders emphasized punitive policies, and were intent on weakening the elements of German power; and British leaders sought not only to curb German power but to encourage the political reconstruction of Germany along the lines of the British model. Allied policymakers thus saw themselves in the role of absolute rulers, and considered cooperative acquiescence to be the proper role for their German counter-players. Germans who failed to play this role were subject to Allied sanctions such as removal from office or denial of the facilities they needed to carry on political activities.

As tension between the Soviet and the Western leaders increased, supervision and direct intervention in German affairs diminished in both parts of Germany, though much more strikingly in the West. The establishment of the German Federal Republic brought with it the termination of Western punitive and tutelary policies. War-crime trials stopped, the last prisoners of war were released, the dismantling of factories for reparations payments ceased, and decision-making authority was largely turned over to the new German government of Chancellor Adenauer. Under American leadership, the new Western policy was to woo the West Germans into a voluntary and intimate partnership against the Soviet bloc. Western leaders and the high commissioners who now replaced the former military governors saw themselves as bargaining collectively with the German leaders for their cooperation and support. The proper or approved role for the German leaders was seen as counter-bargaining in good faith, demanding no unreasonable price for their cooperation, and providing assurances that they would live up to the "contractual agreements" negotiated with their Western partners.

The new relationship made the Western leaders increasingly sensitive to the political attitudes of the West German public, and above all to those of its political leaders. Instead of demanding unquestioning acquiescence, they now sought voluntary cooperation from the emerging West German elites by offering direct and indirect rewards for proper role behavior—that is, behavior consonant with Western plans and expectations. To the West German public, they offered economic assistance, military protection against Soviet attack, and Allied support for German policy goals (above all, reunification and the full recovery of sovereign decision-making power), if, in return, the German people would support Western policies and German leaders whose behavior was approved by the West. To cooperative political leaders, they offered moral and material support, the satisfaction of demands, and high-level consultations in foreign capitals that elevated their status at home and abroad. German political leaders could thus expect very tangible rewards, in terms both of their own personal interests and of those of the groups associated with them, if they played their roles according to Western requirements.

Role Perceptions of the Patriotic Leader

In Schumacher's eyes, the collapse of the Nazi regime ushered in a vitally important period of political realignment. He saw the post-totalitarian era as a crucial conflict for power between those who wished to transform Germany into a peaceful socialist democracy, and those who would impose "reaction" and pseudo-socialism on the nation. The former he identified with the Social Democratic movement and, specifically, its leadership, the latter with "capitalist" and "feudalist" forces and the Communists. As he saw it, Germany was doomed unless Social Democracy gained power as rapidly as possible. Ever conscious of the history of the Weimar Republic, he expected the temporary apathy and demoralization of the masses to be replaced by political reactivation as they responded to postwar social dislocation, economic misery, and foreign intervention in German affairs. Whether this reactivation could be directed toward peaceful social progress (and thus world stability), or whether it would lead to a new totalitarian regime (and thus the final destruction of Germany) depended, he believed, upon who won the battle for power.

Schumacher saw the situation entirely in terms of German developments. To him the occupation was a temporary period of foreign interference during which alien elites tried to determine the future of the German people on the basis of interests that he believed conflicted with the needs of that people. This interpretation led him to regard the goals of a patriotic Social Democratic movement—that is, his own goals—as opposing those of Western capitalism and Soviet Communism alike. He saw the activities of the occupation authorities and other foreign leaders entirely in the context of their apparent impact on the struggle for power in his own country. In his view, neither Germany nor the world could afford another nationalist reaction to the shortsighted policies of foreign elites, and German democracy must not again become identified with capitulation and fulfillment of the victors' terms.

Since he perceived the occupation in these terms, he apparently felt that the victors' claim to determine the fate of Germany rested on little more than the notion that "might makes right." His claim that only he and his party had the "legitimate" right to lead the nation was matched by his contempt and hostility toward foreign leaders who appeared to him to lack the skill, the desire, and above all the moral right to satisfy the needs of the German people. In short, they stood in the way of the necessary, rapid acquisition of power by Schumacher and his Social Democrats.

Schumacher emphatically denied the theory that the Germans' "collective guilt" for Hitler's crimes gave the victors a superior moral claim to rule in Germany. The victors, in his opinion, carried a far greater share of "collective guilt" than the anti-Nazi Social Democrats. "We fought the Nazis ... before anyone else in the world bothered about it," he said at the 1946 party congress, and he told a mass meeting in 1947 that "we opposed the Nazis at great cost when it was still fashionable for the rest of the world to bid for their good will."[5] He was outraged by foreign assertions that the hungry and miserable Germans were simply reaping the fruits of their submission to Hitler. "What he did," he wrote to an old friend in May 1947, "I probably know a great deal better from personal experience than those gentlemen throughout the world who now waste their ink on articles that will some day stand as monuments of human stupidity and heartlessness."* He was convinced that foreign leaders could not understand the basic issues at stake in Germany, and that their meddling efforts to pacify, re-educate, and democratize the German people were certain to backfire unless someone compelled them to do the "right thing." "Four little men" trying "to solve the German problem by tea gossiping," as he described the Foreign Ministers London Conference of February 1948, would never bring about the reunification of Germany.[6]

In general, Schumacher saw foreign leaders and occupation officials as cynical realists engaged in a game of power politics in and over Germany—no matter whether they sought to conceal their real interests by professions of anti-Nazism, anti-capitalism, or anti-Communism. He felt that both Western capitalists and Soviet Communists were bound to act in accordance with their own imperialist and nationalist interests, and that therefore the victor powers neither could nor would make decisions favorable to the interests of the German masses, at least not on their own initiative. If pressed hard enough, they might be induced to act more in accordance with German needs, but this meant taking arms against a sea of troubles.

This image of the occupation authorities appears to have governed Schumacher's thinking from the very start of his postwar career. The Allies' punitive policies immediately confirmed his view. "The victors are now going to make their peace terms, not ours," he asserted in his first public statement on May 6, 1945.[7] Reported American plans to deprive Germany of its industry, French and Soviet proposals to annex German territory, and Soviet and British dismantling of German factories all fitted into the picture. What Schumacher termed "the politics of moralizing property acquisition, justified in the name of sanctimonious morality" but in fact imposed by brute force, appeared to him a manifestation of the most extreme anti-German sentiment on the part of the victor powers.[8] When punitive policies gave way to bargaining moves, the switch confirmed his belief that for the foreign leaders Germany was simply the object of a power struggle. Both East and West, he felt, were trying to lure his countrymen into serving foreign interests at the expense of vital German interests, above all at the expense of a united, sovereign Germany under Social Democratic leadership.

From Schumacher's point of view, there were three possible roles for a German political leader operating in this context. First, he could play the all-out collaborator, the role that Schumacher believed Grotewohl had chosen in the Soviet zone and Adenauer in the West. Second, he could choose the role of the

---

* He expressed much the same sentiment—and contempt—when he told a mass meeting in 1947 that the activities of the victors left him with the impression "that perhaps they did not have quite so good an understanding of certain crucial issues at stake in contemporary Germany as the responsible leaders of the Social Democratic party." *Turm.*, II, 472ff.

entirely uncooperative German nationalist, and accept the temporary antagonism of the occupation powers in the hope of benefiting from the inevitable reaction of the German masses to the occupation and economic misery. This was the role which Hitler had assumed during the Weimar Republic, and which, Schumacher evidently suspected, many of Hitler's former followers were eager to assume in post-Nazi Germany. Finally, there was the role of the patriotic leader, neither a slavish collaborator nor an unreconstructed nationalist, but the defender of the real interests of the German people. This was the role he chose for himself.

It is possible to reconstruct a fairly clear picture of Schumacher's conception of the patriotic leader's role from his own utterances and the recollections of his associates. The patriotic leader, to Schumacher, was above all a fighter, a militant defender of his people's true interests. His image of this role assumed that dissension between the patriotic leader and the representatives of foreign interests was unavoidable. The role committed its incumbent to fight collaborators as well as rigid nationalists, and accordingly it was essential that the patriotic leader identify himself to his countrymen as the militant representative of their best interests. It was a role that demanded fearless, self-assertive behavior toward foreign counter-players at the risk of inviting hostile reactions and sanctions. It assumed the superiority of active opposition over accommodating cooperation, but it rejected sterile negativism; the Social Democratic party and its leaders, Schumacher asserted repeatedly, were always prepared to cooperate with the occupation authorities if cooperation served German interests. "We are not accommodating, but we are realistic," he said at the Nuremberg party congress of 1947.[9]

Proper behavior for the patriotic leader was evidently prescribed within the limits of what Schumacher perceived as inviolate principles on the one hand, and grand strategy for the conquest of power on the other. Insofar as he believed cooperation could be reconciled with such behavior, he did not hesitate to collaborate with the occupation authorities. From the very beginning he declared himself willing to cooperate in the political reconstruction of Germany, and endorsed the moral obligation of the German people to make "just" restitution for Nazi crimes.[10] Moreover, he continued to consider it realistic to participate in political reconstruction even when it became apparent that the creation of a separate West German state would aggravate the division of Germany. But he adamantly opposed cooperation with the occupation authorities when he believed it to be unprincipled or prejudicial to German and Social Democratic interests. From his point of view such opposition was always constructive, and he indignantly rejected accusations that his behavior toward foreign leaders was irresponsible and negative. According to his conception of the patriotic leader's role, his behavior was aimed at preserving vital interests, upholding sacred principles, and achieving goals which, in the last analysis, he perceived as positive contributions to international peace and understanding.

To many observers this patriotic stance seemed to be simply a tactical expedient; others felt that Schumacher, like many Social Democrats, assumed this role because he had learned from experiences in the Weimar Republic and the Nazi era not to underestimate the nationalist emotions of the Germans. Tactical considerations as well as the "lessons of the past" were no doubt contributing factors; but it is also clear that already in the pre-Hitler period he had held views that led him to assume this role. The political environment of his youth and his intellectual development as a student and young politician had conditioned him for it. He was prepared to play the role when he entered upon his post-totalitarian career, he found his party on the whole ready to support him in it, and he was only too willing to interpret the situation in Germany as demanding it.

Schumacher's performance as patriotic leader followed a consistent theme, with minor variations dictated by particular circumstances. This theme was his insistence that the German people must be masters of their own fate, and that those he identified as the true defenders of the national interest were the only ones legitimately entitled to act on the people's behalf.[11] "Every country is above all concerned about its own position, and forward-looking people in all countries perceive the defense of the world-wide freedom in terms of the needs of their own nation," he told the Bundestag in November 1950.[12] He frequently insisted that he, too, wanted the states of Europe to surrender their sovereignty to a larger community of nations, but he also insisted that the unification of Europe depended upon strictly equal rights for all countries, Germany not excepted.

Schumacher's claim that Germany had an important part to play in European and world affairs were dangerous words so soon after the fall of the Nazi regime. He explained, however, that the task he envisaged for the country was not a nationalist one in the traditional sense of the word, for the "new Germany" was to become the nucleus of a democratic and socialist Europe, a third force between the capitalist United States and the Stalinist Soviet Union. Germans needed the opportunity and the leadership to transform their country from a threat to international peace into a "positive element" in the world. The occupation powers could provide the opportunity; the Social Democrats, and they alone, the leadership. The future of German democracy, and therefore of international stability, was directly dependent on the "creation of a new spirit of national self-confidence" in a demoralized German people, a spirit "equally far removed from the irresponsible arrogance of the past" as from unquestioning submission to the Big Four; it was not necessary "to see a revelation of the European spirit" in every Allied demand for German concessions.[13]

1. Age 6

2. Student, Halle, 1915

3. Flag dedication ceremony of the Reichsbanner, Stuttgart, 1925;
   Schumacher fifth from left

4. Württemberg, 1924

5. Official portrait after election to Reichstag, 1930

6. Schumacher leads the Reichsbanner through the streets of Stuttgart, 1931

7. Addressing a meeting, Frankfurt, 1947

8. About 1947

9. Return to Stuttgart, 1945 or 1946

10. About 1948

11. With Annemarie Renger, 1949

12. Casting his ballot, Bundestag election, 1949

13. With Adenauer, about 1950

14. Addressing a meeting,
about 1951

15 About 1951

16. Deathbed, 1952

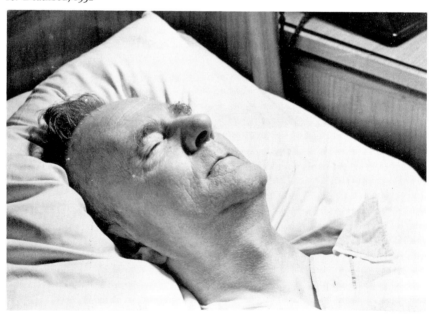

According to Schumacher, the creation of a peaceful, democratic, and co-operative Germany required that the country be led by a party which was trusted by Germans not only in the Western zones but in the Soviet section, and which was neither the willing nor the unwilling tool of foreign interests. "The world should understand," he wrote in 1946, "that only he who can gain for his people the self-esteem they require will win their confidence."[14] Accordingly, he defined it as the duty of the S.P.D. to be "the political party of the German patriots," the party that repudiated "the policy of national capitulation" dictated by the victor powers. He asserted that this position was perfectly consistent with the internationalism of the German Social Democrats, since love of country and defense of its interests were basic ingredients of socialist internationalism. Socialist patriotism and socialist internationalism, in his view, were complementary, not mutually exclusive, sentiments. "The essence of socialism," he told a meeting of European socialists in 1951, "is the morality of equal rights and equal responsibilities for all men," for freedom meant "self-determination" and cooperation between equals, not the supremacy of some and the submission of others.[15] Socialist internationalism, he claimed, meant "cooperation between nations effectively equal in rights and mutual self-esteem."[16] Given this essential harmony, German Social Democrats could be loyal to their own country and at the same time to the ideals of international socialist solidarity and world citizenship. Thus, to be a good German was to be a patriotic Social Democrat, and a true socialist in France or Britain, by the same token, could not support the exploitation of the German people by the enemies of democratic socialism inside or outside Germany.

The German Social Democrats, Schumacher declared, could not and would not become "patriots of other states," who served alien interests at the expense of their own working class. That role he assigned to his principal domestic opponents, the Communists and Christian Democrats, whom he portrayed as the collaborationist opposites of the patriotic Social Democrats. Both he described as allies of hostile alien interests, who, despite the differences in their objectives, were very much alike in their hatred of democracy and their dependence on foreign powers. Thus he wrote in 1947: "Tried friends and path-makers of the Third Reich, who have fought all their lives against democracy, find a home in the Christian Democratic Union," which "can depend on the support of foreign propertied elements allied to it by social bonds and material interests," and "the direct support of the Roman Catholic Church and other clerical institutions." Similarly, "the dictatorial mortal enemies of democracy in the Communist camp" were "after all merely the creatures of Russian foreign policy." Both collaborationist groups received the plaudits of foreign opinion, whereas the only truly internationalist and democratic party was denounced as nationalistic and got little sympathy abroad.[17]

"We shall not sell ourselves," he told a mass meeting in Frankfurt in 1947.

"We shall rely on our own best judgment to pursue the task we have set our-selves: to be free, self-reliant, and independent in the face of all foreign and domestic forces.... It is of vital national importance for the German people to have a party that still has the courage to fight for the right to freedom and in-dependence."[18] The S.P.D., ran his favorite slogan in 1945, was "neither Rus-sian nor British, French nor American, but spoke solely on behalf of the new Germany."[19]

Schumacher insisted that Social Democrats must demonstrate their inde-pendence from foreign interests in all their actions. Those who lacked the courage to tell occupation officials to their face what they dared to say in party meetings did not belong in the S.P.D., he announced at the first postwar con-gress in 1946,[20] and he harshly denounced party members who advocated a more cooperative attitude. "We are prepared to cooperate," he said repeatedly; but from his battle against Grotewohl at the beginning of his postwar career to the fight against Western integration in the last years of his life, the accent was on non-cooperation whenever his objectives came into conflict with those of non-Germans, including foreign socialists.

In reply to charges that he was a nationalist, Schumacher said that this cal-umny had been initiated by the Communists in 1945 when he fought against Soviet domination of the German workers movement, and was then picked up by malicious or ignorant Westerners. He claimed to be too truly patriotic to be a nationalist, and endeavored to establish a clear distinction between socialist patriotism and "reactionary nationalism," such as that of the Nazis. He dis-tinguished between *nationalistisch* and *national,* the former being identified with aggressive nationalism, and the latter with real love for one's country. Aggressive nationalism was a sickness, a "mortal danger" for the German peo-ple, and it was therefore the duty of Social Democratic patriots to oppose it with all their might, "whether it be the neo-nationalism of the Communists or the traditional nationalism of the capitalists."[21] A good German could only be patriotic, never *nationalistisch,* he asserted, and the Social Democratic party would under no circumstances use nationalistic appeals or accept nationalist support. Patriotism and nationalism were thus portrayed as irreconcilable op-posites, just as patriotism and internationalism were said to be basically com-plementary. To fight for socialism and democracy in one's own country was to strive for the welfare of the working people everywhere; to oppose nationalism was to fight against their exploiters everywhere. The German Social Demo-crats wanted to safeguard the welfare of the German "working people," and it was slanderous to attach the nationalist label to their actions. Schumacher insisted that he and his party repudiated the exploitation of other people as much as they repudiated the exploitation of their own, and wanted for the Ger-mans no more and no less than they believed every people was entitled to.[22]

In his first public statements after the war, Schumacher acknowledged that the Germans' failure to revolt against Hitler denied them the right to self-

government, but he soon altered his tune. The behavior of the occupation powers had forced him to revise his position, he said. Admittedly they had liberated
the German people from Nazi oppression, but they had spoiled the good work
by substituting their own brand of despotism, which neither understood nor
cared about the measures that had to be taken to create the new Germany. He
complained that the Allies not only denied German anti-Nazis their legitimate
part in the political reconstruction of the country, but treated them with such
arrogance and contempt that it needed much more than good will to muster
up a cooperative spirit. "The system of military governments cannot be exactly
admired as the ultimate and most perfect form of democracy," he told fellow
Social Democrats at the party congress in Düsseldorf in 1948.[23] He said that
stupidity and hostility marked the behavior of the occupation authorities toward the German people in general and the patriotic Social Democratic leadership in particular. Above all, he objected to what he described as their attempt
to force Germans to become their agents in the execution of foolish or pernicious policies. Schumacher declared that total victory also meant total responsibility, and you could hardly ask a people to take responsibility for carrying out
policies that they had had no hand in making.[24]

According to Schumacher, the reunification of Germany was the S.P.D.'s
primary and mandatory goal. From his first proclamation in the summer of
1945 to his last public statement seven years later, he maintained that this problem was basic to all others, and should therefore form the basis of all relations
with the occupation authorities and other foreign leaders. "We cannot regard
as a friend of the German people anyone whose political actions deny or hinder
German unity," he declared in the Bundestag on September 29, 1949,[25] and he
savagely criticized both Soviet and Western leaders for perpetuating the division of Germany by action or inaction. Reunification, he declared time and
again, was the most urgent and patriotic task for a German leader, one that
only selfish politicians and abject collaborators could ignore. He exhorted
members of his own and other parties to subordinate local and regional interests to this larger goal, and explained his opposition to various Allied proposals—to strengthen the Länder, to internationalize the Saar and Ruhr industrial regions, and to associate the "temporary" West German Republic intimately with the Western powers—in terms of such patriotic motives.

Schumacher repeatedly warned his fellow Germans that they could depend
neither upon the inevitability of history nor upon the good will of foreign powers to bring about a reunited Germany. Such dependence would be fatal. The
battle for reunification demanded constant determined action by all German
patriots, and above all by responsible leaders in West Germany, whose duty
it was to prod the great powers into negotiating reunification. "Many Germans...do not realize that the world is very well able to survive without a
unified Germany," he warned as early as the summer of 1945;[26] in fact, many
powers might prefer to maintain the status quo. It was up to German patriots

to see that neither German nor foreign leaders, nor the public, ever lost sight of the problem or the need for its speedy solution. It was a dangerous illusion for Germans to consider reunification the responsibility of Americans, Russians, or any other foreigners; it was the responsibility of the German people themselves.[27] The Social Democrats were leading the fight because they alone realized that a truly democratic and socialist Germany depended upon reunification, and that a divided Germany was a perpetual threat to domestic and international stability. Since this was their goal, they were deeply committed to liberating the Germans at present under Soviet rule. Freedom for the working men of East Germany was the first essential step toward reunification. To fight for their liberation was thus the highest moral and patriotic duty of Social Democrats and all other "good Germans" who wanted a free and peaceful world. Therefore, according to Schumacher, it was false and evil to identify the Social Democratic battle for reunification with negative obstructionism and aggressive nationalism.

In Schumacher's view, the occupation powers were doing nothing to advance reunification, in fact they were hindering it. He held them responsible for the deepening division of the country, the continued enslavement of his fellow Germans under the Communists, and the separation of the Social Democratic leadership from its supporters in East Germany. In his speeches he pictured the Social Democratic leadership as engaged in a duel with the occupying powers and their German collaborators, a duel whose object was to induce them to agree on the re-establishment of a unified and independent nation. Admittedly the victors could not be forced into negotiating an agreement, but he maintained that by a persistent militant effort they could be prodded into doing so. He constantly stressed the urgent need for action in this area, but he failed to present a solution that both East and West would be likely to accept. He insisted that free elections in the Soviet zone were an essential first step if the Germans living there were to be included in a free and democratic Germany, but he tended to overlook the obstacles. The inconsistency of his emphasis led some observers to suppose that he actually held little hope for early reunification, and was merely trying to exploit popular sentiment in West Germany in his drive for power. Others thought that he was motivated entirely by a determination to press for reunification regardless of the immediate political consequences, and regarded his behavior as an example of his inflexibility. Schumacher apparently did not enlighten his critics, but simply stuck to his demand that the occupying powers re-establish a unified Germany.

This meant, in his view, that the Allies should put an end to what he termed their brutal and unjust punitive policies. He said it was the duty of the Social Democratic leadership to provide for Germany's spiritual and material recovery by protecting her against the rapacity of the conquerors. He acknowledged that the German people must make amends for Nazi crimes, but he categorically denied their collective guilt. Punitive measures taken by the victor powers against the entire German people on the grounds that all were guilty seemed to him dangerous and cynical; mass punishment would block spiritual and political recovery by uniting its victims in nationalistic resentment. To expel millions of Germans from their homes in East Germany, to punish the "little Nazis" while letting many of the big ones go free, to use prisoners of war as "slave labor"—all constituted an immense wrong. One could not hope to "erase the injustice of the past with the injustice of the present."[28] He agreed that Germany's war-making capacity should be eliminated, and that restitution should be made to the victims of Nazi aggression. But he denounced what he described as the plundering of vital German economic resources and the alienation of German lands and property by "moralizing" foreign powers who justified their greed in the name of reparations and indemnification. "We have the honest intention to pay reparations," he is reported to have said, "but we warn all victors, big and little, not to rip pieces from the German people, leaving wounds which will fester for many years to come."[29]

As the leader of a party primarily identified with the interests of the industrial workers, he objected in particular to what he termed the "insane" policy of dismantling German factories and exploiting German coal mines and other economic resources for the benefit of "foreign interests" basically opposed to a democratic and socialist Germany. The German people needed these resources if they were to recover from the devastation Hitler had brought upon them and build a new Germany. But the occupation powers seemed determined to deny them the opportunity to reconstruct their country, and by direct and indirect measures did everything possible to undermine the position of the Social Democratic patriots whose task it was to direct economic and political reconstruction.

In sum, Schumacher's behavior toward the occupation powers was militant and self-assertive, and he advocated this attitude for all true patriots. In his relationship with the occupation authorities and foreign leaders this hostile, aggressive behavior almost invariably provoked strong reactions, with results that were usually frustrating for his drive for power.

The Patriotic Leader and the Soviet Union

Schumacher emphatically and categorically rejected the role of a Soviet collaborationist. "We have no reason to help any country—no matter how many deceptive and diversionary pseudo-socialist ideologies it may advance—to become the most powerful nation on earth, and to exploit Germany and the socialist idea for its own ends," he declared in January 1946.[30] His attitude was not anti-Russian, he said; it was merely the reaction of a patriotic Social Democrat, who could see how the Soviet leadership was trying to keep Germany in a state of permanent chaos, and the Soviet zone enslaved, in order to transform the entire country into a Soviet satellite. As he was fond of reminding his Western critics, he had fought against Soviet expansionism when less perceptive Westerners still had hopes of cooperating with Russia—if necessary at Germany's expense. All too long, he maintained, the German Social Democrats had had to stand alone in opposition to the ambitions of the Soviet Union, the only victor power to have any clear plans for postwar Germany. The Social Democratic leadership had always recognized the Soviet leadership's intentions to use its base in East Germany for westward expansion, and had fought every move in this direction, beginning with the battle against the creation of the Socialist Unity Party and the establishment of a satellite dictatorship in the Soviet zone.

He felt that Soviet and Communist attacks against him were entirely deserved in view of his behavior as a patriotic Social Democratic leader. Many of the obstacles blocking his rise to power he attributed to his uncompromising opposition to the actions of the Soviet leadership and its Communist collaborators in the Soviet and Western zones. That he was decried as a nationalist he traced to his leadership of the fight against amalgamating the Social Democrats with the Communists. He blamed the growing division of his country— with its attendant handicaps to him and the S.P.D.—on the deliberate refusal of the Soviet Union to negotiate in good faith with the Western powers. And he felt not only that Soviet actions denied the S.P.D. the support of millions of actual and potential adherents in East Germany, but that the need constantly to defend German and Social Democratic interests against Russian and Communist attack weakened the S.P.D. in its fight against foreign and domestic capitalist and reactionary opponents in West Germany.

In particular, he denounced what he described as Soviet and Communist attempts to pervert prevailing socialist and patriotic sentiment in Germany. In his view, the enslavement of the East Germans was being used to blackmail patriotic West Germans to support Communist reunification schemes that were designed to enslave all Germans. The anti-capitalist sentiment of the masses in West Germany, and their longing for German unity, peace, and social and economic betterment, were being cynically exploited to weaken resistance to Soviet expansionism. Therefore it was essential that the Social Democratic leadership be given the opportunity in West Germany to put into effect the only program that could save Germany and Europe from Soviet penetration. The Social Democrats, he said, recognized the justice of Russian demands for protection against future German aggression, and were prepared to agree to the security arrangements needed to induce the Soviet Union to loosen, and eventually relinquish, its hold on East Germany. But they were not willing to stand by and watch the exploitation and perpetuation of misery and disorganization in Germany for the benefit of Russian imperialism.

Schumacher's behavior in regard to the Soviet leadership and its German supporters thus expressed intense hostility, mingled with respect, toward a powerful and determined opponent. His public statements portrayed a militant Social Democratic leadership of a reunited Germany as the only real defense against the subjugation of Germany and Europe by the Soviet Union. Neither building West Germany into a forward bastion of Western capitalism nor accepting reunification on Soviet terms would serve the purpose. He justified his opposition to the former course on the grounds that by encouraging the recovery of West German capitalism and trying to transform the Federal Republic into a stronghold of the "Free World," the Western powers were playing into Soviet hands. He opposed the latter course, he said, because he refused to buy Soviet agreement to the reunification of Germany at the expense of inalienable German rights, above all of individual and national freedom. When in November 1950 he told the Bundestag that the Western powers should refuse even to consider negotiations until the Soviet Union had agreed to "the same degree of personal and political freedom and equality in all four zones and in Berlin,"[31] he was merely reiterating a position that he had maintained consistently since 1945. Reunification was impossible as long as free elections could not be held in the Soviet zone, an event which, he implied, would not only terminate Soviet control but result in an overwhelming Social Democratic victory over Communists and "reactionaries" alike. German unity "in peace and freedom," in other words, meant the establishment of an anti-Communist socialist democracy of some seventy million people at the borders of the Soviet bloc, a democracy that would be economically strong and free enough to pursue policies orientated toward the West rather than the East.

Schumacher was apparently quite unconcerned about the unfavorable reaction that his position provoked among the Soviet leadership and its German supporters. On the contrary, he missed no opportunity to stress his bitter opposition to the expulsion of Germans from Eastern Europe, the annexation of former German lands by Poland and Russia, and what he termed the brutal exploitation of Germans in the Soviet zone. Overtly and covertly, the Social Democratic party under his leadership encouraged the development of an underground movement in the Soviet zone. He himself devoted a great deal of his time to the operations of the party's so-called Eastern Bureau (Ost Büro), which the Soviet authorities regarded as the headquarters for subversive activities in their zone, and when in June 1953, less than a year after his death, the East German workers rose in rebellion, the uprising was immediately attributed to "Schumacher men" by the East German and Russian leadership.

Schumacher's most savage attacks, however, were reserved for the Soviet leaders' German collaborators. Not one to forgive or forget his encounters with the Communists in the Weimar era and the concentration camp, he categorically rejected all Communist proposals for cooperation. The Communists, he declared, were loyal neither to German nor to international proletarian interests, and were nothing but "German-speaking members of the Russian state party."[32] He opposed them not so much for ideological reasons as for the fact that they were abject collaborators; and he expected them to attack him in turn as a true German patriot defending the interests of his people against Soviet designs. Flashes of the young Schumacher reappeared in the savage ridicule of these attacks. Pointing to the Communists as mere mouthpieces of their Soviet masters, he told his fellow Social Democrats in 1948 that he was reminded of an old Russian proverb: "The man who keeps a dog need not bark himself."[33] And in reply to an unfriendly interruption from the leader of the West German Communists in a Bundestag debate, he said that such behavior illustrated the well-known political fact "that there are not only wolves in sheep's clothing, but also sheep in wolves' clothing."[34] The West German Communists were far too weak to constitute a serious threat to Schumacher by themselves. They were his foils, both for attacking the Soviet leadership and for identifying himself and his party as the only truly socialist and patriotic spokesmen for the German working man in all four zones.

This basic pattern of hostility to the Communists can be traced in Schumacher's postwar speeches and activities (see Appendix C for an analysis of his speeches). Almost invariably, he reacted negatively to actions he perceived as emanating directly or indirectly (i.e. through Communist collaborators) from the Soviet Union. Whether they were proposals for four-power talks or for direct negotiations between East and West German leaders, whether they were appeals to proletarian unity or German neutralism, he would term them devious Soviet maneuvers that a patriotic leader must expose and oppose. Every Russian move, he insisted, was contrary to German interests, and everyone who took the slightest step toward cooperating with the Soviet leaders was *ipso facto* working for the destruction of German freedom.

Not surprisingly, Schumacher's behavior aroused correspondingly hostile reactions from his Communist counter-players. German Communists, emphasizing their own patriotism, accused him of betraying Germany and its working class, and trying to perpetuate the division of the nation. Otto Grotewohl, for example, called him a tool of foreign interests, particularly of American "monopoly capitalism,"[35] and the Communist press throughout Europe followed the lead of Soviet news organs in denouncing him as another Hitler, backed by the forces of reactionary capitalism and opposed to international working-class solidarity under Soviet leadership. Czech, Polish, and French Communist publications asserted that he rejected proper claims for German reparations and was plotting the reconquest of lands liberated from Nazi domination.[36]

In short, Schumacher's behavior was utterly self-defeating in terms of gaining Soviet assent for his ambition to obtain decision-making power in a unified German state. He was evidently perceived in Moscow as an opponent of Soviet policy whose aspirations had to be checked. As the foremost exponent of anti-

Communist democratic socialism in Germany, and the highly effective organizer of a strong Social Democratic movement oriented toward goals in direct
conflict with those of the Soviet leadership, he fitted the Communist stereotype
of the German "social fascist" leader who stood in the way of Soviet Communism's westward advance. As long as he rejected collaboration with the Soviet
Union, he could achieve his goals only over the opposition of the Russian leadership or by inducing it to withdraw its opposition. However, neither party
was willing to change its position.

The Patriotic Leader and the Western Allies

Political conditions forced Schumacher to concentrate his activities in the
Western occupation zones, and in his role as patriotic leader to focus on the
behavior of the French, British, and American occupation authorities. In general, as we already briefly noted, his behavior was strongly resented by Western
leaders despite his anti-Soviet and emphatically pro-Western political orientation. After some vague initial intimations, recalling some of his pre-1933 views,
that he would like to see Germany play the role of an intermediary, balancing
power between East and West, he very soon abandoned any thought of political neutrality for Germany. He maintained that "the whole German people in
thought and deed belong to the West,"[37] and claimed that German Social
Democracy was the heir and executor of the Western European democratic
liberal heritage.

However, he tried to distinguish between a general cultural and political
affinity with the Western democracies and specific agreement with the actions
of Western leaders, including fellow European socialists. "As Europeans, as
Germans, and as Social Democrats we want to cooperate with the Western
democracies," he told the Commonwealth Club in San Francisco in the fall
of 1947, "but we are not prepared to accept unquestioningly a foreign political
system as a model for ourselves."[38] He bitterly objected to what he termed
"moralistic" Western pressure on the Social Democrats to choose between
Western freedom and Soviet slavery, to demand professions of loyalty to democracy and hostility to Communism from men whose records spoke louder
than any fair-weather words could speak. "The politics of either-or, the cliché
antithesis of East versus West," was in his view a primitive oversimplification,
a political polarization entirely unacceptable to patriotic Social Democrats who
aimed to eliminate, not to deepen, the division of their country.[39] For the Social
Democratic leadership the needs of the German working people came before
all other interests, and the Western leaders must be made to realize that the
satisfaction of these German needs was in truth in their interest, too. In the face
of growing Western pressure to commit himself clearly, Schumacher asserted
the patriotic leader's right and ability to maintain maximum independence of
action in the East-West conflict for the benefit of his country and its people.

He made it plain that he did not trust Western leaders. As he told an interviewer shortly before his death in 1952, he felt that they were pursuing their interests at German expense.* Whether he described their actions as bungling, cynical, or shortsighted, his comments almost invariably reflected a deep suspicion of their motives and intense irritation with their actions. The Western occupation powers should never forget, he said at the Düsseldorf national congress of the S.P.D. in September 1948, that Germans who had any pride could have had no more confidence in the occupation authorities than the latter had in them.[40] He indicated that such mutual confidence was lacking, and that the Social Democratic leadership found it difficult to live up to its desire for cooperation when the occupation powers constantly frustrated the realization of German, i.e. Social Democratic, interests. The new Germany could not be formed by powers who, on the basis of Germany's unconditional surrender, arrogantly claimed the right to tell Germans what they must do, and who had only their own narrow self-interest at heart. As long as they persisted in policies that he described as "managing and exploiting Germany," and refused to place full confidence in those Germans who alone could transform the country into a democratic and peaceful nation, their "political and military conceptions" would continue to be the principal target of Social Democratic strategy.[41]

Schumacher's behavior toward the Western leaders was self-assertive to the point of claiming superior wisdom. He denounced scathingly what he termed their insistence that they always knew better than Germany's "legitimate" leaders what was best for German and world interests. Before 1945 he had himself been inclined to consider the Germans particularly stupid in political matters, he told an interviewer in 1952, but since he had observed the occupation powers in action, he had learned that Germans had by no means a monopoly on political ineptitude.[42] In addition to his public statements, cryptic notes in his appointments diary indicate that he believed it incumbent upon him to tell bungling Western leaders what German interests required, and if necessary to compel them to adjust their political actions accordingly. He wanted them to turn over the decision-making power in West Germany to the Social Democratic leadership as soon as possible. Though Western leaders might not realize it, such a course would in truth be to their own best interests, not only because the Social Democrats would follow policies that were to Western advantage, but because alien military governments could never transform Germany into

---

* Asked about his view on the reported use of German limousines by occupation officials, Schumacher replied: "It would be all right if it were only a matter of going for drives at our expense; ... but they now want to compete for political power at our expense as well." Kaufmann Int. Sharing the widespread but mistaken German belief that West Germans were paying all the occupation costs (see Davison, p. 266), Schumacher told a press conference in September 1951 that the extravagance and luxurious living of the occupation powers made it all the more difficult to make the improvements necessary in German social conditions to strengthen democracy. See the newsletter of the S.P.D., *Sopade*, No. 913, Sept. 1951, p. 4.

a true democracy or command the loyalty of its people. The less they sought to govern, the more likely the Germans would be to cooperate.

Schumacher chose to clash with the Western occupation powers on three main issues. First, he charged that Western elites sought to prevent, or at least handicap, German economic recovery and the restoration of independent decision-making power to Germans in domestic and foreign affairs. Second, he criticized Western policies in German political reorganization and reconstruction. Third, he fiercely opposed efforts to cement the West German Federal Republic to the Western camp by means of intimate economic and military ties to France, Italy, and the Benelux states.

We have already referred to Schumacher's bitter criticism of Allied efforts in the early years of the occupation to make Germany pay reparations for Nazi aggression. He was no less vehement in his denunciation of the West than of the East in this respect. In particular he condemned the dismantling of factories and other industrial installations by the West, and what he charged were French efforts permanently to deprive the German people of control over the Ruhr and Saar industrial complexes. As patriotic leader, he claimed that the Western powers were trying to enfeeble Germany forever by alienating lands that were legitimately hers. He also accused them of helping the Soviet Union to keep Germany divided because at heart they were not particularly eager to see the country unified. When in 1950 the Western powers moved to tie the newly created Federal Republic to the states of Western and Southern continental Europe, he was apparently convinced that behind the move lay a Roman Catholic–capitalist conspiracy to separate West Germany permanently from the predominantly Protestant parts of Germany that were under Soviet control.

From the very first Schumacher accused the occupation authorities of deliberately blocking Social Democratic efforts to achieve a genuine democratization of West Germany. He believed that the French and Americans were trying to frustrate his efforts to create the militant, centrally directed Social Democratic party that was needed to achieve his goals. He resented French and American support of Social Democrats who opposed him in Bavaria and other places, and felt that Western efforts to encourage the independence of Social Democrats in public office, particularly chiefs of state governments, were directed specifically against him and his attempts to create a strongly led party and a centralized state. He claimed, too, that the Western powers failed to support him properly in his fight against the Soviet Union and its German collaborators. When Western policy became openly anti-Communist in the spring of 1948, he charged that for almost three years the Western powers had freely allowed the Communists to delude and terrorize the Germans, leaving it to the S.P.D. to carry on the fight alone.[48] It was the resistance of the German workers, not "the machine guns and steel helmets of certain countries to the west of us," that had kept the Soviet Union from extending its dominion to the Atlantic Ocean after the war, he asserted in January 1950.[44] A clerical and capitalist anti-Communism would be self-defeating in Germany, he said, for it would only drive the masses into the totalitarian camp. Genuine anti-Communism and support for democracy demanded support for the Social Democratic party, its leadership, and its goals. The Western powers, he charged, not only withheld such support, but were strengthening the very forces of reaction that had brought Hitler to power, and were preparing the road for Communism by their anti-social policies.

Schumacher blamed the occupation powers for deliberately preventing a genuine political and social revolution in post-totalitarian Germany. In his speeches between 1945 and 1948 he asserted that the country was in a state of "latent revolution" that was held in check only by artificial constraints imposed by the occupation authorities. "We are faced with the unique opportunity to deprive the remnants of the big business cliques in West Germany of their power," he told the Nuremberg S.P.D. congress in 1947.[45] If in 1918–19 it had been the German people themselves who failed to carry through a genuine revolution, this time it was the fault of occupation powers that the forces of big business and reaction could not be eliminated once and for all. Schumacher's speeches in these years reflected his growing irritation over Allied refusal to permit the Social Democratic leadership to take control and effect the necessary changes in German society, and guide the supposedly dissatisfied masses toward a new Germany. While the Soviet Union stifled revolutionary sentiments in its zone by terrorism, he said, in West Germany the occupation powers preached democracy but allowed the capitalist and reactionary sponsors and benefactors of the Nazi regime to regain power and influence.[46] "After 1945 there was the opportunity to begin a new political era in Germany," he told the party congress in 1948, apparently implying that by now the opportunity had been lost.[47] Similarly, in December 1949, after failing to win the first federal election, the S.P.D. leadership asserted that "the psychologically favorable moment for decisive steps toward the democratization and social reconstruction of Germany" had passed, and that "reactionary elements" were rapidly staging a comeback in West Germany because the occupation authorities had blocked Social Democratic efforts to introduce land reform, give the workers greater influence over the economy, and socialize key industries.[48]

With his own very definite ideas about what was needed to create a genuinely democratic Germany, Schumacher had only contempt for initial Western efforts to denazify and re-educate the Germans, and weaken the power of big business by decartelization and similar economic reforms. He regarded it as either foolish or hypocritical to try to effect changes that could come about only by the socialization of key industries, economic democracy, and centralized control over the economy by a Social Democratic central government. He felt that the Western powers were at best very naïve to attempt to shape the new Germany in the image of their own, supposedly superior, economic and political systems. He and his supporters were outraged when United States influence blocked almost successful Social Democratic efforts to introduce socialization in Hesse in 1946, and in North Rhine–Westphalia in 1947–48. American-sponsored agreements to place the Ruhr industries under international control were in his eyes pernicious schemes to block socialization permanently and allow international capitalism to exploit the property of the German working people. It was for this reason that he called Adenauer "the Chancellor of the Allies" when in 1949 Adenauer concluded the Petersberg Agreement for an International Ruhr Authority, and subsequently fought bitterly against the creation of the European Coal and Steel Community as a super-cartel of European capitalists.

Conflicting ideas about how to reconstruct German governmental institutions caused continuous friction between Schumacher and the American and French authorities during the first four years of the occupation. Attributing many of the evils of the past to an all-powerful central German government, French and American decision-makers, and ultimately the British Labour government, favored a strongly decentralized Germany with broad powers reserved for the constituent Länder. Accordingly, political reconstruction in the French and American zones began with the establishment of governments in states that were either re-established or newly created by the occupation authorities. Until the establishment of the Federal Republic in 1949, the Western occupation powers, particularly the French and Americans, considered these Länder governments the sole representatives of the German people, and recognized political parties only as participants in state government and politics. When the occupation authorities decided to establish first the Bizonal Economic Council for the British and American zones, and subsequently the Parliamentary Council to draft a constitution for a single West German state, they called upon the Länder to appoint and send delegates to these bodies, rather than permitting direct popular elections. They thus underscored the preeminence of the states in the federal system they were trying to establish. Finally, when the Basic Law for the new Federal Republic was drafted, the French and Americans strove to give the constituent Länder broad powers vis-à-vis the federal government.

Schumacher, by contrast, wanted political reconstruction to bypass the Länder, and move as quickly as possible toward the establishment of a strong central government with a popularly elected national legislature and a powerful chief executive. As the chairman of the only interzonal, centrally directed political movement in these early years, he declared that only political parties with national goals, rather than Länder governments identified with regional interests, could be instrumental in shaping the new Germany. From his point of view, a view that assumed the pro-socialist sentiments of the German people, this was the fastest and perhaps the only road to power in Germany—at any rate in the Western portions of the country. To build up powerful Länder before creating a central government, and then to place the creation of a federal government in the hands of the state governments, was directly contrary to this strategy.* Here he expressed not only personal but traditional Social Democratic goals. Since its creation in 1875, the party had opposed particularist and autonomist sentiments in South Germany and the Rhineland, and had maintained that the German people could get responsible democratic rule only from a central government and a legislature of popularly elected representatives nominated by national parties. Already as a young socialist in Stuttgart, Schumacher had identified himself with this position, and had bitterly attacked South German and Rhenish autonomists and proponents of federalism, of whom Adenauer, then Lord Mayor of Cologne, had been one of the best known.

Evidently sensitive to foreign and German memories of extreme centralism under the Nazis, Schumacher asserted that the S.P.D. did not seek to establish a unitary state with an all-powerful national government, and agreed that the new Germany would probably have to be a federation with certain administrative powers reserved to the Länder. He recognized the existence of ethnic and cultural boundaries justifying the survival of traditional states in West Germany, but asserted that "a Rhineland and a Bavaria, a Hannover and a Hesse, are not ends in themselves. They must not serve themselves and their separate interests. They can only be component parts of a future Germany; they should only serve as stepping stones toward the reorganization of the Reich. The creation of national unity takes precedence over Länder politics."[49]

He made a sharp distinction between the establishment of a federal state in which the national government was supreme, and a confederation in which the central authority was at the mercy of the autonomous constituent states. Accordingly, he strongly opposed what he described as the reactionary, particularist, and separatist tendencies of certain Allied and West German leaders. Those who held such views, he asserted, were trying to prevent the establishment of the strong central government that alone could defend the interests of *all* Germans against foreign and domestic enemies. Particularism, he said,

---

* In taking this position, Schumacher indignantly rejected accusations—not only from Allied quarters and other political parties, but from certain Bavarian Social Democrats as well—that he sought to restore Prussian supremacy in Germany. Apart from the fact, he said, that he emphatically opposed such a notion, Prussia was dead (see his remarks as chairman of the special committee "Reorganisaton der Länder" in the British Zonal Advisory Council, 1st session, Aug. 6–7, 1946, Archiv Bundestag, Bonn). He sought to distinguish clearly between his own plan for a centralized German government under Social Democratic leadership and Communist proposals for a unitary German state. The latter he labeled an attempt to revive "bankrupt Prussianism under the aegis of the hammer and sickle." *Turm.*, II, 47, 90.

was the doctrine of those German states' righters who wanted to protect their property against the claims of the national community, while separatism was particularism compounded by the attempts of foreign powers to take such vital areas as the Rhine, the Ruhr, and the Saar away from the German people by carving up Germany into a number of weak states. It was but a short step from advocating federalism to serving particularism, he told the S.P.D. congress in 1946, and "I have seen many a supporter of particularism end up as a separatist."[50] As long as a German Reich existed only as an ideal and not as a fact, it was essential that good patriots keep the aspirations of the German people focused on the restoration of a united country, rather than on subordinate Länder and zonal issues; however, the final determination of the structure of the new Germany must await the re-establishment of a national government, he said at a meeting of the British Zonal Advisory Council.[51]

In his role as patriotic leader, Schumacher attacked all Allied actions and proposals that seemed to him to prejudge the future structure of Germany in favor of the states or regional organizations. Already in August 1945 he had denounced a suggestion that he attributed to the Lord Mayor of Cologne, Konrad Adenauer, that the three Western zones be turned into independent states.[52] In 1946 he described a reported proposal for a South German Confederation as a "fantastic notion."[53] He was critical of the new state boundaries drawn by the Allies because they seemed to favor anti-socialist and particularist forces, and of some of the new Länder constitutions because they appeared to him to give the states too much autonomy. In 1946 he attacked the creation of the Länderat, an advisory council of the three Länder chiefs in the American zone, as "false and dangerous" because it encouraged centrifugal tendencies that opposed the creation of a unitary state.[54]

As Western policies after 1946 assumed a more definite pattern under American direction, Schumacher expressed increasing hostility toward the Western occupation powers. He indicated that their efforts to use West Germany as a forward bastion against the Soviet Union conflicted directly with the aspirations of the Social Democratic party. From 1947 onward, practically every major Western action seems to have deepened his conviction that Western capitalists, together with their German collaborators, were just as determined to frustrate the ambitions of the patriotic S.P.D. leadership as the Communists in the East. All this shouting about Social Democratic nationalism, he wrote to a German journalist early in 1949, was "simply an attempt to humble us, to force upon us a mood of contrition."[55] If earlier he had tended to describe the Western occupation powers as fools and bunglers, he now claimed that they were deliberately seeking to restore "capitalists" and "reactionary Clericals" to power. He complained of constant Allied interference in German politics and internal Social Democratic affairs, and made no secret of his belief that Roman Catholics within the leadership of the Western occupation authorities were conspiring with clergy and politicians of their faith in Germany and Western Europe on behalf of an unholy alliance between a "black" and a "capitalist" international against Social Democratic German patriots.[56] His reaction to this apparent conspiracy was to become increasingly belligerent and intransigent in his relationship with the representatives of the Western powers. Under the circumstances, he said, militant opposition to Western actions was mandatory for any self-respecting Social Democrat.

With the creation of the Bizonal Economic Council in 1947, the relationship between Schumacher and the Western occupation authorities became set in the pattern it was to maintain until his death. The Economic Council, established despite Soviet warnings that it would deepen the division of Germany, was elected by the Länder parliaments in the British and American zones. It was given authority over the economic life of most of West Germany, and soon became the nucleus of the future West German government. Political alignments crystallized, and the anti-socialist coalition that was to govern the country began to emerge. According to Harold Zink, the chief historian of American military government in Germany, the Council was "a political structure in almost every sense," particularly after its powers were increased in 1948. "All that was needed to have a full-fledged government in the merged British and American zones was a change in terminology and a slight extension in the scope of the bizonal institution."[57]

Schumacher, who maintained that the Social Democrats refused to play zonal or interzonal politics because they concentrated on "German politics," did not welcome this development. He tried to distinguish between the political and administrative functions of the Council (a distinction that was entirely inconsistent with his views about the close interrelationship between the two functions), and declared that if this new Allied creation were content to be no more than a non-political administrative body to assist economic recovery, the Social Democrats were ready to cooperate; but they would strongly oppose any action that aided Soviet efforts to deepen the division of Germany. Actually, he seems to have been well aware of the political significance of the Council, although in retrospect some of his associates thought that he underestimated the importance of the Council in general. Failing to gain control of the key economic posts in the Council's Executive Committee, he decided to take the S.P.D. into opposition against the "bourgeois collaborationists," thereby initiating a policy of negation that his party was to pursue for many years to come. Thereafter he justified his generally uncooperative attitude toward Western efforts to create a strong West German state on the ground that the Western Allies were helping the Soviets to perpetuate the division of Germany and assisting anti-democratic collaborationist forces on both the right and the left.

Since the Allies were determined to proceed with their plans to establish a

West German state, Schumacher was confronted by a conflict between his patriotic refusal to collaborate and his desire to take advantage of conditions that he believed would soon bring the Social Democrats to power. Faced with the choice of refusing to take part in any further political reconstruction under Western auspices, thus denying himself and his party the opportunity to shape the new political institutions in accordance with his objectives, or throwing himself into the political struggle over shaping these new institutions, he chose the latter course. However, he still sought to adjust his actions to his perception of the patriotic leader's role and the need for consistent, militant action.

Disputes over the Federal Republic

In the spring of 1948, American decision-makers, who viewed the Soviet threat to West Germany with growing alarm, induced the rather reluctant British and French leaders to join them in asking the minister-presidents of the eleven Länder to convene a constituent assembly to set up a West German federal republic. In return, the Germans were promised that an Occupation Statute would be drawn up, under which Allied controls over German decisions would be considerably relaxed. The Allies had just imposed a drastic currency reform, which Schumacher was convinced would increase pro-socialist sentiment in West Germany, and he therefore moved boldly. When the minister-presidents met in July 1948 and turned down the Western demands on the grounds that they threatened to deepen the East-West split, Schumacher's influence seemed all too apparent. In view of increasing tensions with the Soviet Union, highlighted by the Berlin blockade, the American initiators felt that the minister-presidents had displayed "a catastrophic disregard of the total European situation." Moreover, this allegedly irresponsible behavior was seen as being largely due to "the intransigence of the Socialist party leadership."[58] The U.S. Military Governor, General Lucius Clay, to whom Schumacher was only a party boss in the British zone, was particularly outraged that the chiefs of popularly elected state governments had shirked what he believed to be their duty, and had yielded to the illegitimate dictates of a party leader without a popular mandate.* It was the first but by no means the last open clash between Schumacher and Western leaders. Clay made a determined effort to offset this "disastrously irresponsible German move," which British and French leaders were quite willing to abide by. He apparently took it as a personal slight.[59] He succeeded in forcing a compromise, under which the minister-presidents agreed to ask the state legislatures to elect a Parliamentary Council that would draft a Basic Law for a "provisional" West German state.

* Clay's suspicions were apparently quite justified. Schumacher directed the actions of those Social Democratic minister-presidents who attended the meeting, and was evidently able to persuade the rest to go along.

The Social Democrats lacked a majority in the Parliamentary Council that met in Bonn from September 1948 to May 1949. Schumacher himself did not participate in its deliberations, being confined to his bed in Hannover for most of the period by the amputation of his right leg. However, he was in full command of the Social Democratic delegation, and insisted that his deputies in Bonn take no action without his approval. He made his position clear from the outset in the keynote address that was read for him at the S.P.D. national congress at the beginning of September. He declared that the Social Democrats would not let the Western Allies saddle them with the responsibility for the "political and administrative reorganization of West Germany," or compel them to cooperate with the West's collaborators in the Council. The S.P.D.'s primary aim, he said, continued to be reunification with the Soviet zone, and the party would do nothing to relieve the Allied powers of their responsibility to heal the breach they had caused. However, he announced that the Social Democrats were willing to help formulate a set of rules for the temporary governance of West Germany by German decision-makers pending the establishment of a reunited Germany.[60]

The actions of the Social Democrats in the Parliamentary Council led one American observer to conclude that their principal aim was to create a political structure for West Germany that could be extended to East Germany once the country was reunited.[61] Under Schumacher's direction, they claimed to speak both for West and East Germans in striving for the establishment of political institutions that would meet German rather than foreign interests. According to Adenauer, who was Chairman of the Council, all the German participants believed that West and East Germany would be reunited before long.[62] However, Schumacher's strategy had a more immediate goal, it appears. In the opinion of several observers who were not only close to him but intimately involved in the discussions, he still believed that political developments in West Germany favored a Social Democratic victory in the forthcoming elections for a West German parliament, and thus the creation of a government under his leadership. This perspective appears to have decisively influenced his view of proper Social Democratic behavior toward the Western powers and their German supporters in the Council. He seems to have been determined to impress upon the prospective voters that the Social Democrats alone were the true defenders of the national interest, and therefore deserved their support. In addition, his belief in impending victory accentuated his bitter clashes with the American and French military governors over the distribution of powers in the new state.

Since thus far Schumacher had been frustrated by Allied limitations on central party control over Social Democratic officeholders in the Länder, and Allied insistence that socialization measures had to await the formation of a German government, he was now determined to obtain for the new government, and especially its chief, the extensive powers that he believed were essential to put his program into effect. The Americans and the French, however, wanted to reserve substantial powers for the Länder on the grounds that only thus would German democracy be safeguarded from a return of the evils attributed to past centralized control. To Schumacher, this stand seemed to favor the particularist and anti-socialist forces of "reaction" and foreign interests that were intent on keeping Germany permanently weak and the Social Democrats out of power. As a result, intense friction developed between him and the French and American military governments, which several times threatened to halt negotiations altogether. He accused the two Western powers of intervening openly in favor of the "reactionary" federalists, particularly the Christian Democrats led by Konrad Adenauer and their Bavarian Christian Socialist affiliate, because these groups were willing to collaborate. Whereas it was Adenauer's strategy to go along with French and American demands for a federation with strong component states and a comparatively weak central government, Schumacher was trying to force the military governors to yield to his demands for a more centralized government. The French were apparently quite ready to see the negotiations fail; the Americans were evidently eager to gain speedy and overwhelming approval in the Parliamentary Council for the new constitution, the Basic Law; and the British maintained a benevolent neutrality toward the Social Democratic demands. Schumacher obviously counted on differences among the Allies, and on American eagerness for Social Democratic agreement, to help him win his objectives.

Near the very end of the negotiations the Western Allies gave Schumacher an opportunity to demonstrate his thesis that only the insistent demands of a militant patriotic leader could make foreign powers revise their position in favor of the Germans. The issue in question was the distribution of powers between the federal government and the states, in particular the distribution of financial authority. The Social Democrats, despite the opposition of the Christian Democratic and Bavarian federalists, had succeeded in pushing through the Council a constitutional draft that gave the federal government financial supremacy with regard to the collection and apportioning of taxes. In March 1949, however, the military governors demanded greater fiscal powers for the states. Under Adenauer's leadership, the Christian Democrats proposed to meet Allied wishes, but Schumacher flatly refused to make any concessions. Instead, on April 20, 1949, he announced dramatically that the Social Democrats would not endorse the Basic Law unless the powers of the upper house (representing the state governments) were drastically curbed and the federal government given undisputed financial supremacy. The S.P.D., he declared, refused to be a tool of foreign or particularist interests, or to yield to Allied pressure as the Christian Democrats did. He asserted that his party's determination to defend the national interest was inflexible, that its patriotic principles were immutable, and that its record of militant opposition to Western and Soviet designs against Germany contrasted sharply with the actions of Christian Democratic and Communist collaborationists. Three days later the Western Allies capitulated, and publicly accepted Schumacher's demand for the financial supremacy of the federal government.*

This triumph was to have far-reaching consequences for future relations between Schumacher and the Western powers. Schumacher exploited his victory to the full in the election campaign that followed, and he kept referring to it subsequently to support his contention that only firmness produced results with the Western powers. His deputies later said that this was more than a tactical gesture. They felt that he really did believe that an unyielding stand would make the opponent give way, and that the incident strengthened his conviction that the strategy he had adopted from the start was correct. This strengthened conviction subsequently made him even more inflexible in his relationship with Western as well as German political opponents. But while Schumacher could claim credit for the creation of a relatively strong central government, his more accommodating opponent, Konrad Adenauer, proved to be the principal beneficiary of his action. When Adenauer became the leader of the new government, he was able to take advantage not only of the powers Schumacher had intended for himself, but of the hostility the dispute created between Schumacher and the Western leaders, particularly the Americans. A relationship already marked by suspicion and lack of cordiality was now characterized by intense hostility. Adenauer, by contrast, seemed to Western leaders reasonable, cooperative, and understanding.

We shall examine Schumacher's duel with Chancellor Adenauer more closely in the next chapter. What interests us at this point are the repercussions of the conflict in Schumacher's relationship with the Western powers. It was a conflict in which both leaders focused on foreign policy issues, and in which Schumacher emphasized for the German public his role as the patriotic leader fighting for German interests against a collaborationist chancellor. This strategy made it difficult, if not impossible, for Schumacher to support Western proposals that Adenauer had accepted (even if he had been inclined to do so); and, conversely, it led him almost automatically to oppose any suggestions made by Adenauer and accepted by Western leaders. In his determination to accentuate the difference between himself and Adenauer, Schumacher seemed in Western eyes to be playing an entirely negative role during the last years of his life. It was of course an image that Adenauer was only too ready to underscore to further his own purposes. Indeed, Schu-

---

* Adenauer's supporters later asserted that Schumacher had had advance knowledge that the Allies would yield if he stood firm, but the evidence is far from conclusive. Other sources claim that General Clay, the American Military Governor, had instructions to yield but hoped to compel Schumacher to submit to Allied demands.

macher provided him with an ideal foil, for he could always conjure up the threatening image of the opposition leader when bargaining with Western powers, just as Schumacher tended to use the Communists.*

At issue, as stated earlier, was the association of the new Federal Republic with the Western alliance and its integration into Western Europe. The Adenauer government cooperated closely with Western leaders in promoting these plans, while Schumacher strongly opposed them. As we noted, Schumacher rejected both a Soviet orientation and political neutralism; but the demands of his role as patriotic leader in the duel with Adenauer—"the Chancellor of the Allies," as he called him—caused him to oppose every step that led toward the integration of the Federal Republic into the Western camp. The Occupation Statute, the Petersberg Agreement for an International Ruhr Authority, German membership in the consultative Council of Europe, participation in the European Coal and Steel Community, and finally the proposals for participation in a European Defense Community—all were vehemently and unsuccessfully opposed as schemes to keep Germany weak, divided, and under capitalist domination. He accused Adenauer of acting against the interests of the German people, in both West and East Germany, because he was entering into agreements that denied the Federal Republic equality with other European powers and the sovereign right to freedom of action; each new agreement, according to Schumacher, placed additional obstacles in the way of German reunification. Adenauer, he claimed, was simply the tool of his Western masters, who did not hesitate to intervene for him in strictly German political matters and exert heavy pressure on his behalf.

This conflict reached its climax in 1950 and 1951, after Adenauer agreed to Allied proposals for the armament of West Germany. Schumacher rejected Western efforts to gain the support also of the Social Democrats. He declared that a German defense contribution might be desirable, but it must not take the discriminatory form proposed by the Allies. He stipulated conditions. If the Allies wanted German soldiers to defend the West, they must first of all assume the same responsibilities and the same risks they asked of the West Germans.

Confident that he was rapidly recovering from his stroke of December 1951, as his associates recalled, Schumacher prepared himself to re-enter the arena against Adenauer and the Western powers. The preface that he wrote for his party's new program in July 1952 was apparently designed to sound the keynote for a renewed onslaught against the advocates of Western integration in the skirmishes that were bound to precede the 1953 campaign for

---

* According to some of Schumacher's associates, Schumacher had deliberately provided this service for the Chancellor, and had even complained that Adenauer did not properly exploit the opportunity to gain greater concessions from the Allies. However, such arguments are probably rather labored efforts to rationalize what appeared to be highly self-defeating behavior.

the election of a new parliament. Sensing a very strong popular sentiment against rearmament, particularly in the form agreed upon by Adenauer and the Western powers, he wrote: "What has happened so far in the various parts of Germany is only provisional. These provisional arrangements cannot assume final character in relation to the German nation as a whole. Only a united people is entitled to determine and give final shape to its future policies and economy."[63]

A few weeks earlier he had already put the West on guard by commenting that seventy million Germans in a united Germany would view the "practical possibilities of making their weight felt" in a rather different light from the man who had just signed the European Defense Community Treaty without consulting them.[64] The actions of the cooperative chancellor of West Germany, like those of Schumacher's old rival Otto Grotewohl, were likely to be repudiated by an all-German national government under Social Democratic leadership, he warned. The S.P.D., the party of the German patriots, would "fight against attempts to integrate any part of Germany with other nations in advance of German reunification";[65] it would fight any and all agreements that did not "leave open and even strengthen the possibilities of German unity."[66] Not only did he demand complete equality for German contingents in a European army, but he asked that West German forces be increased while rearmament took place so that West Germans would be able to make an immediate and successful counterattack should Russia strike. The German people, he said, regardless of what had happened in the past, were entitled to the same rights and opportunities in their defense as the British, French, or American poeple. "As long as the others do not demonstrate their solidarity with us by their deeds, we shall withhold our agreement to a German military contribution," he told a meeting of party leaders in March 1951.[67] It seems probable, though proof is lacking, that he knew the Western forces would not be reinforced while the Korean War was in progress.

Since his conditions were not met, Schumacher opposed all other proposals that were put forward in 1951 for a European army. He rejected the French Pleven Plan as entirely unacceptable; and after further negotiations had led to an agreement to form a European Defense Community with German contingents, he announced that if he became chancellor, he would not only oppose the formal signing and ratification of the treaty, but repudiate it on behalf of the German people, who, he charged, had not been allowed to express their views. When Adenauer signed in 1952, Schumacher declared that anyone who accepted this action no longer had the right to call himself a German.[68] To Americans, such remarks "nearly coincided with Communist propaganda" against German rearmament.[69] Though some Western leaders, including U.S. High Commissioner McCloy, doubted that Schumacher would in fact carry out his threats, his behavior hardly made them look any more kindly upon the possibility of his replacing Adenauer in the chancellorship. For, as Schumacher said in a filmed interview on August 20, 1952, German reunification was "a more urgent and important aim for the pacification and reconstruction of Europe" than the integration of a rump Germany with other European countries.[70] A few hours later "the man in the way" was dead—to the unquestionable relief of most Western leaders.

Schumacher's relations with influential Western leaders had been mostly indirect. Unlike other important German political figures such as Adenauer and Reuter, he met very few prominent Western decision-makers, and there was little opportunity to correct respective stereotyped images. Contact was made principally through intermediaries in the military governments, journalists, and occasional Western visitors to Germany. Schumacher paid two brief visits to Britain in 1946 and 1948 on the invitation of the Labour party, but met none of the principal leaders of the Labour government. In the fall of 1947 he spent three weeks in the United States at the invitation of the American Federation of Labor, but his contacts were virtually limited to American labor leaders and German refugees; he had no opportunity to meet American government leaders.* France he never visited at all. Since he had had no previous opportunity to get to know Western countries at first hand, his image of his Western counter-players was formed by parochial stereotyped preconceptions that were little changed by his postwar experiences or his impressions of the behavior of Americans, Englishmen, and Frenchmen in occupied Germany—most of them members of the occupation forces and military governments. The Western leaders, for their part, viewed his activities through the prism of postwar hostility and suspicion toward Germans in general, and the reports of Allied officials, who, in many instances, had little use for the Social Democratic leader.

Schumacher's Relationship with French Leaders

Schumacher's relationship with the French leaders was bad from the start and remained so until his death. In terms of French objectives, the Christian Democratic Union seemed to many French officials more trustworthy and deserving of support than its major rival, the S.P.D. Since they intended to encourage the federalist and even autonomist sentiments that had been traditionally strong in the Rhineland, Baden, and Württemberg, they found the religious and political identification of the C.D.U. leadership more congenial than Schumacher's patriotic posture. They strongly opposed ties between the S.P.D. leadership in Hannover and the Länder organizations in their zone, and for a long time Schumacher and his supporters were forced to operate

---

* An analysis of Schumacher's appointments diary bears this out. His principal non-government contacts were Irvin Brown and Jay Lovestone, two representatives of the American Federation of Labor, the former a trade union leader, the latter an ex-leader of the American Communist party.

almost covertly there. Schumacher depended heavily upon the cooperation of such S.P.D. leaders in the French zone as Carlo Schmid in Baden, Franz Bögler in Rhineland-Pfalz, and Erwin Schoettle in Württemberg. Until the establishment of the Federal Republic, the French authorities would not recognize him as the leader of the S.P.D., and as late as April 1947 they refused him even the right to address a public meeting in their zone.[71]

Schumacher apparently saw French policy in Germany as conforming faithfully to his image of the French as implacable foes of German interests. The harshly punitive actions of the French occupation forces, and the French government's pronouncements on its plans for the future of his country, seem to have reinforced the stereotyped image of nationalistic "French ruling circles" that he had held as a young politician in Stuttgart twenty years earlier. In his eyes, de Gaulle's demands for a weak Germany, for placing the Rhineland and the Saar as separate political entities under permanent French control, and for internationalizing the Ruhr, the industrial heart of Germany, spelled the final destruction of his country. He regarded the Franco-Russian Treaty of 1945 and French and Russian opposition to German unification as clear evidence that France, like Soviet Russia, was intent upon satisfying interests directly opposed to those of the German people.

Though French policy relaxed after the first two or three years of the occupation, Schumacher maintained that basically it had not changed, as French insistence upon a decentralized German state during the 1948–49 dispute over the Basic Law had proved. He claimed that French proposals in the early 1950's for the economic and military integration of the new German state with other European nations were aimed at keeping Germany permanently feeble, divided, and under French domination. He complained that Britain and the United States acceded far too readily to French demands that were designed merely to strengthen France and its unstable governments—at Germany's expense.

French antagonism toward him personally was evidently not unwelcome to Schumacher. To be identified as the principal opponent of French interests in Germany fitted his perception of his role as patriotic leader. He cited French criticism of himself to support his assertion that he was the principal defender of German interests. Germans were reminded that it had been primarily France and Russia that had sought to block the organization of a strong Social Democratic movement after the war. According to his view, their common hostility toward Germany's "legitimate" non-collaborationist leaders was much the same as hostility toward the German people themselves.

Behavior that to Schumacher was legitimate and proper in terms of his role perceptions was, however, highly illegitimate and improper from the French point of view. Communist as well as right-wing papers in France called him a pan-German nationalist, a new Bismarck or Hitler, in almost identical language. French leaders of widely varying viewpoints were united in describing his behavior as outrageous, for France was declared to be entitled to retribution and compensation and iron-clad assurances against the revival of a powerful and threatening Germany. Privately and publicly, they typed him as the traditional arrogant Prussian nationalist, consumed by hatred and contempt for the hereditary foe (*Erbfeind*). It was primarily the French who perceived in Schumacher a possible leader for the new Germany; they saw his behavior as clearly hostile to their country's interests, and decided he was not the sort of man they would like to have at the head of the government. Almost any other German leader, but particularly the Francophile Adenauer, would have been preferable—even to Schumacher's fellow socialists, the leaders of the S.F.I.O. (Section Française de l'Internationale Ouvrière).

As key participants in postwar French governments, French Socialists took a leading part in formulating policy toward Germany. Generally, though not invariably, S.F.I.O. leaders in the government supported prevalent French views on the treatment of Germany, and consequently they had frequent clashes with Schumacher. Jules Moch, whose son had been killed by the Germans, and Guy Mollet, General Secretary of the S.F.I.O. and a strong supporter of Western European integration, apparently disliked the German "comrade" intensely—a sentiment that the latter reciprocated. Professions of solidarity at meetings of European socialist leaders could not conceal strongly conflicting viewpoints. According to Schumacher, the French Socialist leaders were pursuing a narrow nationalist course, and giving aid and comfort to his German opponents who collaborated with France. He said that a weak French Socialist leadership, unable to cope with a powerful Communist movement on the left and the Gaullist nationalists on the right, was maneuvering desperately to make common cause with reactionary capitalists and Roman Catholics at the expense of the German workers.* To the leaders of the S.F.I.O., however, it seemed that Schumacher was antagonistic to both French and international socialist interests. Salomon Grumbach, the S.F.I.O. leader who made a genuine effort to bridge the differences, had concluded by 1951 that Schumacher's intransigence made the task well-nigh impossible.[72]

Schumacher had few direct contacts with the principal French leaders.† He never visited France, and seems to have been entirely unable to understand the French point of view. His infrequent contacts were chiefly with a few officials of the French occupation authorities, and his relations with them were consistently marred by mutual animosity. He accused the French of constant interference in "internal" German politics on behalf of his opponents. His

---

* For example, Schumacher attacked Jules Moch in March 1951, claiming that the S.F.I.O. leader wanted to use the Germans as cannon fodder should Russia attack the West. See *Turm.*, II, 257.
† He met none of the French premiers, and had only one meeting, in January 1951, with Robert Schuman, the chief architect of Western European integration.

long feud with André François-Poncet, the French High Commissioner, with whom he conferred only three times according to his appointments diary, came to a climax in 1951 in connection with the Schuman Plan and West German armament. Infuriated by the High Commissioner's reported comparison between the "patriot" Adenauer and the "Faustian schizophrenic" Schumacher, the Social Democratic leader declared at a press conference that the German people had had more than enough of the didactic pronouncements of a man whose record of "appeasement" as French ambassador to Nazi Germany from 1933 to 1940 made him a "misplaced person" in his present position.[73] His criticism was to no avail. The French government was apparently well satisfied with the activities of its chief representative in Germany. However, further relations between the two men were for all practical purposes severed entirely.

Schumacher's Relationship with British Leaders

The relationship with the British occupation authorities seemed to begin more auspiciously. The Labour party's accession to power in the summer of 1945 came at a most opportune moment from Schumacher's point of view. His base of operation and the industrial areas from which the S.P.D. had traditionally drawn most of its strength in West Germany were in the British zone, and apparently he hoped to receive discreet support from his fellow socialists in Britain in his drive for power. Many of the political officers of the military government showed a sympathetic attitude toward the Social Democrats, and favored them when appointing Germans to local government positions.* Quite a few of the leaders in the reorganized S.P.D. in the British zone had lived for a number of years as exiles in Britain, and others had received special political training in British prisoner-of-war centers. British occupation officials believed that most of the former exiles had been deeply impressed by "the British way of life" and would now strive to introduce it into German politics.†

Schumacher, who had been quick to enlist the support of many such former exiles, profited from the benevolent British attitude. Men who worked with him in this period credited the local occupation officials with helping him

---

* "In spite of the insistence on neutrality in our high-minded objectives," recalled one such officer later, "very many Military Government officers came to find themselves more in sympathy with the Social Democrats than with the other parties." The Social Democrats seemed to them "to have more in common with the average Englishman than most other kinds of German. Those of us who had only a superficial knowledge of recent German history admired the stand they had taken against the rise of Nazism and the moral courage shown by leaders who had preferred either to go into exile or face arrest and the concentration camp rather than throw in their lot with a dictatorial regime they despised and loathed." Ebsworth, p. 26.

† In fact, such sympathies apparently led these officials to overestimate the popularity of the Social Democrats in assigning local government positions. Elections in the spring of 1946 proved the S.P.D. weaker than had been thought, and led to the replacement of a number of Social Democrats by members of other parties in local governments. See Ebsworth, pp. 50–51.

considerably in his organization of the party both in Hannover and in the British zone in general. The chief political officer of Hannover's military government came to know him well, and fifteen years later still spoke of him with admiring enthusiasm.

After his election to the chairmanship of the S.P.D., Schumacher's claim to prominence was given a considerable boost when the Labour party invited him to London in December 1946. The first German political leader to visit Britain in almost a decade, he had an opportunity to introduce himself to the British public and the leaders of the Labour party. He was hailed in the Labour press as the spokesman for the new Germany and an ideal leader for its new government. He was treated as if he were the chief of a friendly state, wrote the independent *Observer*, rather than merely the leader of a political party.[74] The visit received considerable notice in Germany—one paper called it the beginning of a resumption of German foreign relations.[75] Upon his return Schumacher wrote to an old friend in the United States that the trip was seen as a success by most Germans, but "naturally" there had been criticism as well. "However," he added significantly, "such criticism is as necessary as the applause." Both reactions helped to establish his reputation at home and abroad. A second journey to Britain followed in March 1948, but was cut short when Schumacher fell ill and had to return to Hannover for immediate treatment to his leg.

The manifestations of sympathy in Britain led Schumacher's German opponents, as well as some French and American officials, to identify him as the protégé, even the stooge, of the Labour government. Schumacher considered it necessary to deny this vehemently. Thus in August 1946, when Adenauer, as leader of the Christian Democrats in the British zone, called him an agent of the Labour party, he asserted that such accusations were cynical efforts to mobilize a new German nationalism against the S.P.D. "We Social Democrats," he said, "are more independent of foreign influences than any of our opponents."[76] And in the years that followed he lost no opportunity to emphasize his independence from the British authorities, and his growing differences with them.

Such support as Schumacher and his party may have received from the British was probably of little significance in the long run. Contrary to American and French suspicions, direct assistance was negligible. The professional military men and colonial officials who actually controlled the day-to-day operations of the British occupation authority had no particular sympathy for the Social Democrats or their leader. Until 1949 the direction of British policy in Germany was largely in the hands of General Brian Robertson, a professional soldier, and thereafter of Sir Ivon Kirkpatrick, a senior civil servant who heartily disliked Schumacher. The British soldiers and civil servants sent to Germany generally tried to be completely neutral toward all German political groups, but the S.P.D. leadership had many grievances about the way this neutrality was exercised, according to an authoritative American observer.* High officials in the British and American military government later agreed that despite the sympathy of a number of Labour party leaders, the Labour government carefully refrained from giving direct support to the Social Democratic leadership. "If anything," observed one former U.S. official, "Mr. Ernest Bevin leaned in the other direction."[77] Bevin, next to Prime Minister Attlee the most powerful figure in the Labour government, was Foreign Secretary from 1945 to 1951, and in this capacity apparently wielded greater influence over British policy in Germany than any other Labour leader, not excepting Attlee or John B. Hynd, the minister formally in charge of German affairs. According to Sir Ivon Kirkpatrick, perhaps Bevin's closest assistant in the Foreign Office, Bevin had little liking for the German Social Democrats because he had never forgiven them for supporting the imperial German government when it went to war in 1914. "He felt betrayed, and it made him more anti-German than anything else the Germans ever did." Kirkpatrick claimed that Bevin's experiences with the Social Democrats, particularly with their leader, confirmed him in his "gloomy view" of them, and he found it much easier to deal with Adenauer than with Schumacher.[78] Whatever the reason, Bevin's foreign policy gave German Social Democrats little to cheer about.

Some of Schumacher's principal deputies had come to know Bevin in their exile in Britain and thought of him as a friend of German Social Democracy. They were therefore shocked and deeply disappointed by his unfriendly attitude after the war. Bevin refused to see Schumacher on his London visits in 1946 and 1948. A meeting was arranged in May 1949, but it failed to create greater understanding and cooperation between two strong and stubborn personalities. Schumacher blamed Bevin for the disputes that increasingly clouded his relations with the Labour government. He alleged that the Labour government's subservience to American and French wishes had caused it to veto socialization of key industries in the British zone, and to support Ameri-

* Richard M. Scammon, in Litchfield, ed., p. 479. For example, in July 1946 the British Military Governor, General Robertson, summoned both Schumacher and Adenauer in order to announce to them the formation of the new state of North Rhineland–Westphalia, in the British zone. This sudden reorganization on the part of the British was apparently intended to discourage French plans for separating the industrial Ruhr area from the rest of West Germany. However, the effect on internal German politics was to give Adenauer's C.D.U. something of an advantage because it could rely on its supporters in the Catholic strongholds of the Rhineland to outvote the Social Democrats in the industrial centers of Westphalia (Heidenheimer, p. 81, n. 3). Not surprisingly, therefore, Adenauer received Robertson's announcement with enthusiasm, and Schumacher with annoyance. Schumacher, it seems, feared that hereafter Germany would be governed by "three cardinals," Frings in Cologne, Faulhaber in Munich, and the Communist "Cardinal Wilhelm Pieck" in the Soviet zone. This account is based on a protocol of the S.P.D., apparently taken by Schumacher's deputy Heine, and included in S.P.D., Pers. Archiv, K.S., Bd. IX, Bonn.

can plans for reorganizing West Germany and integrating it with Roman Catholic, capitalist-dominated Western European countries. He held Bevin responsible for the removal of German factories from the British zone, charging that the dismantling of "non-military plants" was a blow aimed directly at the German workers and a boon to the S.P.D.'s Communist opponents. It would cost the Social Democrats millions of votes, in his opinion, and gave the lie to Labour's professions of international socialist solidarity.* The British Labour government, he intimated, was more concerned about eliminating the threat of German competition in world markets than establishing a socialist Germany and Europe. British participation was a prerequisite for the unification of Europe, he said, and the Labour party's policy of nationalist isolationism, and its efforts to maintain Britain's position as a major world power, left the Social Democrats at the mercy of anti-socialist interests on the Continent.

Relations between Schumacher and the British occupation authorities grew increasingly worse after Schumacher's last visit to Britain in the spring of 1948. An important British official reportedly denounced him in 1949 as a "dogmatic, doctrinaire, distorted old man with a twisted mind."[79] When the Labour government fell in 1951, Winston Churchill's new Conservative government, and the new High Commissioner in Germany, Sir Ivon Kirkpatrick, made no effort to conceal either their preference for Chancellor Adenauer and his policy of wholehearted cooperation or their dislike for the leader of the Social Democratic opposition.

Schumacher's Relationship with Other European Socialists

Schumacher's relations with socialist leaders in other non-Communist countries were on the whole not much better than his relations with French and British Socialists. It seemed at first that the German Social Democrats might benefit from the postwar upsurge of socialist power in many countries. In Denmark, Norway, and Sweden, democratic socialists controlled the government; in Belgium, the Netherlands, Austria, Switzerland, and Finland, they participated prominently in coalition governments. In Italy, where the socialist movement was split into pro-Communist and anti-Communist parties, the minority Social Democrats played a key part in coalition governments. In December 1947, after some initial opposition, the S.P.D. was admitted to the Comiscon, a loose association of socialist parties, and in June 1951 the

---

* The job of dismantling German "war-production" plants for reparations happened to fall particularly to the British, in whose zone the majority of such plants were located. The Labour government argued that it was committed to proceed under its international agreements, but this argument made little impression upon workers who were put out of work. Sporadic wildcat strikes and demonstrations were climaxed in March 1950 by riots at the former Hermann Göring Works in Watenstadt-Salzgitter; the British High Commissioner was forced to send in troops to restore order before the dismantling could proceed. For Schumacher's reactions, see *Turm.*, II, 126, 429, 437.

German party played host to the reorganization meeting of the Socialist International in Frankfurt.* At the meetings of these groups, Schumacher tried to gain support for his objectives; but as on his 1946 and 1948 visits to Britain, his visit to the Scandinavian countries in 1947, and his conferences with European socialist leaders who came to see him, he had little success.

To start with, there were ambivalent sentiments toward the German Social Democrats. On the one hand, the strong anti-Nazi record of their leadership, associations dating back to the Weimar era, common imprisonment in Nazi concentration camps, and contacts developed by the anti-Nazi exiles during the war had earned Schumacher and his party a certain amount of sympathy. On the other hand, they had to face the strong anti-German sentiment of many European socialists—aggravated in a number of cases by intense Communist pressure—that had been created by the war, or that even dated back to World War I. Many socialist leaders had been killed or imprisoned by the Nazis; others had fought against them with the Communists in underground movements or had been driven from their countries by invading Nazi armies. Many had lost close relatives and friends, or suffered in other ways at German hands. "My international socialism stops at the Germans," observed one British socialist. "I don't trust any of them."[80] On top of this, the policies pursued by most European socialist leaders, in and out of government, were more or less in conflict with the strategy that Schumacher followed as a German patriotic leader. In the Western countries the tendency was to work with parties to the right of the socialists in support of American efforts to build up the economic and military strength of non-Communist Europe. Most European socialists, including the exiled leaders of the Eastern European socialist parties, supported the North Atlantic Treaty Organization and the integration of the German Federal Republic into Western Europe. Those who were opposed, like the Nenni socialists in Italy, were often Communist sympathizers. Thus Schumacher's demands for German reunification and the recovery of East German territory now controlled by Russia and Poland aroused little sympathy, while his reservations about reparations in many cases provoked anger.

It was a situation containing many causes for friction, and Schumacher's behavior did nothing to ease it—at least this was the opinion of many of his own associates as well as foreign socialists who had tried to act as intermediaries, such as the Frenchman Samuel Grumbach, and the Austrian Benedict Kautsky who had come to know and respect Schumacher in the concentration camp. He seemed to them unwilling or unable to adjust his vision. He was openly contemptuous of Italian and French socialists, who, he asserted, could not match the German Social Democrats' effective resistance to Com-

---

* The Comiscon, or Committee of the International Socialist Conference, officially existed between 1947 and 1951; it was succeeded in 1951 by the Socialist International, which is still sometimes referred to as Comiscon.

munist pressure. He charged that socialist leaders in Western and Northern Europe were either indifferent or opposed to the interests of the S.P.D., whose devotion to the cause of international socialism they had absolutely no reason to doubt. Their own behavior, he said, gave them no excuse for denouncing him as a nationalist.

Schumacher's determination to play the patriotic leader, even on his few visits abroad, was hardly calculated to win support from men who were already suspicious of the German Social Democrats. His trip to Denmark, Norway, and Sweden in 1947, like his visits to Britain, had few positive results. The Scandinavian socialist leaders apparently found it hard to reconcile Schumacher's actions with their own views about the proper behavior for a German Social Democrat. Hans Hedthoft, the Danish socialist leader, seems to have disliked him intensely. Dutch and Belgian socialist leaders evidently found his behavior equally disagreeable. The leader of the Dutch socialists, Koos Vorrink, who had suffered bitterly in a Nazi concentration camp, was led to denounce him as a German nationalist who had no right to demand the support of other socialists.[81] Paul-Henri Spaak, the Belgian socialist leader and foreign minister, and like Vorrink a strong advocate of West German integration with other Western European countries, found himself in opposition to a man he professed otherwise to respect and even admire.

Formal professions of friendship, respect, and socialist solidarity could not hide the differences that developed over the years between Schumacher and other European socialist leaders. His emphatic rejection of the "collective guilt" thesis that so many European socialists supported, and his appeals to former "little Nazis," seemed to them only additional evidence that here was not the promising "new" German leadership he claimed to represent. Conflicting personal and group goals and role perceptions were never reconciled; indeed there appeared to be a mutual inability, even unwillingness, to understand and try to eliminate these differences. As a result, when Schumacher died, most European socialist leaders were apparently no more distressed than his non-socialist opponents.

Schumacher's Relationship with American Leaders

This conflict of perceptions and failure of communication was undoubtedly most injurious to Schumacher's ambitions in his relations with the leaders and representatives of the senior partner in the Western alliance—the United States. American values were completely alien to him. His references to the Western traditions of democracy and liberty, as well as to Western capitalism, were always to European experiences like the French Revolution. He complained that Americans did not understand German conditions and needs, but he himself was entirely unable to comprehend American attitudes and behavior. The United States was a *terra incognita,* and his closest advisers were equally unfamiliar with the country and its people. Social Democratic leaders who had closer contact with Americans—such as Brauer, Reuter, Hoegner, and Kaisen—had little influence on his views. Most of them, in fact, he deeply distrusted, not least because their contact with American occupation officials and government leaders was closer than his. With the exception of the mutually unsatisfactory encounter with Secretary of State Acheson, he apparently had no direct contact with major American decision-makers. His one visit to the United States, in 1947, was considered a fiasco by both sides.

Thus Schumacher's image of the Americans and the Americans' image of him were based principally on encounters with American journalists and officials in Germany. Both sides gained increasingly unfavorable impressions from these contacts. At first the picture of Schumacher in the accounts of American journalists contained rather contradictory elements, but as he came to be identified more and more as "the man in the way," the image became pretty consistent. "I gather from the American press that some papers perceive the situation correctly, but others are striving to make me out a complete fool or devil," he wrote to a friend in 1947. Indeed, while some accounts in this period referred to him as "Germany's staunchest democrat" and praised his ability and intelligence, others were already extremely critical.* One leading journalist referred to him as "a narrow-minded pedant who has little to offer beyond a party patriotism that is more interested in justifying the actions of pre-1933 Social Democracy than in dealing with the realities of a new era."[82] Another called him "an autocrat of autocrats," and "a powerful rabble-rouser" whose intense nationalism made him stoop "to the most chauvinistic tricks to win popular support." The only thing that prevented him from becoming another Hitler, a Frenchman is quoted as saying, "was his crippled right arm, which he could not raise above his shoulder."[83]

As Schumacher came more and more into open opposition with American policy in Germany, his image in the United States became correspondingly blacker. Particularly in comparison with Chancellor Adenauer, the picture was almost entirely negative. In 1950 a political scientist called his behavior "rigid, hysterical, and lacking in political prudence."[84] In 1952, another commentator described him as "a politician of uncontrollable temperament, with

* According to Drew Middleton, then the *New York Times*'s chief correspondent in Germany, the "demagogic overtones" of Schumacher's speeches "should not blind Americans to the ability and intelligence" of the S.P.D. leader. "He impresses me as the most dynamic and independent of German politicians and certainly as the toughest. . . . Although he is adept at all sorts of political stratagems and maneuvers, on the whole he has clung to his political beliefs despite Nazi torture and the not inconsiderable pressure placed upon any German politician by the occupation. . . . He is a man whom it is difficult not to admire but equally difficult to like" (*The Struggle for Germany,* pp. 226–27).

a dangerous flair for demagogic argumentation," whose belligerent anti-Western nationalism distinguished him from Adenauer, a "statesman in whom the democratic powers could put their trust."[85] *Time* identified him as "the gospel preacher of revived German nationalism," and "the reincarnation of the rabble-rousers who...led Germany down to catastrophe."[86] Leo Lania, in an article devoted to Schumacher, declared that he was a "self-righteous, intolerant, fanatic authoritarian," who reminded him in a most frightening way of the late Führer.[87] When he died, an obituary article in the *New York Herald Tribune* summed up the prevalent Amercian view by calling him "a disruptive force in the reconstruction of Europe," and the "most difficult and frustrating of German political leaders."[88]

Such descriptions were not calculated to change Schumacher's belief that American "capitalists" were ignorant of German conditions and implacably hostile toward the Social Democratic leadership. The mounting attacks in the American press, he wrote to a friend in the United States in January 1951, showed a complete lack of understanding of German politics; such criticism would gain the United States no new friends in Germany, and would lose them many old ones.

The unfavorable picture of Schumacher in the United States reflected the view of high American officials in Germany. Before the establishment of the Federal Republic in 1949 they refused to acknowledge his claim to speak for Social Democrats in the American zone and looked with disfavor upon his efforts to take a leading part in the political reconstruction of Germany. Some American officials reportedly compared his activities to those of Hitler before he seized power.[89] He came to be seen as the most powerful German opponent of American policies, and as a trouble-maker who refused to play the cooperative role that, in the view of U.S. officials, was the only legitimate one for a German politician. His attacks on American and Western policies, his clashes with the American military government over economic and political reconstruction, and his refusal to cooperate until decision-making power was turned over to the "proper" German leaders soon led them to conclude that a Germany led by Schumacher would be contrary to American interests.

As we have noted, Schumacher's relations with General Clay, the American Military Governor until the Federal Republic was established, were exceptionally bad. The two men apparently met only a few times, and not at all during their critical conflict over the structure of the new Federal Republic.* Schumacher's name is mentioned only twice, in passing, in Clay's account of his administration in Germany,[90] but this seems to be a reflection more of dis-

---

* Schumacher's appointments calendar notes only four meetings, one in 1946, two in early 1947, and one in October 1950 (presumably Clay's formal leave-taking when he gave up his post).

cretion than of indifference. The conflict between him and Schumacher during 1948 and 1949 was no less intense for being waged at a distance and through deputies, according to contemporary observers. Schumacher, who overestimated his popular support (as the federal elections of August 1949 were to show), saw Clay as the man principally responsible for the failure of socialization measures in the British and American zones, and for the frustration of the Social Democratic drive for power in West Germany. Clay, who for his part apparently underestimated Schumacher's influence during the deliberations of the Basic Law, came to look upon him as an uncompromising, zealous fanatic, possessed of "only one arm but a dozen elbows" and entirely unfitted to become the leader of Germany.[91] Clay evidently regarded the creation of the Federal Republic as the culmination of his work in Germany, and Schumacher's successful opposition to the American conception of the coming state seems to have led him and his advisers to fear and distrust what they felt was the authoritarian and nationalist character of the Social Democratic leadership.[92] Forced to accept Schumacher's conditions in order to save the basic concept of a West German state, they apparently could not forgive him the victory he proudly claimed. If the outcome left Schumacher with the impression that firmness could always gain concessions from the Western powers, it left United States officials with a feeling of bitterness toward Schumacher that was to increase in the disputes that followed.

After the Federal Republic had been established, Schumacher's fight against American efforts to tie it to the Allied camp by political and economic unification with the rest of Europe and by rearmament earned him U.S. recognition as leader of the opposition in effect as well as in name. If his accession to leadership in the new state had seemed undesirable before, it now appeared out of the question to American leaders who accepted at face value his declarations that he would repudiate Adenauer's "illegitimate" agreements as soon as he should come to power.* He was treated as an outsider in American negotiations with Adenauer, and was granted no more than the courtesy of periodic meetings with U.S. officials, apparently more for informative than consultative purposes. General Clay's successor, U.S. High Commissioner John J. McCloy made more of an effort than his British and French colleagues to maintain contact with the leader of the opposition, both personally and through his representatives, but the attitude of McCloy's superiors, as well as that of Adenauer and Schumacher himself, seems to have made it difficult

---

* However, according to a story that appeared on June 10, 1952, in the semi-official paper of the U.S. High Commissioner, *Die Neue Zeitung*, High Commissioner John J. McCloy did not share the fear that a Social Democratic government under Schumacher would carry out Schumacher's threat to repudiate the European Defense Community Treaty or otherwise make drastic changes in German foreign policy. Schumacher might seek certain modifications, McCloy was reported as saying, but in general he would take a far more positive position than the one he was maintaining as leader of the opposition.

to do more than engage in a formal exchange of views.* To the American State Department, Schumacher had become "the one man menacing the unity of Western Europe."[93] To Schumacher, the American leaders were primarily a group of Wall Street lawyers and bankers (as indeed many of them were), who were determined to frustrate his ambition to represent the "true" interests of the German people.

The beliefs on which Schumacher based his interpretation of the postwar political context for his activities as a patriotic leader predisposed him to be highly suspicious of American policy in Germany. Whether American policy-makers were aware of it or not, in Schumacher's view their actions were dictated by the necessities of American capitalism in the postwar world. A patriotic German leader was bound to come into conflict with the policies of the largest capitalist nation in the world, according to this interpretation, because the interests of American capitalism were fundamentally at variance with those of the German working people after the war. He therefore saw it as his duty to oppose and force the modification of any American policies in Germany that appeared to conflict with German interests. The German Social Democrats shared with the Americans a belief in the desirability of a democratic order, he asserted, but democracy in postwar Germany could not be modeled on the American capitalist model, since ideological, political, and economic conditions in the two countries were fundamentally different. The German workers would fight for democracy, but not the capitalist version.[94]

This belief in a fundamental conflict between Social Democratic and American interests appears to have provided the general basis for Schumacher's behavior toward American leaders. His interpretation of specific American actions caused this attitude to crystallize into hostility toward United States policy and opinion leaders. Thus he welcomed American food shipments in 1946, but at the same time asserted that American farmers were profiting from German starvation by the sale of agricultural surplus goods. American economic aid to Germany, he said, was an instrument of American capitalism used to compel a destitute people to comply with its wishes. In his view, selfish but not very astute power politics lay behind the Americans' support both of "unjust" French claims against Germany and of the demands of his "collaborationist" opponents inside and outside the S.P.D. A narrow, short-sighted view of American interests, he felt, guided American policy-makers in their efforts to block the endeavors of patriotic Germans to establish German democracy on firm anti-Communist foundations. Thus during

* Schumacher's appointments diary indicates thirteen meetings with McCloy between September 13, 1949, and December 7, 1951 (when Schumacher was incapacitated by a stroke), and almost weekly meetings with one or another of his deputies, such as Charles W. Thayer, who from 1950 to 1952 was chief of the Liaison Division of the Political Affairs Division in the Office of the U.S. High Commissioner for Germany.

the first years he characterized American efforts to "democratize" as naïve, and during the later years as just as undiscerningly anti-Communist. In effect, he said, the crude anti-Communist crusade of American policy-makers served merely to aid and comfort the sworn foes of democracy, the "reactionaries" behind Adenauer and the Communists. He claimed that American pressure for European integration and German rearmament was directed against the reunification of Germany and the democratization of the country through socialism. The United States, he asserted, was forcing upon West Germany policies that a German democrat and patriot was compelled to oppose.

In sum, Schumacher's relationship with American leaders was marked by increasing distrust, hostility, and misunderstanding. To Schumacher in his role as patriotic leader, United States policy seemed a mixture of personal vindictiveness, stupidity, and cynical pursuit of national capitalistic interests. To American officials and opinion leaders, Schumacher's behavior appeared irrational, parochial, and increasingly threatening to United States objectives in Germany. In the end the relationship became so polarized that most American policy-makers judged it necessary to frustrate Schumacher's drive for power if United States interests were to be protected. Whether this view was justified is irrelevant for our purposes. What matters here is that Schumacher's ambitions encountered strong opposition from the Americans, who, by virtue of their overwhelming influence over Western German politics, were in effect the king-makers in West Germany.

The Patriotic Leader: An Assessment

I have attempted to show in this chapter that Schumacher's differences with the leaders of the occupation powers and other foreign states were based primarily on conflicting conceptions of the legitimate role for a German political leader. Soviet and Western leaders expected a man in this role to cooperate with the occupation authorities, and if he did not, they considered his behavior improper and illegitimate. Of course, the criteria for evaluating such behavior varied according to differences and changes in the objectives of the respective foreign leaders. In 1945 Konrad Adenauer was appointed Lord Mayor of Cologne by the American military government, only to be removed from office by the British when they took over, because they considered his behavior uncooperative. Subsequent developments caused the British to change their minds, and to agree with their Western allies that Adenauer was most cooperative and his behavior legitimate. If the Chancellor was seen as a "good German" by the West because his political activities in that office satisfied their expectations, Premier Otto Grotewohl of the German Democratic Republic was equally satisfactory from the Soviet point of view. He played his role legitimately by agreeing to merge the Social Democrats with the Communists, and then by faithfully cooperating with the occupation authorities as leader of the new Unity party and as premier.

Kurt Schumacher, as we have noted, used entirely different criteria in evaluating the legitimacy or illegitimacy of a German political leader's behavior in his relations with non-Germans. For him, legitimacy was evaluated according to the expectations he identified with the position of the patriotic leader. That is, a "good" German fought for what Schumacher perceived as the rights and interests of the German "working people" against foreigners whom he considered more or less hostile to the satisfaction of these values. The patriotic leader, the epitome of the good German, would cooperate if his cooperation could be reconciled with this role; but whenever the actions of foreign leaders and occupation officials conflicted with German rights and interests, he was committed to oppose them. Thus illegitimate behavior for a patriotic leader was behavior that violated these normative expectations, such as the deliberate sacrifice of basic principles for the sake of personal gain or an "opportunistic" compromise.

Schumacher's determination to play the role of patriotic leader in the proper manner led him to clash with all four occupation powers—to the apparent detriment of his political ambitions. His consistent refusal to play a role sanctioned as legitimate by the Western or Soviet leaders resulted in his condemnation by them both. Unlike Grotewohl, he would not collaborate with the Soviet Union, and unlike Adenauer, he refused to cooperate with the Western powers; instead he attacked both Soviet and Western actions, and made demands that neither East nor West could accept. This behavior earned him the distrust and enmity of the Soviet authorities, the Western authorities, and many fellow socialists. The Western powers, whose support he needed, came to look upon him as a disruptive force because, as one perceptive American observer put it, "he upset their plans and refused to look through their eyes at the mass of complications in [Western] efforts to make Germany safe for democracy."[95]

In view of Schumacher's professed ambitions to achieve power for himself and his party in a united Germany, or at least in its Western portions, his behavior seemed irrational to many observers. However, it might be better to call it dysfunctional in terms of his manifest goals and the political setting, for rationality is a misleading concept in this context. From Schumacher's point of view, his behavior was perfectly rational: he refused to cooperate with the occupation authorities because the role sanctioned by them was illegitimate according to his criteria. His behavior was dysfunctional under the political conditions of postwar Germany because he could not achieve his goals under the prevailing power alignments. His attitude toward the Soviet Union ruled out help from that quarter, and the Soviet leadership was obviously determined to deny him the support of Social Democratic adherents in East Germany. The Western powers refused to sanction his efforts to introduce drastic political and economic changes that he believed would further the Social Democratic cause, and opposed his attempts to keep the Federal Republic free from foreign commitments that would limit its future freedom of action.

What induced Schumacher to adopt and cling determinedly to a role that in this sense was clearly dysfunctional for his goals? His interpretation of the political situation seems to have been one reason, and certain personality characteristics another. Let us recall that Schumacher's assessment of the postwar situation was characterized by two basic factors. First, he saw the relationship between the Germans and the victorious powers as a fundamental power conflict. He believed that because of economic and political conditions in the postwar world, foreign interests were bound to attempt to exploit German human and physical resources and to oppose the satisfaction of "German interests." He seems to have interpreted the actions of foreign leaders strictly in accordance with Marxist as well as national preconceptions and stereotypes, and to have been unable or unwilling to revise his views even in the face of appeals from friendly foreign visitors, such as fellow socialists. These visitors, like many of Schumacher's colleagues in the S.P.D., were struck by his inability to communicate with non-Germans—literally as well as figuratively. Not only were foreign listeners unfavorably impressed by his manner of addressing German audiences (some claimed to be reminded of Hitler's harangues), but even when he spoke specifically to foreigners, he seemed entirely unaware of a possible difference in outlook. This was particularly evident on his visits to the United States and Scandinavia. In retrospect it seemed to many of his former associates that besides being exceedingly parochial in his assessment of non-Germans, he lacked the ability to put himself in their place, the ability that would enable him to understand their attitudes and behavior. In sharp contrast not only to Adenauer but also to such fellow Social Democratic leaders as Reuter, his manner of speaking, his brusqueness, his apparent inflexibility of thought and action, his deafness to "reason," his frequent displays of temper, and his self-righteousness proved exceedingly irritating to foreign listeners.

Second, Schumacher's chief concern was not the opinion of foreigners, but that of the German people on both sides of the Iron Curtain. He chose to reject an international dialogue, as an astute German observer noted, in favor of a monologue addressed to the German masses.[96] Though his words and actions appeared to stress foreign relations, he was in fact primarily concerned with their domestic impact. According to his interpretation of the political context, the future of Germany, the S.P.D., and its leaders was ultimately in the hands of the German masses. Non-German factors were of only secondary and derivative significance, for in the last analysis domestic political developments would control whether Germany were reunified or remained divided, whether the masses rallied behind the Social Democrats or their nationalist, Communist, or "reactionary capitalist" opponents, whether the country became a social democracy or reverted to autocracy.

When Schumacher asserted that Germany's future was in the hands of the occupation powers, he apparently meant this only in a conditional sense; in the end, the mobilization of German mass opinion would force these same hands. He evidently feared that the mobilization might be undertaken by either the Communists or a new right-wing nationalist movement, rather than by the Social Democrats. Therefore he lashed out at unity appeals from the Communist leaders of the Soviet zone as well as the nationalist agitation of right-wing groups in West Germany.

Schumacher's performance in the role of patriotic leader conformed to personality characteristics that we have already detected in his earlier career. He seemed determined to carry out a preconceived and inflexible strategy based on the conviction that he was right and his cause was right; that was all he needed to know. His open assertion of superiority was coupled with a strong emphasis on the need for absolute consistency in tactical matters. He insisted that he could not allow the sacrifice of basic principles for temporary advantages, and flatly rejected offers of compromise. He stressed the necessity for militant behavior toward opponents, and the virtues of intransigence and toughness in negotiations with the occupation powers. He showed a singular inability to bargain with his foreign counter-players, to persuade or charm them into letting him have his way, preferring to be defeated than seem to be yielding. He lacked finesse and was apparently well aware of it, but according to his principal deputy he was unable to alter his behavior even when his logical mind seemed to urge it. A Frenchman called him "Germany's de Gaulle," and indeed the two men seem to have certain traits in common that were particularly evident in their relations with foreign leaders.[97] The difference, as it turned out, was that political conditions twice rewarded the French patriotic leader's stance with success, whereas Schumacher's hour of triumph never came. We shall have occasion to examine this point again in the next chapter.

EIGHT

The Champion of the Common Man

In 1947 the British military government conducted an opinion survey that asked Germans to name the man they most admired. Only one German political figure was mentioned in the answers: Kurt Schumacher.[1] About the same time a similar survey in the American zone showed that 40 per cent of the respondents had heard of Schumacher, Adenauer's name not even being mentioned.[2] He appeared to be by far the best-known and most respected political leader, and when people spoke about the S.P.D., they thought of it as "Schumacher's party."[3] Moreover, this party had shown unprecedented strength in West Germany in the first postwar elections, and appeared to have overwhelming latent support in the Soviet zone (where it had been outlawed in 1946). In every respect, Schumacher seemed to be the most obvious candidate for the leadership of a new German government.

Yet when he died in August 1952, another opinion survey showed that only about one-fourth of West German adults supported the S.P.D., and that only one per cent thought that the death of its leader would make any difference in their attitude toward the party.[4] In the election for the second Bundestag a year later, less than 30 per cent of the electors voted for "Schumacher's party," as the S.P.D. had deliberately designated itself, while over 60 per cent supported the conservative, anti-socialist coalition led by Chancellor Adenauer. Schumacher's failure to be accepted by the people as their champion, and the dysfunctionality of his behavior toward relevant domestic counter-players, will be examined in this chapter.

The Role of the People's Champion

The role of Tribune, the defender of the common people against exploitation by the privileged classes, has existed since the days of ancient Rome. Particularly in periods of transition and political instability, when the old institutionalized norms and roles have broken down and new patterns have not yet become established, many an aspiring political leader has assumed this role in his bid for power. For Kurt Schumacher it was evidently the pivotal role in his fight for the leadership of postwar Germany. His pre-Nazi career and his imprisonment in the concentration camp had prepared him for it, his declared aspirations and personal inclinations seemed to demand it, and his performance both as a party leader and as a patriotic leader was conditioned by it. As the people's leader he expected to gain the support that he needed to defeat his opponents conclusively.

Guided by the lessons of the past, which he had studied so thoroughly in the concentration camp, and by his perception of postwar conditions, Schumacher adopted the role of people's champion as soon as American troops occupied Hannover in April 1945. As we noted in Chapter 5, he thought that poverty, hunger, and foreign occupation would create in the "proletarized" German masses an overwhelming desire for strong leadership and a political movement that promised not only to liberate them from foreign rule, but to show them the way to economic recovery and social justice. Anticipating a period of political instability until a new German government could be established, he was determined that he and his party should fulfill these expectations of the masses, and thereby gain the support that would sweep the Social Democrats into power.

Schumacher was by no means alone in his view that Germany faced a period of prolonged socio-economic instability and political crisis. Most of the old norms and patterns of behavior seemed to have lost their validity in the chaotic conditions following total defeat and the collapse of the all-pervasive Hitler regime. Those institutional structures that had not been deliberately destroyed by the occupation powers seemed unsuited to the new conditions. Most articulate Germans agreed that their country was undergoing a fundamental social and political transformation, and expected radically new patterns to emerge. However, such patterns could not emerge without leadership, and the political parties sanctioned by the occupation authorities sought to move into the vacuum left by the destruction of the Nazi elite.

The new political leaders could not foresee that the division of Germany would last. They regarded the political structures imposed by the occupation authorities as temporary, artificial creations, sooner or later to be replaced by structures more in accord with German values and developments. Initially, most of the new leaders declared themselves in favor of a drastic new beginning, a system as far removed as possible from the authoritarian institutions of the past. Social Democrats, Christian Democrats, and Communists were united in demanding a demilitarized and democratic Germany, and far-reaching social and economic changes to meet the people's assumed demand for peace, security, and unity. Opinion polls in the Western zones appeared to substantiate this image of mass opinion.

For Schumacher, this period of transition presented the Social Democrats with a unique opportunity to win the class struggle in Germany by mobilizing the masses. Economic conditions were not likely to improve until there were thoroughgoing reforms by a socialist government; foreign oppression and un-relieved misery would keep the country in a state of social disorganization, and mass unrest would increase as the shock of defeat and occupation wore off; the Allies' restrictions on economic recovery and exaction of reparations were bound to intensify resentment against both them and their German collabo-rators as millions of refugees from East Europe swelled the huge number of unemployed. Under these circumstances, he asserted, the rising anti-capitalist and nationalist sentiments of the German people in all occupation zones awaited the authoritative leadership that under similar circumstances Hitler had once provided.

Thus the crucial issue for Schumacher was who would inherit the leader-ship of post-Nazi Germany: the Social Democrats, who were alone compe-tent and morally "legitimized" to succeed Hitler, or their allegedly unquali-fied anti-democratic rivals, who would lead the German masses to their doom. Recalling the alignment of forces in the last years of the Weimar Republic, he considered the Social Democrats to be confronted once more by an unholy alliance between Communist and "bourgeois" authoritarians. The remnants of the propertied bourgeoisie he described as fighting a desperate struggle in defense of their vested interests against the impoverished multitude. These forces, who in the past had used National Socialism to beguile the masses, now found it more opportune to proclaim themselves as the champions of Christianity and free enterprise, he said. The great danger, he told the party congress in 1946, was that their true nature might not be recognized by the leaderless masses, especially since they enjoyed powerful support from the Roman Catholic Church.[5] The Communists, for their part, he saw as wel-coming the activities of the "bourgeois reactionaries" because these promised to ease their task of consolidating their position in the Soviet zone and extend-ing it westward with pseudo-socialist, pseudo-democratic, and pseudo-patriotic appeals to the masses.

This situation demanded, in Schumacher's view, that the Social Democrats offer the confused, impoverished, and desperate masses a focal point around which to rally as they emerged from political apathy in search of a means to escape their condition. Obviously recalling what seemed to him analogous conditions in the Weimar era, particularly in the years immediately preceding the Nazi regime, he held that the inevitable reactivation of the masses would give the leadership of Germany to the man and the party who could capture their imagination and affection, and give shape to their temporarily con-fused emotions. To be effective, such a leader had to become clearly identified with a high moral purpose and unselfish devotion to the interests of the "little man," and with a dynamic determination to obtain power on his behalf. The masses were to view him as their champion, who needed support in his battle against their enemies. The evil forces needed to be exposed and clearly identified, and the battle lines sharply drawn, if those who hid their anti-democratic intentions behind appeals for socialist or Christian unity were to be prevented from once again confusing the real issues, and once again exploiting the misery and disorientation of the masses for their selfish ends.[6]

Most Germans, Schumacher felt, were disposed to follow a fearless and aggressive leader clearly identified with their interests, and he was only too ready to play the role. He bid for their support by taking every opportunity to accentuate his implacable hostility toward those he called their enemies. He took every care to prevent any confusion about the character of the opposing camps and insisted time and again that there could be no compromise between them. And as champion of the masses, this meant that there could be no compromise between him and his foes; only complete submission to his demands would do. He would be the lion rather than the fox, roaring for all to hear, in the expectation that he could waken and rally the exploited German people, and lead them to victory.

The Bid for Mass Support

In his role as champion of the masses Schumacher addressed himself to Germans in all parts of the country. He was barred from campaigning in the Soviet zone, but far from forgetting the East Germans, he seems to have kept them constantly in mind as a silent but presumably attentive audience that some day might become vocal again. He apparently hoped that the highly unstable economic and political conditions in the Soviet zone would induce the Russians to seek to extricate themselves from an increasingly untenable position—provided they were given a way out.

It was apparently this belief, in which he may have been encouraged by his agents in East Germany, that led him to oppose any Western action likely to rule out the possibility of changing the bases of negotiation with the Soviet Union. If the demands of the Russians for insurance against new German aggression and for economic aid to their war-ravaged country could be satisfied in some other way, they might be persuaded to abandon their German collaborators and agree to the reunification of Germany. The Nazi-Soviet Pact of 1939 was by no means the only instance of a drastic reversal in Soviet policy. He considered it imperative that those he viewed as his clientele in the Soviet zone regain political freedom, both because this was their right, and because he was convinced that free elections in all of Germany would bring to power the patriotic, democratic, and socialist champion of the people.

In the meantime he concentrated his efforts on the Western zones. Political developments there were going to be of decisive importance for the future of all Germany, he said; a peaceful, democratic, and socialist West Germany would prove such an irresistible magnet for the East Germans that the Russians would find it difficult to resist for long the pressure for reunification. The Social Democrats were willing to cooperate in establishing a "temporary" West German state, he explained in 1948 and 1949, because it offered them a chance to initiate in two-thirds of Germany the revolutionary changes they expected to be extended ultimately to the entire country. To obtain control of the government of a West German state seemed to Schumacher the most direct road to power.

The accent was on dynamic action. The role of the Tribune was far removed from the gradualist, Fabian outlook that had guided the political behavior of the leadership of the Weimar S.P.D. He pushed himself to the very limits of the physical strength of a crippled, ailing man to focus public attention upon his activities. Even when the amputation of his leg forced him to make no public appearances for almost a year, he managed to keep his name constantly in the limelight. A stream of press releases and dramatic declarations flowed from his sickbed, and the S.P.D. was no less Schumacher's party for the physical absence of its leader.

He was determined not to repeat the mistakes of 1918–19, when the Social Democrats' failure to take advantage of the temporary disorganization of German political life had given their opponents the chance to recover. In 1919 the Majority and the Independent Social Democrats had been supported by almost half the electorate, only to lose much of that support soon after. This time he hoped to act so quickly that his party would have obtained and consolidated its power before rival aspirants had gathered strength, and before political conditions had become less favorable. Though these ambitions had been dealt a severe blow in 1946 by the creation of the Socialist Unity party and the outlawing of the S.P.D. in the Soviet zone, Schumacher evidently believed that the right strategy and tactics would still carry him and his party to victory in West Germany. He constantly demanded that the occupation powers quickly restore power to a German national government, and welcomed the opportunity that came at last in 1949 to obtain the endorsement of the West German electorate at the polls.

But the decision had to come soon. If delayed for too long, the opportunity presented by the conditions of the present transitional period would be lost. Schumacher's speeches and articles in these years constantly emphasize the need to mobilize the masses quickly and obtain a decision at the polls. To what extent his warnings about the restoration of "reactionary capitalism" in West Germany and the consolidation of "Stalinist Communism" in the Soviet zone were real fears, and to what extent they were specters conjured up to obtain support, is difficult to say. Probably they were both. He was apparently trying to call public attention to threats that to him seemed real enough, and in doing so to turn his warnings into self-denying prophecies. He seems to have feared that if the period of transition were allowed to give way to permanent new political structures fashioned by the occupation powers and their German collaborators, even a subsequent Social Democratic government would find it difficult, if not impossible, to reverse these developments. As the Weimar experience seemed to prove, hostile administrative and judicial officials solidly installed in key positions could effectively sabotage all meaningful reforms. Big business interests, supported by foreign associates, might finance radical right-wing groups, and, finally, the impoverished masses might once again turn to Communist and nationalist demagogues for salvation.

In the first postwar years the S.P.D. seemed to be in an exceptionally favorable position. A well-organized, united Social Democratic movement under a strong and dynamic leader seemed to be faced with only weak opposition from disorganized and divided rivals. There was no longer a powerful radical left-wing movement, as there had been in the Weimar Republic, to compete for the "proletarian" votes. The Communists were too closely identified with the misbehavior of Russian troops at the end of the war, with Soviet punitive policies and threats, and above all with the collaborationist Socialist Unity party in the Soviet zone to command a substantial following in West Germany. Though they managed to win close to two million votes in the state diet elections of 1946 and 1947, this compared poorly with more than seven million Social Democratic votes; and thereafter there was every indication that the K.P.D. would lose most of its supporters to the Social Democrats. To the right of the S.P.D., various competing groups and leaders seemed to Schumacher likely to revert to the pre-Nazi pattern of a large number of comparatively small economic, religious, and regional interest parties who fought amongst themselves for the dwindling "bourgeois" votes. That these groups could unite for any length of time against the Social Democrats and mobilize mass support appeared most unlikely, especially if the S.P.D. continued to refuse to collaborate with the Communists and thereby denied them cause to unite.

The Christian Democrats

Of these parties the newly established Christian Democratic Union was by far the most important rival of the S.P.D. Opinion polls and election results indicated that the two parties were about equally popular in these years. However, the C.D.U. lacked the S.P.D.'s disciplined and loyal mass membership, its organizational strength, and its cohesion. Nor did it have a leader who could match Schumacher's popularity and fame. In fact, it was as yet little more than a working alliance of various local and regional groups, who, despite a few vague principles held in common, were determined to guard their freedom to pursue separate interests and tactics. Most of its prominent figures were former Weimar politicians, who seemed too old, infirm, and jealous of each other to give the party strong leadership. Because many of them had been associated with the pre-1933 Center party, it seemed to Schumacher that the C.D.U. was the successor of that party as the political arm of the Roman Catholic Church.

In fact the C.D.U. in the various West German states and in Berlin represented many shades of political opinion.* It contained survivors of anti-resistance groups and concentration camps, people who had occupied prominent economic and administrative positions in the Third Reich, and people who had managed to remain neutral during the Nazi regime. Some of its leaders were trade union veterans, and others belonged to the remnants of the old aristocratic and big business elites. Some were close to the Roman Catholic hierarchy; others were prominent in the Protestant Church. A left wing favored a certain amount of socialization and the establishment of a democratic welfare state along the lines proposed by the S.P.D., and wanted to cooperate closely with that party; a right wing proposed far more conservative goals for German society, including sharp restrictions on state intervention in economic and cultural affairs. In South Germany the party's spokesmen wanted the new Germany to be a highly decentralized federation of autonomous states; in North Germany they demanded a unitary state. In Berlin Christian Democrats sought to maintain close contacts with the C.D.U. in the Soviet zone, and hoped to establish a reunited Reich; in Munich their Christian Socialist colleagues had little sympathy for such "Prussian" notions.[7]

Schumacher at first scoffed at the efforts of the C.D.U. founders to forge out of these diverse factions a right-of-center mass movement that would offset the Social Democratic attempt to mobilize the German people. A two-party system was impossible in Germany because traditional social patterns were against it, he asserted in August 1945. Religious cleavages going back to the Reformation were simply too deep to enable a party he identified with political Catholicism to attract any significant support from Protestants.[8] Germany's political history, he felt, proved that efforts to unite so many diverse interests in the name of "Christian" and pro-capitalist principles were bound to fail. Since capitalism seemed to him thoroughly discredited among the German people, he felt that no "bourgeois" party had any real future as such. The impoverished masses could no longer be recruited to support the remnants of the old landed aristocracy and big business interests, even if these elements did have the Roman Catholic Church behind them. Indeed, Catholic action

* The Bavarian branch of the C.D.U. called itself the Christian Social Union (C.S.U.).

was likely to do the C.D.U. more harm than good because it would turn Protestants and anti-clericals against it. He told the S.P.D. national congress in May 1946 that the sizable vote for candidates running under the Christian Democratic label in various states was no real proof of strength or staying power. A political organism might appear strong, and yet be basically soft and flabby because it lacked muscle; the C.D.U. was likely to fall apart once it became clearly identified with its reactionary Roman Catholic and capitalist sponsors.[9]

To achieve this identification was one of Schumacher's principle aims.[10] He asserted that the Social Democrats would have been ready to cooperate with those "honest and decent elements" in the other camp that shared their general objectives, but that the growing dominance of big business and Roman Catholic interests in the C.D.U. and the collaborationist activities of its leaders demanded categorical opposition. The S.P.D., according to Schumacher, could only work with parties who accepted its legitimate right to assume the leadership of Germany. As long as the C.D.U. and other "bourgeois" parties refused to accept this, and insisted on equating the defense of private property with the welfare of the people, there was little likelihood of cooperation. Differences between the Social Democratic party and these parties, he insisted, could not be resolved until they discarded their reactionary goals and leaders. Only then would they be fit partners for the S.P.D.[11]

Schumacher continually elaborated on this theme. The C.D.U., he told his German audiences, was a refuge for anti-democratic reactionaries and collaborators; it was controlled by unprincipled remnants of the big industrialists who had brought Hitler to power, and by the clergy, who had done next to nothing to oppose him. Its slogan "Christianity or Socialism," he said, was a vicious calumny designed to turn Catholics and Protestants against a party that was free of clerical influence but welcomed adherents of all faiths. There was no room for either Christian or anti-Christian parties in the new Germany, only for patriotic, democratic parties dedicated to the interests of the German people.

Schumacher was particularly vehement on this subject of alleged clerical, especially Roman Catholic, influence in the C.D.U. Evidently resentful that the Western military governments had allowed the Roman Catholic and Protestant Churches to play an important part in the reorganization of German society, he demanded that the clergy maintain strict neutrality in the battle for political power. By meddling in political affairs, he said, they were provoking a major conflict between Church and people that was not in the interest of either Christianity or Germany. It would be far better for all concerned if they kept out of politics, instead of putting the religious faith of their flocks to a severe test by supporting the Christian Democratic enemies of the people. The Social Democrats, not the clergy, were legitimized to undertake the political reconstruction of Germany, he claimed; for they alone had earned that right by sacrifice and battle against both Nazi and Soviet authoritarianism. The clergy, he said, had discovered their anti-Nazi sentiments only after the Hitler regime had begun to attack the Churches. Social Democrats, regardless of their personal beliefs, respected every man's right to worship as he pleased, and accepted Christian principles as an integral part of German culture; this tolerant attitude, he asserted, deserved reciprocal tolerance from the clergy.[12]

Schumacher was especially opposed to the efforts of the clergy to influence the structure of the postwar German educational system. The worst offender in his eyes was the Roman Catholic Church, which fought hard to preserve denominational schools and other traditional educational privileges of the major Churches. In particular, it demanded that parents have the legal right to decide by majority vote whether schools in their community should be denominational or interdenominational (the latter providing religious instruction as part of the curriculum). The Christian Democrats championed the demands of the Churches, and the Social Democrats opposed them. This led to bitter exchanges. Christian Democrats and religious leaders united in condemning the Social Democrats as anti-Christian crypto-Bolshevists. Both sides appealed to the court of public opinion, making this a major issue in the developing battle for control of the new West German government. Schumacher, charging that the Roman Catholic Church had become "the fifth occupation power," asked the voters to repudiate the clerical forces aligned behind the C.D.U., while bishops and priests asked them to support the only truly Christian party.

Schumacher's vehemence on the subject of clerical influence did not mean that he went lightly on his other main charge, his identification of the C.D.U. as the party of big business (*Unternehmerpartei*). He asked the electorate to support him in his fight to liberate the toiling masses from their capitalist exploiters once and for all. As soon as the Social Democrats came to power, he said, they would socialize all key industries, and purge the defenders of big business and reactionary capitalism from all positions of influence. Those who had profited from the Nazi system and postwar misery would be made to surrender their ill-gotten gains, and exploitation would end forever if the impoverished many would support their champion against the wealthy few. He was their Tribune, and the C.D.U. their enemy; to support Social Democracy was the road to salvation, whereas Christian Democracy would prolong mass misery indefinitely.

Clearly, Schumacher used these tactics because he felt sure of the strength of anti-capitalist and anti-clerical sentiment in the country. Although almost half the population of West Germany was at least nominally Roman Catholic, he seems to have thought that by identifying the C.D.U. as the party of big business, he would capture the votes of Roman Catholics who favored a democratic social welfare state. Conversely, his claim that the C.D.U. was a creature of the Catholic hierarchy was aimed at anti-clerical and anti-Catholic elements. In particular, he apparently hoped to attract support from the millions of Protestant refugees and from younger voters who had been taught by the Nazi regime to despise the Churches.

Such expectations seem to have been reinforced by the initial trend of the state diet elections. By 1947 the S.P.D. had surpassed its pre-1933 strength throughout West Germany, and in the British zone it was the strongest party. In predominantly rural Schleswig-Holstein, which before 1933 had been a stronghold of the right-wing parties, it captured 44.4 per cent of the votes in the state diet election of April 1947, whereas the C.D.U. got only 34.5 per cent. Schumacher, like many other observers, apparently attributed this victory to support from the large proportion of Protestant refugees among the voters, and relied on benefiting from a similar reversal of traditional voting patterns in other parts of West Germany.

Political Action in the Länder

He conducted his campaign on two levels. On one level of the polity, he tried to establish the role relationship between the leader and his counterplayers, which involved aligning the people behind their champion in opposition to his foes. This took the form of direct appeals to the voters, as well as dramatic displays of differences between the Tribune and political actors identified as hostile to the people's interest. On a higher level of the polity, he tried to influence the emerging administrative and political patterns in order to establish firm foundations for a nation-wide reorganization of German society. He approached this task by way of immediate action in the various Länder. The two aspects of his strategy proceeded hand in hand. Where Social Democrats already had the necessary power, Schumacher wanted them to push through immediate, drastic reforms, compelling other groups to go along. Where they could not obtain such power, he thought it better to go into opposition and promise the voters satisfaction as soon as a Social Democratic government had been elected.

In several states the Social Democrats attempted to start the socialization of key industries. In Hesse they were blocked by a veto of General Clay, the American Military Governor, who objected to such attempts to influence the evolving structure of the German economy. In North Rhine–Westphalia a socialization law was passed after a prolonged battle with conservative C.D.U. forces led by Adenauer; but it was subsequently vetoed by British military government on the grounds that "the question of socialization must be considered by a German government, and not by a 'Land' government."[13]

Prodded by their national chairman, the Social Democrats also moved to gain control of the police, public administration, and key economic posts in the states. Schumacher thought that the economic and interior ministries in the Länder governments were of basic importance in the battle for power, and demanded that in negotiating coalition governments with other parties, the Social Democrats insist on these posts. In most cases these tactics were successful, and by December 1947 eight of eleven economic ministries and eight of nine interior ministries were headed by members of Schumacher's party. Where these demands were not met, the S.P.D. usually followed its chairman's instruction to assume the part of a strong opposition and offer itself to the voters as an alternative to the ruling "bourgeois" government.

The purpose of these tactics was apparently not merely to place Social Democrats as rapidly as possible in key positions in the evolving governmental structure, but to compel the bourgeois parties to take a clear stand either for or against the political and economic reforms that Schumacher declared to be essential. If some of them came out in support of the Social Democratic demands, this would presumably lead to a split in the bourgeois camp, force those elements anxious for cooperation with the S.P.D. to follow its leadership in opposition to the conservative forces, which would thus be isolated. If they came out against the reforms, the German masses would be presented with a clear choice between the party that had their interests at heart and those that did not. As we noted in Chapter 7, such tactics led to serious clashes between Schumacher and the Western occupation powers. They also established the relationship between the Tribune and rival political actors in the battle for control of the West German polity.

The Bourgeois Coalition

Schumacher's first opportunity to move beyond the level of political action in the states came with the establishment of the Bizonal Economic Council in Frankfurt in 1947. When, over the objections of the Soviet Union, the British and Americans decided to merge the economic administration of their zones, and give a German administrative agency and economic council far-reaching powers to reorganize and supervise economic affairs, a major step toward establishing a West German government had clearly been made. The new institution offered aspirants for the leadership their first real opportunity to bid for power, and marked the beginning of the open duel between Schumacher and Adenauer, who was now emerging as leader of the C.D.U. in the British zone and skillful architect of unity in the "bourgeois" camp. Neither man was a delegate to the Economic Council, but both strongly influenced the political alignment that emerged from its deliberations. For both of them it provided an opportunity to marshall their forces within and without their respective parties.[14]

Out of the 52 delegates sent by the state parliaments to the Council, the

S.P.D. and the C.D.U. (together with its Bavarian Christian Social affiliate) each had 20 representatives. When the Council assembled in June 1947, the main question was whether the two parties would form a coalition—as they had done in many states—and divide the five positions in the executive directorate between them, thus shutting out the other parties. The S.P.D. was too weak to form a majority without the help of some of the "bourgeois" parties, but the C.D.U. could do without the S.P.D. by forming a coalition with some of the smaller anti-socialist parties. Nevertheless, according to the leader of the C.D.U. faction in the Council, the Christian Democrats were generally in favor of forming a coalition with the S.P.D.[15]

Apparently quite a few Social Democrats also favored a coalition on the grounds that the public interest demanded that the major parties cooperate in alleviating the economic situation and present a united front toward the occupation powers. To some, too, such a coalition seemed the best way to obtain maximum influence and still retain the support of the voters. However, this was not Schumacher's view. As he saw the situation, unless the S.P.D. could dominate the bizonal economic administration, it would be far better not to compromise its campaign by forming a coalition with the "politically incompetent and impotent representatives of German big business and the bourgeois parties."[16] He therefore instructed the Social Democrats in the Council to state that they would join a coalition only if they were given the key posts for economics and finance in the five-man administrative directorate. This the C.D.U. refused on the grounds that the S.P.D. already controlled all the economic ministries in the state governments of the British and American zones. However, it offered to compromise on a "non-party man" for the economic directorate, or a Social Democrat if the S.P.D. would in return surrender three of its economic ministries in the states to the C.D.U. Schumacher rejected this offer. Such a deal suited neither his strategy nor his image of his role as unyielding champion of the people. If he could not have his way, it would be better to saddle the bourgeois parties with responsibility for an undertaking which, he is said to have thought, would in any case fail.

According to a number of Social Democrats who were deeply involved in these deliberations, Schumacher thought that further deterioration in economic conditions would make a farce out of efforts to re-establish a capitalist economy in West Germany. He apparently did not think that the decisions of the Economic Council and its administrative directorate would prove of lasting importance, or that a coalition with a party represented by high-level industrialists and bankers would work. He distrusted the bargain offers of prominent Roman Catholics like Adenauer and his friend the Cologne banker Robert Pferdmenges, and of industrialists like Günther Henle, Wilhelm Nägel, and Erich Kohler, who were among the leaders of the C.D.U. in the Council. As he told one of his deputies in Frankfurt, collaboration with such men would only compromise the popular image of the Social Democrats. Let the incompetent and discredited defenders of the old capitalist and reactionary order and their Western backers wear themselves out in tackling problems which could not be solved except by measures that went against their cherished values. Let them assume the blame for actions that would inevitably fail to make a real improvement in the condition of the masses: an uncompromised Social Democratic party would be all the more certain to profit from the people's subsequent disillusionment.

Schumacher's decision was undoubtedly welcomed by the leaders of the conservative wing of the C.D.U., who also wanted an open battle with the Social Democrats. His intransigence persuaded those in the C.D.U. who had wanted cooperation with the S.P.D. to agree to the formation of a right-of-center "bourgeois" coalition with the Free Democratic Party (F.D.P.) and the small German Party (D.P.), an alliance that was to survive for almost a decade. In particular, he seems to have played directly into the hands of Adenauer, who, at the head of the conservative forces in his party, now began to move toward the leadership of this coalition. Under his guidance, the C.D.U. and its lesser allies succeeded in electing a five-man economic directorate for "Bizonia," which Arnold J. Heidenheimer has described as being, in effect, the first C.D.U. cabinet on an interzonal level. "Its formation marked, first, the C.D.U.'s willingness to assume responsibility at a difficult and risky time ... and second, the beginning of an increasing split between ... the C.D.U.-dominated 'government' bench, and the 'opposition' Socialists."[17] When in 1948 the powers of the Council were enlarged by the two occupation powers and it became the chief agency for distributing American Marshall Plan aid in Germany, suggestions by some Christian Democrats that the S.P.D. be brought into the coalition were squelched by Adenauer's conservative faction. Dominant elements on both sides now were determined to let the voters have an unequivocal choice in the forthcoming elections.

Although the S.P.D. pledged itself to be "constructive" in its opposition, and did in fact contribute a good deal to the deliberations of the Council on technical economic questions, its political strategy up to the 1949 election followed the firm Schumacher line. The party chairman established this position as soon as the crucial coalition issue had been decided. Now that big-business interests in the C.D.U. had triumphed, he announced in July 1947, the battle lines in the class struggle were clearly drawn.[18] There was no longer any ambiguity about the true nature of the C.D.U. or its determination to wage an unrelenting class struggle against the toiling masses. By refusing the legitimate Social Democratic demand for the economic directorate, it had rejected out-of-hand the S.P.D.'s offer to "cooperate honestly and loyally with all forces that sought to provide for the survival of the German people." Cooperation was no longer possible: the C.D.U. stood revealed as a "totalitarian party" just like the Communists, and the speeches of such prominent C.D.U. supporters as Cardinal Frings of Cologne merely served to underscore the party's "anti-democratic character." Together with its ally, the Free Democratic party, it had become the "administrator of the demands of the remaining forces of German capitalism."

Schumacher claimed that these two parties, having already greatly profited from the prohibition of the S.P.D. in the Soviet zone, now sought to profit from a division of Germany into a Communist and a capitalist part. "Without any sense of responsibility toward the whole of Germany," he charged, they were deepening the gulf that divided the nation by pursuing economic policies on behalf of "private capital." But Germany had become too poor to afford such policies of "exploitation and monopoly profit accumulation," and the "interests of the masses" were now in "sharpest conflict with the class policies of the bourgeois parties." The German people were told that now more than ever the S.P.D. would fight to give them real democracy and socialism, firm in the knowledge that the decision in Frankfurt was just one more temporary move in the rearguard battle of reaction. Soon, he promised, these provisional arrangements would be terminated and a "socialist order" would take over.

The preceding episode has been examined rather closely because Schumacher's decision to take his party into opposition not only marks a decisive turn in postwar German politics, but illustrates very clearly his perception of his own role and that of his counter-players: the mass of the German people and his apparent rivals in the struggle for power in Germany. One has the impression that he sought and welcomed a decision that placed the S.P.D. in opposition to the "bourgeois coalition," just as earlier he had insisted on a categorical break with the proponents of a united front with the Communists. His arguments and subsequent actions indicate that he deliberately avoided a coalition with the Christian Democrats and joint responsibility with the occupation powers for the measures taken to combat economic chaos. It was indeed no coincidence that the negotiations broke down, as he claimed at the 1948 party congress; but the cause of the breakdown was not necessarily the bourgeois parties' determination to fight a ruthless class war against the toiling masses.[19] Rather, Schumacher's entire perception of the postwar situation and the necessary distribution of roles arising from it appears to have demanded a position that barred compromise.

On the face of it, his decision followed logically from his belief that the "proletarization" of the Germans was proceeding apace. The economic situation of the great mass of the people seemed unlikely to improve in the immediate future, he felt, and their proletarization would soon lead them to react against occupation and exploitation. Schumacher never forgot, as cannot be too often stressed, the political disadvantages under which he and his party had labored during the crises of the Weimar era, when the Social Democrats were blamed by the voters for the nation's political and economic instability. This time, it seemed, by avoiding participation in an enterprise that he regarded as bankrupt from the start, the Social Democrats might profit from the people's discontent.

However, there seems to have been also a strong personal element in Schumacher's choice. The role of the belligerent opposition leader was apparently far more satisfying to him than the entirely unaccustomed role of partner in a coalition, especially when his associates struck him as thoroughly untrustworthy. All his previous behavior points to such a conclusion. Just as he had refused to collaborate with Grotewohl and the Communists, he now preferred to play the unambiguous role of the anti-bourgeois champion of the masses in a straight battle for control in West Germany. In short, by refusing to participate in the coalition, he chose to play a role that not only seemed highly functional to him in terms of his objectives, but was also apparently highly congenial to him in terms of his personality characteristics.

Vox Populi, Vox Dei

As the interregnum in West Germany drew to a close and the occupation powers indicated their intention to establish a new German government, the polarization of the rival camps became complete. In the spring of 1948, Ludwig Erhard, an outspoken proponent of "free enterprise capitalism," was chosen by the dominant C.D.U.-F.D.P. coalition to become economic director of the Economic Council, which was taking on increasing importance in the zonal administration. He immediately put forward a proposal to remove existing economic controls, and stimulate economic expansion by a policy based on the classic principles of a free market economy. The Social Democrats objected to the proposal on the grounds that apart from creating great social inequities, such a policy would not work. When the coalition adopted Erhard's policy in spite of their objections, they promised to "remind the voters which party was responsible for their plight."[20]

Erhard's plans were designed to tie in with the drastic currency reform that the Western occupation authorities imposed in June 1948. The C.D.U.-F.D.P. coalition authorized him to lift economic controls so that supply and demand might determine prices, and to ease up on taxation so that profits could be ploughed back into business expansion. In terms of the total economy, the combined results of the currency reform and Erhard's policies were spectacular. Industrial production rose from 54 per cent of the 1936 level in June 1948 to 84 per cent in February 1949, and had risen above 100 per cent before the year was out.[21] However, the impact on the mass of the people appeared to support Schumacher's expectation that they would rapidly become proletarized, and that their economic condition would deteriorate in direct relation to the growing wealth of a small group of aggressive entrepreneurs. The Erhard policy and the currency reform seemed to benefit only producers and merchants who had refused to sell their real assets before the almost worthless old Reichsmark gave way to the new Deutsche Mark, which was pegged at one-tenth of its value by military government decree. The "little people," whose champion Schumacher claimed to be, lost almost all their savings, and found their real income from wages, pensions, and so forth enormously reduced. Unemployment rose from 450,000 to 1,300,000 in a year.[22] Only the new rich or those who had something to sell could afford to buy the luxury goods that suddenly crowded the shops, or to rent the villas that suddenly became available in a country where in 1950 a quarter of the population still "shared their living-space with friends, relatives, or strangers, or lived in bunkers and cellars."[23]

Schumacher was convinced that victory could not elude him now. His expectations seemed confirmed, and his strategy in the Economic Council fully vindicated. He anticipated that the discontented workers, refugees, pensioners, and other victims of the new economic policy would now rally to the Social Democrats, that the S.P.D. would emerge as the strongest party in the election of a West German parliament, and that he would become the first chancellor of the German Federal Republic.[24] The trend of mass opinion seemed to favor the champion of the people and his party, whereas the C.D.U. and its allies appeared to be saddled with the responsibility for a harsh new policy that penalized the little man. Not only had they ignored Social Democratic warnings that Erhard's program would cause grave social injustices, but they had also refused to approve a *Lastenausgleich,* i.e. legislation to offset some of the worst inequities arising from the currency reform. Thus, in accordance with Marxist theory, the rich were getting richer and the poor poorer, and the bourgeois parties appeared to care more for the rapacious entrepreneurs than for the suffering multitude.

Outraged by what he regarded as unbearable social injustice and irresponsible ineptitude, Schumacher was convinced that the mass of the people shared his sentiments, and would turn against the bourgeois coalition and the occupation powers in the upcoming election. He obviously welcomed the polarization of political forces, for it fitted his image of a decisive "class struggle" between a small group of exploiters and the exploited masses. Political tension was increasing, he reported in December 1948 to his former girl friend in the United States. The Social Democrats, he wrote, not the Communists, had become the chief target of the selfish bourgeois groups whose lack of responsibility was so conspicuous. For his part, cooperation with these unprincipled champions of clerical and capitalist "reaction" had become impossible. Both sides had made their position clear; the decision whether West Germany was to be ruined by incompetent reactionaries and exploited by German and foreign capitalists, or achieve social justice, reunification with the Soviet zone, and freedom from foreign control under a Social Democratic government was now up to the voters. And which way the decision would go seemed clear to him: the masses would not accept the thesis that economic recovery required sacrifices from them and profits for "the beneficiaries of the Third Reich"; they could be made to realize that the Social Democratic way was the only road to political and economic recovery and true democracy in Germany.[25]

So certain was Schumacher that he would head the new government that he not only agreed to Social Democratic participation in drafting the Basic Law for the new Federal Republic, but insisted on provision being made for a very strong executive. Although he did not himself participate in the deliberations of the Parliamentary Council that drafted the new constitution in 1948 and 1949, he supervised the Social Democratic delegation from his sickbed in Hannover. As in the Economic Council, both Social Democrats and Christian Democrats were represented in equal numbers among the delegates elected by the state legislatures; but this time they cooperated to an unusual degree because each group thought it would control the new government. Where differences developed, Schumacher's party invariably insisted on strong authority for the central government, particularly for the executive branch and its chief.

Schumacher apparently thought that the election would result in the fractionalization of the anti-socialist groups and the break-up of the C.D.U.-led bourgeois coalition, allowing him to form either a weakly opposed minority government or a coalition incorporating some minor parties and, perhaps, dissident deputies from the left wing of the C.D.U. Therefore he agreed with Adenauer, the Council's president, that the chancellor should be assigned a dominant position, and showed no particular interest in the position of the opposition in the new governmental set-up, as his chief deputies in the Parliamentary Council later recalled. Social Democrats and Christian Democrats joined forces to pass Article 67 of the Basic Law, which made it extremely difficult for the Bundestag to overthrow the chancellor by providing that a successor could be elected only by so-called "constructive vote of no confidence." They also agreed to give the chancellor supreme authority over the policies of the government, complete freedom to pick and dismiss his ministers, and the right to demand that the president dissolve a legislature that refused to cooperate with him but could not agree on an alternative chancellor.

In the spring of 1949 Schumacher resumed direct leadership of the Social Democratic campaign for the West German Bundestag elections that would take place in August. He believed that he had greatly increased his chances of success by his apparent triumph over the Western occupation powers and Adenauer's Christian Democratic leadership in the dispute over the distribution of powers in the Parliamentary Council.[26] His firm stand, he felt, had established him in the eyes of the masses as the defender of German national interest, and his principal Christian Democratic rival as an untrustworthy, opportunist collaborator. This belief, as well as his conviction that mass discontent with the economic policies of the bourgeois coalition strongly favored the Social Democrats, evidently reinforced his inclination to wage a bold and savage campaign, particularly against Adenauer, who was clearly his only serious rival. As the campaign advanced, it developed more and more into a bitter personal duel between the two men.[27]

The result of the elections came as a great shock to Schumacher and his supporters. Only 29 per cent of the voters supported them, whereas Adenauer's party received 31 per cent of the votes and eight more seats in the new legislature (see Table 6). The masses had failed to respond to the appeals of the man and the party who claimed to be their champions, and in almost all areas where the Social Democrats had shown promising strength in earlier elections (for example, Lower Saxony and Schleswig-Holstein), their share of the votes had dropped drastically. For Schumacher, according to one of his deputies, it was the greatest disappointment of his life.

TABLE 6

BUNDESTAG ELECTION, AUGUST 14, 1949

Party	Total votes	Per cent	Seats
Christian Democrats (C.D.U./C.S.U.)	7,359,084	31.0	139
Social Democrats (S.P.D.)	6,934,975	29.2	131
Free Democrats (F.D.P.)	2,829,920	11.9	52
Communists (K.D.P.)	1,361,706	5.7	15
Bavarian Party (B.P.)	986,478	4.2	17
German Party (D.P.)	939,934	4.0	17
Center Party (Z.)	727,505	3.1	10
Reconstruction League (W.A.V.)	681,888	2.9	12
German Reich Party (D.R.P.)	429,031	1.8	5
Others	1,491,877	6.2	4
Total	23,742,398	100.0	402

SOURCE: Litchfield, p. 506.

What had gone wrong? To Schumacher it seemed that once again, as in the last days of the Weimar Republic, the politically unenlightened had been seduced by the forces of reaction to vote against their own best interests. "The large turnout deprived us of a victory," he explained in a letter to his former girl friend in the United States. "Only a small proportion of the new voters and those mobilized by non-political forces turned to us." After twelve years of totalitarian rule and four more of military government, the German people, supported in their ignorance by the refugees from Eastern Europe, had remained politically disoriented despite the strenuous efforts of the Social Demo-crats to give them guidance. The Western occupation powers were to blame, he asserted, because they had not only neglected to support the democratic forces in Germany, but actively handicapped them by their policies.[28] And the Roman Catholic clergy were to blame because they had diverted the mass of the faithful from demanding satisfaction of their economic needs by inten-sive agitation on behalf of the "Christian" party.* Only their strong interven-tion, he said, had "saved the Christian Democrats from a major defeat."[29]

What had not been wrong, according to Schumacher, was his strategy and role conceptions in the fight for power. "Of course, the political task before us remains unchanged," he wrote to the United States immediately after the election. In public he declared that the Social Democrats would fight on un-daunted; after all, they had won greater support in West Germany than ever before, and there was certainly no reason to capitulate. A battle had been lost, but the "class war" would continue with even greater intensity. The reaction-aries would now feel even freer to pursue their selfish aims at the expense of the working masses, with catastrophic results. Economic expansion had al-ready slowed down to an "extraordinary and dangerous" extent, he told a Social Democratic conference in January 1950, and the only economic cer-tainty was unemployment. He insisted that the intensification of the class struggle demanded that the Social Democrats become even more aggressive. Comparing the present situation with that of 1923–24, when a similar cur-rency reform was instituted, he claimed that in this new class war the S.P.D. had already given a better account of itself, under far more difficult conditions, than in the 1923–24 situation. "This," he told his fellow Social Democrats, "should give us the strength to see how much can be achieved today if one is really determined to fight, and if this determination also leads one to try to reach the apolitical masses by exercising a natural, magnetic influence upon them."[30]

The Tribune as Leader of the Opposition

Immediately after the August 1949 election there was once again talk about a "grand coalition" between the C.D.U. and the S.P.D. A number of leading personalities of both parties (particularly in the many states where such coali-tions had ruled for years) and the chiefs of the trade unions strongly favored such a course. The difficult economic and political tasks facing the new gov-ernment were said to demand that the disputes of the campaign be put aside, and the major parties combine their forces to push the reconstruction of West Germany and the reunification of the entire country. The public interest, it was said, required that partisan controversy yield to the needs of a national emergency, as it had done in wartime Britain and contemporary Austria.

* This claim was partially borne out by the figures, which showed that the predominantly Roman Catholic areas provided the votes necessary to give the C.D.U. its narrow lead.

Such suggestions were entirely unacceptable to the two men who were now to play the leading roles in structuring the relationship between government and opposition in the new state. Both Adenauer and Schumacher had previously shown little liking for such coalitions at the state and local level, and now saw their opportunity to impose upon the polity their own conceptions of the political patterns they thought should prevail. Apart from the fact that personal hostility ruled out their cooperating in the same government, both leaders believed that a coalition at the federal level would seriously interfere with their efforts to dictate policy in their respective parties, and particularly to impose their strategy upon the state leaders, who up to now had shown considerable reluctance to accept their direction. Above all, both men were convinced that the achievement of their personal and their political goals would be hindered by such an alliance.

The two enemies were therefore in agreement that Social Democratic participation in the new federal government was out of the question, and that it would be far better to follow the pattern of conflict that had existed in the past. Both men asserted that the country would be better served if the coalition that had ruled the Frankfurt Economic Council for the preceding two years were now to form the new government as well, with the S.P.D. maintaining the part of the principal opposition party. In the preceding election campaign they had presented the positions of their parties on domestic and foreign affairs as irreconcilable; a coalition in which they did not actively participate would have implied a repudiation of their leadership, and one in which they did take part, a retreat from these categorical positions. For Schumacher, at least, this was impossible. Not only was he not the man to retreat from a firmly taken position, but his unaltered perception of his political task demanded that he and his party appear consistent, and therefore reliable, in the eyes of the people. Adenauer was quick to see his advantage, and used Schumacher's attitude to strengthen his own position. It was neither the first nor the last time.

As Adenauer moved rapidly and adroitly after the election of August 1949 to assure himself the support of his party and its partners in the Economic Council for a conservative coalition under his leadership, Schumacher proceeded simultaneously to establish himself as the leader of the opposition. Even before the S.P.D. executive committee met at the end of the month in Bad Dürkheim to adopt his 16-point opposition program, the party chairman had publicly committed the Social Democrats to support the role he now intended to play. As he told his biographer later, the grand design was already firmly fixed in his mind on election night.[81] Immediately after the election, one of his principal assistants, Fritz Heine, declared on behalf of the S.P.D. that control of the economic ministry would be a minimum condition for Social Democratic participation in a coalition with the C.D.U., obviously an unacceptable demand in the light of past developments and the nature of the election campaign. At the same time, the S.P.D. headquarters in Hannover publicly repudiated a statement by the Social Democratic minister-president of Hesse, Christian Stock, in favor of such a coalition.[32] What followed at Bad Dürkheim was thus only a formal declaration of the principles that the opposition party was to follow in its fight against the Adenauer government. The traditional Social Democratic procedures had to be observed, but that the executive committee, and subsequently the newly elected S.P.D. Bundestag deputies, would accept the "Schumacher course" was a foregone conclusion. Therefore, as Klaus Schütz has pointed out, the subsequent Social Democratic assertion that Adenauer's ill will had blocked a coalition government was merely a quibble, since Schumacher had deliberately stipulated unacceptable conditions and insisted that only the adoption of the entire S.P.D. program could overcome "present chaotic conditions."[33]

The Schumacher Course

Schumacher's first opportunity to present himself as leader of the major opposition to Adenauer's "bourgeois" coalition arrived even before the election of the new chancellor on September 15. On September 12, the Federal Convention (*Bundesversammlung*), consisting of the new deputies and an equal number of representatives chosen by the state diets, met to elect the federal president. Although the Basic Law provided the president with practically no power to influence government policies, both Adenauer and Schumacher used the occasion to establish their positions. The future chancellor had agreed with his intended Free Democratic coalition partners to back one of their leaders, Theodor Heuss, for the position, in return for their support of an Adenauer government. There was opposition to this arrangement in his own party, and some Christian Democratic leaders proposed that the S.P.D. be given at least nominal responsibility in the government by letting a "moderate" Social Democrat, such as Wilhelm Kaisen, fill the office. Both Adenauer and Schumacher found this entirely unacceptable.

As we have seen, Schumacher insisted, over the opposition of leading figures in his party, that he himself contest the office against the candidate of the bourgeois parties.[34] By forcing a clear division in the Federal Convention, he wanted to demonstrate dramatically the strategy of opposition that he intended to follow in his efforts to reverse the electorate's decision of August 14. He deliberately invited defeat in the contest with Heuss, ostensibly to show that the Social Democrats would not compromise in their attempt to obtain control of the government. When Heuss failed to obtain a majority in the first ballot, though he defeated Schumacher in the second by a vote of 416 to 312, to Schumacher's way of thinking this was a promising beginning for the new phase in his fight for power. His belief that the new coalition rested on weak foundations was apparently confirmed when three days later Adenauer was elected chancellor by the precarious margin of one vote.

Both chancellor and opposition leader now stepped into positions that largely remained to be molded by their incumbents. They had considerable liberty to interpret roles and political relationships that were not yet firmly institutionalized, and to pattern the formal structures outlined in the Basic Law. The architects of the constitution had been more concerned with avoiding the structural defects they perceived in the Weimar system than with establishing political patterns for the future. Because direct democracy was thought to have led to the instability, and ultimately the destruction, of the Weimar Republic, they denied the voters an opportunity to participate directly in political activities through referenda, plebiscites, and the popular election of the president. Because a highly fractionalized multi-party system was believed to have led to governmental instability and frequent elections, they had provided the chancellor with strong powers, and had made it practically impossible for the president, and exceedingly difficult for the legislature, to remove him between general elections. Finally, little thought had been given to the role of the opposition. Implicitly it was viewed more as a negative than as a positive factor in the conduct of government, no doubt because of the destructive activities of the radical opposition parties in the Weimar era.

We already noted earlier the general context within which Adenauer and Schumacher now attempted to structure the roles of the principle political actors, especially the role relationship between the chancellor and the principal opposition leader. Between 1949 and 1952 the underlying socio-economic and political patterns were emerging only slowly, almost imperceptibly, seeming to provide determined political actors with considerable opportunities to influence the course of their development. Economic recovery still seemed an uncertain matter, with the real upsurge to come later. The ordinary West German consumer had as yet to experience any major and direct economic benefits; unemployment remained high, 9 per cent of the labor force still being unemployed in 1951.[35] Wages, salaries, and pension payments barely increased, in sharp contrast with the rising profits of industrial and commercial enterprises; expanding production was chiefly devoted to capital goods and export items, rather than to housing and consumer goods for the low income groups; taxes fell most heavily on those least able to pay them. With the emergence of an extremely wealthy new business elite, the divergence in income and standards of living became even more pronounced—refugees, one-fourth of the population, having a particularly hard time. Tensions between the new rich and the very poor, between native West Germans and refugees, between the urban and rural sectors, remained very high. German reunification seemed a major political issue as a growing flood of refugees gave evidence of mounting unrest in the Soviet-occupied areas of Germany. The establishment of the German Democratic Republic—simultaneously with that of the German Federal Republic—promised new terror and oppression in East Germany, with the attendant possibility of the rise of a new anti-Communist, radically nationalist movement in West Germany. The establishment of NATO in 1949 in response to presumed Soviet threats of aggression, and the outbreak of the Korean conflict a year later, produced not only new and severe tensions between East and West, but a rising fear in West Germany of another war in Europe. The stability of the late 1950's and early 1960's was still a long way off.

Right up to his death, Schumacher insisted on following with unswerving determination the grand strategic design that he had adopted right after the election. In his public utterances as well as in private conversations with his lieutenants, he made it plain that he could see nothing in the new situation to warrant changing either his strategy or his role as aggressive champion of the working masses. He refused to admit that he might be swimming against the stream, and stressed that all signs pointed to continued economic and political instability. Industrial recovery under Economic Minister Erhard's free market policy was most unlikely, according to his interpretation; and even if massive American aid under the Marshall Plan should boost the economy, social unrest and intense class conflict would continue because the ruling groups in West Germany would never let the masses share the benefits of economic expansion under a capitalist system. As for political developments: the Chancellor was in his seventies and not immortal; moreover, his majority seemed to Schumacher to rest on a brittle alliance of basically hostile groups, and on an electoral fluke that was unlikely to recur if those who had voted for the C.D.U. could be shown that they had been duped.

Schumacher apparently remained hopeful that Adenauer's coalition government would be unable to satisfy the conflicting demands that its various domestic and foreign sponsors pressed on it. He seems to have felt that despite powerful support from "reactionaries" at home and abroad, the aged Chancellor and his party were bound to compromise themselves in the eyes of the voters before long, and that the merciless criticism of the opposition would speed their collapse. His own task in the role of champion of the common man and patriotic defender of the national interest was to show the West German masses that an uncompromised alternative leadership stood ready to guide them to a better future.

Schumacher may have nursed some hopes that the rise of new parties competing with the C.D.U., as well as growing dissension between the left and right wings of the C.D.U., would not only bring the ruling coalition to grief, but perhaps provide him with the opportunity to overcome the constitutional obstacle of the "constructive vote of no-confidence."* He seems to have tried

---

* The most prominent of these new parties were the refugee party, the Bund der Heimatlosen und Entrechteten (B.H.E.), and the right-wing Socialist Reichs party (S.R.P.). The B.H.E. made its first appearance in the Schleswig-Holstein election of July 1950, winning almost a quarter of the votes (more than the C.D.U., but less than the S.P.D.). In the Länder elections of 1951, the S.R.P. won 11 per cent of the votes in Lower Saxony, and 8 per cent in the city-state of Bremen.

to bring public pressure to bear both upon non-socialist deputies in the lower house and upon representatives of certain state governments in the upper house with a view to weakening the parliamentary position of the Adenauer government. More explicitly, however, he relied on winning a series of impressive victories in state elections in the expectation that these would lead to a Social Democratic triumph in another federal election if the Bundestag should be dissolved, or at least by the time of the next regular election in 1953. Now as before, he wanted to mobilize the masses so he might obtain complete power to reconstruct Germany, and to dismantle the economic and political structures erected by the occupation powers and their German collaborators, which, he declared, had no place in a democratic, socialist society. Anything less, it appears, he would not accept.*

Though seven other, if much smaller, parties (including the Communists) also opposed the three-party Adenauer government, Schumacher claimed for himself and the S.P.D. the legitimate right to speak for all Germans whose interests were not properly represented, including those living in the German Democratic Republic. The government, he maintained, represented only a minority, which for the moment had the power to make decisions on behalf of the German people; but the opposition, in representing the public interest, was every bit as important, and as much entitled to respect and attention. The duty of the government was to act in a responsible manner on behalf of all Germans; that of the opposition to prod the government whenever it considered it remiss in its task, and to point out its shortcomings to the voters. The civic duty of an opposition, Schumacher said in his opening address to the Bundestag in September 1949, was not to shield the government, or make its life easier, or share responsibility for actions that it was afraid to take alone; rather, its duty was to compel the government to defend itself constantly against criticism that the opposition was bound to offer on behalf of those Germans whose interests were being neglected. The Social Democrats, he said, were committed to the German people as a whole to prevent the stabilization of political conditions, to prevent the efforts of the ruling groups to restore the social order of the past, and to do their best to keep German politics in a state of flux so that the path would be kept open for future changes. In this sense, he claimed, the Social Democrats were not "merely the negation of the government, but an independent force," and in this spirit they would play the role of the opposition "with the aim that some day the policies of democratic socialism will be supported by a majority in this legislature."[36]

Which of the two, government or opposition, had established the better

---

* Schütz, in Lange, p. 246. As Schütz points out, it is uncertain to what extent Schumacher really believed that he might obtain a dissolution, and to what extent he was putting up this argument merely for the sake of the voters. Some of his remarks in this period seem to indicate that he may have thought that the president could dissolve the chamber on his own (as was possible in the Weimar era), despite the constitutional requirements giving the chancellor a decisive voice in this matter.

record, which was more deserving of support, this was to be the issue before the voter at the next election, Schumacher told his fellow Social Democrats in January 1950. The goal, he said, was to seize, not share, controlling power in the state; to eliminate, not tolerate, the political influence of big industry in the federal government. This was his justification for a strategy of categorical and belligerent opposition: "With any less forceful or firm position, we shall permit Germany's development toward democracy to take the wrong turn and to fall into the abyss."[37] The Adenauer government, he said, was paving the way for a new totalitarian regime because it was the creature of blind and selfish capitalist and reactionary groups; its laissez-faire policies, its neglect of the millions who were destitute and exploited, and its lack of initiative and planless drifting threatened to open the floodgates of discontent for the benefit of the reviving forces of Nazism on the right and "national bolshevism" on the left. These forces, he said, stood waiting in the wings, ready to profit from the present government's failure to give the German people social justice and security or to promote the cause of German reunification.

The opposition was thus said to be the guardian of democracy, and its behavior to be responsible, statesmanlike, and patriotic. According to Schumacher, anti-capitalist and patriotic sentiments, which he had always claimed lay dormant in the German masses, were still waiting to be aroused by a leader and party who knew how to cue them. The great danger, as he saw it, was that this might be the wrong man and the wrong party; the lessons of the past were all too plain.* Only the Social Democrats, he said, stood between an incompetent and stupid capitalist government that was rapidly approaching bankruptcy and the specter of a new totalitarian regime. Not for his own gain or partisan interest, but only for the good of the German people was he fighting his battle against Adenauer and his supporters. "It is a moral and national obligation toward our people," he told a group of Social Democratic leaders in March 1951, "to show those who made such a fateful mistake on August 14, 1949, the true contours and political profiles of the parties so that they may know whose policies will help them and whose hurt them."[38]

By continuing to play his role of Tribune, Schumacher still hoped to attract the support of patriots and anti-clericals, of young idealists and impoverished refugees. His uncompromising opposition to the new ruling elites, he apparently thought, might yet allow him to mobilize the young students and the old pensioners, the intellectuals who were dismayed by the conservative policies of the Adenauer government, and the "proletarians" who needed to be

---

* Not only did Schumacher constantly point to the threat of an upsurge of pro-Communist sentiments in West Germany, but he paid a great deal of attention to the new, if still rather small, extreme right-wing groups such as the S.R.P. He asserted, for example, that Otto Strasser, a former Nazi leader who had broken with Hitler before 1933 and now sought to return to Germany after almost twenty years of exile, was trying to become the leader of a neo-Nazi mass movement.

shown their true "class interests." His speeches in parliament and on the hustings, his writings, and his demonstrations of categorical belligerency toward the government, the occupation powers, and the Communists were addressed to these groups—not to the foreign and German elites that were Adenauer's main concern. This, for him, was the audience that really mattered; this, to his way of thinking, justified his role performance as the opposition leader. These voters were the counter-players toward which his performance was directed, whose expectations he sought to make congruent with his own by asserting the legitimacy of his purpose and the corresponding propriety of his behavior. If he could persuade them to accept his leadership, he would at last realize the goal he had set himself and his party; and he felt, apparently, that his best chance of persuading them was to present himself as the intransigent opponent of those he identified as the enemies of the German people, in particular Konrad Adenauer.

The Duel with Adenauer

The bitter personal antagonism that developed between these two stubborn and strong-willed men provides an excellent example of how such a conflict can influence political developments. Both men perceived this conflict in terms of a battle between two irreconcilable political *Weltanschauungen,* which could end only with the absolute triumph of one or the other view; both did their best to accentuate these differences, and to persuade other political actors to see the battle in this unequivocal light. Those observers who have thought that the situation in postwar Germany required close cooperation between the major political parties have viewed the Schumacher-Adenauer enmity as a great misfortune. Others, looking back upon it in later years, believe that the long-run effect was in fact beneficial because it had a decisive influence on the development of a stable, two-party political system. What seems certain is that the personal duel between the two leaders did much to destroy the rather widespread desire for political unity of the early postwar period, and to deepen the gulf between the major parties of West Germany, a division that was to last for many years after Schumacher's death.

As many observers have pointed out, the two men's radically different backgrounds set them in opposition from the moment they first met in the German Advisory Council of the British zone in 1946. Adenauer, who was nineteen years Schumacher's senior, had grown up in the conservative, upper-middle-class atmosphere of the Roman Catholic stronghold of Cologne. The dominant political figure of his youth was Bismarck. A few years before Adenauer's birth, Bismarck's conflict with the German Roman Catholics had led to the rise of the Center party, and Adenauer early became an active participant in the party's battles against the Protestant Prussian Junkers and the anti-clerical Social Democrats. He came to dislike both the "blue" and the "red" Prussians intensely, and felt a far closer affinity with his coreligionists in Western and Southern Latin Europe than with his compatriots across the Elbe. The world of Berlin and East Germany, young Schumacher's world, was alien to him—an outpost of Western civilization in a Slavic world shaped by Byzantine and Asian despots. The Rhineland, where he grew up and lived his entire life, seemed not to belong to Prussia (which had annexed it after the Napoleonic wars), but to the civilization of Western Europe oriented toward Rome rather than Berlin and Moscow.[39] It was from the East, rather than the West, that the war clouds seemed to come when fighting broke out in 1914. In 1917, when Adenauer was forty-one, he became lord mayor of Cologne, having been prominent in the municipal government of his home town for some years past; he held this position without interruption until the Nazis removed him in 1933.

As a powerful lord mayor and a leading figure in the Center party, Adenauer was prominent in politics when Schumacher was still a novice; on two occasions he was even considered for the chancellorship. His party, though not one of the largest, held a key position, which it exploited to the full by a highly flexible course of action that allied it sometimes with the Social Democrats, sometimes with parties to the right of them. Adenauer belonged to the conservative wing that was reluctant to cooperate with the S.P.D., but he was also opposed to the strong national state advocated by most right-wing parties. In the political wars of the period, he became known as a skillful and agile politician. When the Center party dissolved itself after Hitler came to power and Adenauer was forced to retire, he withdrew to a small village near Cologne to raise roses. There he lived quietly throughout the Nazi era, with the exception of a brief period in 1944, when he was imprisoned following the abortive putsch to overthrow Hitler (in which, however, he had not been involved). The next year, at the age of sixty-nine, he emerged from retirement to resume the mayoralty of Cologne for a short time, and, more important, to become one of the founders of the Christian Democratic Union. Within a year he had become its leader in the British occupation zone, and one of the principal aspirants for the national leadership.

Adenauer's success in welding the diverse elements of the new C.D.U. into a unified movement, and in putting together the coalition that eventually allowed him to form a government, proved that he had lost none of his skill for political maneuvering. He quickly managed to dispose of his rivals for the leadership of his party (largely by playing off various factions against each other), and established his dominance over its regional leaders even before control of the chancellor's office enabled him to become the undisputed chief of the Christian Democrats in form as well as in fact. With equal skill he succeeded in obtaining the support of the Roman Catholic Church and powerful business groups, and the cooperation of the Free Democrats and the German party, in creating his coalition against the Social Democrats. At the same time he managed the difficult feat of pleasing the occupation powers, particularly the French and the Americans, without losing the allegiance of his German supporters. In all these endeavors he showed himself highly adaptable to political circumstances, and quick to shift his tactics when his relationship with other political actors seemed to demand it. His basic strategy, however, remained constant: to obtain power for himself by manipulating various political elements that he was not strong enough to control.

Adenauer, like Schumacher, wanted to obtain the leadership in West Germany so that he might direct the nation's political reconstruction. But whereas Schumacher believed this to be primarily a matter of internal economic reforms by a sovereign German government, Adenauer showed little interest in economic affairs and looked beyond the borders of Germany in his vision of the future. Though Adenauer was not very explicit in spelling out his program, leaving it to political developments to provide him with the opportunities to demonstrate by concrete action what he sought to accomplish, he indicated from the start that he did not share Schumacher's desire for the reestablishment of an independent and unified Germany under a strong central government. Rather, he hoped to see all, or at least the better part, of Germany incorporated into an organic union with the Latin and Roman Catholic countries of continental Western and Southern Europe. He therefore favored close cooperation with Roman Catholic leaders and groups in these countries who professed similar aims, and indicated his willingness to collaborate with foreign governments and leaders who opposed the re-establishment of the old Reich. But, characteristically, he was always prepared to soft-pedal these intentions when immediate tactical considerations seemed to demand it, as, for example, in bidding for the support of domestic groups who did not share his sentiments for Western European union, such as the leaders of the refugee organizations, the Protestant Church, certain business interests, and what remained of the old military elite.

Unlike Schumacher, Adenauer sought to gain power in Germany by negotiations with the leading political actors rather than by constant appeals to the masses; German and foreign leaders were the ones who mattered. Apparently quite ready to risk temporary unpopularity, he showed little concern—to the point of disdain—about mass reactions to a tactical move that he believed really necessary. Except when an electoral campaign compelled him to face the voters, he preferred to stay out of the limelight in maneuvering for dominance first in the C.D.U. and then in the "bourgeois" coalition that gave him the chancellorship by the narrowest of margins. It was only after he became the chief of the new government that he deliberately thrust himself forward as leader of the German people. At the time of his election, an opinion survey showed that only 37 per cent of a representative sample of West German voters could name the new chancellor, while 50 per cent had absolutely no idea who he was.[40]

Here was a man whose background, outlook, and political behavior were radically different from Schumacher's. Both men were more or less authoritarian in their perception of the relationship between leader and masses, but whereas Schumacher's perception of his relationship with those he aspired to lead was charismatic, in the Weberian sense, Adenauer's was traditionalist. Schumacher sought to gain support for himself by playing the role of the Tribune, because he believed he was dealing with a people prone to hero worship, particularly in time of crisis; Adenauer, by contrast, played the role of the stern patriarch who demanded respect rather than love, obedience rather than enthusiasm. Fundamentally, both men were equally inflexible in pursuing their objectives, but whereas Schumacher felt obliged constantly to demonstrate his determination to stand firm, Adenauer sought to achieve his ends by appearing always ready to make tactical concessions if it seemed expedient; he stood firm only when his drive for power seemed directly threatened.

In comparing the political approach of the two men, Machiavelli's distinction between the lion and the fox comes to mind. Schumacher, whose entire political career had been one of opposition, chose to play the lion in postwar German politics. He welcomed conflict, and insisted on rigid adherence to political principles, which, he always insisted, were not up for sale. He despised political "deals" and bargaining, and adopted an all-or-nothing approach. Claiming that there could be no middle ground between absolute opposition and complete power for the Social Democrats, no compromise between a reactionary capitalist society and a democratic socialist one, no choice between subservience to foreign interest and national self-determination, he expressed far more than campaign oratory; he wanted either complete authority to reorganize Germany or no responsibility at all. It was either the "Schumacher course" or a course without Schumacher, he told his fellow Social Democrats in his role as party leader; as patriotic leader he informed the occupation powers that total victory meant total responsibility for Germany's fate until power was turned over to a German government; as leader of the opposition he asserted that the power to govern meant absolute responsibility or complete disregard of the wishes of the people. This either-or, black-or-white dichotomy was fundamental to his entire political style.

Adenauer, by contrast, stressed tactical flexibility. Where Schumacher insisted on a clear-cut yes or no, he was always ready to say "maybe," never seeming to shut the door to an alternative arrangement or a new combination. Rather than meet an obstacle head-on, he preferred to evade or circumvent it, even if it took longer to reach his goal. Rather than let matters come to an open clash, he sought to cooperate with German and foreign leaders whose cooperation he valued, waiting for his opportunity to dismantle an arrangement he disliked, or allowing time to erode it. If Schumacher's weapon was the battering ram, Adenauer's was the rapier.

How did such different counter-players view each other? Adenauer's official biographer later claimed that the Christian Democratic leader "always felt great respect for the uncompromising strength of character of this fanatical man, and ... set great store by Schumacher's judgment."[41] If so, he kept such sentiments well concealed during Schumacher's lifetime. Rather, he indicated that Schumacher represented for him everything he had come to despise: Prussian arrogance, anti-clericalism, radical socialism, and demagogic nationalism. One of his cabinet ministers later attributed Adenauer's hostility to the fact that Schumacher made no effort to hide his contempt for a man who had not suffered under Hitler. Finally, we can imagine the reaction of a man who believed that a good political leader should always keep his emotions under control to a man who, when they met, "spoke with a loud, animated voice, his face twitching with nervous tension and his left hand underlining his words with emphatic gestures."[42]

But Adenauer must have realized that he owed a great deal to Schumacher in furthering his own ambitions, for it would seem that he needed just such an opponent. Without his aggressive opposition and categorical refusal to make concessions, Adenauer might have found it a great deal more difficult to gain recognition in his own party, among other German groups, and with foreign leaders. By focusing his attacks on Adenauer and his supporters, Schumacher helped an initially rather obscure, aged survivor of the Weimar era to make a spectacular comeback. His opposition helped Adenauer to unite the diverse groups around him against the threat of a Social Democratic government. It tended to neutralize differences between conservative business leaders and Christian trade unionists, between Protestants and Roman Catholics, between clericals and anti-clericals, in the alliance that Adenauer forged first within his party, and then with others.[43] It helped him, too, in his relationship with the occupation authorities and other foreign leaders, who came to regard him as exceedingly cooperative in comparison with the Social Democratic leader. Adenauer may have disliked Schumacher as a man, but he probably was most grateful for the part he chose to play as his chief opponent.

As for Schumacher, his intense hostility toward his great rival helped feed the flame of his determination to overcome all obstacles on the road to power, a flame that fanned into an all-consuming white heat during the last three years of his life. Long before the two fought the dramatic duel between chancellor and opposition, he had come to identify Adenauer as his chief opponent in the struggle for power, and to view him with the same mixture of contempt and uncompromising hostility that characterized his attitude toward all those who appeared to him to be illegitimately challenging his claim for leadership. We noted this attitude in his relationship with men he perceived as his rivals in the Social Democratic party, and in his dealings with the military governors; in the case of Adenauer, it was greatly intensified by the undeniable success of the challenge, a success achieved by methods that Schumacher considered highly immoral and despicably devious. This contempt for Adenauer was so great that according to many of Schumacher's associates, it blinded him to the Christian Democratic leader's political ability, and led him to overestimate the potential opposition against him among the German masses.

To Schumacher, Adenauer represented the very worst aspects of the supposedly thoroughly discredited reactionary elements in the nation who had done little or nothing to oppose Hitler, and who now sought to stage a comeback by opportunistically collaborating with the Western "capitalist" powers and exploiting the division of Germany. He associated him with the separatists who in the early days of the Weimar Republic had collaborated with the French, and with the discredited anti-socialist leaders who, it seemed to him, had helped destroy the Republic and bring Hitler to power. He saw him now as the stooge of the Western powers and of an unholy alliance between German and foreign reactionaries, as an opportunist hypocrite, without patriotism or moral integrity, who sought by devious methods to obtain a position for which Schumacher considered himself, both intellectually and morally, much better qualified. He looked upon Adenauer as a sly but superannuated municipal administrator whose traditionalist and conservative parochial outlook and intellectual limitations made it impossible for him to see beyond the realm of petty political intrigue, or to comprehend the larger historical forces that for Schumacher determined the course of German and world developments. He felt that Adenauer lacked the vision, the ability, and the dedication that were absolutely essential for the man who was to guide Germany in this period of crisis. He despised him as a man who had demonstrated his love for Germany neither on the battlefield nor in the concentration camp, but had sat out both wars in comfort and managed to coexist with a totalitarian regime that left him in peace to tend his garden on the Rhine. More shame and less arrogance, the former concentrationnaire repeatedly proclaimed, were qualities that he looked for in vain in a *Mitläufer* of the Nazis who had no legitimate right to lay claim to leadership in Germany.[44]

According to Schumacher's associates, he realized that "objectively," from a Marxist point of view, Adenauer was no more than an instrument of larger social and economic forces. Schumacher's Marxism, however, was not sufficiently orthodox to allow him to take the proper "scientific," impersonal view; besides, his personal involvement in the battle was too great. His propensity to reduce political controversy to the level of individual conflict was here reinforced by the image of a successful opponent who represented for him not merely the forces of reaction, but a personal enemy whom he hated with increasing passion. Schumacher seemed to realize that Adenauer was his superior as a tactician. Cold and dispassionate even at the height of controversy, Adenauer invariably managed to provoke him into angry public outbursts that Schumacher himself later recognized as grave tactical mistakes. To proclaim in public what he thought and said in private was certainly honest, but Schumacher knew that it made him appear intemperate and impetuous in comparison with his opponent. But he apparently found it insufferable that a man he considered utterly cynical and untrustworthy should be trusted by Germans and foreign leaders when he, Schumacher, found difficulty in obtaining their trust. His tendency to speak his mind and react vigorously to provocation and unfair behavior, he felt, was being exploited by Adenauer so that he should appear in false light before the public. But he could not resist the urge to hit back when he believed he had been dealt another unfair blow by a rival he considered so far beneath himself. Schumacher may have found such outbursts emotionally satisfying insofar as they relieved inner tensions, but he must have realized that his behavior was dysfunctional in terms of his efforts to gain the trust of the German people. Perhaps he secretly envied Adenauer's tactical skill and self-control, especially since he was convinced that his was the better cause and he the better man to lead the country. But he believed that his role as aggressive defender of national and working-class interests nonetheless demanded and justified his belligerency toward Adenauer, and that his own display of integrity and courage would lead the German people to repudiate the false prophet they were following.

Schumacher's conflict with Adenauer began at about the time that his battle with Grotewohl ended. As leaders of the two main parties in the British zone, they met in March 1946 in the Advisory Council, to which the military government had appointed a number of prominent German political figures. According to one of Adenauer's associates in the Council, Schumacher already told Adenauer on this occasion that cooperation between the two parties was possible only if the C.D.U. accepted Social Democratic leadership. "Every objective observer will admit," Schumacher is supposed to have said, "that the S.P.D. is the largest party with the greatest future, and that it will remain so."[45] Adenauer reportedly did not agree, and the two men went their separate ways.

At first, however, Adenauer was careful to avoid saying openly that he, too, would cooperate only on his own terms. Rather, he asserted frequently that he thought the two parties should work together in the difficult task of reconstruction.[46] But at the same time he persuaded the C.D.U. leadership in the British zone to forbid lower party units from entering into election alliances with either the Communists or the Social Democrats, while permitting them to do so under certain circumstances with anti-socialist parties.[47] In terms of Schumacher's strategy to polarize political forces, this was not necessarily an unwelcome development, but he nonetheless attacked Adenauer for attempting to crush left-wingers in the C.D.U. who sympathized with certain Social Democratic aims. He also denounced him for attempting to pin a collaborationist label on the S.P.D., for lack of courage in criticizing the occupation powers, and for his attempt to block socialization in the British zone.

As we have seen, in the summer of 1947 Adenauer's tactical skill and Schumacher's intransigence led to the alliance between the Christian Democrats, the Free Democrats, and the small German party in the Frankfurt Economic Council, with the S.P.D. assuming the part of the principal opposition. A year later the 72-year-old Adenauer emerged as the leader of this coalition in the capacity of President of the Parliamentary Council in Bonn, in which position he repeatedly clashed with the Social Democrats, who were being directed by Schumacher from his sickbed in Hannover. Adenauer was careful to conduct his maneuvers out of the public view, and repeatedly switched his stand—particularly on the issue of federalism—in order to accommodate himself to Western Allied wishes on the one hand, and those of his party and the coalition he sought to unify on the other. Schumacher sought unsuccessfully to exploit Adenauer's vacillation by claiming that his behind-the-scenes collaboration with the Allies showed him to be not only an opportunist, but an untrustworthy spokesman for the German people and their representatives in the Parliamentary Council.* He pursued this theme in the 1949 election campaign, again with no success. When he entered the Bundestag as leader of the opposition, he was convinced that the removal of the new chancellor was essential. Adenauer appeared to him as much "the man in the way" with regard to the realization of his own aspirations as he himself was for the Western powers.

For calling Adenauer "the Chancellor of the Allies" in a stormy all-night session of the Bundestag in September 1949, Schumacher became the first deputy to be formally excluded for a time. The incident established the hostile atmosphere that characterized the next two years. With their troops solidly aligned behind them, the two men dominated political life inside and outside parliament. Dissident members of both the ruling coalition and the opposition party were whipped into line in the name of solidarity against the opponent. In both camps, state and local leaders who still wanted to cooperate found it in-

* Thus Schumacher held that Adenauer had deliberately misinterpreted the explicit agreement of the parties in the Council to bar Allied intervention in their deliberations, when, in December 1948, he requested the Western military governors to adjudicate certain differences among the delegates. Schumacher suspected that Adenauer hoped that the military governors would rule in favor of the Christian Democrats on issues in which they were in a minority. A similar "crisis of confidence" occurred in March and April of 1949, when Adenauer tried to induce the Council to accept Allied proposals on the distribution of financial powers between the states and the federal government in the future Federal Republic, proposals that were opposed by a majority in the Council. Schumacher believed, as we have seen, that his categorical opposition induced the Allies to give way, thoroughly discrediting Adenauer and boosting his own stock with the voters.

creasingly difficult to do so in the face of a conflict that their national leadership sought to impose upon their parties at even the lowest level of the polity. Both chancellor and opposition leader wanted to focus public attention on their conflict, and to exclude any appearance of the slightest concession or compromise.

As time went on, it became clear that the occupant of the chancellor's office had considerable tactical advantages over the opposition leader. Adenauer staffed his administration with members of the coalition parties and old-guard civil servants who shared his own conservative orientation. With the exception of a few so-called *Konzessions-Sozis* (Social Democrats who were given positions as a gesture toward national unity), most of the top federal administrators were men selected as much for their loyalty to the government as for their technical skills. Ties based on shared experiences, common social background, and similar values bound them to the parties and interest groups who supported the government. As a result, the opposition was almost entirely cut off from access to and information about the executive branch, except when and where it suited the Chancellor.

Although Adenauer would occasionally "consult" with Schumacher (apparently on the urging of the Allied High Commissioners), and periodically "inform" him personally or in a letter about certain of his policies, neither man seems to have found these contacts particularly productive. Schumacher constantly complained that the government did not consult the opposition on policy-making, but when he met Adenauer privately, he usually came away with the impression that he had been told nothing but platitudes.* Both in their meetings and in their exchanges of letters, the two leaders apparently spoke at each other, rather than with each other, restating more or less irreconcilable positions they had already taken or intended to take in public.[48] There appeared to be no bases or desire for agreement; the dialogue was largely confined to direct or indirect hostile exchanges in the Bundestag, in the mass media, and at public meetings. It is doubtful whether Schumacher really thought he could influence the Chancellor's policies, as he claimed was his intention, or for that matter whether he really tried. Both men distrusted each other far too much to confide in one another, or to come to any agreement on the "national interest." Schumacher, in particular, seems always to have feared that Adenauer would trap him in private conversations into taking a position that could be used against him, and he apparently avoided meeting him in the absence of witnesses.

Excluded from the decision-making process and compelled to leave the political initiative to the head of government, Schumacher and his party could

---

* Schumacher's appointments calendar indicates fewer and fewer of such meetings. Whereas the two men appear to have met for private talks 12 times in the period from September to December 1949, in all of 1950 only 14 meetings were noted, and only 7 in 1951. (There were apparently no meetings after Schumacher's stroke in December 1951.)

criticize only whatever issues Adenauer cared to bring before parliament. And these, they felt, were all too few. Again and again Schumacher and his followers charged that Adenauer was deliberately withholding vital information, and was violating his constitutional duty to keep both houses of parliament informed about affairs of state, particularly on the conduct of negotiations with the Western allies. As Schumacher said in the Bundestag in June 1950: "I believe that a man who tries to use the instrument of parliamentary democracy needs to have a better understanding of how the functions between government and opposition are divided."[49] The only course for the opposition, in Schumacher's opinion, was to reject every major measure on which the opposition had not been properly consulted (which meant the budget as well as every major foreign policy agreement), and to repudiate as unconstitutional every "executive agreement" with the Western powers that the Chancellor did not present to parliament, such as the Petersberg Agreement in 1949 and the Saar Agreement in 1950. The main issue was not the formal constitutional question of the power of parliament and the rights of the opposition, since the framers of the constitution had hardly entered into the question of the status of the opposition; rather, it was Adenauer's structuring of the chancellor's role, and with it that of the opposition leader.

Champion of the National Interest

Schumacher, sitting way beneath the government bench in the Bundestag like a student in school, had now to learn from Adenauer what could be done with the great authority that the Basic Law had vested in the chancellor. Adenauer showed no compunction to use this power to the full, regardless of the opposition's criticism, since he was confident that his majority would keep him in office at least until the next regular election in 1953. In the area of foreign affairs, which very soon became the chief source of controversy between government and opposition, his authority was vast because undefined. The Allied powers gradually granted the federal government legal authority to conduct its own foreign policy, and thus the de facto administration of this important matter was successfully claimed by the Chancellor under a very vaguely defined mandate. He and his personal assistants, rather than any minister responsible to parliament, negotiated the important foreign-policy agreements that were made in these years, leaving the opposition leader only the freedom to appeal to the public to repudiate the government at the next election. This risk Adenauer was perfectly willing to take.

Thus, whereas the government majority and the opposition cooperated on a number of minor and uncontroversial domestic matters, with the notable exception of the Codetermination Law of 1951* they collaborated on hardly

---

* For a discussion of this law, see p. 254 below.

any issue that was of political importance.[50] To some observers, particularly in the American High Commission, this seemed to augur well for the development of German democracy.[51] To Schumacher, however, the way Adenauer was playing the game was neither in the spirit of parliamentary democracy nor likely to further its development. The Chancellor's policies, he said, and the manner in which they were executed in defiance of the will of the German people and their elected representatives, were threatening to take Germany back to a totalitarian regime by the well-trodden road of the authoritarian state. "We have already outdone the authoritarian state of William II," he said near the end of his life, "and the parallels with the Austrian corporate state of 1934 are increasing. This is how fascism in Europe has in each case begun."[52] Under Adenauer, he said, gross incompetence was wedded to irresponsible power, just as it had been under Brüning, Papen, and Schleicher, the last chancellors of the Weimar Republic. He claimed that an arrogant bureaucracy and undemocratic judiciary, most of whose leading members were said to have served Hitler loyally, were once again ignoring their duty to people and state, and that reactionary clericalism and capitalism were having a field day at the expense of the masses under a chancellor who was selling out the national interests to the lowest foreign bidder.

Although much of this was probably political oratory, Schumacher clearly did believe that it was his duty as a German patriot and democratic socialist to block the pernicious forces of reaction that Adenauer was resurrecting. He evidently had come to identify himself so closely with his role of Tribune that he believed that his stand transcended any personal motives, and that it was his duty to persevere in his uncompromising battle against Adenauer, no matter what might happen to his health or at the next election. Retreat he could not and would not. Unable to affect the present, he kept his eyes on the future —if not his own, then that of Germany. "Remember just one thing," he told his colleagues: "politics concern not merely the present, but also the morrow and what comes after."[53]

It has puzzled some observers that a party which in the days before Schumacher's leadership had made domestic affairs its particular concern should now have allowed foreign policy to become so important. The answer seems to be that the S.P.D. had little choice once it had accepted Schumacher's strategy of categorical opposition to the Adenauer government. The Social Democrats had apparently hoped to wage their battle on social and economic issues, particularly the latter, but international developments and the Chancellor's ability to choose the battleground compelled them to focus on matters relating to West and East Germany's relations with foreign powers.*

---

* In the program for the opposition that Schumacher had presented to the S.P.D. executive committee at Bad Dürkheim, domestic issues definitely took precedence over foreign policy matters, in line with his tactics preceding the election of 1949. Most of the 16 points that were then enumer-

Neither Adenauer nor Schumacher wanted to appear responsible for op-posing domestic measures that were demanded by important sections of the public—for example, home construction, equalization of economic burdens, and codetermination for the workers in the iron and steel industries. Conse-quently, Social Democrats and Christian Democrats united a number of times against some of the minor parties in passing domestic legislation, each side subsequently trying to obtain the credit for itself. Despite Adenauer's con-servative orientation on matters of social and economic reform, he was ob-viously determined not to permit Schumacher to use the people's social and economic distress against him. He led his party in embracing trade union and refugee demands, asserting that the Christian Democrats had no desire to neglect essential reforms for the sake of partisan controversy. As relations be-tween the two leaders became increasingly bitter, Adenauer and his followers managed to maneuver the Social Democrats into opposing measures that were obviously popular, largely because Schumacher had committed the S.P.D. to a role of categorical opposition.

To justify their behavior, Schumacher and his supporters maintained that foreign policy issues and major domestic issues had become inseparable: both were now determined by factors outside Germany. Adenauer and the Western powers linked the future development of the Federal Republic and German reunification to intimate association between West Germany and the Western powers; full sovereignty, economic recovery, and permanent security against Soviet aggression were said to depend on close and loyal cooperation between the Federal Republic and the West; reunification was said to demand that West Germany become so strong that the areas under Soviet control would sooner or later be drawn into the Federal Republic.

Schumacher's counter-argument held that the only real chance for reunifi-cation lay in keeping the Federal Republic entirely free from entangling com-mitments to the Western powers, and in concentrating on domestic socio-economic and political reforms that would make it difficult for the Soviet Union to resist East German demands for joining a well-developed West German democratic society. Adenauer's enthusiastic acceptance of American leadership, he said, as well as his efforts to cooperate closely with "Christian" conservative parties in Latin Europe against the "threat of Bolshevism," gravely endangered the chances of reunification, and denied Germans the

---

ated as the basis of Social Democratic policy dealt with demands for extensive social and economic reforms, ranging from public ownership of basic industries and economic planning to immediate improvements in housing, social security, and economic welfare for the masses. Only three points related in any sense to relations with other nations: the Social Democratic demand for the inclusion of Berlin in the Federal Republic, which the occupation powers opposed; the demand for the abolition of the remaining vestiges of Western control in the Federal Republic; and Social Demo-cratic opposition to the claims of Russia and Poland to the territories of the old Reich beyond the Oder-Neisse line and French claims to the Saar.

right to make full use of their resources and opportunities to further their national interests. Adenauer asserted that it was above all necessary to earn the trust and confidence of the Western powers if West Germany was to be rehabilitated and escape the fate of East Germany; reunification took a secondary place in his program. The Social Democrats, by contrast, argued that such policies resulted in abject collaboration at the expense of the German nation. Instead of striving to meet every Western demand to the point of anticipating the wishes of the occupation powers (as Adenauer was alleged to do), a patriotic German leader should take full advantage of the international situation by fighting for German interests, and by making no concessions that were not clearly in those interests. According to Schumacher, the Western powers needed German friendship at least as much as the Germans needed Western military protection and economic assistance, and therefore there was no need to rush into signing every piece of paper they presented; a chancellor who failed to see this was unfit to represent the German people.

It was for this reason that Schumacher called Adenauer "the Chancellor of the Allies" when he accepted the Petersberg Agreement in November 1949.* He charged that by signing, without even consulting parliament or the opposition, Adenauer had concluded a deal between German and Western big business interests at the expense of the German "working people." According to Schumacher, he had given away a major bargaining weapon by accepting international control over the Ruhr, supposedly the last important ace in the hands of the German people, without even trying to fight for maximum concessions in return.

In shifting from attacks on the social and economic policies of the Adenauer government to denouncing its foreign policy, the Social Democrats stressed two principal arguments—with increasing emphasis on the second.† The first was that Adenauer's policies sought to place West Germany under the control of a reactionary international coalition—variously described as under American or French leadership—between the Roman Catholic Church and Western industrialists. This, it was argued, not only threatened the establishment of a truly democratic (i.e. socialist) Germany, but would revive strong authoritarian, anti-capitalist, and radical nationalist sentiments. This was the princi-

---

* This agreement between the Chancellor and the three Western High Commissioners went a long way toward satisfying Social Democratic demands for an end to the dismantling of German industries, but it also provided that in return the Federal Republic would participate in an international authority that was to allocate the industrial resources of the Ruhr among German and foreign customers, and set the pattern for closer economic coordination between West Germany and the rest of Western continental Europe.

† This shift in emphasis from domestic to foreign policy issues can be traced by the dominant themes in Schumacher's speeches: until about the middle of 1950, internal social and economic developments were the principal focus of his remarks; thereafter foreign relations became his chief concern. See Appendix C.

pal argument advanced in 1949–50 against the Petersberg Agreement, against Adenauer's decision to take the Federal Republic into the Council of Europe, and against his enthusiastic acceptance of Robert Schuman's proposal for a European Coal and Steel Community. The second major argument, which became increasingly important as Adenauer pushed through his policy of European integration and military collaboration with the West, went beyond the alleged impact of his foreign policy on internal developments in the Federal Republic. According to this argument, not only was the Chancellor surrendering vital German resources to foreign control in order to sustain himself in power with Western help, but his policies were seriously endangering the chances for German reunification.

Schumacher, as we noted in previous chapters, claimed to favor international friendship and European unity at least as much as Adenauer, but disapproved of the Chancellor's methods of getting it. He argued that reunification had to be the first and foremost goal of a truly "German" foreign policy, even at the risk of offending the Western powers. He pointed out that according to the Basic Law the Federal government was only a "provisional" structure, and therefore its principal goal had to be reunification. Any policy that sought to establish West Germany as a permanent state or transform it into a military bastion of the West was in direct conflict with this goal, since it would make the "liberation" of the East Germans far more difficult, perhaps impossible. Accordingly, the Federal government, as the representative of both West and East Germans, was morally and legally obligated to keep the situation fluid, and to explore and exploit every opportunity that might further this supreme goal of the German people. To accept the *de facto* annexation of the Saar by France and to offer German troops to the Americans were said to be actions that ran directly contrary to these mandatory objectives of a genuine "German" foreign policy. The West German government could claim to be the "legitimate" spokesman of the German people, Schumacher declared in a radio broadcast in August 1951, only if it acted at all times as the temporary representative of the whole of Germany; the Adenauer government's failure to obey this mandate deprived it of legitimacy.[54] A government that committed the people of West Germany to make a military contribution to a European Defense Community, he said in May 1952 when Adenauer was preparing to sign the E.D.C. Treaty, forfeited the right to call itself a German government.[55]

This shift in the role of the Tribune from champion of the working people to champion of the national interests of all Germans was probably the product of a complex mixture of personal sentiments, Social Democratic values, and tactical considerations. Whatever its causes, it made Schumacher's actions in these last years appear to many observers not nearly so consistent and logical as they seemed to him.

The party, however, was behind Schumacher. Many of his deputies were, like him, natives of East Germany and Berlin, and longed to see these areas reunited with the Western sections—not only because of personal attachments, but because they believed that this would bring them to power. For reasons they considered inimical to the establishment of a united and socialist Germany, and by methods they found despicably devious, Adenauer appeared to them to be doing his best to prevent this. Thus, the more successful the Chancellor was, the more outraged the Social Democrats became, and the more determined to overthrow him. If we add to these sentiments Schumacher's personal hostility toward Adenauer and his personal determination to defeat him, we may see why the opposition leader's choice of role behavior was so satisfying to both him and his supporters.

On tactical grounds, the shift from a predominantly class-oriented struggle to a more explicitly patriotic appeal was virtually mandatory in terms of Schumacher's strategy to mobilize mass support. This strategy, it will be recalled, demanded that the Social Democrats demonstrate at all times their unwavering, categorical opposition to any course chosen by the Chancellor. Since Adenauer and the Western powers had made foreign policy the key issue in the conflict, the opposition had to accept this choice of battleground. Its expectation, apparently, was that it would be able to stimulate and exploit West German resentment against Adenauer's collaboration with the Western powers. Schumacher seems to have hoped that as Tribune of the German people he might succeed in rallying neutralist, pacifist, patriotic, and anti-authoritarian sentiments in West Germany behind him. This became particularly evident in the battle over West German rearmament.

The Battle Over Rearmament

"Schumacher thinks his turn has come," wrote a German journalist when the rearmament issue suddenly came to the fore in the fall of 1950.[56] The strong public reaction against Adenauer's agreement with the Western powers to provide German soldiers for N.A.T.O. seemed to confirm Schumacher's expectation that the electoral verdict of the previous year might be reversed. As long as there had seemed to be complete agreement among German and Western leaders that West Germany should remain disarmed indefinitely, the matter had not offered itself as an issue.[57] All this changed dramatically when it became known that Adenauer had not only acquiesced in American demands, but anticipated them by secretly initiating an offer to provide German troops.

Poll results showed that mass opinion in West Germany emphatically rejected rearmament. Opposition to it increased from 45 per cent in the fall of 1950 to 50 per cent in 1951; only 22–26 per cent of those questioned in various surveys approved. According to a survey of the U.S. High Commission in

January 1951, 46 per cent of the respondents thought it would be better to "try to unite with East Germany, and as a neutral nation . . . keep out of conflicts between East and West." Although the more affluent favored rearmament, the low-income groups overwhelmingly opposed it, as did most Protestants.[58] Other surveys showed that general support for Adenauer's policies and for his party had dropped drastically; the S.P.D. was suddenly the most popular party, supported in 1951 by between 36 and 38 per cent of respondents.[59] The Social Democrats made important gains in the state diet elections of November 1950 in Hesse and Württemberg, and for the first time in history achieved a plurality in Bavaria, formerly a stronghold of the Christian Social Union. According to a study made by the U.S. High Commission in the spring of 1951, a redistribution of Bundestag seats on the bases of these elections would have resulted in a drastic reversal of the position of the two major parties, with 150–55 of the 402 seats going to the S.P.D., and only 130 to the C.D.U.[60]

Schumacher demanded immediate new federal elections. The mandate of 1949 had been invalidated by Adenauer's action, he claimed, and the government had lost the confidence of an overwhelming proportion of the electorate. The state election results, he said, showed that dissatisfaction with the government was reaching boiling point, that the people were realizing at last that "the way the Federal Republic is at present governed is impossible."[61] In the Bundestag and at mass rallies, in broadsides and in the press, he and his supporters demanded that the voters be immediately allowed to express their opinion of the Chancellor's rearmament policies. In a state that was supposed to be a democracy, the people should have the chance to determine their fate, rather than have it decided for them. If Schumacher really expected Adenauer to yield, his hopes were quickly quashed. Adenauer made it clear that no matter what the temper of mass opinion, he had no intention of resigning or agreeing to new elections, and he was supported in his stand by a majority in the Bundestag. This left Schumacher no choice but to try to sustain the momentum of popular resentment through the various state diet elections up to the next regular federal election in 1953.

On this issue, as on others, Schumacher's aim was to demonstrate his categorical opposition to the Adenauer policies, rather than to make out a case for pacifism. Although he had repeatedly expressed his opposition to the reestablishment of an army under the control of the old "reactionary" military elite, he had not rejected the idea of rearmament out of hand. He would not allow "a single German proletarian" to sacrifice his life for a foreign power, he said in 1946;[62] but even before the armament issue became relevant, he and other S.P.D. leaders had indicated that the S.P.D. might agree to the participation of a sovereign German state in some sort of collective security arrangement in which their country would be accepted as an equal.[63] He declared that it was the duty of all Germans, particularly the workers, to defend their country and their liberty; but, as he had told the party congress in May 1950, it was also their right to receive assurances that Germany would be spared renewed destruction and "senseless sacrifices."[64] He now maintained that if sacrifices were to be required, the German people had to be given firm guarantees that they would be fighting to save their own country, not other countries, from destruction; and it was the responsibility of the Chancellor and the Western Allies to provide such guarantees.

Schumacher's arguments against rearmament—at least in the form proposed by Adenauer and the Western powers—were many. He objected to the reestablishment of military forces under the control of the old military elite; he rejected the proposed inclusion of German contingents in a European army under N.A.T.O. command as denying equality to the Germans; he declared that West Germany needed adequate defenses against Soviet attack, but that it would provide its own soldiers only if the Western powers gave assurances that they were prepared to take the same risks and make the same sacrifices in case of war as the Germans. He demanded massive Western reinforcements to guarantee that the first and decisive battle would be fought on the Federal Republic's eastern borders, and that the country would not be left to face total destruction by a Western retreat across the Rhine.

All told, his position was by no means clear. Perhaps he did not want it to be, and perhaps his feelings were in any case mixed. For one thing, he was trying to reconcile the interests of rather divergent groups—neutralists, pacifists, ex-generals, and anti-militarists, for example. But this hardly explains the ambiguity in his proposal to defend West Germany in case of war by a massive attack to which the East Germans would fall victim along with the Russians. For another, he seems to have found it difficult to reconcile his determination to oppose Adenauer's policies at any cost with his apparent wish to have an active part in formulating plans for West Germany's defense and in developing the new German forces. One of his associates was later to recall that efforts to make Schumacher face the contradictions in his arguments were quite in vain. He either would not or could not acknowledge them.

It is practically impossible to determine Schumacher's actual position on rearmament in view of the many different objections he raised. To many, including some of his own supporters, his demand for massive Western reinforcements seemed a red herring in light of the United States' heavy military commitments in Korea and elsewhere, and the evident unwillingness of other Western powers to meet such demands. After all, he had nothing to lose, and possibly a good deal to gain, by raising conditions that might seem reasonable enough to many Germans but were bound to be rejected by Adenauer and the Allies. This would have been a tactic consistent with his strategy against Adenauer, in this case designed to attract the many young West Germans who opposed rearmament. Such a tactic might have been intended to identify Adenauer even more closely with abject capitulation to the Western powers, while the Tribune of the German people remained unsullied by the kind of concessions to foreign demands that Schumacher believed had contributed to the downfall of the Weimar S.P.D. Publicly, at least, he rejected all suggestions that the Social Democrats take part in formulating plans for rearmament on the grounds that there could be no "collaboration on capitulation."[65]

Some observers, including apparently American High Commissioner Mc-Cloy, believed that Schumacher was reconciled to rearmament but wanted to compel Adenauer to exact the highest possible price for it from the West. The difference between Chancellor and opposition leader on this issue, it seemed to them, was one of degree, not kind, tactical, not fundamental. "The choice between Schumacher and Adenauer is a choice between two different defense ministers," asserted one German journalist.[66] Schumacher said that his opposition to rearmament "under present conditions" was motivated neither by neutralist nor by pacifist sentiments. His notes and letters dealing with the issue indicate that he believed himself to be playing a positive role, since he saw his demands as serving to strengthen the German bargaining power in negotiations with the West. There were obvious difficulties and differences, he wrote to Sir Ivon Kirkpatrick, the British High Commissioner, in November 1950, but good will on both sides should lead to successful negotiations.

Although publicly Schumacher refused to assume any responsibility for the government's policy, he was ready to meet frequently with Adenauer's military advisers to discuss armament questions and argue his proposals.[67] His arguments seemed reasonable enough, and in certain respects quite close to those of former members of the old military elite. He evidently entered into these discussions with keen interest, and displayed a familiarity with military details that impressed and surprised his conversation partners.* In short, there seemed to be some reason for believing that he would accept rearmament if at least some of his conditions were met—particularly his insistence on equal status for West Germany in an international military organization and his demand for a "democratic" defense establishment.† Perhaps he would have if he had become Adenauer's successor; but as opposition leader he remained adamantly opposed to the proposed European Defense Community. In May 1952, when the E.D.C. treaty was about to be signed, he declared categorically that he would repudiate it should he become chancellor.

---

* One of Adenauer's military advisers reportedly remarked after one such meeting that Schumacher would have made an excellent general staff officer.

† After all, he had bitterly opposed Adenauer on the question of membership in the Council of Europe, but had later permitted his party to be represented. Perhaps in this case, too, some observers felt, he would reconcile himself to the situation, and agree to having Germans serve in the proposed European army.

In conversations with his associates, and with visitors from abroad who tried to persuade him to change his position, Schumacher always insisted that he could not accept rearmament because it would destroy all hopes for reunification. He asserted that the Soviet Union might yet agree to some sort of arrangement that would allow East Germany to rejoin West Germany, and that therefore everything should be done to induce the Russians to explore such a possibility, and absolutely nothing to discourage them. To raise the question of West German rearmament was one thing—perhaps even a useful bargaining point—but to put it into effect was quite another. He may have been encouraged by various Russian and Russian-inspired statements at this time to believe that the Soviet leaders were sufficiently concerned about the prospect of a rearmed West Germany in N.A.T.O. to consider the establishment of a neutral, reunited Germany.

On the other hand, Schumacher made it clear that he opposed any measure that would permanently associate the Federal Republic with the Western Alliance and a European Community stopping at the Elbe. There seemed no room in such arrangements for German reunification, and he insisted that therefore he could not accept them.

In terms also of Schumacher's battle against the return of "reactionary" groups, rearmament was undesirable: it threatened to restore to positions of influence members of the old military elite. With the past authoritarian attitude of the German officer corps only too clearly in mind, he and apparently most Social Democrats feared that Adenauer's allegedly incompetent rule, together with American pressure for speedy rearmament, would enable a new military elite to unite with the other reactionary forces once again to stifle German democracy.

Finally, Schumacher appears to have become increasingly adamant in his stand as he endeavored to remain consistent in his relationship with Adenauer, a consistency that he required both to satisfy his own needs and to live up to his role as Tribune of the German people. Much as he may have enjoyed playing the military expert in discussions with Adenauer's advisers, he was apparently constantly afraid that the Chancellor would trap him into appearing to go along with his plans. As we noted, he deeply distrusted Adenauer, and he seems to have leaned over backward to dissociate himself from his policies. Moreover, his perception of his role demanded that he remain consistent in his behavior as the unyielding opposition leader. With public sentiment running high against rearmament, he could not afford to give an inch to a chancellor who seemed indifferent to the will of the people, but all too eager to please his Western friends.

As his associates recalled later, Schumacher's moods in his three-year battle to displace Adenauer alternated between feelings of bitter frustration and savage determination to defeat his rival. He clung to the belief that somehow or other he would achieve this goal, new obstacles notwithstanding. After his stroke in December 1951, he would not admit to anyone—probably not even to himself—that he had reached the end of his physical resources. His profound belief in his personal mission would not allow him to withdraw from the battle even now; he struggled on against partial paralysis and aphasia to force his body to submit to the psychological imperatives of his drive for power. "If he lives long enough," wrote an American journalist who interviewed him shortly before his death, "he will be the Chancellor of Germany in . . . 1953."[68] The statement may well have represented Schumacher's personal view; his death in August 1952 spared him the blow of Adenauer's great triumph in the 1953 elections.

The Champion of the Common Man: An Assessment

It is now apparent—as it was not at the time (either to Schumacher or to most of his contemporaries)—that the society which emerged in West Germany after the collapse of the totalitarian system was radically different from that which had provided the Social Democratic leader with his frame of reference for choosing and assigning political roles. Not only had the collapse of the Nazi regime created the need for new norms and new structures, but those of the pre-Nazi era had become largely irrelevant. As a result of extensive geographic and social shifts in the German population, many of the regional and class differences that had sustained political alignments before 1933 were no longer particularly significant. A society long dominated by an alliance between Prussian aristocrats and conservative industrialists collapsed; the Nazis and the war had initiated the destruction of the old order, and the dissolution of Prussia, the division of Germany, and other actions of the victor powers completed it. Cut off from the old Prussian areas in Eastern and Central Germany, and deprived of Berlin as a political focal point, West Germany gave birth to a society that had only the vaguest resemblance to the society in which Schumacher had received his political training. What emerged was a transitional society with new structures, new norms, and a few symbolic ties to the past to give a little stability amidst all the change. In what has been called Germany's "second industrial revolution," economic chaos was succeeded by a rapid process of modernization, which was set in motion by extensive American financial aid and the governing coalition's economic policies. In 1949, if not before, the West Germans emerged from the anomie of the beginning phase of this transitional process to embrace the norms of a new, pluralistic, and achievement-oriented society, dominated by a coalition between the survivors of some of the old elites and the new-rich beneficiaries of economic recovery.[69]

How much could Schumacher, or for that matter any other Social Democratic leader, have accomplished under the circumstances? Some have argued that under prevailing conditions Schumacher's aspirations were doomed from the start. "Left to their own devices the German people would undoubtedly have chosen social democracy as their main political belief," claimed an American observer in 1950, reflecting a popular view among German Social Democrats.[70] In other words, it was felt that factors entirely beyond the control of the S.P.D. leadership, particularly international developments, had interfered decisively against the cause.

There is no doubt that the conditions under which Schumacher labored were far from ideal. As we have already noted, he was hampered by the fact that the traditional centers of Social Democratic strength in Central Germany and Berlin could not give him their support, by the opposition of important German as well as foreign leaders who regarded a Social Democratic national government as a threat to their vital interests, and so on. Yet these situational factors cannot, by themselves, explain Schumacher's failure. It seems to me that he himself contributed significantly to the frustration of his aspirations— at least in West Germany—by the manner in which he sought to realize them. Not only was the context in which he tried to play the militant champion of the working masses unsuited to the performance of this role, but it provided severe political sanctions for the actor who insisted on playing the part. In this instance, as in his decision to play the patriotic leader in his relationship with the occupation authorities, his role choice was based on a seriously disoriented perception of political reality. His evaluation of various situations, his definition and assignment of roles, and his own political responses resulted in an increasing incongruence between his perceptions and expectations and those of his relevant counter-players. Faced with highly dynamic political developments, he appeared unable to adjust his outlook and actions accordingly.

Schumacher's performance in the role of champion of the masses did not correspond with the behavior that most West Germans seem to have expected of a leader they were prepared to entrust with authoritative decision-making power. The masses he wanted to mobilize remained unmoved or reacted negatively to his performance; potential supporters were put off rather than attracted by his actions; and his opponents were aroused to unite against him rather than being intimidated by his behavior. In fact, it seems that his leadership of the S.P.D. reinforced the widespread impression that the Social Democrats were not qualified to govern the country. Even many of those who respected him, and admired his intellect, courage, and firmly held convictions, seem to have come to the conclusion that he was unqualified for leadership. Since this appraisal may seem severe (though it is in no sense to be taken as a moral judgment), it seems advisable to pursue it further. First, therefore, let us examine his efforts to mobilize the masses, and then his tactics toward certain elite elements in West Germany.

The Climate of Mass Opinion

We noted that Schumacher deliberately chose to play the role of militant champion of the masses on the strength of expected mass reaction, an expectation based in part on his analysis of past experiences, in part on his perception of future socio-economic developments. Apparently not even the outcome of the 1949 election could shake his belief in this role and the strategy he associated with it. Time and again he interpreted postwar political developments in terms of developments in the Weimar era, discovering analogous patterns and anticipating that once again the economically destitute and politically disoriented masses would seek a champion to lead them out of chaos. This retrospective orientation included the belief that economic developments would lead to a major political crisis whose effects might be even more severe than the one that brought Hitler to power. Refusing to accept evidence to the contrary, he structured his strategy in expectation of the crisis for which he waited in vain.* Thus his actions and the strategy he imposed on his party were oriented toward an image of the future based on the past.

Schumacher was by no means alone in expecting a people who in the past had shown themselves highly susceptible to charismatic leadership to respond to the appeal of a dynamic Tribune. Particularly in the difficult first years, he seemed to quite a number of observers ideally equipped to mobilize effective and enthusiastic mass support. As a living symbol of uncompromising opposition to the Nazi regime and an unrivaled orator, the gaunt cripple appeared to possess both the instrumental and the affective qualities necessary to come to power in his defeated, devastated, and occupied country.

But the political mood of most West Germans was highly unfavorable for the role of a militant Tribune, even before the new norms became established. It was radically different from the mood of the 1920's and 1930's, and it seems doubtful whether even a severe new economic crisis in 1950 or 1951 would have caused it to conform more closely with Schumacher's expectations. Temporary resentment against specific actions of the dominant decision-makers—first the Western military government, later the Adenauer coalition—did not significantly affect expectations that were fundamentally at variance with Schumacher's strategy and behavior. The masses he sought to mobilize by calling them to battle against foreign and domestic "reactionaries" and "exploiters" had no taste for conflict, and longed only for a period of quiescence

---

* His error, here, was perhaps not so much his initial view of the impending economic crisis and its political repercussions as his failure to modify this frame of reference in the light of contradictory developments. It should be recalled that until 1951 the economic position of West Germany was most precarious, general postwar problems being aggravated by an extremely inequitable tax policy that favored the highest income groups. Had it not been for the outbreak of the Korean War and its impact on the German economy, German industry might have expanded far more slowly, perhaps even suffering a severe setback. The Korean conflict, however, immensely boosted Erhard's export drive and the growth of the gross national product, while self-restraint on the part of labor and the influx of refugees from the Soviet zone helped to keep industrial overheads low. I am indebted for information on this point to Professor Karl W. Roskamp of Wayne State University; see his "Distribution of Tax Burden in a Rapidly Growing Economy: West Germany in 1950," *National Tax Journal*, XVI (1963), 20–35.

and stability after their emotionally exhausting and disastrous experience with a charismatic leader. Their reaction to the chaotic conditions of the postwar years was mostly a self-centered determination to put the past behind them, and to achieve as rapidly as possible social and economic security for themselves and their immediate families. What Otto Kirchheimer has fitly described as a "trend toward privatization, a turning inward of interests and a concentration on private affairs," caused most West Germans to avoid political involvement and collective political action.[71] They were quite content to let a small, active political elite do their fighting for them, an outlook that was diametrically opposed to Schumacher's perception of their role in relation to his own and that of his opponents.

Attitude surveys as well as studies of overt mass behavior indicated that the "little man" neither understood nor particularly cared about the issues that Schumacher called vitally important. To the man in the street, a job, better wages, and better housing had far greater immediacy and significance than equality, reunification, and sovereignty for his country.* For the most part, the people did not consider themselves "proletarians," and had no wish to take part in a class struggle against "reactionary capitalists."† They were unmoved by the bitter conflicts over the economic and political reorganization of West Germany; and they cared little or not at all whether the Federal Republic joined a European Coal and Steel Community.‡ The rearmament issue briefly aroused their opposition, but once the matter had been settled they came to acquiesce in this as in other decisions of the political leadership. An almost passionate desire not to become involved again in politics led them to

---

* Asked what they considered "the most important problem for the West German population," 23 per cent of the respondents in an opinion survey in the summer of 1951 mentioned high taxes and prices, low wages, and lack of money; 16 per cent named improvement of economic conditions and living standards, 15 per cent the elimination of unemployment, 9 per cent the solution of the refugee problem, and 6 per cent the need for extensive building to answer housing problems. Only 6 per cent considered the division of their country most important, only 4 per cent the recovery of German sovereignty, and only 2 per cent defense against Communism. O.M.G.U.S., *Opinon Survey Reports,* Series 2, No. 91.

According to another survey, taken in October 1951, 45 per cent of a representative cross section of West Germans considered economic problems the most important issue, whereas only 18 per cent named reunification, and a mere 5 per cent matters relating to the country's relations with the Western powers, such as the termination of the occupation, a peace treaty, and equality for Germany. Noelle and Neumann, p. 392. See also *Der Spiegel,* April 17, 1952, citing E.M.N.I.D. polls for January 1950–January 1952.

† Asked whether they considered a class struggle necessary or harmful, 45 per cent of the respondents in a 1950 opinion survey considered it harmful, 21 per cent necessary, and 12 per cent declared that the concept meant nothing to them. Noelle and Neumann, p. 385.

‡ In March 1949, at the very height of Schumacher's dispute with General Clay over the distribution of powers between the Länder and the federal government, 40 per cent of the respondents in an opinion survey expressed complete indifference about the contents of the new constitution, 33 per cent professed to be moderately interested, and only 21 per cent claimed to be very interested (*ibid.,* p. 157). For data on the E.C.S.C. issue, see *ibid.,* pp. 343f.

accept more or less apathetically the actions of the military governments and the Adenauer government. Their experiences both during the Nazi regime and under the occupation made them feel that in such matters discretion was the better part of valor.

Respectability and personal well-being were the dominant social values to emerge out of chaos in the transitional society of postwar West Germany. The attainment of both came more and more to be associated with conformity to the norms established by the Western occupation powers and by those Germans who enjoyed their favor, such as certain religious and business leaders. Cooperation with the Western leaders no longer carried a popular stigma as it had done in Weimar days, but appeared to be the way to higher status and material advancement. "Western democracy," "Christian principles," and "individual enterprise" assumed symbolic meanings that carried a far greater positive weight in attracting the masses than "patriotism" and "socialism." Far from being resented, wealth, power, and social status came to be admired as proof of the achievement of respectability and security—goals to which almost everyone aspired. "Proper" political behavior came to mean compliance with the wishes of the foreign and domestic leaders who appeared to have the means to apply both negative and positive sanctions—above all, compliance with the wishes of United States leaders. The overwhelming majority of West Germans, including most Social Democratic supporters, were not willing to risk American displeasure. Their desire to maintain the good will of the Western power that clearly had the greatest ability to give them political and economic security was far stronger than their dissatisfaction with specific Western policies, and induced them even to accept the Americans' demands for rearmament.*

Apparently, the rather vague "anti-capitalist" and "socialist" sentiments that were held by many West Germans did not mean that they wanted direct political action to be taken to alter the distribution of power or establish a Social Democratic commonwealth.† The considerable support that had existed in the first years for the socialization of basic industries melted away rapidly as the new middle-class norms were reinforced by the evidence of gradual economic recovery.‡ An opinion survey in April 1952 showed that 38 per cent of

* At the very height of popular opposition to rearmament, opinion surveys indicated that West Germans would nevertheless prefer to make the military contribution demanded by the United States than forgo Western, and particularly American, support for the sake of furthering reunification or conciliating the Soviet Union. See Noelle and Neumann, p. 349.

† An opinion survey in October 1947 indicated that only 10 per cent of adults in the American zone wanted a "socialist republic," whereas 56 per cent preferred just a "democratic republic." Even among S.P.D. supporters only 20 per cent favored the former as against 64 per cent favoring the latter. O.M.G.U.S., *Opinion Survey Reports*, Series 1, No. 74.

‡ Opinion surveys in the American zone indicated that whereas in 1947 some 49 per cent of adults favored the socialization of basic industries and only 24 per cent definitely opposed it, by 1950 support had shrunk to 28 per cent and opposition increased to 37 per cent. By 1952 even S.P.D. supporters were lukewarm: only 25 per cent thought the workers would be better off under sociali-

the respondents wanted their national government to include more "socialist principles" in its policies, but only one per cent associated these with "socialization" and a "planned economy." The rest associated them with social welfare legislation and government measures to boost incomes, lower prices, and raise their personal standard of living.[72]

Obviously this outlook of the masses was a far cry from Schumacher's perception of the situation. The Germans he sought to mobilize did not share his interpretation of legitimate and illegitimate political behavior, and the public image that he projected in his role as champion of the working people appears to have provoked negative rather than positive responses. A majority of West Germans did not perceive him as competent to satisfy their interests, and the issues on which he chose to make his bid for their support lacked appeal. His failure was demonstrated only too clearly by election results and opinion polls.

The role of champion of the people, to succeed, demanded that the masses Schumacher sought to mobilize behind his leadership achieve a sense of identification with him and his goals. But for the average West German, it seems, Schumacher was a deviant type—a man whose intellectual and idiosyncratic qualities put him out of touch with the people's everyday needs. There are times and situations when group sentiment may favor the deviant as a candidate for leadership, since he is believed to have the unusual gifts required to deal with extraordinary problems. To a certain extent, as we noted, Schumacher's authority within the S.P.D. was based on such expectations. However, the ordinary West German farmer, worker, or shopkeeper—probably even the rank-and-file Social Democrat—looked for entirely different qualities in a national leader. Such people looked for a man who seemed sober and reliable, and whose characteristics, instead of setting him apart from the masses, would allow the ordinary citizen, longing for respectability, to identify with him because he was seen as a normative model. He had to display commonplace, unspectacular traits, and at the same time appear competent to deal with community problems that the "little man" felt unable to deal with himself. He had to appear pragmatic rather than dogmatic, sober rather than passionate, flexible rather than rigid. Neither Schumacher's role choice nor the image he projected was congruent with these expectations.

Schumacher's decision to obtain power in Germany by democratic methods meant that he had to persuade a majority of the voters in a comparatively amorphous transitional society that he could satisfy a wide variety of interests. But his approach was ill-chosen. His arguments were incomprehensible to many, and his political style too radical, negative, and aggressive. His emphasis on German patriotism did not produce the expected emotional response; his appeal to the "proletarized" masses to join him in a class struggle repelled

---

zation, while 60 per cent did not think so; 29 per cent still wanted basic industries to be socialized, but 42 per cent were definitely opposed to any form of socialization. *Ibid.*, Series 1, No. 60; Series 2, Nos. 27 and 147.

rather than attracted his audience, since both native West Germans and refugees for the most part identified themselves and their interests with what they considered "middle-class" norms. His fierce attacks on the clergy antagonized not merely the devout members of the Churches (above all, Roman Catholic women), but also Roman Catholics and Protestants whose religious beliefs were more nominal but who identified support of "Christian principles" with social respectability, anti-Communism, and American benevolence.

Schumacher's demands for a radical purge of the "beneficiaries" of the Nazi regime, and his summons to Germans who had not fought against the Nazis to achieve moral regeneration by supporting him, evoked little sympathy outside his own party. Many thought it best not only to forgive but to forget their own and others' past sins. To them, apparently, Schumacher's claim to govern Germany on the strength of his anti-Nazi record, and to pass judgment on all whose record was not as pure as his own, seemed arrogant and self-righteous.* His stand, after all, had been atypical, and they found it more congenial to identify themselves with political leaders whose records, like their own, were not spotless.[73]

Schumacher was aware of this outlook among older Germans, and as we have seen, he tried in particular to obtain the support of the younger generation, i.e. Germans under thirty. But the younger Germans, who felt no personal responsibility for the Nazi past, did not look to him for leadership any more than their elders. Most of them had little interest in politics, and were far too preoccupied with personal problems to pay him much attention. In the disrupted postwar world, family ties were for many of them the only bonds that mattered, and the conflict between the generations that had played so important a part in Weimar politics was conspicuously absent. As a result, there was no strong desire to repudiate the values of the older generation.

For most of the small minority of young Germans who were interested in politics, Schumacher soon came to seem quite as dated in his notions as those he criticized for their "reactionary" outlook. His image of a "new" Social Democratic leadership failed to be convincing, and many of them turned away from a man who had initially impressed them. For young Germans, who had not experienced the trauma of Hitler's accession to power, Schumacher's "lessons of the past" held little meaning, so that they often found his outlook in-

---

* It seems that among Germans who preferred to forget their own part in Hitler's rule, the concentration camp veteran evoked feelings of acute discomfort, which they sought to assuage by rejecting him for ostensibly entirely different reasons, such as his alleged radicalism. The coming into play of such defense mechanisms made it difficult for Schumacher—in many cases probably impossible—to gain the allegiance of people who had in any way been involved in the Nazi regime, or at least had done nothing to oppose it. Not only his record but his physical appearance seemed an implicit condemnation of those who had not suffered as much. Whereas this sense of guilt induced in Schumacher's admirers even greater admiration for him, it led other Germans to reject him as a symbolic reminder of their own culpability.

comprehensible.* They regarded his emphasis on the past and traditional Social Democratic objectives as largely irrelevant in their day, his patriotic stance as misplaced in the context of postwar German politics, and his attempt to play the Tribune as inappropriate for a generation that had come to distrust heroic leaders. Sobered by the Nazi catastrophe and a disastrous war, such young Germans "no longer had any sympathy for petty nationalism," as one of them wrote in 1947. The time was past, they felt, for traditions, dogmatic *Weltanschauungen,* and the petty squabbles of political leaders.[74]

So the masses were probably never in the state of "latent revolution" in which Schumacher diagnosed them to be. All the average West German wanted, it seems, was the chance to rebuild his home. He wanted authoritative direction rather than mass participation; he looked for a leader or leaders who could provide him quickly with the peace and security he longed for. Some Social Democratic leaders—Reuter, Kaisen, and Brauer, for example—seem to some extent to have met these expectations. Schumacher, however, failed entirely, and when he died, opinion surveys showed him to be even less popular than the party he had led. Most West Germans found it impossible to identify themselves with the man who wanted to be their champion, and with the goals he wanted them to seek.[75]

The leaders of the major "bourgeois" parties, particularly the leaders of the C.D.U., were more realistic in their perception of the expectations of the "little man." The C.D.U. leadership showed itself keenly sensitive to the trend of mass opinion, and highly competent in exploiting and structuring it in the battle for power with the Social Democrats. From the very start, in naming their new party, the C.D.U. leaders chose a symbolic name, which proved "to have just the right combination of fixed meaning and flexibility" for a party trying to attract a broad segment of the population.[76] The heterogeneity of the C.D.U. and its leadership, and its deliberately vague programmatic goals, turned out to be a definite asset. Unencumbered by cherished traditions and strong in-group feelings, the C.D.U. leaders were quickly able to overcome whatever advantages a superior organization and a large core of loyal party members may have initially given the S.P.D. They succeeded in preventing the splintering of the nonsocialist camp, and in persuading more and more West Germans that they could satisfy their expectations for "proper" national leadership and public policy decisions. Thus the C.D.U. succeeded where the S.P.D., under Schumacher's firm leadership, failed: it managed to mobilize

* Thus one young man, who had been an ardent Nazi youth leader but had become bitterly disillusioned with the regime, recalled that in a series of conversations that he and his friends had had with Schumacher, Schumacher spoke to them in what seemed an alien language. His references to the class struggle in Germany struck them as meaningless and entirely inappropriate to contemporary conditions. For his part, Schumacher seemed unable to understand their pragmatic and non-Marxist outlook, leaving both parties to these conversations dissatisfied.

both elite and mass support because the flexible and pragmatic conduct of its leaders promised to satisfy a wide variety of interests. In 1949 this promise was still largely unfulfilled, but four years later the party could point to concrete results. The beginnings of economic and political recovery were by that time clearly visible, and a majority of the voters attributed them directly to the conduct of the C.D.U.

Adenauer's triumph not only over Schumacher but also over other rival aspirants for the leadership of West Germany (including other Christian Democrats) can be attributed to a number of complex and interrelated elements. Favorable situational factors—not least Schumacher's conduct and strategy—were no doubt of considerable significance; but by themselves they no more explain why Adenauer succeeded than why Schumacher failed. In his case, too, the central actor's orientation, his choice of political roles, and his performance of these roles are highly relevant.

Like Schumacher, Adenauer was apparently motivated to select and play certain roles because they suited his personality needs as well as his perception of the political context in which he sought to realize his aspirations. However, his role choices and performances proved to be highly functional in terms of his aspirations, not merely with members of his own party (as in Schumacher's case), but in his relationships with other politically significant actors. In dealing with other Christian Democrats, with members of the new elites, and with Western leaders, as well as in his relationship with the masses, he displayed a keen awareness of objective political reality, an acute sensitivity to the expectations of other actors, and great flexibility in adjusting his actions to the immediate demands of a situation. In this sense, what has been called his political genius was his ability to adapt his behavior to the expectations of other actors when he needed their support, to persuade others to adjust their expectations to conform with his role (and thus accept his role assignments), and, finally, to turn to his own advantage the role choice and behavior of opponents—above all, the role choice of Schumacher. His enemies were given an acceptable alternative that allowed them to turn negative sentiments, such as hostility toward Schumacher or Social Democracy in general, into positive identification with the leader of a common cause. Others, even if they were not particularly attracted to Adenauer personally, were persuaded by his actions that he was highly competent to further their interests. Lastly, he was able to accomplish what Schumacher could not: he managed to gain the effective support of a large number of voters because he apparently satisfied their demand for authoritative, paternalistic leadership.

The significance of the personality variable in political orientation and behavior was strikingly evident in Schumacher and Adenauer's relationship with other political actors. Schumacher, as we have seen, chose to make a frontal assault on the positions of power, expecting to override all opposition by uncompromising militancy. Ostensibly to obtain the support of the masses, he struck out at those he termed their enemies: Western leaders, "bourgeois politicians," clergymen, business leaders, and all those who would not submit to his demands. Adenauer chose an entirely different approach. For him the significant counter-players were not the masses, but a comparatively small group of Western officials and German leaders whose support he regarded as sufficient to obtain his goal. He apparently believed that the masses would follow rather than determine the actions of this small but politically attentive group; and to win its favor, he was quite ready to risk temporary unpopularity with the masses. This approach, it seems, was motivated not merely by political astuteness, but by personality traits and a social background that were radically different from Schumacher's. The patrician from Cologne evidently found it more congenial, as well as more effective, to exercise his political skills and persuasive powers in private meetings with Western officials, German politicians, and business and religious leaders than to woo the masses. He seems to have felt himself more at home in such settings than in front of a mass audience or a microphone. The role of the militant Tribune was entirely alien to him.

Yet it was Adenauer who won the support, and eventually the grudging affection, of the masses. Practically unknown to most of the voters when he assumed the chancellorship, he gradually gained mass approval for his interpretation of the chancellor's role and for his policies.* When chancellor and opposition leader entered upon their open battle after the election of 1949, and for some time thereafter, their popularity among the masses was about equal.† Adenauer's rising popularity suffered a setback when he first proposed West German rearmament, and a poll in December 1950 showed that while 40 per cent of the voters endorsed him as the head of the government, an equal proportion preferred Schumacher in that position.[77] However, despite the fact that the S.P.D. remained for some time the more popular of the two parties, its leader rapidly lost most of the mass support he had personally enjoyed. In 1952, shortly before Schumacher's death, a poll revealed that only 12 per cent of West Germans considered him the most capable political leader in Germany, whereas 33 per cent named Adenauer.[78]

Adenauer undoubtedly profited from the fact that the position of the chan-

---

* Before the rearmament issue temporarily turned mass opinion against Adenauer, a poll in May 1950 revealed that mass satisfaction with his conduct of the government was as great among Social Democrats as among Christian Democrats. O.M.G.U.S., *Opinion Survey Reports*, Series 2, No. 28. After resentment against rearmament had abated, another poll, taken in the fall of 1951, indicated that 51 per cent of West German adults considered the Chancellor's policies good for the country, and only 14 per cent disapproved of them. Among S.P.D. supporters, 50 per cent generally favored these policies, and only 22 per cent disapproved. *Ibid.*, Series 2, No. 106.

† According to an opinion poll in the fall of 1949 that asked respondents to name the person in public life who enjoyed their "greatest sympathy," 8 per cent named the new chancellor, and 7 per cent the leader of the opposition. Most respondents ignored German political figures altogether, some naming foreign leaders, and others scientists, movie stars, etc. Lorenz, *Die Persönlichkeit in der Volksmeinung.*

cellor was favored by the new institutional structures, and that of the opposition leader placed in a negative light. Yet there was more to it than this. Less extreme in his behavior than Schumacher, more successful in his dealings with other actors, Adenauer was apparently more in sympathy with the desire of the masses for stability, material betterment, and a burying of the Nazi past. Schumacher seemed to be a misfit in postwar German society, whereas Adenauer, stern and sober, emerged in the public mind as the ideal man to direct the difficult transition from chaos to middle-class stability in a safe and orderly manner.

Relations with the West German Elites

Let us now turn from Schumacher's efforts to mobilize the masses to his relationship with individual actors and groups who played leading parts in the politics of post-totalitarian Germany. Here, again, we find that his insensitivity to the attitude of other actors, his negative evaluation of their abilities, and his monistic interpretation of roles and role relationships in his fight for a Social Democratic commonwealth helped to alienate the S.P.D. national leadership from the new elites, and apparently caused Schumacher to embrace all the more emphatically his self-assigned role as champion of the inarticulate masses. His orientation seems to have allowed little room for maneuver or compromise in dealing with members of these elites, when these very qualities seem to have been mandatory under the existing political conditions.

As in his relationship with the East German elite, Schumacher's behavior toward his principal counter-players in West German politics suggests that he was unwilling to accept them as either worthy allies or honorable opponents, or to concede to them the high moral purpose, selfless idealism, and iron determination that he considered essential qualifications for national leadership. The evidence available to us from interviews and other sources indicates that he was convinced that he alone possessed these qualifications, and that he looked upon those who questioned his preeminence as fools or knaves—making little effort to conceal his contempt for the former and his hatred for the latter. In fact, he showed himself contemptuous or hostile toward all those who would not accept his definition of the political situation, or his assignment of roles in the effort to establish a Social Democratic commonwealth.

In view of the enormous difficulties that in any case confronted Schumacher in the face of apathy among the masses and antagonism from foreign leaders, his behavior toward key counter-players in West Germany appears singularly inept. By playing the defender of the masses against both foreign and West German elites, he denied himself, in effect, any alternative or even complementary method of reaching his goal. Not surprisingly, his uncompromising belligerency toward these counter-players, and his firm resolve not to yield to their demands, provoked increasingly hostile reactions from them. They came to the conclusion that his goals were in fundamental conflict with their own, and that a government under his leadership would be a catastrophe. These negative responses, in turn, confirmed Schumacher's belief that all individuals or groups who questioned his authority were irreconcilably opposed to his cause, and that the Social Democrats had to subjugate these hostile elements through the mobilization of the masses.

This conflict between Schumacher's image of "proper" roles and the way his counter-players perceived them had two results. First, it prevented effective cooperation between the S.P.D. leadership and the leaders of other groups who shared many of the Social Democratic objectives, but not Schumacher's role perceptions. Second, it helped to neutralize differences among non-Socialist leaders, who came to look upon Schumacher as their common enemy. His bitter hostility toward those members of the new elites whom he denounced as reactionaries, unpatriotic collaborators, and unregenerated Nazis, and his virulent opposition to domestic and foreign policies favored by other leaders conjured up frightening visions of a Germany under his leadership. As a result, men of otherwise widely divergent views were drawn together in a common effort to keep him from reaching his goal. To paraphrase Lenin's well-known statement about the relationship between the proletariat and its revolutionary vanguard, we might say that Schumacher's actions helped to push elites of conservative orientation (already more or less spontaneously opposed to a Social Democratic Germany) into actively supporting his rivals, above all Konrad Adenauer. Religious leaders came to associate him with extreme anti-clericalism, business leaders accepted at face value his promises that he would expropriate the "big capitalists," and leading officials feared his threat to purge all alleged Nazi collaborators from public service.[79]

Schumacher's orientation and strategy in the role of Tribune meant in effect that he refused to negotiate with other leaders who would not accept his supremacy, since in his view there was nothing to hold them to their word, or to conciliate groups that to his way of thinking stood in the way of his aspirations. This led him repeatedly to reject offers of collaboration on the grounds that the men who made these offers were to be neither trusted nor respected as potential partners in the fight for a united, democratic, and socialist Germany. His refusal to make what he called "opportunistic concessions" to the leaders of other parties and groups was later judged his greatest shortcoming by observers intimately involved in such negotiations. It seemed to them that he denied himself and his party numerous opportunities to move closer to the acquisition of national power, or even to influence political developments in general, by refusing to negotiate with groups that were willing to collaborate with the S.P.D. but not to accede to all his claims.

Time and again, tentative offers of collaboration from leaders who claimed to share many of his objectives and who sought a national coalition of the major democratic parties and groups foundered on his insistence that there could be no intermediary position between unconditional acceptance and total rejection of Social Democratic leadership and goals.* He dismissed appeals for common action from certain non-Socialist leaders as meaningless as long as they would not openly renounce the "reactionaries" in the bourgeois camp and acknowledge the S.P.D.'s claim to primacy. Well-meaning though such men might be, he said, when the chips were down, they invariably capitulated to the reactionaries, and therefore their promises had no validity.[80] But it seemed to many observers that it was Schumacher's own uncompromising stance that helped to weaken the position of these leaders, and to strengthen those elements within their groups that were opposed to cooperation with the S.P.D.

Schumacher's intransigence, along with mounting pressure from conservative opponents of collaboration among the elites, doomed efforts to build a national coalition of anti-Nazi and anti-Communist parties. His rigidly bipolar conception of a struggle for the allegiance of the masses and the power to shape Germany's future prevented men like Brauer, Kaisen, and Reuter in the S.P.D., and Karl Arnold and Jacob Kaiser in the C.D.U., from persisting with their efforts to create in national affairs a coalition arrangement that worked well enough in many Länder.† Not only did Schumacher's be-

---

* A number of Schumacher's former deputies, as well as other people who had been involved in such negotiations, stressed in particular his failure to join a coalition in the Frankfurt Economic Council in 1947, and his precipitate decision to go into opposition when the federal government was formed in 1949. It has also been pointed out that he took no action in 1950 and 1951 to exploit undeniable tensions within the Adenauer government, or to explore the possibilities of building a counter-coalition around a compromise candidate to replace the Chancellor by a vote in the Bundestag. See Gerhard Schulz, in Lange, p. 105 (as well as the references cited there in note 348), and Lange himself in *ibid.*, p. 397.

† Arnold and Kaiser were perhaps the most prominent members of the C.D.U.'s left wing, which was recruited largely from the Catholic anti-Nazi resistance movement. It drew its chief support from Christian trade union leaders and certain lay leaders of both the Roman Catholic and the Protestant Churches who favored close collaboration with the S.P.D. From 1947 to 1950, Arnold was the head of the coalition between the C.D.U., the S.P.D., and some minor parties that governed in North Rhine–Westphalia; Kaiser had been one of the founders and leaders of the C.D.U. in the Soviet zone, and, after his flight to West Berlin in 1947, played a prominent role in the West German C.D.U. in opposing the ascendancy of Adenauer. Schumacher's unconcealed contempt for Kaiser—who considered himself every bit as good an anti-Nazi, anti-Communist, and German patriot, and therefore perfectly qualified for a position of leadership—made a bitter enemy of a man who might have been a valuable ally. Schumacher's disparaging comments about Kaiser's efforts to function as the C.D.U. leader in the Soviet zone, and his subsequent efforts to contest Adenauer's bid to head the West German C.D.U., struck Kaiser as being a direct challenge to Kaiser's claim to be "a self-sacrificing, obdurate champion of German reunification." Reportedly, Schumacher's behavior was decisive in quenching Kaiser's enthusiasm for cooperation with the S.P.D., and caused him to give Adenauer his assent for the exclusion of the Social Democrats from the coalition government that was formed in 1949, in which Kaiser became the representative of the C.D.U. left wing as Minister of All-German Affairs. Heidenheimer, p. 155. See also, *ibid.*, pp. 107 and 176, and "Adenauer und der Föderalismus," *Der Spiegel*, No. 44 (1961), p. 66.

havior seem arrogant, but it invoked memories of the late Führer. "We are up against a man who, just like Hitler, demands complete and exclusive power," a Bavarian Christian Socialist leader told his associates after a meeting with Schumacher.[81] In contrast to many of the Social Democratic officeholders in the Länder, Schumacher appeared to these men incapable of cooperation, and therefore ill-qualified for national leadership. As long as he dominated the S.P.D., they came to believe, genuine collaboration between the Social Democratic leadership and the leaders of other parties was just about impossible.

Similar issues arose in Schumacher's relationship with the religious elites that played so important a part in postwar German politics. Members of both major Churches were anxious to establish ties with the S.P.D. leadership, but Schumacher's attitude was as inflexible as ever. He maintained that he welcomed "genuine Christians" into the ranks of the S.P.D., and initially even gave considerable encouragement to a small group in the party that sought to overcome the traditional cleavage between the S.P.D. and the Churches. However, his determined opposition to religious leaders who sought to participate in political reconstruction, and his refusal to grant the Churches the right to pursue their interests through political action, helped to revive the old differences over the relationship between Church and state, and ruined all efforts at cooperation.

Schumacher's failure with respect to the Churches was twofold. First, he chose to ignore the considerable influence that religious leaders exerted on the postwar attitudes both of the masses and of German and foreign elites. Second, he utterly failed to appreciate the motives of the men who sought to overcome both the anti-clerical orientation of most old Social Democrats and the anti-Socialist views of most clerical leaders. To him it was primarily a tactical question; to those who labored in vain to form an alliance between the major Churches and the democratic political parties and trade unions, it was the foundation for a progressive, peaceful, and democratic Germany. This small but initially quite influential group of religious leaders, journalists, and educators—most of them former members of the anti-Nazi resistance and survivors of Hitler's concentration camps—believed that political and religious organizations could and should collaborate closely. However, Schumacher's analysis of the postwar situation led him to the conclusion that traditional differences between the major Churches and the Social Democratic movement remained too deep and too fraught with emotion to permit genuine and constructive cooperation.[82] Insofar as this was true, his own attitude was certainly a contributing factor. His bitter dispute with religious leaders over educational and cultural issues drove potential allies into the camp of the conservative coalition that opposed him.

Schumacher was obviously unable to view the postwar activities of the

Roman Catholic clerical and lay leaders dispassionately, or even pragmatically in terms of his immediate political aspirations. Contacts with Roman Catholic leaders in the concentration camp had apparently not altered the decidely negative image of the Roman Catholic Church that he had formed as a youth in Kulm and a young politician in Stuttgart. His interpretation of the Church's objectives and activities in postwar Germany fitted into these earlier impressions; "the fifth occupation power" was for him a pernicious reactionary force whose devious stratagems, employed in the name of "Christian civilization," prevented reunification and the establishment of a Social Democratic commonwealth. The prestige and influence of the Roman Catholic hierarchy and its prominent supporters among both German and foreign elites seemed to him entirely unmerited; his criticism became increasingly bitter as he came to see in this church the mainstay of the forces successfully blocking his aspirations.

In the opinion of some astute and well-placed observers, these attacks contributed significantly to the defeat of the S.P.D. in the 1949 election. There is no way of knowing whether Schumacher realized this, but in any case he continued his battle with unabated fervor. Not only did his actions reinforce traditional antipathies toward the Roman Catholic Church within the S.P.D., but they obscured his strongly anti-Communist and basically tolerant attitude toward religious beliefs. Roman Catholic political leaders, trade unionists, and journalists—who otherwise sympathized with many of his goals—were evidently driven by his criticism of the Church to rally to its defense and to align themselves with his conservative opponents. In effect, he accentuated cleavages that he professed to regret, strengthened ties that he preferred to see broken, and made it increasingly difficult for Roman Catholics to cooperate with a party whose leader insisted on identifying himself as the bitter opponent of perhaps the most powerful interest group in postwar West Germany.

The Protestants in West Germany, most of them members of the Evangelical Church, slightly exceeded the Roman Catholics in number, but their leaders were far less active in politics than the Catholic clergy. This was due to the rather wide divergence among them about the proper role of the Churches in politics, as well as the comparatively decentralized structure of the German Evangelical Church and relatively weak influence that its leaders exerted on the political views of the nominal Protestant majority. Some Protestant ministers and lay leaders joined the S.P.D., but a larger number joined the C.D.U. Though Schumacher's relations with the Evangelical Church never became as acrimonious as his relations with the Catholic Church, he failed to obtain its support, thus allowing Adenauer's conservative coalition to lay claim to the benevolent backing of both major religious organizations. Some tentative contacts that the Council of the German Evangelical Church established with the S.P.D. leadership in 1947 failed to yield concrete results. Schumacher's clashes with conservative Protestant lay leaders over social and economic questions were apparently exacerbated by his caustic comments about collaboration between Lutheran ministers and the Nazis, and his disparaging remarks about the postwar political activities of anti-Nazi Protestant lay leaders associated with the anti-Socialist parties. Specific conflicts over such issues as religious instruction and the relation between Church and state in the new West German polity—conflicts that were deliberately emphasized by the Adenauer camp—proved more significant in Schumacher's relationship with Protestant leaders than common interests in reunification with the predominantly Protestant Soviet zone.

Here, too, Schumacher's misreading of postwar developments, particularly his overestimation of old and new differences between Roman Catholics and Protestants, led him to underestimate the abilities of his counter-players and the public's desire for domestic peace on the basis of "Christian principles." In this instance, too, the C.D.U. leadership saw the wisdom of appearing conciliatory, and took great pains to demonstrate a balance of Catholic and Protestant interests in its program and composition. Its foresight was rewarded in the rearmament controversy of 1950–52. Despite strong opposition to Adenauer's proposal, particularly among Protestants, Schumacher was unable to win even a minority of Protestant leaders to his side. Discussions between Martin Niemöller's wing of the Evangelical Church in Hesse and the S.P.D. leadership showed that the pronounced pacifist, neutralist, and anti-Adenauer orientation of Niemöller's group was not enough to induce it to support Schumacher's leadership claims.*

Schumacher's attempt to exploit the rearmament controversy against Adenauer also briefly raised the possibility of support from members of the old military elite. Most of these men were Protestants, and, like Schumacher and the majority of S.P.D. leaders, came from areas now separated from West Germany by Soviet rule. A number of former generals and general staff officers objected to the recruitment of German soldiers into a European army on

---

* According to one of Schumacher's principal deputies, Schumacher nourished some hope that Niemöller and other members of his group might strengthen support for the S.P.D. among Protestant leaders in general. These men had opposed Hitler on religious grounds, and many of them now occupied influential positions in the Council of the Evangelical Church. According to Schumacher's appointments calendar and surviving correspondence, he did try to arrange a few meetings with Niemöller and other members of the group (particularly in 1950–51), apparently with the idea of sounding out their views on possible cooperation. However, not only was their influence among other Protestants weaker than Schumacher apparently thought (especially in north Germany), but they seem to have had no particular desire to join forces with him. Neither side appears to have attached a great deal of importance to these conversations, to judge by the correspondence relating to it in the Schumacher file of the S.P.D. archives. In this connection, see *Turm.*, I, 132, 366 (the sole references to Schumacher's contacts with Protestant religious leaders by one of his principal biographers); also F. H. Allemann, "Das deutsche Parteiensystem," pp. 250f, and Erbe, p. 93.

grounds that in many respects corresponded with Schumacher's criticism in his role of defender of German interests.[83] However, it was hard to reconcile the effort to appear the uncompromising Tribune of the anti-militarist masses with the effort to win support from the old military elite. Briefly and secretly, Schumacher sought contacts with some of the ex-generals whose opinions seemed suddenly of considerable significance in German politics. Their views seemed likely to carry weight not only among veterans organizations, but also among the old Wehrmacht officers (who would have to take charge of a new German military organization) and among members of the political elites temporarily disconcerted by Adenauer's move.

Schumacher's motives in this episode are not clear. He may genuinely have wanted to gain support for his opposition to rearmament, or he may have wanted to establish contact with an influential group with whom he would have to work should he succeed Adenauer. In any case, while he denounced "remilitarization" in public, he not only discussed rearmament with Adenauer's military advisers, but sought contact with other former senior officers, including such outspoken Adenauer critics as Hitler's ex-generals Halder and Guderian. In the fall of 1950, his appointments calendar and correspondence reveal a number of meetings with former senior officers, but apparently as soon as rumors about these secret talks leaked out, he was forced to abandon his plan. He made an attempt to distinguish between "good" and "bad" generals, but it seems that he was unable to reconcile, either to his satisfaction or to that of the pacifists in his party, behavior that was hardly consistent with that of a Tribune striving to mobilize the masses against rearmament.* The contacts with the ex-generals were not developed further, his opposition to

* On November 4, 1950, Gerhart Gleissberg, editor-in-chief of the S.P.D.'s official organ, the Neue Vorwärts, wrote to Schumacher with regard to an article that had appeared in the party paper the previous day under the title "Distanz." He had been told, he said, that Schumacher had strongly criticized the article on the grounds that it seemed to vilify the entire old military elite, and that it would harm negotiations which were in progress with a number of former military leaders. Gleissberg, claiming to have been unaware of these negotiations, offered to publish a statement that the piece was not meant as a wholesale condemnation of all former generals. Schumacher's first major speech on the rearmament issue in the Bundestag on November 8, 1950, was couched in terms apparently designed to further negotiations and win support from former Wehrmacht leaders (see Turm., II, 466).

On December 29, 1950, Schumacher protested in a letter to Hans Böckler, chairman of the German Confederation of Trade Unions (D.G.B.), against apparent trade union opposition to the employment of a former general, Siegfried Westphal, by the Ruhrstahl-AG in Witten. The fact that the man had been a general, Schumacher wrote, was not enough to condemn him, particularly since he had never been a Nazi. At a moment when the rearmament controversy seemed to create the possibility of an understanding with members of the old military elite, whose views on the subject were close to those of the S.P.D. and the trade unions, it would not only be a moral injustice but "a definite political error" to prevent the employment of a man who had the confidence of a group of military men "who are important to us [auf die wir wert legen]." My information about these contacts with former high officers of the Wehrmacht is derived from a number of letters in Schumacher's correspondence (made available to me by Frau Annemarie Renger and the S.P.D. in Bonn), his appointments calendar, and several interviews.

rearmament became more categorical, and both sides came to find more to criticize than to praise in each other's position.*

Relations with the Trade Union Leadership

Finally, there was the crucial relationship with the trade union leaders. Of all the elites, the trade union leadership was the most obvious ally for a Social Democratic leader, not only as the means of approaching the workers, but as the key link for forming an alliance with other groups that favored an egalitarian political and socio-economic order for the new Germany. The postwar labor movement in West Germany represented a break with the traditions of European labor. Whereas in other countries the trade union movement continued to be closely affiliated with specific political parties (and in the Soviet zone became an arm of the ruling Socialist Unity party), in West Germany the survivors of the pre-1933 Social Democratic, Christian, and Democratic (Hirsch-Dunker) unions joined together to establish an organization pledged to political neutrality with regard to party affiliation. They believed that Hitler's rise to power and the abject surrender of the German trade unions in 1933 had been due as much to weaknesses of a divided labor movement as to the help Hitler had received from "reactionary" employers, and consequently they were resolved to build a new movement that would be dominated by no party, but would cooperate freely with any group ready to support its claim to a key position in society.

This new orientation allowed trade unionists who had long been associated with the S.P.D. to join with Christian trade unionists who had close links with the C.D.U. and the Churches in forging powerful state and zonal organizations, which in 1949 they managed to merge in a national body, the German Confederation of Trade Unions or Deutsche Gewerkschaftsbund (D.G.B.). The workers responded to this new image of a united and inde-

---

* As we indicated in our earlier discussion of the rearmament issue, Schumacher displayed a quite uncharacteristic ambivalence with respect to military matters and military men. Whereas he apparently had little difficulty in fitting other issues and relationships into his general orientation, in the instance of the old military elite he seems to have had unusual trouble in determining his position. Conflicting perceptions seem to have been the cause of the trouble. On the one hand, as a Social Democrat, he distrusted these ex-generals and ex-colonels because he identified them with the traditional anti-democratic attitudes of the German officer corps. Yet, on the other hand, he appears to have enjoyed and welcomed his meetings with, for example, Adenauer's military advisers more than he enjoyed many of his contacts with fellow victims of Nazi persecution, who seemingly had a much stronger claim to his respect. He displayed in this instance a quite atypical eagerness to achieve an understanding, showing respect and friendliness rather than contempt and hostility. More than in most of his relationships, he seems to have looked upon them as worthy counterplayers.

The explanation, perhaps, is that these men operated in an area in which he did not claim superior competence. His realm was politics, theirs military affairs; by recognizing their ability, he did not risk detracting from his own. It is interesting to note, too, that this respect for military men was an attitude that he shared with certain earlier Social Democratic leaders, notably Lassalle, Noske, and Ebert.

pendent labor movement. Though the D.G.B. became primarily an organization of industrial workers (salaried employees and civil servants formed separate confederations), by the time of Schumacher's death it had more members than the combined total of all trade unions in the whole of Germany in 1933. With six million members behind them—about ten times as many as in the S.P.D.—its leaders were representing over 38 per cent of the West German labor force, and, more important, a majority of the workers in the key industrial sector.[84]

Although many of the labor leaders were veterans of the S.P.D., and although most industrial workers voted for the party, there was considerable friction between the trade union leadership and Schumacher. His perception of the role it should play and its proper relationship with the party proved to be increasingly at variance with the ideas of the labor leaders. This incongruence not merely interfered with Schumacher's efforts to mobilize the working masses, particularly the industrial workers, behind his leadership, but on several important occasions led to an open conflict between him and the labor leaders, thus making it impossible for the latter to serve as a link between him and the leaders of the C.D.U. and other groups favoring cooperation with the S.P.D. Although Social Democratic and trade union leaders cooperated closely on many occasions, particularly in the Länder, Schumacher's views on national and foreign policy issues ultimately led to estrangement.

Although personal animosities contributed, this alienation was caused chiefly by fundamentally different interpretations of the "lessons of the past" and labor's needs and opportunities in postwar Germany. For Hans Böckler, the man at the center of the new movement, and for a majority of the trade union leaders, it was essential for the success of their enterprise that personal sympathies for the S.P.D., C.D.U., or any other group be kept out of the picture.* Their task, as they saw it, was to strengthen the newly found unity of German labor, and to speak on behalf of the industrial workers rather than for a political party. Pragmatic in outlook and highly sensitive to the fragility of their experiment, they deliberately sought to gain the support not only of Social Democratic workers, but of those who opposed the S.P.D. and its leader. They were determined to avoid any entanglements that might invalidate their claim to speak as an independent force. They were therefore eager to strike a balance between the two major parties, and welcomed the fact that there were trade union members in both the S.P.D. and the C.D.U. They were ready to

---

* Born in 1875, a year before Adenauer, Böckler had been a member of the S.P.D. and the metal workers' union since 1894—a year before Schumacher's birth. He became a trade union official in 1903, and served as a member of the Reichstag from 1928 to 1933; he was briefly arrested when Hitler came to power, and spent the remainder of the Nazi era in retirement. Apparently with the support of Schumacher's foe Carl Severing, he emerged in 1945 as a leading force in the new united trade union movement; in 1947 he was elected chairman of the united labor movement in the British zone, and in 1949 he became the first chairman of the D.G.B.

collaborate with both parties, as well as with the occupation authorities, the employers, and the Churches, whenever such a course seemed likely to further their immediate goal to obtain maximum economic and political advantage during this period of transition.

The lessons of the past caused Schumacher to take an entirely different view of the situation. For him the labor movement represented an effective instrument for mobilizing the German workers behind the political leadership of their Social Democratic champion. He therefore believed it incumbent upon Social Democratic trade union leaders to accept the guidance of their party's chief spokesman, and to support him loyally in his battle on behalf of the German working class. He took the Leninist view that there was no place for a "trade union mentality," which diverted the laboring masses from the overriding necessity to obtain political power. He did not follow Lenin in advocating a proletarian dictatorship; but he did feel that the tactics being used by the trade union leadership were directly contrary to what the situation required. The notion of a truly independent labor movement seemed to him a pernicious fallacy in view of the innate character of German capitalism. Convinced that a militant class struggle was mandatory in this context if the German "working masses" were to escape capitalist exploitation and gain true economic and political freedom, he looked upon trade union efforts to obtain as much as possible under prevailing conditions by bargaining and compromise as dangerously shortsighted opportunism. A "politically neutral" labor movement was all very well, he said at the 1947 S.P.D. congress in Nuremberg, but labor could not hope to achieve this by excessive tolerance toward the opponents of Social Democracy. Rather, it was the duty of all good trade unionists to devote themselves to rallying the workers behind the banner of Social Democracy.[85]

Seconded by a minority of trade union leaders who had formerly belonged to the anti-reformist wing of the party and by dissident radical socialist and Communist groups, Schumacher made strenuous efforts to impose his strategy and role assignments on the leaders of the new labor movement. He apparently came to look upon Böckler and his supporters as competitors in his bid for the allegiance of the workers, reviving an age-old conflict between S.P.D. trade unionists and S.P.D. intellectuals. Memories of these past differences and of the break between the party and trade union leaders over collaboration with Hitler in 1933 probably deepened the new cleavages. Now as then, mutual antipathies between "opportunistic" labor leaders and "doctrinaire" socialist intellectuals ruined a potentially useful relationship. Schumacher's appointments calendar notes only a few private talks with Böckler between 1945 and 1949—hardly evidence of a very active association between the man who saw himself as champion of the German workers and the most influential member of the trade union movement.

Schumacher's opposition failed to deter Böckler and his group from pushing ahead with their own strategy. Despite the workers' economic misery, unemployment, and considerable unrest over the dismantling of factories and the 1948 currency reform, they succeeded in avoiding serious conflicts with the Western occupation authorities and the non-Socialist elites, and in gaining acceptance as labor's legitimate spokesmen in the emerging pluralist society. Working to establish the trade union leadership as a partner with other elites in the political and economic reconstruction of the nation, they relegated their initial demand for the destruction of capitalist power positions by the socialization of key industries to a mere formality. Instead, the keystone of their policy became economic democracy by means of codetermination in the management of major private enterprises (*Mittbestimmungsrecht*). Marx claimed that the first industrial revolution had alienated the worker from his job and other groups in society; it seemed to these labor leaders that West Germany's second industrial revolution should achieve for the worker, not dominion over other groups, but full participation in the decision-making process—through his trade union spokesmen. By striving to reconcile the workers' interests with those of other organized groups, the labor leaders succeeded, where the Social Democratic leadership failed, in establishing themselves as the reasonable and cooperative representatives of these interests. Always ready to parley and negotiate, Böckler and his associates achieved a good working relationship not only with important C.D.U. leaders, but with a number of business and religious leaders as well, who came to accept codetermination as a reasonable demand. This favorable result reinforced the labor leaders' determination to pursue a policy of bargaining and compromise, and their attitude became increasingly at variance with Schumacher's strategy and role assignments.*

Schumacher's defeat in the 1949 election, Adenauer's elevation to the key decision-making office in the new Federal Republic, and the balance of forces in the Bundestag made it all the more imperative in the eyes of the leaders of the new D.G.B. to play an independent role.† Their chief aim at this point

---

* See Hirsch-Weber, p. 77, and Office of the U.S. High Commissioner for Germany, *Labor Problems,* pp. 43ff. It seems that this new orientation of German labor leaders was to some extent due to the influence of American trade union principles, which varied considerably from the traditional politically oriented ones of German and European labor movements. Anti-Nazi exiles who returned from the United States, as well as German trade unionists sent to the U.S. by the American military government, had become familiar with American trade union practices, and U.S. labor advisers in the military government encouraged the new trend.

† At the founding congress of the D.G.B. in Munich in October 1949, Schumacher's candidate for the deputy chairmanship, Willy Richter (a member of the S.P.D. steering committee in the Bundestag), was defeated by Georg Reuter, a strong advocate of trade union independence. The vote was 279 for Reuter, 239 for Richter. At the time, the deputy chairmanship seemed very important, since Böckler was seventy-four and in poor health. Sigmund ("Siggi") Neumann, Schumacher's chief adviser on trade union matters, characterized Reuter in a memorandum for his chief as "a

was to obtain federal legislation confirming the codetermination in the iron, steel, and coal industries that had been introduced by the Western military governments. To get this passed in the Bundestag required not only S.P.D. support but C.D.U. votes as well, and these, it was soon discovered, would be forthcoming only if the Chancellor agreed. In the course of negotiations with the Chancellor in 1949, the D.G.B. leaders gave their support to the Petersberg Agreement between Adenauer and the Western High Commissioners by agreeing to fill one of the three German seats on the International Ruhr Authority. To Schumacher and his supporters, endorsement of an agreement that had just led the Social Democratic leader to call Adenauer "the Chancellor of the Allies" seemed a highly partisan move.* In a letter to Böckler written in January 1950, Schumacher complained that Georg Reuter, the deputy chairman of the D.G.B., had placed himself and the labor confederation behind an article in a Swiss *Fabrikantenblatt*, the *St. Galler Tageblatt*, criticizing the S.P.D.'s opposition. He held that this constituted "a most serious violation of trade union neutrality toward the political parties" to the disadvantage of the Social Democratic leadership.[86] At this very moment however, Böckler—backed by the threat of a strike in the critical iron, steel, and coal industries—succeeded in winning Adenauer's support for a codetermination law. The Chancellor swung his party behind the law, assuring its passage in April 1950.

Almost immediately a new conflict developed when the D.G.B. leaders supported Adenauer and opposed Schumacher on the proposed creation of a European Coal and Steel Community. In contrast to Schumacher's increasingly adamant opposition, the D.G.B. leaders welcomed the proposal on the grounds that it would remove Allied controls over German production and give organized labor as well as their country a greater voice in European affairs. Carrying their political orientation in the codetermination struggle into foreign affairs, they participated actively in the negotiations leading to acceptance of the E.C.S.C. by the Bundestag, despite the bitter protests of Schumacher.[87] Schumacher committed a grave error, in the subsequent view of one of his closest parliamentary advisers, by not adapting his position to the labor leaders'

---

man of great ability but also the possessor of very strong elbows." ("Ein Mann sowohl mit grossen Fähigkeiten als auch mit ausserordentlichen starken Elbogen.") K.S. File, S.P.D. Pers. Archiv/Bonn.

* In a letter written to Schumacher on December 2, 1949, Neumann labeled it a "capitulation to the Adenauer Government." He described Böckler as "so enamored with his creation, the unified labor movement, that he is evidently prepared to sacrifice the [real] political interests of the trade union to this chimera of labor unity." He went on to say that "the trade union movement is far too valuable to be left solely in the hands of an unpolitical trade union leadership," since it was in the very nature of such labor leaders to practice the worst type of opportunism in pursuit of immediate goals, only to fail when it came to defending labor's long-term interests. Neumann was undoubtedly reflecting his chief's sentiments in these statements. K.S. File, S.P.D. Pers. Archiv/Bonn.

stand, thus permitting Adenauer to add yet another group to his coalition against the S.P.D.

What Schumacher refused to recognize was that the D.G.B. leadership had the power to play off the S.P.D. against the C.D.U. He would not accommodate himself to a situation he thought wrong, and persisted in his efforts to bend the labor leadership to his wishes. When Böckler died, in February 1951, Schumacher apparently expected that Adenauer's rearmament plans, as well as the failure of the Böckler group to win the Chancellor's support for "progressive" legislation protecting the workers' rights in business enterprises (*Betriebsverfassungsgesetz*), would arouse strong opposition from rank-and-file trade unionists, and that this would strengthen his own hand. When an Extraordinary Congress of the D.G.B. met in Essen in June 1951 to choose a new chairman, Schumacher backed Walter Freitag, co-chairman of the powerful and militant Metal Workers' Union and an S.P.D. Bundestag deputy. According to jottings that Schumacher made in his appointments calendar for his speech before the Congress, he wanted the Confederation "to become more active in politics than in the past": that is, less "neutral" in favor of the C.D.U., and more so in favor of the S.P.D. In return for S.P.D. support, he noted, the D.G.B. was for its part obligated to back the Social Democratic leadership, not to agitate against it. But once again his efforts to induce Social Democratic members of the D.G.B. leadership to accept the role he had assigned them and use their majority to support his own ends proved to be in vain. Christian Fette, a member of the S.P.D. but of Böckler's orientation on the relationship between party and D.G.B., was elected over Schumacher's man Freitag, reaffirming the independent line of the trade union leadership.

Subsequent notations in Schumacher's appointments calendar indicate that his relationship with Fette and his supporters was no better than his relations with Böckler had been. Fette's failure to accept Schumacher's view of the "real tasks" of the D.G.B., the "proper" role of its chairman in his relationship with the S.P.D. leader, and the "new political tactic" that the D.G.B. should adopt in gratitude for the party's support made Schumacher regard him as a weakling "scared of his own courage." To him the "real chairman" of the D.G.B. was Hans vom Hoff, an enthusiastic supporter of European economic integration, and in Schumacher's eyes an *eminence grise* consumed by "burning ambition."[88] Fette's failure to move Adenauer on new labor legislation and his vacillating position on rearmament led to his replacement by Freitag in October 1952—two months after Schumacher's death. Thereafter cooperation between the trade unions and the party increased as differences between the labor leaders and Adenauer became more marked. It seems idle to speculate whether such a development would have taken place had

Schumacher lived, or what the consequences would have been if it had.* More relevant is the fact that during his lifetime Schumacher's uncompromising and inflexible position seems to have aggravated major conflicts with a powerful elite when a more conciliatory attitude might have served much better.

Our assessment of Schumacher's performance as champion of the common man has led us to conclude that both his choice of role and his behavior in that role were dysfunctional in terms of his declared aspirations. To mobilize the masses and overwhelm opposing or ambivalent elites demanded a climate of opinion that disposed these masses toward intense, partisan involvement in the political process, and strong positive emotions toward the man who aspired to lead them. In the last years of the Weimar Republic such ardent, if diffuse, mass involvement, triggered by immense dissatisfaction with prevailing political and socio-economic conditions, permitted Hitler, and to a lesser extent the Communists, to mobilize mass support behind extremist opposition to the existing regime. This intense partisanship on the part of the masses had, in turn, compelled most of the elites to capitulate, and to accept, even support, Hitler as Germany's leader.

Contrary to Schumacher's expectations, the climate of mass opinion in post-Nazi West Germany was entirely different from that in pre-Nazi times. An extremely low level of political interest and a very high level of political tolerance on the part of the masses disposed them to resist efforts to involve them in bitter political conflicts, and allowed politically active German and foreign elites correspondingly greater freedom of maneuver. Since the apolitical masses were, in effect, willing to accept any measures that promised them stability and security, leading political actors, freed from public pressure to maintain partisan consistency, were able to further their basic aspirations by means of flexible coalitions and unconventional alignments. These conditions were probably the best possible in a situation demanding the orderly but rapid change of a complex society faced with many potentially explosive problems.[89]

They were not, however, the best conditions for the role Schumacher had chosen. His orientation seemed unsuited for the times: it was too Marxist for anti-Marxists, too nationalistic for internationalists and "Europeans," too socialist for non-socialists, too egalitarian for conservatives, too democratic for authoritarians, and too antiquated for youth. To obtain elite support under prevailing conditions was certainly a most difficult undertaking, but Schumacher appears to have written off the possibility from the start. He constantly sought to demonstrate his determination to fight anyone who stood in

---

* Suffice it to note that the increase in trade union support for the S.P.D. after Schumacher's death (1) coincided with a weakening of the D.G.B.'s membership and power, (2) did not prevent Adenauer from increasing both his mass and his elite support, and (3) failed to save the Social Democrats from stunning electoral defeats in 1953 and 1957.

his way, and was all too ready to attribute the worst motives to men he saw as questioning his claim to leadership. As a result, the masses as well as the elites were left with the impression that he was unfit for the office he sought to occupy.

We have repeatedly referred to an apparent conflict between Schumacher's declared objectives and his actual behavior. Since he was neither a political novice nor a fool, but in many respects (particularly in the capacity of party leader) astute, skillful, and intellectually gifted, the apparent "irrationality" of his actions puzzled many of his contemporaries. Was he aware of the full inconsistency of his attitude and behavior? On the one hand, he evidently realized that the collapse of the Nazi regime implied a radical transformation of German society; on the other, he seemed unable to accept that the "lessons of the past" had little relevance for the present and future. On the one hand, he seemed to recognize the growing power of leading political actors who did not share his aspirations; on the other, he engaged in behavior that seemed to invite their opposition. Some contemporary observers suspected that his apparent irrationality was in fact a deliberate pose to win the support of Germans whom he believed to be susceptible to this sort of appeal, and to frighten others into making concessions to him. Others thought that his ambivalence was due to a conflict between his political ambitions and his highly moralistic outlook. To my mind, both interpretations are valid, but I feel that his ambivalence had deeper roots as well.

Schumacher, as we noted, was by no means entirely unaware of the political dysfunctionality of certain of his actions, and came to regret them; but he seemed unable to learn from these experiences. He was repeatedly beset by doubts whether his battle could be won, only to throw himself with renewed determination into the fight. He seemed neither able to change his methods nor to abandon the struggle. These behavior patterns suggest that an outlook and actions which were dysfunctional in terms of his expressed goals may have been highly functional in terms of the "inner man." The power drive, which we have hypothesized governed his behavior, thus seems to have had a logic of its own. Occasionally the requirements of the political situation coincided with the requirements of the inner man; but often, especially in the last years of Schumacher's life, there appears to have been a serious incongruence. It is this interrelationship between personality needs, role choice and behavior, and political context that we shall now examine more closely in Chapter 9.

NINE

Political Behavior and Personality

Schumacher in Perspective

Shortly before midnight on August 20, 1952, Kurt Schumacher was found dead in his bed. His death was universally acknowledged as a major event in postwar German politics. "His name will remain linked with the history of this era," Chancellor Adenauer wired from a vacation retreat in Switzerland.[1] But few were willing to follow President Heuss's advice to leave it to future historians to "explain and evaluate the man and his deeds in the context of our era, the validity or incorrectness of his judgments, the appropriateness or inappropriateness of his assessment of men and events." "Who in these confused times," Heuss asked at Schumacher's funeral, "can be certain of the right standards by which to judge him?"[2] He had been too important and controversial a figure to allow the world to defer judgment. His personality, the issues he had raised, and the battles he had fought had made a deep impression on his fellow actors, and they felt impelled to evaluate his actions for themselves and for posterity.

To Schumacher's admirers the man and his deeds carried a high symbolic content, and for political as well as personal reasons they were determined to commemorate him as a heroic figure. According to Erich Ollenhauer, Schumacher's deputy and now his successor as leader of the S.P.D., "He was one of the greatest hopes of German and European democracy and libertarian and democratic world socialism."[3] He was said to have rendered the German people "great services" by his ceaseless battle against the nation's enemies. He had fought for his principles without ever thinking of himself, and it was all the more to his credit if unprincipled enemies and an unappreciative world failed to recognize his unrivaled integrity. But he would not be forgotten; a heroic figure in unheroic times, according to these admirers, he would live on as "The Guardian of Democracy," who gave "A Life for Germany," to quote the titles of the two biographical studies published soon after his death. It was he who was said to have been primarily responsible for repelling Soviet efforts to subjugate the entire German people, for establishing democracy in West Germany on firm foundations, and for making the Western powers and their

German collaborators abandon their efforts to deny West Germany equality and freedom. According to this version, he should be remembered for all time as a great patriot who had fought for the restoration of a united Germany, and as a great socialist who had tried to give his people liberty, democracy, and social justice, and the world a peaceful Germany. If he had failed to accomplish all he set out to do, this was seen as a condemnation of his less discerning and less dedicated contemporaries, not as a reflection on him.[4]

Others were less convinced of Schumacher's stature. To some he was a demagogue; to others a fanatic or psychopath. Many could not forget personal injuries, and many (though not all) who had believed him to be wrong in his lifetime saw no reason to revise their judgment after his death (see Table 7).

TABLE 7

"As I Remember Him"—The Schumacher Image in Retrospect
(Evaluation by informants interviewed 1959–60)

Characterization	Source
Pre-1933 Period	
Great man (impressive, tolerant, determined, energetic, generous, courageous, impulsive)	Female relatives, friends, secretary
Great political leader (militant, courageous, great orator, great intellect, fascinating)	Fellow S.P.D. members
Politically inept (disloyal, opinionated, intolerant)	S.P.D. leaders
Nazi Period	
Impressive personality (strong, respected, born leader, fascinating, admirable, great intellect, courageous, uncompromising, sensitive, good comrade, morale builder)	Fellow prisoners in the concentration camp
Postwar Period	
Great political leader (uncompromising, intellectual giant, inspiring, fascinating, witty, dynamic, militant, lonely, impulsive, dedicated, forceful, moralist, heroic, great orator)	Close political associates and other S.P.D. members, minor Western military government officers, and some major political opponents outside the S.P.D.
Authoritarian dogmatist and bigot (tenacious, dedicated, inconsistent, intolerant, unrealistic, arrogant, self-willed, intelligent, ambitious, sarcastic, cynical, opinionated, destructive, full of hatred, opportunistic, uncontrollable temper, irresponsible, power-mad, Prussian)	Opponents in the S.P.D., some major political opponents outside the S.P.D., and a number of Western military government officers

For them he remained a blinded Ajax slaughtering sheep in the belief that they were Trojan enemies, or a Don Quixote tilting at windmills. Others conceded that he had been highly intelligent, sincere, and upright, and, in Adenauer's words, dedicated "to what he believed to be politically proper for his party and the German people."[5] But they took a more negative view than his admirers of his uncompromising attitudes and aggressive political behavior. Many who respected his zeal and courage felt at the same time that his behavior was inappropriate if not irresponsible and destructive in the post-totalitarian setting.

"It is not impossible," wrote a leading American newspaper after Schumacher's death, "that he may prove to have been historically correct"; but in another place it also noted that "perhaps history will write him down as a potentially great statesman who suffered the misfortune of becoming a physical and spiritual casualty of the Nazi regime."[6] According to a liberal Catholic German journal, "He was a great party leader . . . because in his brash way he was pure and sincere," but his uncompromising intolerance was declared to have kept him from being a true statesman.[7] It seemed to such observers that other German political leaders had shown a far greater sense of responsibility, moderation, and tolerance. Almost ten years later, General Clay, the former American Military Governor, described him as a "highly intelligent, very tense, and courageous" man, "a truly major figure in the reforming of political life and activity in West Germany." But it seemed to him that other German leaders had had a better understanding of "the part that compromise must play in a democracy." For his part, Clay had found Schumacher "difficult to work with, as his almost fanatic zeal left him little room to compromise."[8] Clay's successor, John J. McCloy, considered "Germany and the West" in Schumacher's debt "for his statesmanlike position" in leading "his great party in the direction of freedom," and for his "firm stand against Communism" at a time when "the German people, particularly the workers, might [have been] open to Communist persuasion" owing to the "moral turbulence, physical destruction, and economic ruin" bequeathed them by the Nazi regime. Unlike some who had once tilted lances with Schumacher, McCloy believed that there could be no question about his honesty and integrity. He "always seemed to me a powerful individual whose life was dedicated to politics and the political objectives in which he believed," McCloy recalled, but this "intensity of views" seemed often to deny him "objectivity and toleration of others."[9]

Such differences of perception applied not only to Schumacher's political actions, but to his more specifically personal characteristics as well. Whereas some remembered him as a sensitive and considerate person, others considered him arrogant and ruthless. Some who had known him personally called him a fanatic, whereas others insisted that it was "superficial" to describe "a man of great warmth and understanding" as a fanatic.[10] A prominent British newspaper correspondent had found him to be an "intensely shy, humorous, and friendly man."[11] But American journalists "could detect in him no human warmth," and saw him as a man of "wit but no humor, heart but little geniality."[12] Some obituary writers described him as a person who "impressed without evoking particularly affectionate feelings," who aroused respect and sympathy, but little fondness among those who came into contact with him.[13] Others again maintained that he was "far more flexible" in private "than many believed who only knew him as a public speaker."[14]

These and other published and unpublished observations reflect that in death as in life Schumacher evoked widely different and conflicting reactions, especially among those who had had direct personal contact with him. Even after a decade or more, the Schumacher image remained vivid for those who had come to know him well—a measure of the impact he had had upon them. Whether they had worshiped or hated him, supported or opposed his views and actions, in most cases the vividness of this image appeared to correspond to the degree of emotional involvement with the man and his policies. Despite the passage of time, many still found it difficult to view him dispassionately, and few appeared to have altered their views over the years (see Table 7). In 1963, one of Schumacher's closest postwar associates claimed to be "still too close to the man and the situation at the time" to obtain an objective picture; a non-involved observer might have greater success, he suggested.

But if non-involvement perhaps allows greater objectivity, it also deprives the non-participant observer of the insight derived from personal contact and shared experiences. Inadequate information and conflicting accounts about this complex, enigmatic figure emphasize the limitations that non-involvement places upon efforts to understand and evaluate Schumacher's postwar behavior. Those who claim to have "known" him may very well charge that the non-participant observer shows a lack of "feeling" for his subject, and cannot really understand him or the context in which he was operating. Schumacher's admirers may say that he deserved better, his critics that he deserved worse at the hands of a biographer. The non-involved observer's efforts to avoid normative judgments and the intrusion of personal values in his assessment inevitably invite such criticism, but he must be willing to accept this if he is to be true to his resolve to strive for objectivity.

Perhaps we are still too close to the political events of Schumacher's time to attempt an objective analysis. Yet other considerations suggest that we may be almost too late to attempt it. Many of the people who could have provided important information have died; moreover, changes in German politics have obscured the figure of Schumacher to a point at which, only a dozen years after his death, he seems to belong to a distant, indistinct past. Overshadowed by Adenauer and the achievements with which he has been credited during his fourteen years as chancellor, Schumacher and the issues that concerned him appear to have little significance today. Even the S.P.D. has undergone vast changes since Schumacher's death, and the tenth anniversary of that event was allowed to pass almost unnoticed by what was once "Schumacher's party." In the face of new problems, many S.P.D. leaders seem to remember Kurt Schumacher with respect, but also as a symbol of political ineptitude.

Whereas Adenauer's record has generally been accepted in Germany and abroad as having earned him a permanent place in history as the chief architect of postwar recovery and political reconstruction, it may be Schumacher's fate to be remembered, if at all, as no more than one of Adenauer's unsuccessful rivals. "His hour never came," one obituary stated;[15] and Heuss, in his funeral oration, called Schumacher "a tragically incomplete man," who never had an opportunity to prove himself a constructive statesman.[16] The few years had not been enough, according to another obituary, to indicate how far he might have influenced the course of German history had he lived to become chancellor. "We got to know Schumacher more as a nay-sayer than as a constructive leader."[17] Perhaps this will remain his image.

In the analysis to follow, no effort will be made to establish Schumacher's "proper" place in history. The object of this study, as was stated at the outset, is to examine Schumacher's activities as a case study of the interaction between a major political actor and his political environment. What we shall now attempt to do is to make explicit what has been left more or less implicit in the preceding chapters, namely the interrelationship between personality syndromes, roles, and political context in Schumacher's postwar career. First we shall consider his various role choices and consequent behavior in terms of their effectiveness for his manifest political goals. This will be followed by an analysis of these role choices and performances in terms of their effectiveness for latent personality needs.

Political Leadership, Roles, and Setting

In terms of the conceptual scheme presented in Chapter 1, Schumacher (the central actor) was a candidate for the leadership of post-totalitarian Germany (the focal position) who chose for himself and assigned to the incumbents of other positions in the polity (the relevant counter-players) various roles that seemed to him appropriate for the achievement of his manifest goals in various settings. For analytical purposes, we treated these role assignments as conscious and deliberate but separate actions, conditioned by the central actor's perception of the situation, his manifest goals, and the means he believed to be available to him to achieve them. Empirically, however, they were fused. For Schumacher, the attitudinal and behavioral patterns that we isolated and turned into arbitrary abstractions were inextricably related to his primary focal position as an aspirant for the post-totalitarian leadership. He did not see himself now as party leader, now as patriotic leader, now as champion of the common man; he saw himself as playing all these roles simultaneously.

In Chapter 5, and in greater detail in the chapters that followed, we presented the objective setting in which Schumacher was compelled to operate, his interpretation of that setting, his manifest goals, and his perception of the actions necessary to achieve them. In a country controlled by foreign powers and under conditions of extreme socio-economic dislocation and rapid political change, he operated in a setting characterized by comparatively unstructured political patterns and roles, and a degree of access to political participation and positions of power unprecedented in the history of modern Germany. However, certain factors imposed limitations upon the freedom of action of an aspiring leader: (1) the presence of foreign occupation powers with the ability to impose far-reaching sanctions; and (2) certain surviving patterns of earlier German socio-political alignments and norms, which soon fused with new alignments and norms that developed as a result of the collapse of the Nazi regime and the subsequent disputes and divergent actions of the occupation powers. Under these conditions, the primary tasks that confronted the aspiring leader were (1) to identify those actors who had the power to promote or block his efforts to obtain the position to which he aspired; (2) to create and encourage among them a consensus of favorable expectations toward himself in such a position; and (3) to discourage and destroy such expectations toward all rival candidates for the position. In short, he had to establish in these vitally influential counter-players the confidence that he could satisfy their values better than any of his rivals, and he had to deny his rivals the opportunity to establish themselves as more competent than he.

For Schumacher, as the central actor in our analysis, there existed in the objective environment two major sets of other actors with whom he had to deal in order to obtain their support or to deny them an opportunity to block his ambitions. First, there were the counter-players of the in-group within which he sought to exercise leadership: the members of the S.P.D., and particularly the incumbents of positions of influence within the party. Second, there were the counter-players outside the party who could affect his efforts to exercise leadership in all of Germany, or at least the Western parts: the members of other political and non-political groups inside and outside Germany who occupied positions of influence in the larger setting. This second group of actors consisted of the leaders of the foreign occupation powers and their principal representatives in Germany; other non-German leaders and elites who directly or indirectly associated the satisfaction of certain of their values with developments in Germany and the nature of its leadership; and Germans with a direct or indirect interest in and influence over domestic political developments, particularly certain elites but also members of the mass public in both the Western and the Soviet zones of occupation.

In Schumacher's interpretation of the environment in which he would have to operate in order to obtain positions of leadership in party and country, there seem to have been two main factors affecting his choice of roles and perception of counter-roles. First, German counter-players and what he took to be their expectations and values had for him far greater relevance than non-German. Second, he expected his relationships with other leading political actors to be marked more by conflict than by cooperation, for he assumed a fundamental difference of interests and goals. He regarded German politics as a dialectic conflict between the forces of reaction and the forces of progress, a conflict which, with the collapse of the Nazi regime, seemed to have reached a decisive phase. Since he identified himself with the forces of progress, he believed that he must inevitably clash with his reactionary foes. Similarly, international relations seemed to him fundamentally a conflict between national leaders who were more or less conscious of their opposing interests, with *Realpolitik* as the norm and Germany in a key position. According to this view, a German leader who sought to exploit the situation in the interests of his own nation was bound to come into bitter conflict with foreign counter-players who were inevitably pursuing their own national interests.

Schumacher's postwar statements and actions suggest that his assessment of the political situation provided him with a rational and logical link between his goal as an aspiring leader and his various roles in that focal position. He believed, it seems, that the situation required three main conditions if a Social Democratic government were to assume power in Germany. First, there had to be a person capable of providing symbolic as well as instrumental leadership for a people who were prone to respond to authoritative guidance in times of crisis, and who were certain to demand it again under present conditions. The collapse of the Nazi regime and the occupation of Germany appeared to him to have created a situation in which "everything depended on the initiative of the right leader," to borrow a statement from his doctoral dissertation.[18] This was the man with the moral, intellectual, and political qualifications to understand conditions and establish objectives, "to recognize the dialectic possibilities imminent in the situation and to force them to result in the kind of synthesis he wanted,"[19] to move events rather than be moved by them. In short, this was the man Schumacher believed himself to be, or at least wanted to be.

Second, such a leader needed an organizational instrument, an efficient and disciplined political movement committed to his strategic objectives and consisting of men and women dedicated to the common cause. This, of course, was Schumacher's image of the kind of Social Democratic party that he believed essential for the acquisition of power and the creation of a sovereign, united, democratic, and socialist Germany.

Last, the aspiring leader needed overwhelming mass support, in Schumacher's view, if power was to come to him legitimately. Accordingly, he was far more concerned with what he assumed to be the mood, aspirations, and demands of the mass of the German people than with the values of German and non-German elites, and was quite prepared to sacrifice the good will of the latter to obtain that of the former.

On the strength of these images, Schumacher evidently chose to play the three roles that we examined in detail in preceding chapters, and that we shall now consider in terms of their effectiveness for a man aspiring to become postwar leader of Germany.

Focusing first on Schumacher's relationship with his counter-players in the Social Democratic party, the in-group within which he actually exercised leadership, we find that here, apparently, a general congruence of role and value perceptions made his choice and performance of *the role of monocratic leader* functional in terms of his aspiration to become Germany's leader as well. In his fight for the party chairmanship against Grotewohl, and subsequently as the incumbent of this position, he was able to create and maintain a very high consensus of positive expectations toward himself and his performance among his in-group counter-players, and to gain general acceptance of his role assignments in relevant role-sets. He succeeded in establishing among party members the confidence that he could satisfy their values better than anyone else, and he consequently obtained widespread support for his perception of goal and instrumental values in the fight for power in Germany.

There appear to be three main categories of orientation toward Schumacher that explain why he was accepted by most Social Democrats in his role of monocratic leader.[20] Party members, it seems, perceived him *cognitively* on the basis of performance criteria as an effective instrumental leader, *evaluatively* on the basis of his personal record as a positive moral symbol of leadership, and *affectively* on the basis of emotional ties between themselves and him as a positive expressive symbol of leadership. These attitudes occasionally operated singly, but more often in combination.

When I say that Schumacher was perceived cognitively as an effective instrumental leader on the basis of performance criteria, I mean that Social Democrats looked upon him as a man who knew what to do and how to do it in the postwar situation facing their party. Thus, as chairman of the S.P.D. and its principal spokesman in relations with the political out-group environment, he provided party members, particularly the rank-and-file, with an authoritative frame of reference that enabled them to interpret political actions and events relating to the perceived external task of the S.P.D. in postwar Germany. In this sense he was perceived impersonally as the legitimate incumbent of the party chairmanship, who was entitled to loyal and disciplined support as a task-oriented agent of the party membership striving for the realization of group goals. Such cognitive orientations toward him appear to have been particularly strong among the "old-timers," who constituted the majority of party officials and members after the war, and who brought into the post-totalitarian political arena an institutionalized image of the relationship between party leadership and followers that was based on Social Democratic norms of the pre-totalitarian era.

For very many Social Democrats, Schumacher's personal record as a crippled war veteran, as a socialist militant before 1933, and as a martyr of the Nazi concentration camps made him appear a strong moral symbol of leadership. That is, he was perceived evaluatively as a man who symbolized standards of right and wrong values and behavior for those who identified themselves directly, or through him, with the Social Democratic anti-Nazi counter-elite and its presumed mandate to rule postwar Germany. He was respected and admired as a living symbol of the resurrected party, of its egalitarian, patriotic, and democratic principles, and of militant opposition to its "unworthy" reactionary and pseudo-socialist German and foreign opponents. In this sense, his drive for power in Germany was identified with the gratification of group norms based on more or less abstract ideals and visions associated with the principles of German and international democratic socialism.

Finally, for an undetermined number of party members, Schumacher represented not only a moral but an expressive symbol of leadership. Particularly among his closest political associates, he was evidently perceived affectively as a man whose personal impact evoked strong positive emotional responses. That is, he was appreciated not just because he was the party chairman or a moral symbol, but because these counter-players found personal emotional gratification in being associated with him, and feared emotional deprivation if they should quarrel with him or refuse to accept his role assignments and goals. Thus, whereas as an instrumental leader and a moral symbol he was accepted as a monocratic leader because he seemed to represent the group and was identified with it by the members on the strength of values held in common, as an expressive symbol of leadership he was accepted on the strength of the difference between himself and those who were emotionally tied to him. As I tried to indicate in earlier chapters, such affective criteria seem to have governed not only Schumacher's relationship with his comitatus of younger "brothers and sisters" in the postwar era, but his relationships with his admirers in the concentration camp and his immediate entourage in Stuttgart (see Table 7, p. 260).

Only a small minority of Social Democrats appear to have viewed Schumacher's role choice and behavior as monocratic leader with comparative indifference because neither his role assignments nor his performance had any particular relevance for them. However, it would probably be more accurate to speak of degrees of involvement, since what Schumacher said and did was of constant concern to only a few party members, the others giving him their attention according to the situation of the moment and their sense of involvement in it. As for a negative reaction, a minority of S.P.D. members, most of them public officeholders, rejected Schumacher's role assignments and performance with varying degrees of vehemence. Some did so on the basis of performance criteria alone; others on the basis of evaluative moral standards and/or affective expressive criteria as well. When evaluative and affective standards came into play, it seems that Schumacher was usually the initiator of actions that gave rise to feelings of resentment and even hatred on the part of S.P.D. members. When influential Social Democrats were involved, these actions often proved dysfunctional in terms of his manifest goals because they alienated persons whose support he needed.

As we turn from the in-group setting to the out-group setting, we find that Schumacher's relations with his counter-players were marked by a high degree of incongruence of role and value perceptions, and a consequent high degree of dysfunctionality of role choice and behavior. His inflexible determination to adhere to role assignments relating to his decision to play *the role of patriotic leader* in his dealings with non-German counter-players evidently led to increasing incongruence between his perception of roles and objectives, and that of foreign political actors who had a high degree of influence on the structuring of political patterns and the means to impose deprivational sanctions upon an aspiring leader. Instead of seeking to create among them a consensus of favorable expectations toward himself in the position of Germany's future leader, he chose to view most of his important foreign counter-players as foes or fools whose good will was neither to be expected nor to be obtained, but who might be prodded to move in a desired direction by playing on their fear of Communism, revived German nationalism, or "capitalist encirclement." The failure of Soviet as well as Western leaders to respond to his efforts to influence their behavior and their increasing hostility toward him seems merely to have confirmed his belief that he was engaged in conflict made inevitable by a basic difference of values. As for the leading foreign actors who associated the satisfaction of their interests in Germany with the nature of its dominant leadership, his behavior served to encourage unfavorable expectations toward him and more favorable expectations toward his rivals. Thus under prevailing international conditions, the role of the patriotic leader, and above all Schumacher's rigid adherence to perspectives and behavior that he related to this role, proved highly ineffective.

If we analyze the orientations of these counter-players toward the patriotic leader in terms of the same criteria we employed in considering his image among Social Democrats, we find that cognitively his performance came increasingly to be viewed as highly inept, and as proof that he was obviously incompetent to deal with international issues requiring "effective" German leadership. That is, he was seen by most of his non-German counter-players as incapable of competent actions identified by them with the realization of their interests in Germany, and his behavior as patriotic leader was interpreted as promising them even greater difficulties should he realize his aspirations. Unlike Pieck, Ulbricht, and Grotewohl (from the Soviet point of view), or Adenauer, Erhard, and Reuter (from the Western point of view) he appeared to know neither what needed to be done in Germany nor how to do it, and he was perceived as an obstacle rather than an aid in terms of such instrumental criteria.

Evaluatively, Soviet and Communist leaders repudiated Schumacher from the start of his postwar career as a positive moral symbol of world leadership; Western leaders were initially more ambivalent, but before long most of them also rejected him as such. As he took actions that brought him increasingly into conflict with symbolic moral values dear to the hearts of his Western counter-players, Frenchmen came to look upon him as an unregenerated Prussian nationalist, Americans as an opponent of free enterprise democracy and its defense against Communism, while to various other Western leaders he seemed to challenge deeply felt religious and ideological beliefs. His posture as a patriotic German leader seemed immoral to the foreign victims of Nazi aggression and persecution, as well as to the proponents of German participation in a Communist or anti-Communist international organization. In short, although these foreign actors adhered to widely differing national and international moral symbols, Schumacher's activities produced a far-reaching consensus among them that he was a "bad" rather than a "good" German.

Finally, the patriotic leader was viewed affectively by very many non-Germans as a negative expressive symbol. That is, his deeds apparently provoked strong antagonistic feelings among individual foreign counter-players, such as Bevin, Mollet, and other European socialist "comrades." Prominent occupation officials and foreign opinion leaders who had a strong emotional and personal involvement in the political reconstruction of post-Nazi Germany, and in the policies and actions that Schumacher deliberately chose to oppose, seem to have felt him to be a threat to the gratification of personal values identified by them with measures to punish or reform the Germans. Beyond this, his behavior was frequently taken to be personally offensive. He seemed arrogant to those who expected deference, demanding to those who expected gratitude, and impenitent to those who expected him to assume a share of the Germans' "collective guilt."

In his relationship with his German counter-players outside the S.P.D., Schumacher's decision to mobilize mass support by playing *the role of the champion of the common man,* and his rigid adherence to role projections and actions that he associated with it, also appear to have defeated his aspirations for the national leadership. Incongruence between his perception of the objective political context, role relationships, and relevant values and that of other politically relevant German actors appears to have contributed significantly to his failure to obtain either the elite or the mass support needed to achieve his goal. Here, as in the relationship with his non-German counter-players, he persistently overlooked or deliberately ignored all three tasks that we previously identified as crucial for success under prevailing conditions. He failed to identify those political actors who had the power to help him obtain his goal, and chose instead to appeal to the largely inert masses. He failed to create a broad consensus of favorable expectations among those actors who occupied positions of influence, inviting instead deprivational sanctions from members of key elites, and encouraging more favorable expectations toward his rival Adenauer among elites and mass public alike. As I tried to show in Chapter 8, his role performance as champion of the common man not only failed to elicit the intended mass response, but stimulated highly negative ex-pectations and responses from more attentive German counter-players, for whom his activities had greater relevance because they seemed to threaten the denial of values important to them. His attacks on various interest groups prodded their members into lending support to his opponents. Moreover, he appeared unable or unwilling to adjust his orientation to the dynamics of po-litical change, a limitation that was particularly noticeable after develop-ments in 1948 and 1949 radically altered the conditions under which he was compelled to fight for the leadership.

Insofar as Schumacher's role choice and assignments may have been condi-tioned by expectations relating to counter-players in the Soviet zone, lack of empirical evidence prevents us from assessing the effectiveness of a role that may have been oriented, at least in part, toward a nation-wide mass audience on both sides of the Elbe.* However, since our analysis is confined to his efforts to become the leader of West Germany alone, such considerations are irrelevant. There, as we noted, the prevailing climate of mass opinion proved to be a major impediment to the successful mobilization of the "people" by their self-proclaimed "champion." Most of the time, Schumacher's appeals either had little relevance for members of the mass public, or else were incon-gruent with their own perceptions. Among members of the politically at-tentive public outside the S.P.D., reactions were highly ambivalent and often decidedly negative.

Cognitively, Schumacher's performance was perceived in increasingly negative terms. To more and more Germans, it seems, he appeared incompe-tent to deal with issues that in their view demanded effective instrumental

---

* The vehement attacks directed against Schumacher by leaders of the Socialist Unity party and other Communist spokesmen might be taken to indicate a positive mass response in the Soviet zone to his bid for leadership. He was blamed by them for unrest in the zone, and the uprising of 1953, ten months after his death, was attributed to "Schumacher's men." If the revolt had taken place during his lifetime, it might have provided more convincing evidence of his appeal beyond the Elbe.

leadership, such as political and economic reconstruction. His refusal to co-operate with other political actors except on his own terms, his determination to pursue a strategy of conflict with important German and foreign leaders, and in general his aggressive political style appeared even to those who in other respects sympathized with his values to be directly contrary to the proper behavior for a German party leader—in particular, one who sought to obtain the highest political office in an occupied, destitute, and disorganized country.

This emphasis on effective instrumental leadership appears to have turned against Schumacher even many Germans who accepted him evaluatively as a moral symbol of leadership on the strength of his anti-Nazi and anti-Communist record. Communists, right-wing conservatives, and latent Nazis rejected him totally as a positive moral symbol. For those who were more ambivalent in their moral values, his negative attitude toward cherished traditional norms, particularly religious values, as well as his apparent stand against certain new post-totalitarian norms, such as success ethics or the principle of European unification, seemed to outbalance his acknowledged moral virtues. In general, given the moral climate of postwar West Germany, it was apparently a disadvantage for an aspiring leader to be associated with the standards of a comparatively small minority (in Schumacher's case, the anti-Nazi socialists), since this made him seem a deviant in the eyes of most of his countrymen. To have been truly perceived as a popular symbol of moral leadership, it seems, he would have had to satisfy a much broader range of moral values, almost to the point of being all things to all men.

Finally, it appears that the man who sought to gain the support of the German masses in the role of their champion was not perceived affectively by most of them as an expressive symbol of charismatic leadership, such as Hitler may have been. For non-socialists he failed to overcome the image of a party leader representing a special interest group, and thus lacked positive emotional appeal. For some of them, particularly for those of his German counter-players whom he attacked personally as immoral, opportunist, and corrupt, he became in fact an extremely negative expressive symbol. By questioning the purity of their motives and policies, he aroused strongly antagonistic emotional responses that transcended purely rational considerations. Thus Heuss, it seems, deeply resented Schumacher's decision to contest his election as federal president in 1949; and Kaiser, as we noted, was led by the aspersions that Schumacher cast on his record and motives to throw his support to Adenauer. There is a good deal of evidence to indicate that in quite a few other instances, too, Schumacher's display of open contempt and hostility toward influential counter-players, and the provocative actions that evoked images of Hitler, not only lost him potential allies but made him new enemies. Under prevailing political conditions he could ill afford to make them.

As we noted in the introductory chapter, the socio-political environment limits a political actor's freedom to choose roles that will advance his ambitions. The successful leader in a group setting is the man whose role assignments and actions are accepted by his relevant counter-players because they are perceived by them as satisfying, or leading to the satisfaction, of values that are important to them. As Table 8 indicates, Schumacher was "a great party leader" in the sense that he managed to create or exploit a general congruence of role and value expectations in the S.P.D., which allowed him to function successfully as its monocratic leader. But at the same time he imposed upon himself far-reaching limitations upon his relationship with out-group actors by his role choice. His belief that the drive for power under prevailing conditions required not only a militant leader but a disciplined organization led him to fall in with in-group norms and institutional patterns that militated against his efforts to obtain the support of the masses outside the S.P.D. His emphasis on the mandate of the Social Democrats to determine the future of Germany and on the class struggle against "reactionaries" apparently suited the mood of most in-group members and strengthened consensus behind his leadership, but it also accentuated a sense of exclusiveness that set Social Democrats apart from out-group actors. Thus, the priority he gave to fighting and winning a battle for power that he saw as an all-or-nothing contest apparently made him neglect building up a popular social reform move-

TABLE 8

FUNCTIONALITY AND DYSFUNCTIONALITY OF SCHUMACHER'S ROLE CHOICES AND
PERFORMANCES AS AN ASPIRANT FOR POSTWAR LEADERSHIP

| Context | Role-set | | Central actor's role choice | Congruence/ incongruence of reciprocal orientations toward chief roles in set | Functionality/ dysfunctionality of role choice & performance by cent. actor |
	Central actor's position	Counter-players' position			
Social Democratic party	Party chairman	Party members, officials, & public office holders	Monocratic leader	General congruence	Mainly functional
Occupied Germany in world politics	Chairman of major West German political party	Leaders and representatives of non-German governments, parties, & interest groups	Patriotic leader	High incongruence	Highly dysfunctional
Intra-German politics	Chairman of major West German political party	Leaders of German governments, parties, interest groups, opinion leaders & mass publics	Champion of the common man	General incongruence	Mainly dysfunctional

ment in favor of establishing an efficient organization of loyal functionaries. The result, it seems, was that he found it increasingly difficult to reconcile the role of monocratic S.P.D. leader with that of champion of the common man, to maintain a favorable consensus within a party composed mostly of "old-timers" and at the same time to use his energies to obtain the support of the non-socialist masses.

As Table 8 also shows, outside the S.P.D. Schumacher failed to create a favorable congruence of role and value expectations that might have permitted him to function more successfully as an aspirant for the national leadership. Although the comparatively unstructured out-group context allowed him—and his competitors—considerable freedom to choose roles and actions, his interpretation of this context, his projection of roles, and his perception of the values of other political actors seem to have led him to take actions that proved in effect goal-denying. The image he chose to present, the values he advanced, and the actions he took failed to elicit the responses necessary to advance his drive for power because they were either not relevant in terms of the norms and expectations of his counter-players or perceived as conflicting with them. Given the outlook of those of his counter-players who determined the rules of the game in postwar German politics, Schumacher's determination to play the game according to a different, preconceived set of rules was hardly likely to yield him the desired rewards. In this sense, he was neither a "great political leader" nor a "statesman." But let us keep in mind the criteria for our assessment; perhaps he may be said to have possessed qualities of greatness not encompassed by the standards we have used here. We shall return to this question in the last chapter. At this point let us consider personality factors that may help to explain his behavior.

The Personality Variable

It has been one of the basic contentions of this study that to understand Schumacher's postwar political behavior we must take account of his personality characteristics. This is a risky and, of necessity, conjectural undertaking, for neither the theoretical tools nor the data available to us seem really adequate for the task. But surely it is worth the effort if we are to try to understand not only *what* Schumacher did, but *why* he did it. By shifting our focus from the objective political environment to the complexities of Schumacher's psychological environment, we may be able at least to infer a relationship between his responses to the context in which he had to operate and the configurations of his personality.

For many observers, particularly Schumacher's postwar critics and admirers, his behavior presented no puzzle. According to some of his severest critics, behavior that often seemed inexplicable was actually nothing but a studied effort to imitate Adolf Hitler. Admirers, too, saw nothing irrational in his actions.

They claimed that he was in fact far more perceptive and realistic than most of his opponents and critics because he saw more clearly than they the dangers inherent in certain postwar political developments and the urgent necessity for a determined effort to prevent Germany and the world from drifting into another catastrophe. Some political analysts were content to dismiss him as a hard-headed politician who lost his bid for power because others simply proved more adept than he at the game of postwar German politics. Others, noting his rigid and uncompromising behavior, attributed it to his "Prussianism." For President Heuss, for example, a South German who had known Schumacher over three decades, he was a typical product of West Prussia, a region that bred just such tough and "realistic" politicians.[21] To some non-Germans, particularly Americans, he was an "authoritarian personality," who typified the "obsessive-compulsive" traits that they associated with the German "national character." Quite a number of observers attributed his behavior to a Hegelian and/or Marxist philosophical orientation, while others stressed his alleged bonds to Lutheranism, all of them belief systems identified with self-righteous rigidity.

Whereas most of the above interpretations explained Schumacher's behavior primarily in terms of his social and intellectual antecedents, others put greater stress on specific personality traits, particularly his alleged "irrationality." They noted, for example, that he had been in rebellion against prevailing societal and political norms all his adult life, and had been a deviant type even within his own party and in the universe of Hitler's concentration camps. They also frequently asserted that his long imprisonment had wrought a fundamental transformation in his character. His suffering in the concentration camps was said to have produced physical and mental disturbances which, in the last years of his life at least, led to behavior bordering on the psychotic. Frustrated and exhausted, he was likened to a blinded gladiator who strikes out wildly in every direction, hoping to hit the many enemies he senses about him. "His tempestuous personality, his premonition of a disaster he was desperately trying to prevent, and his knowledge of his approaching death" allegedly "drove him into hasty outbursts which later no one regretted more than he."[22] Ultimately the burdens of his pain-wracked, crippled body and his desperate efforts to master them were said to have overwhelmed him, and to have led him to behave in a highly "irrational" manner in the last years.[23]

Many of these interpretations point to what may indeed have been very important causes of Schumacher's postwar behavior. But it also seems that they focus on certain pieces of the puzzle, leaving other questions unanswered. For example, did Schumacher's behavior really undergo significant changes, and if so, at what point in time? Was his alleged political "irrationality" entirely the product of his concentration camp experiences and postwar physical complaints, or was it perhaps rooted in earlier experiences shaping his personality? If he was just "a typical Prussian," "Marxist," "authoritarian German," or "concentrationnaire," how are we to explain that others with similar backgrounds did not behave in a similar way? If the threat of his approaching death drove him into frantic efforts to achieve his goals before it was too late, how are we to explain the calm behavior of much older men, such as Adenauer, who may have had as much reason to engage in a "race with death"?

Our examination of Schumacher's manifest attitudes and actions over a span of some thirty years seems to suggest certain rather distinct personality traits which, in interaction with the various situations in which he had to function, appear to have led to behavior that in some instances proved to be objectively dysfunctional and in others highly functional—both in terms of his manifest political objectives and in terms of his apparent personality needs. Our findings also seem to suggest that although certain attitudes and behavior patterns may have become more pronounced during the last years of his life, they may have already been deeply imbedded in his personality system as structures of vital importance for its proper functioning and adjustment to inner needs. In this case, the orientation and behavior that seem to have distinguished his psychological environment may have been mandatory for him, no matter what the cost to his physical well-being and manifest political aspirations.

As we shall try to indicate in the discussion to follow, Schumacher's behavior and attitude patterns point to *character traits clinically identified with those of an obsessive-compulsive personality striving to adjust to the objective environment in a socially acceptable manner.* Thus our investigation of his developmental history and postwar activities appears to indicate that (1) antecedent personal experiences may have had a strong, perhaps decisive, influence on his postwar psychological environment, and may have prestructured his political role conceptions and behavior patterns; (2) the personality syndrome that he brought to his focal position as an aspirant for the post-totalitarian leadership may have severely restricted his perceptions, interpretations, and choice of responses relating to the political setting in which he had to function; (3) his political style in general and his specific role performances in particular may have reflected strenuous efforts on his part to maintain consistency in his personal beliefs—to the point of satisfying his inner needs at the expense of his political goals.

Characteristic Behavior Patterns

In considering the above hypotheses in greater detail, let us begin with an examination of Schumacher's *expressive style*: that is, not only what he did but how he did it, not only his actions, but the manner in which they were performed.[24] Psychologists and psychiatrists inform us that the nature of a man's overt actions as well as his characteristic style of performance may tell us much about his personality in that they reflect his view of his environment and of his counter-players, even when he deliberately strives to conceal his basic attitudes or is not consciously aware of their full meaning. By beginning with an examination of the general behavior patterns that seem to emerge from Schumacher's associations with other actors and his responses to the objective environment, we may thus be able to delineate characteristic modes of expression, and to infer from them certain attitudes identifying the belief system structuring the psychological environment.

One of Schumacher's postwar lieutenants described him as *homo politicus,* in the sense that there existed for him no life outside the political arena. A commemorative brochure published by the S.P.D. after his death pointed out that for most of his life he had had "neither a family nor anything else usually associated with a private life."[25] He had lived "for politics" and not "of politics," to use Max Weber's terms, leaving his relatives after his death no private possessions to speak of.[26] From the time he entered politics to the day he died, political activities took up most of his waking hours. His associations were almost entirely confined to other political actors; women friends, relatives, and others who did not fall into this category were given less and less of his time, and after the war he excluded them completely. Increasingly, too, he claimed to have no time for relaxation. Journalists, comparing him with other politicians, called him the austere monk among German political leaders. In the twenty years before his death, he apparently took only one vacation, and then only on the insistence of his physicians after his stroke of December 1951. His "marriage to politics," he frequently asserted, demanded all his time and energies; political issues emerged clearly as the focus of his interests in everything he did and said, not only after the war but in Stuttgart and the concentration camp as well.*

His health, too, Schumacher regarded as primarily a political issue. His physical condition and the possibility of his death, he impressed upon associates, had to be viewed exclusively in terms of the realization of his political aspirations. His survival in the concentration camp and his struggle to overcome physical infirmities after the war, he asserted, was of little significance to him personally, but it was of utmost significance to the course of political developments in Germany. In particular, he stressed that he must *appear physically strong* in order to provide the masses he sought to attract with the

---

* "You often inquire about my private life, but I have little to report on it," Schumacher wrote in December 1947 to a woman who had been a close friend in the Weimar days. "I have not seen my relatives in two years for lack of time," he told her, and the assertion is borne out by his crowded appointments calendar. His lieutenants were surprised when once or twice in these years he offered to join them in their regular card game, for it seemed so entirely out of character. Usually, they said, he could not even find the time to attend to all the political matters that he insisted demanded his attention.

image of a vigorous leader capable of giving them authoritative guidance. When he was told in 1948 that to save his life his leg would have to be amputated, he consented reluctantly. The personal discomfort and pain was of no importance, he said, but he feared that he might become an object of pity rather than respect. Would he appear less impressive to the masses he wanted to lead, he asked an old friend, would they respect him less for this additional indication of physical infirmity? As for the possibility of death, this, too, he treated as a political matter. When in 1947 he accidently took an overdose of sedatives on a visit to Berlin and barely recovered (he relied heavily on both sedatives and stimulants to keep himself going in those years), he coolly discussed the political implications of his death with his lieutenants.

Schumacher was a man of *intense political action,* a man who expressed his dedication to politics by participating in them rather than meditating and writing about them. He had, after all, barely found time to earn his doctorate, a title that he employed, as we have seen, exclusively to further his political ambitions. His style of performance was consistently militant. Bitter experience had taught him that "the battle for political progress" demanded that one "fight for every inch of the ground with iron determination," as he said after the war, and never seek "refuge in passivity."[27] Whatever experiences he may have had in mind when he said this, we have seen that from the beginning of his career he was an aggressive political fighter, who seemed to *seek conflict* and showdowns with opponents. Openly contemptuous of other political leaders who were less determined to achieve victory, more ready to compromise, and more willing to evade an open clash, he held that "postponed crises ... are always more destructive in their consequences than those which are boldly faced and thus overcome."[28] This dictum, which he presented to fellow Social Democrats in his first public statement after the fall of the Nazi regime, seems to have been basic to his political activities before as well as after the Third Reich.

While Schumacher maintained that as a democratic socialist he neither would nor could descend to the methods employed by those he denounced as anti-democratic, he claimed at the same time that a vicious opponent deserved no better than Schumacher gave him. His savage hostility toward certain of his foes literally frightened some of his more moderate associates after the war. Not that his aggressiveness began after the war. Already in the Weimar days he had earned himself a reputation as the most belligerent Social Democrat in Württemberg, not only by making savage and often deliberately insulting attacks on other political actors, but by organizing a militant organization to engage in physical combat with Nazi and Communist strong-arm squads. He seemed to enjoy the excitement of battle, and according to one of his early associates, he was never one to moderate his provocative behavior if he could possibly help it. After the fall of the Nazi regime, he was vehement in his insistence that proven anti-Nazi leaders mete out "revolutionary justice" to those he called the "beneficiaries" of the Third Reich and its "sponsors," and exceedingly bitter about the refusal of the occupation powers to let him have his way. He was infuriated by the rise to power, in both the Western and the Soviet zones, of groups that in his view should be barred permanently from participation in political life. His professions of democratic tolerance explicitly did not extend to individuals and groups whom he declared beyond sufferance because they represented values that he said were totally unacceptable to him.

Schumacher was an extremely *self-assertive person,* who evidently refused to accept anyone as his better, *above all in matters relating to politics,* whether political knowledge, skills, morality, or idealism. From the time he began his drive for political power as a young socialist in Württemberg to his last clashes in the battle for leadership in postwar Germany, he seemed constantly intent upon asserting his superiority over other political actors. In his conflicts with rivals inside as well as outside the S.P.D., as in his relationship with his follow-ers, he consistently showed himself absolutely certain that he knew exactly what had to be done and how, and he rarely sought advice or accepted the counsel of anyone who tried to influence him. Not only in public but in private gatherings as well, he stated rather than discussed his views on political issues. On the rare occasions when he professed ignorance, it was usually on non-political matters, such as music and art, which were clearly of little interest to him compared with politics.

Above all, it seemed to many who observed his behavior closely that he re-sented opponents who questioned his courage, political morality, or selfless idealism. In such cases, he tended to throw caution to the wind and to react with impassioned fury, as we saw in his battles with the Nazis and Com-munists before 1933, and in many of his disputes after the war. In the concen-tration camp, too, he seems to have found the taunts and insults of his jailers far more difficult to accept than physical abuse, severe deprivation, or the threat of death. At times his contempt for those he declared to be his inferiors in political courage and morality led him to underestimate the power of op-ponents; but even when it was evidently quite clear to him that his belligerent behavior involved serious dangers for himself and his cause, he seems to have insisted on demonstrating that he was a better man than his foes. It frequently seemed, in fact, that the more powerful the counter-players he chose to attack and hold in contempt, the more determined he became to assert his superior-ity, and the more infuriated by failure to establish clearly that he was the better man and his the better cause. Unlike most other Weimar political leaders, he refused to accept Hitler's victory in Germany as a defeat for himself, literally inviting imprisonment rather than take flight or submit. And unlike many of his countrymen, he would not recognize the authority of the occupation powers to prescribe political beliefs and actions, claiming that it was "an illusion to conclude that victory brings with it superior wisdom."[29]

Statements like these were more than polemics, it seems. They apparently expressed a genuine sense of superiority that characterized Schumacher's political behavior in general. As a young socialist, as a concentration camp prisoner, and as an aspirant to the postwar leadership of Germany, he asserted again and again that he felt it his duty to oppose those persons who, he insisted, were neither morally nor intellectually qualified to wield political power. According to him, Keil, Bazille, Hitler, Grotewohl, Adenauer, and other opponents had to be fought because they were unworthy of exercising the power that had come to them either by trickery or luck.

Constantly alert to challenges from potential or actual rivals, Schumacher *would not share the powers that he claimed for himself.* In Stuttgart as in postwar Germany he surrounded himself with persons who accepted his claims uncritically, and quickly cast out of this inner circle anyone who questioned his authority. Both in his bid for the leadership of the S.P.D. and in his drive for the leadership of his country, he chose for his lieutenants men who faithfully accepted and carried out his wishes. Their assigned task was primarily to assist and inform him, rather than advise him, and he certainly did not welcome unsolicited advice. He demanded that they consult him and keep him informed at all times, but he himself would seek their advice only on matters of detail, not substance. According to one of his principal postwar lieutenants, he would let trusted assistants handle the details of his political decisions and actions, but insisted on reserving for himself the right to plan and direct strategy and tactics. He interpreted his formal powers as party leader very broadly, and was easily annoyed if a subordinate questioned his authority or fumbled in the execution of his instructions. Even when he was seriously ill, he insisted that all substantive political issues be referred to him for decision, and that other Social Democratic leaders keep him fully informed of their intentions and actions. In short, he allowed no doubt about who was in charge.

Another aspect of this self-assertive behavior was Schumacher's persistent *refusal to compromise on political issues that he had declared to be a matter of principle* with him. Principles, he asserted time and again, could not be bargained over, and tolerance in politics was a sign of weakness. A compromise, he said, could only come "at the end of a battle," not at the beginning: "The man who enters a fight intending to compromise is certain to be defeated."[30] But for him the fight seems never to have come to an end, and rare indeed were the occasions when he would retreat on an issue on which he had taken a firm stand. He might engage to a limited extent in tactical maneuvers designed to strengthen his political power, but he seldom made significant concessions. As one observer noted after his death, he seemed to want to provoke his opponents, rather than induce them to seek a solution of differences.[31] In the opinion of some of his closest associates, he may well have been aware that he created new obstacles for himself by behaving in this way, but they had the impression that he was unable to help himself, and at times was actually relieved when an agreement could be avoided and the battle could continue. Whereas before 1945 Schumacher's refusal to compromise his professed principles appears to have served his purposes rather well, in the postwar era it appears to have had less favorable results—though even then it undoubtedly helped him at first, as his battle with Grotewohl demonstrated.

In this connection, let us also note that Schumacher seems to have had great *difficulty in retracting a charge or apologizing*—even when, in the opinion of his lieutenants, political prudence called for such action. Only rarely, such as after his famous charge in 1949 that Adenauer was "the Chancellor of the Allies," could he be induced to retract an insult. He might admit at times that a particularly aggressive attack on a potential ally had been politically unwise, but even then, according to his associates, he found it extremely difficult to recant.

Despite his professed belief in democratic practices, Schumacher displayed throughout his career *a very low degree of tolerance for disagreement* with his views or actions. Hypersensitive to indications of dissent, he could be exceedingly hard on those who disagreed with him. In general, he demanded that others yield to him and accept his views, and persons who failed to comply seem to have provoked bitter attacks from him. He would redouble his efforts to compel them to submit, at whatever political cost to himself and his aspirations, and was infuriated when he failed. We noted such behavior in his controversies with Reuter, Kaisen, Adenauer, and Western occupation officials, and many other, if less prominent, instances could be cited. Although he himself was always in rebellion against his formal superiors, he was acutely sensitive to signs of rebellion against his own claims to leadership. Most of his associates, as many of them admitted later, took care not to disagree with him, for fear of his savage ridicule and anger. Few who sought to change his views in the sphere he claimed as his special competence ever succeeded. Those who did had to learn that he was more likely to resent than appreciate their efforts— even when, perhaps particularly when, they were later proved right.

Schumacher could display deep, even touching, concern for the health and welfare of others, but the objects of such solicitude were almost always *persons who in some way were clearly his inferiors, particularly in political matters*. Adoring women, admiring young socialists, deferential fellow prisoners in the concentration camp, and submissive party officials, they were usually persons who indicated to him that he could do more for them than they for him, whether the service rendered was material or (as oftener the case) emotional. If they helped him to deal with his physical infirmities or in other ways sought to make his life easier, there almost always remained an implicit understanding that such assistance was rendered out of respect for him, not pity. It was mostly in these relationships, apparently, that Schumacher was able to employ a tone of familiarity and to show the warmth that others found lacking in him.

He showed greater concern about the health of such persons than about his own, and sought to provide for their material welfare as best he could. But none of them would ever joke at his expense, or in any way disturb a relationship that was clearly not between equals but between an acknowledged superior and his deferential admirers.

From the time he was a boy, it appears, Schumacher *never really confided in anyone*. His family knew of his thoughts and plans only in the most general terms, and in later years he did not "open up" even to his closest associates. According to people who had worked with him, no one really "knew" what went on in his mind, or what his plans were beyond the political issues of the moment. Not even his closest co-workers after the war could say later what he would have done had he succeeded in his fight to become Germany's leader. He seemed to go out of his way to avoid discussing personal problems and experiences, and to evade questions about his private thoughts. Always ready to speak out on a public issue, he was strikingly reticent about matters that he claimed to be of interest to no one but himself. His letters from the concentration camp to people who were presumably close to him reveal nothing about his thoughts and feelings at the time. Perhaps he did not care to expose them to the eyes of the censor, but his conversations with fellow prisoners were apparently no more revealing. An unbreachable wall seems to have surrounded an inner sanctum of his mind since his youth, leaving him something of an enigma even to his most intimate associates.

Our analysis of Schumacher's expressive style has shown his single-minded dedication to political action (and the fight for authoritative power that it implied), his self-assertiveness and intolerance, and his refusal to give his full confidence to anyone. Why did he adhere so rigidly to these behavior patterns, especially when the results seem to have blocked rather than furthered his ambitions? Why was he apparently unable to profit from potential learning experiences, and why did he persist in behavior that proved increasingly frustrating in terms of his political goals? Why was he unable to establish or maintain political relationships that involved concessions on his part? Why did he appear to go out of his way to show his hatred or contempt for other important political actors, even when there was little apparent cause for such behavior, and it provoked seemingly unnecessary, politically disadvantageous antagonism? Why did he evidently assume the need for political conflict? Why did he persist in efforts to compel others to act—even against him—rather than await the trend of political developments? Was it merely a matter of strategy, as he claimed, or were there other reasons for his efforts to dominate developments? The key to these questions seems to me to lie buried in Schumacher's personality. If we want to try to find it, we must push our analysis further and consider the relationship between his expressive style and belief system, for the outlook that a person brings to various situations determines his choice of responses.

Orientation Patterns and Belief System

Schumacher's behavior, especially during his last years, led a few perceptive observers to suspect that beneath the armor of a tough, extroverted, and calculating political actor lay the highly unstable, tempestuous personality of a man deeply preoccupied with himself and at war with the world. They noted what one of them termed a decided *Zwiespältigkeit,* a tendency to function on two entirely separate levels of action. On one level he seemed intent on following a highly rational course in the battle for political power, on the other he appeared guided more by his emotions than by his reason, by what his friend Ollenhauer called the "inner passion of his political aspirations."[32]

Willy Brandt has spoken of "the almost fanatical tenacity" with which Schumacher clung to his decisions."[33] There were times when Schumacher seemed stubbornly to ignore, even defy, the dictates of political reason in choosing a course of action for himself. This was apparent not only in the postwar years, but also when he refused to avoid certain imprisonment in 1933, and subsequently when he would not follow the example of other anti-Nazis by submitting nominally to the Nazi regime, a course that would have gained him freedom for new political action in exile or the underground movement. Repeatedly throughout his entire political career, emotion rather than logic seemed to influence his choice between alternatives, but he refused to admit that there was such a dichotomy. He acknowledged no conflict between his insistence that the Social Democratic drive for power in Germany was of overriding importance and the tenacity with which he clung to a strategy and tactics that failed to bring him the desired results. On the one hand he insisted that postwar realities created entirely new conditions for the Social Democratic fight for power; on the other he never ceased to harp on the "lessons of the past." He made no effort to conceal his determination to wield power in the name of progress and reform, yet he seemed unable to take the actions that might bring him closer to this goal. The answer to the puzzle lies perhaps in our hypothesis that behavior which may have been self-defeating in terms of Schumacher's manifest aspirations may have served latent personality needs. To consider this matter more closely, let us seek to explore his psychological environment by studying his orientation patterns and the belief system underlying them.

Behavior patterns delineate concrete responses to the objective environment; they are based on the observable output variables of the personality system. When we turn to orientation patterns, however, we venture into an area of analysis that even under the best of circumstances poses difficult problems, for the investigator must rely largely on inference. In Schumacher's case the difficulty is compounded by insufficient empirical data, and we are compelled to rely particularly heavily on inference and analogy. Happily, recent studies by American social psychologists can assist us here.

A person's *psychological environment,* the subjective manner in which he perceives and interprets situational stimuli from the world about him (the objective environment), determines his behavioral responses, and it is from them that we seek to infer his hierarchy of values, his perception of other actors and what they do, and his expectations of potential rewards and punishments for himself if he takes or does not take certain actions. The psychological environment thus incorporates beliefs and expectations that provide a person with guideposts or reference points for understanding men and events, and since these cognitive processes are more or less structured, we can speak of them as *personality orientation patterns. Beliefs,* then, are "those stored memories whose contents specify for the organism what may be expected to happen" on the basis of past learning processes; and they are converted into expectations that influence behavior when they are activated by stimuli originating either inside or outside the organism.[34]

Extensive experimental studies by a number of social psychologists have indicated that personality orientation patterns incorporate a cognitive ego defense mechanism by means of which informational cues from the external environment are filtered out or modified in order to ward off or render harmless items that threaten the equilibrium of the personality system. Human beings appear to view external objects and events in terms of what they believe to be true or untrue, and to react to them in accordance with such beliefs or disbeliefs, as well as in terms of the relevance that such objects and events seem to hold for them with regard to their goals and values. On a deeper, more or less subconscious level of the personality system, orientation patterns are apparently structured to maintain psychic equilibrium. To avoid the serious inner tensions that are caused by cognitive dissonance and belief incongruence, new information tends to be either rejected when it clashes with cherished beliefs, or made to conform with them. It has also been found that the degree to which a person adheres to existing beliefs in the light of new informational cues depends on the nature and strength of his ego defense network. Some persons appear to find it comparatively easy to adjust existing beliefs to new information, and to be highly flexible in reacting to it, either because the information is felt to constitute no serious threat to their self-esteem, or because belief adjustment is discovered to be the best way of relieving tensions produced by temporary belief incongruence. Such persons have been found to be rather open-minded, undogmatic, and quick to adjust to new situations.

Conversely, persons with relatively closed minds tend just as consistently to ignore or distort new information that conflicts with cherished beliefs. They resist adjustment to dynamic external developments, and adhere rigidly to expectations regarding other actors and future developments that are congruent with such beliefs. In such persons, attempts to overcome belief incongruence by adjusting to challenging new information apparently produces greater inner tensions than rejection and non-adjustment because their belief system serves essential ego maintenance functions. In reacting to new developments, they rely far more on memories of past experiences than on available new information, and the expectations influencing their behavior are derived from beliefs that are virtually inviolate for them because they provide "peace of mind." The ego defense mechanism comes into play at this point, when new information challenges firm beliefs, to modify or entirely filter out external cues that are unacceptable in their raw form. Thus, objective situations are made to conform with the all-important belief system by the processing of cognitions in the psychological environment. Resulting rigid attitudes and behavior may seem irrational and prove self-defeating in terms of the person's manifest goals in the objective environment; but he is likely to cling to them nonetheless (and to reject new learning experiences involving rewards and sanctions for himself) because they relate beliefs and expectations that are essential to his personality system and its inner needs.[35]

Roles, which we have defined as expectations toward the incumbents of various positions, appear to play a crucial part in such personality orientation patterns. The central actor's assignment of roles to himself and his counterplayers constitutes an effort on his part to structure social relationships in conformity with his general belief system. His attitude and behavior toward other actors, whether perceived as individuals or collectivities, are conditioned by the extent of his need to accommodate in his personality system tensions arising from the interaction between the "inner man" and the external setting. Accordingly, he views them and their actions cognitively, affectively, and evaluatively in terms of the scope of their apparent significance for himself.[36] He chooses his own roles, projects others upon relevant counter-players, and attempts to respond to various situational cues in accordance with his need for belief congruence and inner tension reduction.

A person's ability to adjust his overt behavior to the expectations and belief systems of his counter-players thus depends greatly on his personality make-up: the extent to which others and their actions create inner tensions for him, the extent to which he can overcome such tensions, and the extent to which he is able to accept or reject sanctions that he applies to himself (as against sanctions that his counter-players are in a position to apply to him). It seems that the greater the actor's sense of personal involvement in a situation is, the more dominant these emotional aspects of his orientation become (with respect both to the situation and to those involved in it), and the more ambiguous the cognitive and evaluative aspects. Also, the less structured by institutionalized social patterns his role perceptions are, the greater the possibility is that subjective personality variables rather than objective situational variables will condition his attitudes and responses. And, finally, the more closed his belief system is with regard to his interpretation of the objective setting, the more inflexible his role assignments are likely to be, and the more limited his ability to adjust his overt actions and style of performance to the expectations of his counter-players. Since these counter-players can block or facilitate his efforts to achieve personal belief congruence and tension reduction, such adjustment becomes doubly important. Severe frustration of externalized efforts to satisfy personal needs may rebound on the "inner man" and result in increased personality tensions, which in turn may yield attitudes and behavior that prove dysfunctional in terms of both manifest and latent functions.* In the light of these theories, let us see what we can infer about Schumacher's orientation pattern and belief system from his behavior over time.

It seems that Schumacher held *very firm beliefs* about the objective environment and his position in it. Throughout his political career, he appears to have searched in a highly selective fashion for evidence in the external environment that would sustain and reinforce these orientations, drawing now upon Marxist theory and now upon more individualistic and voluntaristic interpretations of events.† Potential learning experiences seem to have affected such perceptions only insofar as they served to strengthen existing beliefs, rather than to have modified them significantly. Schumacher seems to have felt irrevocably committed to and involved in an unrelenting, bitter struggle for political power, and this commitment appears to have had a very high emotional content, which manifested itself in his assessment of political issues and actors, and in his increasingly rigid moral standards for evaluating his own attitudes and conduct as well as those of his counter-players.

---

* By *manifest functions* I mean those objective consequences of role choices and performances that are recognized and intended by the central actor in terms of his belief system; by *latent functions* I mean those objective consequences of role choices and performances that contribute to the adjustment and adaptation of the personality system without being consciously perceived or intended as such by the central actor. Thus unintended consequences are latently functional when they serve to satisfy unconscious needs, and dysfunctional when they fail to do so. See Merton, p. 51.

† Schumacher's employment of certain Marxist concepts and theories, especially after 1933, led some observers to regard him as a doctrinaire Marxist. As we have noted, he did indeed emphasize a dialectic analysis of political developments in Nazi and post-Nazi Germany, and particularly in the postwar period he put great stress on what he referred to as the class struggle between the working people and the forces of capitalist reaction. Whereas on the conscious level this may have been a deliberate choice of political strategy (particularly to rally support among the S.P.D. old-timers and to mobilize the "working masses"), our evidence suggests that Marxist interpretations of political developments served primarily to provide him with reinforcement for beliefs that were not rooted in Marxism.

After 1933, theories providing a deterministic interpretation of political developments appear to have provided the concentration camp prisoner, and later the aspirant for the postwar leadership, with belief-sustaining arguments to ward off incongruent information about external developments. Schumacher seems to have selected Marxist arguments and slogans in a highly eclectic manner to provide him with a logical justification for his interpretation of the political environment and his behavior in it. This appears to have been particularly the case in times of personal crisis, as when Hitler's triumph in Germany suddenly put an end to his rise in the S.P.D., and later when his deteriorating physical condition combined with political developments to bring into question his self-assigned mission to transform German society. Thus Marxist beliefs that had been incorporated into the ego defense network appear to have served basically to sustain his psychic equilibrium.

In making such assertions, I am trying to distinguish between the content and the structure of Schumacher's belief system. Manifestly, he was deeply dedicated to democratic principles and practices and emphatically opposed to doctrinaire beliefs. Throughout his life he went out of his way to repudiate dogma: as a young socialist he had ridiculed the theoretical emphasis of certain elements in the S.P.D., calling it the "casuistry of the fathers of the Marxist Church," and after the war he had refused to be bound by any basic Social Democratic program. "One must learn from life as it is" and always face reality, he told fellow Social Democrats in 1946.[37] More than one obituary writer described him as "a man not bound by programs or doctrine."[38] But as a social psychologist has pointed out, "a person may espouse a set of beliefs that are democratic in content," but he may apply them in a manner that is "authoritarian, intolerant of those who disagree with him, and closed in mode of thought and belief."[39] Thus, whereas Schumacher emphatically rejected dogma and doctrines propagated by others, very firm "inner convictions" seem to have ruled his own views and conduct. That is to say, his dogmatism appears to have been highly personal, based on inner rather than external referents, and to have led him to accept no authority as superior to his own subjective insight and interpretations, particularly where politics were concerned.

Basic to a person's belief system is his *self-perception,* the way he views himself as interacting with his perceived counter-players. Schumacher, who reportedly always took himself very seriously, appears on the face of it to have seen himself as a highly task-oriented leader, and to have identified himself entirely, even fatalistically, with serving the cause of progress and freedom in Germany. Assuming a highly moralistic stance, particularly toward other political actors whom he described as amoral Machiavellian manipulators, he "ran the Socialist party as if he were its Moses and its members his Children of Israel," as one observer put it.[40] One might carry this metaphor even further by saying that he apparently wanted to lead not only his party but the entire German "working masses" out of the Egyptian dungeons of their past, through the turbulent seas and arid deserts of postwar socio-economic, moral, and political chaos, and into the promised land of socialist democracy.

This seems to have been no newly found sense of destiny. When Hitler came to power in 1933, Schumacher had informed anxious friends who urged him to save himself by going into exile that he had to stay to uphold a cause that was sacred to him, and set an example for the working masses, who now as never before needed courageous, dedicated leaders. Once imprisoned, he told fellow prisoners and anxious relatives who suggested that he buy his freedom, at least by formal submission to the Nazi regime, that to do so would be to betray his vocation. When at last he was released, apparently a dying man, he told the factory supervisor who had befriended him that his political calling had preordained him to be persecuted by the Hitler dictatorship. When his leg was to be amputated after the war, he said that he had invited this fate when he voluntarily chose to suffer martyrdom for principles he held sacred. "What keeps me going in my position as party chairman is simply a sense of duty toward Social Democracy and the German people," we have already quoted him as saying in a private letter in 1946. "As far as I am personally concerned, I would much rather lead an entirely private life in as minor a position as possible." It seems that he sincerely believed that he was literally laying down his life in the course of carrying out an assignment that was his duty as a soldier in the front ranks of the battle for peace and progress in Germany.

But the assignment was self-imposed; it was Schumacher himself who chose to bear this cross. "He demanded great efforts from his co-workers, but he drove himself most of all," Erich Ollenhauer recalled in his funeral oration. "A more reasonable way of life might have preserved him longer, but then it would not have been Schumacher's way of life—as we knew him, and as he had to be in order to rise to the heights that he alone achieved."[41] Thus it seems that the words "we must" and "we should" that he hurled at others throughout his career were addressed at least as much to himself. Manifestly a task-oriented political actor, he thus appears in fact to have been *highly self-oriented*.

At first glance, this assertion seems to be contradicted by Schumacher's professed identification with the cause he claimed to serve. He emphatically minimized the importance of his own person, ostensibly disliked being the object of hero worship, and, according to one of his biographers, modestly claimed to be no more than a "link in the long chain" of German Social Democratic leaders who had fought for social equality and political progress. But he is also said to have been convinced "that he could do a great many things better than other people" in advancing the cause, and to have sought the power and influence "to mold" political developments, "to change the world" as he saw fit.[42]

Our own investigation indicates that at least since his "marriage to politics" in his late adolescence, the crippled veteran of World War I felt *a sense of intense moral and emotional involvement with his political environment*, which relentlessly drove him to strike out personally against conditions he considered utterly wrong, and to seek the power to change them radically. As a physician might dedicate himself to finding a cure for a fatal disease, or a missionary devote his life to saving souls that would otherwise be eternally damned, so Schumacher seems to have seen it as his calling to give his all to reforming German society. Evidently he was wholly sincere in his conviction that he was singularly well qualified to provide not only the instrumental but the moral and symbolic leadership required by his self-chosen task. This over-whelming sense of duty to the cause he chose to serve apparently induced him to sever the bonds of affection that had bound him to his mother and sisters as a child, and to advise the woman who wanted to marry him to forget him after he was sent to a concentration camp. It also seems to have given him the strength to survive the great physical and psychological strains of his long imprisonment, and to bear the burdens and frustrations of the years that fol-lowed.

If a person's self-perception is the key element in the system of beliefs and expectations that relate directly to his role choices and behavior, his *perception of other relevant actors* seems to be the second most important factor. Social psychologists tell us that a person's behavior toward another person is based upon what he thinks the other is like and what actions he expects of him. An actor's perception of the people and actions that are important to him in his environment seems to relate back to his general belief system and its points of reference. In some instances such images may be based on external refer-ence points, in others on internal ones. Whatever the source, the actor who relies heavily on highly authoritative reference points is likely to possess ex-tremely distinct images and expectations about other actors, and his behavior toward relevant counter-players will be correspondingly unambiguous. "When authority is seen as absolute," according to one social psychologist, it "leads to extreme cognitive distinctions between persons as faithful and unfaithful, or-thodox and heretical, ... friend and enemy." Those who disagree with the actor's absolute authorities for his beliefs "may be rejected as enemies of God, country, mankind, the working class," whereas "those who agree may be ac-cepted, but only as long as, and on the condition that they continue to agree."[43] In Schumacher's case, it seems, inner-directed authoritative absolutes caused him to make *rigid perceptual distinctions between important and unimportant, and trustworthy and untrustworthy, counter-players.*

To the highly self-oriented person, other social objects seem like satellites re-volving strictly about himself, some very close, others barely noticeable, and still others at times invisible and at times extremely visible. To Schumacher, the significance of other actors seems to have varied with their perceived sig-nificance for his assumed political tasks. That is, his reference point for assess-ing the importance of what others said and did was apparently his self-assigned duty to take a leading hand in changing his environment, and he appears to have perceived other actors in strict relation to this sharp and fixed view of himself as a Promethean figure. Such evidence as I was able to collect about his attitudes about others supports this impression rather strongly.

We have noted throughout Schumacher's career a lack of sensitivity to the values and expectations of other actors, and a propensity to assess roles and role performances according to rigid and absolute criteria of significance as well as propriety. Over the years, he seems to have developed an unmistakable tendency to view those about him exclusively in terms of their relevance to his *fight for political power*. Other social objects and what other actors said and did seemed to matter less and less to him if they did not relate to this primary purpose. From the start of his career, he seems to have deliberately kept his interests and social relationships outside politics very much on the light side, apparently finding no difficulty in discarding any associations that got in the way of his political duties. The more pressing the demands of his principal calling were, it appears, the more readily, resolutely, and completely did he divest himself of nonpolitical interests and attachments, and the more sharply did he discriminate between the people and things that mattered and those that did not matter in terms of advancing his cause. In Stuttgart, the demands of his readily assumed and rapidly increasing political responsibilities left him less and less time to indulge his interest in music, art, and literature, or to relax in the company of women, artists, and writers. If he regretted the loss of these pleasures at all, his lust for a different sort of life—the life of a political man—seems to have been ample compensation. After he emerged from his long imprisonment to fight for political power, he claimed no longer to have either the time or the energy for "frivolities" of this nature. He now found his relaxation, he said, in studying election statistics and in informal political discussions with his associates. Political objects thus claimed his primary, and eventually his exclusive, attention.

Within this focus of attention, Schumacher seems to have distinguished rather sharply between generalized collective actors and specific individual actors on the basis of their apparent relevance in his fight for power. In an unpublished interview shortly before his death, he asserted proudly that all his life he had been interested more in ideas than in men. Indeed, analytical constructs seem to have occupied a key position in his belief system, leading him to reify abstract collectivities. His personification of various diffuse national and subnational groups was evidently more than just rhetoric. He apparently perceived such collectivities as "the proletariat," "the reactionaries," and "the American capitalists" as concrete counter-players upon whom he projected roles, and from whom he accordingly expected specific aspirations and behavior patterns. For example, according to associates, he loved the "German people" not so much as flesh-and-blood human beings as an idealized abstraction derived from his patriotism. He spoke of the "little Nazis" who deserved to be forgiven and of the "big capitalists" who should be punished, usually without identifying such groups more specifically. Such stereotyped collective actors seem to have represented for him entirely concrete political objects—either friendly or hostile, either significant or insignificant—to be dealt with according to the position they occupied in his belief system.

At the other extreme, there were actors who evidently occupied very specific places on Schumacher's map of important social objects. These were certain individual actors with whom, it seems, he felt deeply involved emotionally. On the one hand, there were certain close associates, such as the devoted followers who worshiped him as their heroic leader. On the other, there were people whom he took to be personal enemies, such as Reuter. Ostensibly his passionate hatred for the latter category was based on his feeling that they threatened the success of his cause. But as we have seen, his hostility frequently seemed to exceed the limits of purely "rational" disagreements, and to point to deeper and perhaps entirely unconscious emotional attitudes. As we look back, for example, on his disputes with Keil, Grotewohl, and Adenauer, and compare these with his conflicts with Hitler and with various foreign leaders after the war, it seems that the intensity of his negative emotional reactions toward opponents was determined more by the degree to which they seemed *his direct rivals* in the battle for political positions than by differences over goals and policies. This brings us to another distinction that he made among his counterplayers, possibly even more important than that between friend and foe.

To draw *a sharp, unambiguous distinction* between those who supported him in his political battles and those who belonged to the opposing camp seems to have been of immense importance to Schumacher throughout his career, no matter what the particular issue or context. To accentuate this compartmentalization of friend and foe, he would start postwar speeches with the words "My friends and enemies."[44] This, too, might have been merely a rhetorical device, if it had not been for the fact that he seemed constantly to be searching for evidence to support his dichotomy. Boldly stating his own views, he demanded that other political actors respond to him by revealing their "true color"—a wish that probably achieved its most dramatic satisfaction when he was thrown into a Nazi concentration camp. There are numerous indications that he felt more comfortable in facing a forthright, even brutally open opponent than uncertain supporters. As we have noted, he seemed to be put out by ambiguous alignments and ill-defined positions, and to strive for clear-cut divisions, whether in general elections or in representative bodies. In battles with opponents inside as well as outside the S.P.D., Schumacher would time and again insist on a formal vote, even at the risk of revealing divisions that might weaken his position. Fellow Social Democrats who thought such votes unnecessary or undesirable were informed by him that he wanted neither to leave any doubt nor to be left in doubt about *who was for him and who against.* He supported such demands with political arguments, but his insistence may also have been based on the latent need to maintain congruence between his belief system and the objective environment.

Schumacher appears to have assumed that his marriage to politics *committed him irrevocably to participate in a savage battle for power* in Germany. As a young socialist, he told his girl friend that politics was a dirty game unfit for gentlemen, and his experiences during and after the war seem to have strongly reinforced this belief. He apparently believed that his calling obliged him to partake in a conflict which seemed brutal and merciless, in which compromise and tolerance indicated weakness, and in which there could be only total victory or total defeat. Given such assumptions about the political process and the concomitant belief that the differences between the forces of "progress" and the forces of "reaction" were irreconcilable, his firm identification with the former appears to have allowed him no choice but to wage an uncompromising battle against the persons and groups he chose to associate with the latter.

Such personality orientation patterns seem to have made it far easier for Schumacher than for many a liberal democrat to fit Nazi practices into his belief system, for they merely served to confirm his basic view of politics. Similarly, the punitive policies of the occupation powers in the first postwar years appear to have been entirely congruent with his outlook and expectations, whereas subsequent shifts toward more conciliatory policies could apparently be fitted into his belief system only by ignoring some aspects and interpreting others as indicative of weakness or insincerity. And, finally, the need to reconcile highly dynamic political developments with such a basically static and closed belief system seems to go far to explain his postwar behavior toward his domestic political counter-players among both the elites and the masses.

Last of all, let us note that Schumacher evidently sought to reinforce and substantiate his categorical beliefs by placing *great emphasis on the need for consistent attitudes and conduct, on strict distinctions among social objects and values, and on clearly ordered relationships.* The criteria that he applied were based on personal insights rather than on behavioral cues from other actors or groups, and such inner-oriented cognitive distinctions apparently led him to play the "lone wolf" throughout his political career, if not already earlier. At the same time, however, he seems to have considered his deviant attitudes and conduct exemplary. The changes he sought were not in himself, but in an environment that seemed to him to demand drastic alterations to make it conform with his vision of what society and polity should be like. Thus, if he was a deviant, conditions external to himself had forced him to become one.

As we have seen, already as a young socialist in Stuttgart, Schumacher placed great stress on the need for unambiguous distinctions and orderly relationships. For example, he insisted on his right to compartmentalize his life into a private and a public sector, and demanded that his associates in either sphere respect the distinction. Thus he claimed the right to lead rather an unconventional private life outside the S.P.D., unconventional, that is, by party standards; and at the same time he took great pains to keep his political activities separated from his roles as a son and lover.* Similarly, as a concentration camp prisoner, he not only tried to maintain his claim to a private existence in the face of the most extreme pressures, but apparently also differentiated sharply between proper and improper conduct strictly according to his highly individual value system. Isolating himself from his fellow prisoners and refusing to conform even overtly to Nazi norms, he seems to have accepted the norms of both groups only insofar as he could reconcile them with his own beliefs. In the postwar era, these patterns of inner-oriented cognitions and rigid expectations appear to have become primarily more visible, rather than merely more pronounced, though the combined impact of physical illness and political frustrations probably reinforced them as well.

We have already spoken of Schumacher's tendency to discriminate sharply between himself and others, and to distinguish his counter-players according to their perceived importance and worth, ostensibly for reasons of political strategy and tactics. His associates from the period before 1933, as well as fellow prisoners and postwar associates, were later to speak of his *rank consciousness*. One of his postwar lieutenants referred to it as a *Kleiderordnung,* an arrangement of other actors according to their perceived moral stature, intellectual ability, and political importance that was based not so much upon external criteria as upon his personal standards. For example, political actors who, like himself, seemed tough and consistent in their outlook and conduct apparently took a much higher place in this hierarchy than those who appeared to him tolerant and vacillating. He displayed grudging respect for some of his most uncompromising opponents as long as they seemed to him worthy foes, but was infuriated by the political successes of those he considered his inferiors. In particular, he resented counter-players who seemed to have no "right" to regard themselves as his intellectual, moral, or political equals or even superiors—for example, Keil, Grotewohl, Reuter, and Adenauer—and was outraged when he thought his own preeminence in these respects was being questioned by men he despised, such as the Nazi leaders who disputed his patriotism and the Communists who doubted his anti-Nazi record. In such instances, he seemed to his associates to cast reason and caution to the winds, and give his fury free play.†

With firmly fixed images of what his counter-players were like and what

---

* Even after 1933, when for all practical purposes such distinctions no longer had any objective significance, Schumacher still insisted on excluding what he considered private affairs from his political activities. For instance, in the concentration camp, when other prisoners tried to find consolation in affective bonds with their loved ones, he refused to discuss such matters. After the war, when he barely found time for—and perhaps even avoided—meetings with members of his family and former non-political friends, he was careful to note the few such meetings as "private" in his appointments calendar.

† Let us recall in this connection that Schumacher's seemingly stoic acceptance of his imprisonment was shaken when visiting Nazi leaders or guards held him up to ridicule.

behavior could be expected from them, Schumacher evidently sought to fit their actual conduct into his belief system, perceiving and interpreting their behavior accordingly. His formal subordinates and followers were expected to conform with his views of proper role relationships by giving constant evidence of their loyalty to their legitimate leader, and his opponents were expected to reveal themselves as unambiguous foes. Such, it seems, was his view of the immutable order of the world, and his behavior appears to have been designed to maintain it so. Developments that did not fit this view apparently disturbed him greatly, and he seems to have been even more troubled by implications that his own attitudes and behavior were inconsistent or "opportunistically" flexible in terms of his "grand strategy" for the fight for power. Thus, his views and conduct as a young socialist in Stuttgart, as a concentration camp prisoner, and as a leader and aspiring leader in postwar Germany seem to have been governed by a determination to maintain a consistent and orderly relationship between inner-oriented perspectives and the external environment that confirmed and reinforced his belief system.

His associates recalled later that he went to great lengths to give logic to his actions and consistency to his arguments. Known to be a skilled debater, he reportedly girded himself for political encounters like a soldier going into battle, carefully rehearsing not only his own performance but the reaction anticipated from his counter-players, whether at a mass rally or in a meeting with foreign leaders. "War-gaming" such encounters, as several of his lieutenants described it, Schumacher would prepare to present what he considered irrefutable arguments and answers. His speeches were carefully organized around a series of focal themes and arguments, and took into account the anticipated responses of his listeners, including likely counter-sallies.* In the chaotic universe of the concentration camp, he made a deep impression on fellow prisoners with the persuasive logic of his explanations and predictions about the course of political developments, and after the war the brilliance of his intellectual constructions that had already won him prominence in Weimar days undoubtedly helped him greatly in obtaining and maintaining control of the S.P.D. His presentations in party meetings were models of internal consistency even in the eyes of those who considered them illogical with respect to the "real" world. His speeches were almost invariably on an unusually high intellectual level and displayed his extraordinary skill for marshaling detailed facts.

What can we conclude from all this? In general, the structure of Schumacher's orientation patterns suggest that he would have scored very high on the psychological scale for dogmatism, opinionatedness, and other qualities

---

* Shortly before his death, Schumacher told an interviewer that he attributed his skill in parrying the questions of journalists at press conferences to his long training as a political debater and his schooling in Marxist dialectics. Kaufmann Int.

indicating a "closed mind."[45] Despite his strong orientation toward future developments, he relied mostly on memories of past experiences; he analyzed, predicted, and assigned roles on the strength of preconceived expectations, and distorted or rejected new information that challenged his interpretations; he lacked the ability to separate objective informational cues from subjectively perceived sources, and interpreted them more in terms of affective orientations than on their own merit. There is considerable evidence to indicate that he found it exceedingly difficult, at times impossible, to adjust his views about developments in postwar German politics so as to cope with these events effectively in terms of his manifest goals for himself, his party and his country.*

To sum up, our analysis of Schumacher's psychological environment points to *a highly dogmatic personality with an extremely closed belief system.* The evidence suggests (1) that he was basically incapable of accepting new information that contradicted beliefs and expectations that were already firmly established when he began his fight for the postwar leadership; (2) that his rigid behavior was based upon a monolithic, unitary, self-contained, and primarily inner-oriented belief system; (3) that he strove to avoid or relieve inner tensions by maintaining congruence between his beliefs and his actions; (4) that he found it increasingly difficult to maintain such congruence, and therefore psychic stability, during the last years of his life, when his rigid behavior failed to serve its manifest function in the drive for political power; (5) that this conflict, aggravated by his worsening physical condition, produced extreme inner tensions that he tried to relieve by clinging all the more rigidly to established orientation and behavior patterns; and (6) that this effort was not altogether successful, as evidenced by his increasingly tense and "irrational" behavior.

---

* As we have noted, Schumacher's "authoritarian behavior" was frequently likened to Hitler's by postwar critics. But there seems to have been a great difference not only in the apparent content but in the structure of their respective belief systems. Schumacher, as I have stressed, seems to have been entirely sincere in his adherence to democratic principles (though he certainly did not always practice what he preached when it came to running the postwar S.P.D.), whereas Hitler obviously did not share such values. Schumacher was an intellectual, and his speeches and writings were a far cry from Hitler's rantings. Hitler was basically erratic, disorderly, and inconsistent in his behavior, and prone to sudden, unpredictable improvisations. Schumacher, by contrast, utterly lacked such flexibility, and his reactions to specific political events were usually predictable—as perceptive observers, such as Adenauer, discovered. Insisting on a rigidly fixed political strategy, he was capable of only very limited tactical flexibility. His beliefs and expectations allowed him to participate in the establishment of a separate West German state, despite his aversion to collaboration and his insistence on German reunification; also, he sought to negotiate, if half-heartedly, temporary political arrangements with minor "bourgeois" leaders and groups, despite his emphasis on the class struggle in postwar Germany. However, such flexibility was both rare and limited. He drew a rigid line when it came to cooperation with groups and individual leaders in Germany and abroad that involved significant departures from his stand, asserting that he would not yield for the sake of "opportunistic" gains achieved by the surrender of firmly fixed principles.

Political Behavior and Personality Needs

We have reached a point in our analysis at which prudence might advise us to stop. For in turning to the fundamental question of motivation, the investigator is seriously handicapped not only by the fact that he must rely entirely on inference but by his inexpertness. Even for the specialist, motivation represents a highly complex subject, particularly in its latent form. Unconscious motivation, most psychologists and psychiatrists now agree, is a basic component of the personality system, but it is also one that cannot as yet be adequately explained or analyzed. If in the discussion to follow I seem to have thrown caution overboard, the reader should remember that my interpretation of Schumacher's unconscious motivation is at all times deductive and largely impressionistic. It is intended merely to suggest certain lines of thought, and departs deliberately from the rigorous tenets of "scientific politics."

One of the most prominent figures in postwar German politics described Schumacher to me as a man with an unquenchable "thirst for power." This impression was shared not only by people who had known him after the war, but also by those who had known him in the Weimar era. Yet his own description of himself as a modest man was apparently entirely sincere. "Personal ambition," he wrote in a private letter soon after the war, "has mattered very little to me throughout my life."[46] According to Willy Brandt, the man who succeeded him as leader of the S.P.D., "If one wanted to reduce Kurt Schumacher's personality to one short formula one has to say: the dominating feature of his character and the strongest impulse of his life and work was his extraordinary will power."[47] But the goals to which he harnessed this will power apparently had little to do with personal ambition: somebody had to take on the task of leading the fight for democracy and progress in Germany, a fight dictated by historical necessity and moral values, and no one else, he felt, was as competent as he. Finally, as a third observer has pointed out, the man who would never compromise his principles was forever waging a "tragic battle" against politically more powerful opponents, and always discovering new foes blocking the realization of his aspirations for his party and his country.[48]

Taken together, these observations sound the dominant note of Schumacher's political career: an undeviating, uncompromising fight for personal power on behalf of principles that he declared absolutely authoritative and sacred—a fight that he sustained no matter how great the odds against him, no matter how often he was frustrated, no matter how great the drain on his physical resources. Merciless in the demands he made upon himself, he appears to have been driven by a conscience so exacting and authoritative that its commands could not be disregarded except at the cost of extreme inner tensions. Thus conformity with internalized moral standards seems to have been far more significant in influencing his outlook and behavior than expectations of external rewards, and the latent fear of internal sanctions far greater than the conscious fear of external ones. In this sense, we might say that he was not truly free in choosing his particular way of life. Within the extremely severe limits established by inner needs, he tried to adapt himself to the dynamics of developments in the objective environment, but the necessity to avoid internal tensions seems generally to have allowed him little flexibility in pursuing his fight for political power, above all when confronted by situations and actors that he perceived as threats to his self-esteem and aspirations.

Here, it seems to me, was the cause of Schumacher's personal tragedy in his battle for leadership. He wanted to be a Hercules who brought extraordinary powers to the task of cleaning out Augean stables. But pressing personality needs made him a Tantalus instead, frustrated and exhausted by efforts to achieve a goal that compulsive behavior at the same time put out of his reach.

Most of the people who knew Schumacher after the war attributed the inner tensions evidenced by his behavior to physiological causes, to his concentration camp experiences, or to both. These were undoubtedly significant, but to my mind they were not so much the originating sources as factors which *reinforced* psychological tensions that had their genesis in experiences antecedent to his wartime imprisonment and physiological complaints. It seems to me that our own findings indicate long-standing tensions resulting from deep anxieties and latent inner conflicts that had to be managed through exceedingly rigid ego defense structures if psychic equilibrium was to be maintained.*

An enduring state of anxiety appears to produce and maintain a comparatively closed belief system, the latter serving to protect a vulnerable ego against destructive tensions.† We shall consider the possible sources of such anxiety feelings in Schumacher's case shortly. But whatever their origins, they seem to have given rise to psychological tensions that his ego defenses sought to manage by projecting inner conflicts into the external world, and by rationalizing consequent aggressions against external social objects in terms of moral values

---

* By anxiety I here mean "generalized expectations of deprivation from a class of objects to which the actor is attached" either consciously or unconsciously. See Parsons and Shils, eds., p. 13.

† Rokeach, p. 403. When a man cannot face inner conflicts or resolve them by means of compensatory mechanisms, his ego defense network automatically comes into play. Unaware of the fact that an adaptive process takes place, or even that an inner conflict exists, he will strive to reduce anxiety-produced tensions that threaten the stability of his personality system (and thus his sanity). Adaptation takes the form of anxiety-reducing role and goal choices that to his conscious mind seem reasonable, desirable, or even mandatory. In order to be effective, such defenses against ego-threatening stimuli from either within or without the personality system require adaptive choices that satisfy both reason and conscience, and such functional adaptive choices tend to be limited to a class of solutions having common characteristics. See Miller and Swanson, esp. pp. 17–23.

satisfying to a demanding conscience.* Thus, on the conscious level, he regarded his conduct in what he perceived as a fight on behalf of impersonal principles against unethical conditions and immoral opponents as entirely altruistic and even self-abnegating. On another level, however, they seem to have served all-important latent functions of tension reduction and need disposition, and when he spoke of having to do his "duty," it appears that he articulated what in the literature on obsessive-compulsive behavior is referred to as a "command function."

These deductions lead us to hypothesize that *Schumacher's political behavior in postwar Germany may be explained primarily as that of a man compulsively striving to relieve intense personality tensions by means of adaptive mechanisms that had proven effective in the past for maintaining the equilibrium of the personality system.*[49]

A person manifesting obsessive-compulsive traits seeks to overcome doubts about his own intrinsic worth by a very strong sense of purpose and duty in the service of a historical mission. Striving for a reassuring sense of identity, he must be this or that, and once having found satisfactory roles to play, he is forever on guard against departures from who he is and what he should do. He is driven relentlessly by his efforts to fulfill a self-assigned mission, which he feels as a burden imposed on him by authoritative and impersonal external forces, and which he is at pains to show he is trying to satisfy. Such a person is the servant of commands he gives himself because his conscience tells him so, though consciously he feels that they originate with some higher authority, such as some rule or principle that he must follow. He feels himself in his various roles an as agent of such impersonal forces, "a representative to himself of an entirely external office," and will invoke logic, morality, common sense, or some other allegedly authoritative principle in making decisions. Thus, "What may initially have been a decision based simply on his own wish will often be erected into an authoritative principle, and sometimes . . . the act of having made a decision will become sufficient principle in itself, as expressed in such slogans as 'vacillation is weak.' "[50]

Obsessive-compulsive traits manifest themselves, too, by very rigid orientation and reaction patterns, dogmatic self-righteousness, and a distortion of objective reality. The actor's focus of attention is restricted, and he ignores informational cues that do not fit the rules and principles that he accepts as authori-

---

* Aggressiveness is a "disposition to injure or destroy the object felt to be the source of deprivation," and manifests itself "in the organized orientation of action of the need-disposition to remove, injure, or destroy an object." Aggression, withdrawal, avoidance, or passivity are alternative responses to the threat of deprivation; which is chosen "seems to depend on the prevalence of integrative predispositions in the actor's personality system," a factor that may lead to the expression as well as the suppression of aggressive impulses. Parsons and Shils, eds., p. 13.

tative. Highly opinionated, he rationalizes his inflexibility on the grounds that he has to be consistent, strives to have his own way, and finds it a source of intense irritation if others do not behave as expected. He wants others to confirm that he is right, deeply resents criticism, and refuses to accept objective evidence that he may have been wrong. He expects the world to conform to his expectations, while he himself refuses to yield to external forces that he does not accept as authoritative. Finally, obsessive-compulsive traits manifest themselves in inordinate suspiciousness, secretiveness with regard to the person's private thoughts, and a general refusal to confide in others.

I think it is clear that Schumacher's attitudinal and behavior patterns indicate definite obsessive-compulsive traits (and not only in the post-war period), and that these traits manifested themselves particularly in intense self-assertive activity involving rebelliousness and aggressiveness toward established authority and dominant social norms. That is, the perennial outsider, isolated by both physical and psychological characteristics from "ordinary" men, displayed what Parsons has referred to as a highly generalized pattern of need disposition in the form of deviant, compulsive alienation from social objects and normative patterns. The ego defense network of such a person, who must for strong inner reasons compulsively assert his active independence from prevailing norms, functions in such a way as to free him from feelings of dependence on others. In the case of activity-oriented alienative need-disposition patterns, the refusal to conform with the external world becomes compulsive and cumulative. The person in this category is "incorrigibly" aggressive toward other actors, picks fights regardless of the risk, and compulsively seeks "showdowns" even when he can expect serious sanctions in their wake. The consequences of such behavior are new tensions, resulting from the frustration of the conflict between rigid goals and rigid behavior, "the well-known vicious circle ... of deviant behavior patterns."[51]

In a world perceived as a battleground between himself as the agent of mandatory socio-political change, and powerful forces of reaction in his party, his country, and the world, Schumacher apparently sought compulsively to do his "duty"—whether it was to fight for a new S.P.D., suffer in Nazi concentration camps, or exhaust himself in the battle for postwar leadership. But evidently it was also essential for him to be certain not only that he was right to fight, but fit to fight (both physically and intellectually), as indicated by his constant desire to cut a strong as well as a persuasive figure. Prolonged ambiguity in this respect he seems to have found insufferable. Driven by the need to relieve anxiety-produced and anxiety-producing tensions, he made demands upon himself and his environment that ultimately could not be satisfied because they clashed with resilient external social objects and norms. The resulting conflicts between a compulsive drive for political power and rigid orientation and behavior patterns particularly in the last three or four years of his life, apparently led to enormous inner tensions which, reinforced by tension-producing physical complaints, ultimately seem to have destroyed him.

The foregoing discussion should not be taken to mean that I consider Schumacher to have been a psychotic or his behavior pathological. On the contrary, it is my contention that he maintained his psychic equilibrium more or less successfully in the face of intense internal and external pressures by means of tension-reducing adaptive processes that were able to work themselves out in his fight for political power. But let us once again remember that "the function of a behavior in the service of adaptation should be distinguished from its other possible functions."[52] We are concerned here with latent personality functions rather than manifest political functions.

Throughout this study I have suggested that Schumacher's postwar behavior, the main focus of our analysis, can probably be best approached by examining his life before 1945. The process of personality development in the pre-1945 period seems to me at least as important as developments resulting from the interaction of the matured personality with the external environment of postwar politics. A prominent German journalist characterized Schumacher as "a man of extraordinary intelligence, passionate, strong-willed, the born leader, but one who from the start of his [postwar] career carried the mark of tragic failure upon his forehead. . . . Even perceptive observers were unaware of how heavily the endowment of these unusual gifts weighed upon him." The burden was increased, according to this writer, by qualities that perhaps derived from his intelligence—sarcasm, uncontrolled vehemence, and a profound bitterness—qualities that were "inherent in his nature, and that the concentration camp reinforced."[53] Our own findings support this impression. They indicate that what we have referred to as Schumacher's generalized need disposition patterns for rebellion and aggression against the external world were of long standing, reaching back at least to his "marriage to politics" after the loss of his arm, and reflecting subconscious feelings of deep anxiety that derived from a sense of insecurity and inadequacy. Let us now try to review the psychodynamics of his personality development, and consider not only the possible sources of his anxiety feelings, but the adaptive processes chosen, their efficacy in maintaining psychic stability before 1945, and their impact on his postwar behavior.

Trying to trace the developmental history of a highly complex personality back to its origins is like searching for the source of the Nile. The farther back we travel, the harder the task becomes. Tributaries have to be distinguished from the main stream, hidden obstacles that shape direction and strength must be recognized, and indistinct marshes are encountered that conceal the true course entirely. The flow of personality development incorporates congenitally determined factors, maturational factors, and environmental factors, which interact to give shape to the ego and its defenses. Primitive instinctual factors are increasingly replaced or supplemented by effective ego regulations, and defense processes develop both to control instinctual drives and to facilitate their adaptation to the external world. What we call "mental health" involves the reconciliation of environmental and internal demands, and is predicated on the ability of the personality system to deal with environmental situations as well as internal conflicts without producing destructive psychic stresses.[54]

This interplay between inner demands and external environment establishes a definite pattern as the child grows into an adolescent and the adolescent into an adult, just as the small brook cuts a path through the land, gathering force, meeting, avoiding, or overcoming obstacles it encounters, molded by as well as molding its environment according to whether its own force or that of the situational obstacles encountered is stronger. Usually, the stream will adjust to obstacles it cannot overcome or avoid, sometimes almost imperceptibly, and at other times by hurling itself angrily through narrow apertures where external obstacles confine its course. Sometimes, however, the clash of moving body and immovable object will cause a crisis situation that can be resolved only by one or the other giving way. The stream may be halted, impotently lashing against obstacles it cannot surmount or circumvent, but the dam may also burst, flooding the countryside with a force that cannot be contained. It is the function of the ego to mediate between powerful inner personality drives and powerful external social forces seeking to contain them. Tensions produced by frustrations may be "resolved" by surrendering personal needs to societal demands (i.e. by conforming), by turning aggression inward (leading sometimes to a full-blown psychosis, sometimes to suicide), or by turning aggression outward and lashing out against environmental obstacles in an effort to overcome them. Unless some resolution is found, the personality system cannot function efficiently. In this sense, then, *psychologically functional behavior is behavior that allows adjustment by means of ego-satisfying adaptive processes, and prevents inner tensions from destroying the personality system.*[55]

At the beginning of this study I suggested that certain cumulative developments in Schumacher's life prior to 1945 had a decisive impact on the organization of his personality system. In the first place, he may have inherited from his mother a disposition for neurological disturbances. In the second, he was brought up in an environment that may well have given rise to early tension-producing feelings of anxiety and insecurity. The dominant cultural values of pre-war Prussian society were respect for authoritarian father figures, obedience, manliness, order, rejection of "unclean" social objects, and the importance of doing one's duty. Some authors have suggested that such values in themselves lead to anxiety feelings and consequent obsessive-compulsive traits in a child.[56] Although I would not go this far, I do think that a conflict between these values and other influences in Schumacher's early environment may have given rise to anxiety feelings about his own identity. Feminine influences appear to have played a far more important part in his early development than that played by such male figures as father, teachers, and boyhood friends. His adoring mother and older sisters may have given the sensitive child an exaggerated sense of his own importance, and even encouraged narcissistic feelings; but at the same time their influence may have given rise to latent dependency needs and disturbing doubts about his own masculine identity. The boy, growing toward biological manhood and searching for an identity, appears to have felt rather ambivalent toward the members of his immediate family, loving his mother yet striving to adapt himself to cultural norms that emphasized such "manly" virtues as duty and obedience. This ambivalence may have created considerable feelings of anxiety about his "proper" role in life, anxiety that could be resolved neither by identifying with an ambiguous paternal model nor by giving way to demanding feminine influences.

Young Schumacher apparently sought to learn who he was and what he was by searching for an identity outside the family; but here, too, he seems to have encountered only ambiguity. In a community with deep social cleavages, he appears to have found it impossible to identify completely with any particular group. Intent on asserting his individuality and already very much a loner, he lived, as he later put it, *between* the Roman Catholic Polish convent and the German military barracks, literally as well as figuratively. His religious sentiments were not strong enough to draw him to the Lutheran Church, and his awakening social consciousness was apparently still too undeveloped to draw him into youth groups identified with social protest and political reform.

The outbreak of World War I seems to have offered the young man unequivocal opportunity to resolve his search for identity and the anxieties it produced. As a soldier ready to lay down his life for his country, he could find both a masculine and a group identity, and he jumped at this opportunity to distinguish himself in a socially approved manner. As we noted, he volunteered his services at once, and evidently impatient to prove himself, requested transfer to an infantry unit about to go into battle. Not only, however, was this apparent effort to resolve self-doubts and anxieties frustrated, but it seems to have resulted in a traumatic experience that I believe to have been of decisive importance in his personality development.

My contention that the somatic-psychic trauma of the loss of his arm (following upon antecedent anxiety-producing experiences) shaped the pattern of Schumacher's future life may seem a slender reed to lean upon. Admittedly, the case would be stronger if we had more substantiating information, but the circumstantial evidence seems to me persuasive enough to sustain this particular explanation over others. I suggested that this frustration of effort to prove himself a man and find an identity came at a very crucial period in Schumacher's personality development. Instead of resolving his apparent dependency needs and finding an anxiety-relieving secure masculine identity, the adolescent was suddenly confronted by a situation that seems to have given rise to new and even greater anxiety feelings and inner tensions. A sense of competence, of having successfully adapted oneself to the world, is extremely important for psychic stability, psychologists tell us; and, conversely, an experience of incompetence results in a feeling of shame.[57] Young Schumacher, I believe, experienced at this critical stage in his maturation a profound sense of incompetence and shame as a result of an injury felt to be emasculating. To relieve inner tensions and conflicts that seem to have brought him close to a mental breakdown at this point, he had to strive for a new form of adaptation and find inner security in a firm identity that would satisfy his wounded ego. The adaptive choices he could make, however, were limited.

In the first place, situational factors in wartime Germany restricted his opportunities for externalizing his adaptive needs. Second, since he had been brought up in a particular culture and a particular family environment, and presumably had internalized many social and class values of the West Prussian middle class from which he came, he could not simply divest himself of such learned norms but had to make an adaptation satisfying to a conscience that incorporated them. Third, his adaptive choices were restricted by existing ego defenses, particularly those defenses that related to fending off dependency needs aroused by maternal ministrations. Last, his physical condition ruled out certain adaptive choices that might have been ego-satisfying, such as a military career. (We might take note in this connection of his subsequent ambivalent attitude toward military men and military norms). Politics, therefore, may have seemed the best way in which he could assert his masculinity, ward off feminine claims, and at the same time satisfy his conscience.

Schumacher's decision to live for politics represented a choice of adaptive process which, in my view, permitted him to manage tension-producing feelings of self-doubt and inadequacy by proving to himself and others that a one-armed cripple could be strong and powerful in his chosen sphere of competence. However, the choice of a political career cannot be attributed exclusively to the trauma of 1914, or to political conditions in the last war years that might have favored such a choice. For not only had he apparently given some thought to entering politics before the outbreak of war, but the decision seems to have answered certain latent needs that had been present much earlier. The latent component, I believe, manifested itself not so much in the choice as in the nature and style of his whole-hearted commitment to politics. He appears to have obtained ego-satisfying, euphoric feelings from fighting aggressively for political power on behalf of conscience-satisfying principles. As a political man, he was, psychologically speaking, both comparatively safe from disturbing feelings of doubt about his true worth and freed from dependency needs—*as long as he adhered to anxiety-reducing adaptive patterns in his outlook and behavior.*

By joining the S.P.D. in 1918, Schumacher seems to have chosen a self-identity that allowed need dispositions and ego defenses to be accomplished in a morally satisfying manner, for it apparently offered him identification with congenial impersonal principles that his conscience could accept. Other political groups, such as the extremist parties, evidently did not meet such requirements, either because they were anti-democratic or because they were not patriotic enough. As a militant Social Democrat, however, he could rebel against prevalent social norms and authoritative actors, and externalize his aggressive needs by fighting altruistically for such idealized principles as "social justice," "patriotism," and "democracy." Thus a personal need to battle for political power, to prove himself a superior man and obtain deference from others, could be rationalized and intellectualized in terms of a conscience-satisfying moral battle on behalf of the German working people.

Adaptive processes, if they prove successful, typically yield stable perceptual and behavioral patterns that progressively reinforce each other. Situations are increasingly handled in accordance with generalized set expectations and responses that accord with cumulative adaptive patterns. The actor acquires a sense of competence and success (and the psychic stability that comes with it) in the sphere that has become the focus of his adaptive process. In Schumacher's case, it seems that the maturational adaptive process between 1914 and 1933 resulted in the adoption of habitual tension-relieving beliefs and behavior patterns that proved both manifestly and latently functional. It would appear that avoidance of anxiety and tension-producing inner conflicts demanded increasingly strict conformity with the outlook and conduct he found satisfying in his fight for political power. In other words, by 1933 the adaptive process he had apparently chosen many years earlier not only had evolved into a firmly established means for tension-management, but had become *an end unto itself,* vital for the maintenance of psychic equilibrium.

An adaptive process and the ego defenses that accompany it are not necessarily invulnerable against external challenges. A person may suddenly be confronted by a situation that he cannot avoid or ignore, but for which he is not adequately prepared psychologically and with which he cannot cope competently. In Schumacher's case, it seems, the strength of his adaptive and ego defense mechanisms was put to a severe test by what I believe to have been the second major traumatic experience in his development. At the threshold of middle age, almost nineteen years after he had become a cripple, the psychological impact of the establishment of the Nazi regime appears to have posed a severe challenge to the firmly established organization of his personality system. His adaptive drive for political power was abruptly frustrated, and he was faced with the prospect of extreme punitive sanction for non-conformist behavior. His bitter foes among the victorious Nazis made no secret of their intention to take vengeance on a man who had shown himself their inflexible enemy in the past. His reaction, I submit, gave proof of the resilience, strength, and importance of previously established adaptive patterns. By refusing to yield to external pressures, and by adapting himself comparatively successfully to the universe of the concentration camp for ten long years, he showed enormous courage and strength of conviction. But without wanting to seem callous or belittle the suffering he voluntarily took upon himself, I would suggest that at bottom his choice was dictated by the pressure of latent personality needs, and the compulsion to accommodate them by means of firmly established patterns of personality organization and tension management.

The same mechanisms that seem to have enabled Schumacher to deal successfully with anxieties in the past, reinforced by the need to escape the severe threat to psychic equilibrium posed by conditions in the concentration camp, apparently served between 1933 and 1945 to overcome frustrations and adapt the personality system to an external setting extreme in its demands on him. By deliberately inviting imprisonment and accepting it stoically in the face of a constant threat to his survival, it seems to me that he subconsciously avoided potentially dangerous inner tensions relating to anxiety feelings about his true worth as a man. He proved that he was strong, uncompromising, and —as a deliberate deviant—superior to the conformist multitude in Nazi Germany. From his initial decision not to take flight there followed a chain of others (such as his hunger strike), which appear to have formed a set of psychologically functional reaction-formations that differed in content but not in structure from earlier adaptive patterns. The life of the concentrationnaire, with all its unending horrors and potentially anxiety-producing threats to physical and psychic survival, apparently reinforced Schumacher's firm, self-assured, and self-righteous sense of identity as a political man with a mission. In the face of extreme external pressures and severe physiological ailments, this process of adaptation seems to have saved his sanity and perhaps his life as well. He managed not only to maintain his self-respect, but to develop out of this traumatic experience a far more pronounced sense of personal identity and destiny, of competence and power, than he ever had before.

According to men who knew him before as well as after, Schumacher did not change fundamentally during his imprisonment. However, he showed himself afterwards to be far more inflexible in his outlook and behavior, and no longer interested in anything but the single-minded pursuit of his political aspirations. In general, the evidence indicates that this phase of his development did not so much give rise to new personality characteristics as *intensify obsessive-compulsive traits that previously had been less developed and less* *evident.* This happened, it seems, in response to the pressure of new inner tensions that were somatic as well as psychic in their origin and expression.*

Earlier we compared the growth of a personality to that of a river. To pursue this analogy, we might say that although we cannot be certain about the sources which gave initial strength and direction to the course of Kurt Schumacher's personality development, it seems that his marriage to politics in World War I represented a decisive juncture of a number of congenital, maturational, and environmental factors. From this point onward, he apparently developed a specific pattern of behavior that proved both latently and manifestly functional for him up to the time when he began his drive for leadership in postwar Germany at the age of fifty-one. And it was presumably precisely because of its effectiveness that the pattern had already become so firmly established by 1945.

Adaptive processes tend to remain flexible only as long as the actor retains the capacity to absorb and adapt himself to new situations and experiences without

* The exceedingly difficult adaptation process was evidently achieved only at a very high somatic as well as psychic cost. In addition to its psychic impact, life in the concentration camp had somatic consequences which, in turn, apparently reinforced psychic symptoms. The gastric disorders that caused Schumacher excruciating pains until 1947 may have been attributable not only to his hunger strike and malnutrition in the camp, but also to extreme inner tensions that were the result of living for ten years at the brink of death, and being forced to suppress personality needs that demanded expression. Interestingly enough, his stomach ulcers gradually disappeared after the war, cured perhaps as much by opportunities to externalize personality needs and relieve inner tensions as by medical treatment and improved diet.

However, the diet based on milk and other fatty products that was first provided by helpful fellow prisoners and later prescribed by Schumacher's physician may have helped his ulcers but aggravated a more serious vascular condition that probably existed already in a latent state before 1933. This circulatory ailment was diagnosed as the somatic cause of the arterial thrombosis that cost him his leg in 1948, and it probably also led to his stroke in December 1951, and his second, fatal stroke a few months later.

Arterial complaints have been clinically related to a diet rich in animal fats and to heavy use of tobacco. Schumacher, it will be recalled, was a chain smoker, and claimed that smoking helped him overcome nervous tensions dating back to his battlefield injury. His postwar physicians diagnosed his illness as "Bürger's disease" (thromboangitis obliterans), which results from vascular constrictions aggravated by exposure to cold and by heavy smoking. Signs of such circulatory disorders are usually localized in the gastro-intestinal tract, the extremities, and the brain. Symptoms are extremely painful, causing a vicious cycle of agonizing pain, neurological tensions, sleeplessness, and heavy smoking, leading to further pain-producing vascular occlusions, as apparently was the case for Schumacher. Altogether, we seem to have here one of the syndromes in which somatic and psychic, tension-produced and tension-producing, causes and symptoms are too closely interrelated and interacting to be distinguishable.

In attempting this diagnosis, I have relied on personal letters in which Schumacher reported his symptoms to friends, on interviews with various physicians (including Schumacher's), on clinical reports about his condition in the Schumacher File in the S.P.D. archives in Bonn, and on a certain amount of technical literature on arteriosclerosis and related diseases. The interested reader is referred to Russell L. Cecil and Robert E. Loeb, eds., *A Textbook of Medicine,* 5th ed. (London and Philadelphia, 1955), pp. 1381–84, 1398–1403. A number of the items in my Bibliography that relate to life in the concentration camps include references to recent diagnostic studies relevant to Schumacher's case.

creating serious psychic conflicts. However, the more problems he has managed to "solve" to his own inner satisfaction by established procedures in the past, the more difficult it is for him to alter such procedures when facing new situations, even when his reason may tell him that this is necessary in order to achieve conscious aspirations and avoid frustrating experiences and punitive sanctions.[58] As we hypothesized earlier, Schumacher fundamentally lacked the capacity to learn new responses and adopt new orientation and behavior patterns, a lack that put him at a special disadvantage in the postwar situation, which demanded a high degree of flexibility. Suddenly thrust from the highly structured social system of the concentration camp into a comparatively unstructured situation that permitted him a great deal of latitude in terms of the external environment, he apparently made his adaptive choices automatically on the strength of firmly established patterns. Perhaps, by its very nature, the dynamic postwar situation was a source of anxiety, tensions, and inner conflicts for a man who had survived the psychological strains of his long imprisonment by relying on highly rigid adaptive patterns. If so, his need to adhere to these patterns was probably all the more pressing if he was to maintain a secure sense of identity and competence after the war. In short, by 1945 Schumacher seems to have been the prisoner of inner needs that could be accommodated only by conforming absolutely with a firmly patterned personality system.

Schumacher's personal tragedy was that his obsessive drive for power on behalf of a "new" Germany was frustrated not only by objectively unfavorable external conditions, but also by his subjective attitudes and actions. As we have seen, these proved on the whole manifestly functional within the confines of the S.P.D. in helping him gain and maintain the leadership of the party, but manifestly dysfunctional in the larger context of postwar German politics. His beliefs were shared by few of his important counter-players outside the S.P.D., and to the mass of the voters as to German and foreign leaders he seemed stubborn, dogmatic, hostile, and uncooperative.

We have already referred to Schumacher's seeming awareness of a dichotomy between his aspirations and the means he employed to realize them. The dichotomy points to an unresolved inner belief conflict between instrumental values relating to a desire to obtain power and deference on the one hand, and emotional and moral values satisfying to a demanding conscience on the other. Here may have been one of the sources of the tensions that seemed to grip him after the war. Two irreconcilable but equally powerful needs clashed; his compulsive need to be consistent and his obsessive drive for power. Thus he found Adenauer's successful employment of methods that to him seemed immoral and opportunist extremely galling, yet he was unable to emulate them. He had to remain "a man of principles," unbending and tough as steel, despite himself and because of himself. His evident inability to resolve this conflict in the face of cumulative political frustrations may have greatly increased the tension load on the personality system that was demanding relief. Such clashing compulsions seem to have created new feelings of self-doubt, anxiety, incompetence, and inadequacy, as accustomed adaptive patterns failed to function efficiently. His overt reaction was increased goal-denying aggressiveness, resulting in a vicious circle of blocked responses, anxieties, tensions, and behavior that provoked new anxiety-producing external frustrations. In short, he reacted with behavior that was self-defeating both for the inner man and for the political man.

Physical pain and discomfort undoubtedly increased the tension load pressing down upon Schumacher, and probably further reinforced his dependence on adaptive mechanisms that had proved effective in the past. Pain and unavoidable physical dependency on men and women whom he considered his inferiors may have increased his irritability and his sensitivity to alleged insults affecting his self-esteem, particularly in the last years of his life. Perhaps, too, though here the evidence is contradictory, he sensed that the struggle was rapidly exhausting his remaining store of energy. Yet he stubbornly fought on to master mind and body, and when death put an end to the fight, it was his body, not his mind, that finally gave way.

TEN

Conclusion

A political biography, as we noted at the outset, is basically a study of inter-personal relationships. It focuses on a central actor, but examines him in terms of his interaction with other actors against the changing backdrops of the political stage. In a sense we are watching a play in which the leading actor interprets his roles more or less freely, depending on his perception of what the script calls for. A familiar or closely directed script, with well-established roles accepted by all the players, may result in a smooth but routine performance, whereas less tightly structured parts may encourage the central actor to advance a highly personal interpretation both of his own role and of the roles of his counter-players. If his counter-players accept such a novel interpretation and even take from it cues for their own performance, the result may be an original and impressive production that establishes new standards, particularly if the leading actor manages to inspire his fellow players by the superior quality of his performance. If, however, he strikes them as misinterpreting his part and misreading his lines, he will create pandemonium on the stage. For the sake of the rest of the cast and its goals, he is likely to be quickly dropped from the production, if this is possible. If it is not, he may ruin the reputation of the whole company. In politics, as in the theater, good casting is essential.

In a stable political system, institutionalized roles tend to structure reality for a participating actor by defining his expectations to a large extent, and allowing him to predict the behavior of his counter-players with some accuracy. In addition, they help to structure his value system by providing general standards for evaluating his own roles and those of others. Whether he accepts or rejects such roles and standards seems to depend basically upon his personality. The deviant, inspired by standards of his own, rejects them because of components in his personality that prove stronger than the norms acquired in the process of political socialization.

The actor who lacks cognitive sensitivity to political circumstances as they really are is likely to experience considerable personal frustration in his attempt to play leading political roles. The political system or subsystem demands that he adjust his goal-oriented behavior to the expectations of important counter-players, who can advance or frustrate his externalized personal drives. If he cannot make the requisite adjustments in his behavior, he is likely to encounter severe external sanctions, which, in turn, affect his outlook and subsequent conduct. In their more extreme forms, such attitudinal and behavioral patterns may defeat both the personal needs and the public goals of the actor, his personal needs being denied satisfaction in the public sphere because he cannot make the necessary adjustment, or misinterprets informational cues from the situational environment. Thus, insofar as he depends upon the gratification of personality needs by personal success in the political arena, his behavior may prove dysfunctional not only in terms of his personal effectiveness, but in terms of the effectiveness of his group.

The cumulative interaction between inner needs and external situational stimuli—a highly complex process—determines the quality of the political actor, as experiences condition and reinforce his role identifications, philosophy of life, and way of recognizing and responding to informational cues. Personality factors tend to condition his perception of himself and others in a given situation, and cause him to factor out some stimuli, distort others, and admit others intact, a process that will sometimes build up a distinct pattern of behavior over time. Psychologically, the actor finds certain roles and decisional choices more gratifying than others, and he seeks to satisfy certain personality needs and avoid the denial of others. The extent to which he adapts himself to his inner needs on the one hand, and to the demands of the external world on the other, depends on the make-up of his personality. The form that this inner-outer mixture will take in his responses to various situations varies according to the relative influence of his basic impulses, socially implanted values and expectations, and situational cues. An actor's responses may be more or less automatic, either because they are narrowly circumscribed by the situational context, or because they are rigidly structured by his personality characteristics; but they may also result from a considered choice among the alternative courses of action open to him in the light of available information.

The more sensitive to the immediately relevant external environment the political actor is, the more likely he will be to adjust his style of performance to it, and avoid behavior that other actors find disagreeable. The more attuned to personal, internalized motives and needs he is, the more difficult he will find it to make behavioral choices realistically, and advance his manifest aspirations within the objective environment in which he operates. In the one instance, we have an interaction-oriented actor, who leads by readjusting his performance to group demands—in the extreme case, a conformist, who must follow because he wants to lead. Some would call such a political leader opportunistic, others democratic. In the other instance, we have a self-oriented actor, who insists that others adjust their actions to his demands. Some would call him a dedicated idealist, others an autocrat.

The political actor who succeeds in obtaining and wielding power in a political party or larger political unit may thus be a person whose role interpretations are accepted by his counter-players because he satisfies their expectations, or he may be a person who so clearly comprehends the political context that he can adjust his behavior to meet the expectations of these others. The "great leader," speaking in terms of the manifest functionality of political behavior, settles some of his inner problems by not only adapting to the expectations of others, "but in turn changing and controlling his surroundings," as Lucien Pye has observed.[1] Striving to find his own identity, he strikes out against his environment, and succeeds in stimulating a satisfying, positive response in the public arena because he is the right man at the right time.

Postwar Germany offered an aspirant for political leadership considerable leeway in choosing and playing roles likely to bring him success. To revert to the language of the theater, much of the script remained to be written by the actors as they tried out for various parts, though its general outlines were imposed upon them. Surviving elements of past German political cultures and subcultures, as well as the authority of the occupation powers, set limits upon what an aspiring leader could do. But to a large extent political conditions and roles were comparatively unstructured, particularly in the first years, waiting to be molded into more stable patterns by the interaction of leading players, German and non-German. With the benefit of hindsight, we may say that apart from so-called luck, an aspirant for the lead part required certain personal qualities to be successful: (1) strong motivation, and the drive and energy to pursue firmly held goals; (2) the ability to make the most of limited personal and political resources; (3) a keen sense of political reality; (4) sensitivity to the expectations and values of important counter-players; (5) foresight regarding potential opportunities and dangers, watching for what Gaetano Mosca called "atmospheric changes" in the external environment;[2] and (6) the ability to adapt readily to new developments.

Schumacher possessed the first of these qualities in a high degree, and some of the others in sufficient measure to obtain the leadership of the Social Democratic party. However, he was far from adequately equipped to carry his fight for West Germany's postwar leadership to a successful conclusion. Not only were his personal and political resources greatly limited, but he was imprudent in their expenditure, and exhausted his own energies, as well as the store of good will that accrued to him and his party immediately after the war, in futile battles. Above all, he had a poor sense of political reality, was insensitive to the expectations and values of others, lacked foresight, and found it difficult to adapt himself to changing political conditions. In this sense, and for reasons which we have sought to link to his personality organization, he was poorly qualified to obtain the leadership of his country, particularly in comparison with Adenauer, who possessed all these qualities in abundance.

If, as one writer put it, "it was a tragedy that [Schumacher] failed to obtain power and thus specific responsibility for governing," this was above all a great human tragedy.[3] Whether postwar German politics would have taken a different, and some would say "better," course had Schumacher become chancellor is an unanswerable question. Even many of his former lieutenants doubted it as they looked back in later years, some going so far as to say that a Schumacher government would have been "a catastrophe." But whatever one's view, one cannot help feeling sympathy and admiration for a man who, though he may have lacked the attributes needed at this particular time to become the leader of his country, displayed qualities of rare worth.

Here was the dedicated anti-Nazi who many people had hoped would emerge as post-Nazi Germany's new leader, a man who was ready to sacrifice everything, including his life, for what he believed to be a great, democratic cause. Here was a man for whom politics was a calling, in whose entire style of life "the distinction between occupation and calling takes on its full meaning," as Ollenhauer said at his funeral.[4] His record in fighting every form of totalitarianism before as well as after the Nazi regime could hardly be matched either inside or outside the S.P.D. His faith in his destiny had given him the strength to survive Hitler's concentration camps, and when the war ended, he thought of himself as "legitimately" authorized to play a leading part in shaping the new Germany. But "Woe to him who, when the day of his dreams finally came, found it so different from all he had longed for," as a fellow concentration camp survivor so poignantly phrased it.[5] The Germany that emerged after Hitler was a travesty of Schumacher's dreams. His efforts to have it otherwise led only to increasing frustrations, denying him the chance to transform his country into the democratic commonwealth he had envisaged. Defiant to the last, he regretted nothing he had done, only what he was prevented from doing—prevented by both external and internal forces beyond his control.

I have suggested that Schumacher's political behavior after the war was rooted in pressing inner needs, and that conduct that proved dysfunctional in terms of his manifest aspirations was subconsciously structured to be functional at the level of the personality system. I have also suggested that his severe somatic complaints served to reinforce previously established obsessive-compulsive character traits while reducing the store of physical energy available to him to pursue his tasks. As in the case of the polio victim Franklin D. Roosevelt, Schumacher's physical disabilities appear to have strengthened rather than altered already established personality patterns. However, here the similarity seems to end. Roosevelt's adjustment process was apparently facilitated by a secure sense of identity, and unlike Schumacher he had the opportunity to master his physical handicap gradually, under extremely favorable environmental conditions. His adaptation seems to have left him with a superabundance of physical energy, and to have reinforced earlier personality traits that allowed him to be highly flexible, pragmatic, and patient. Whereas outside the party Schumacher's appearance was no particular asset to him, Roosevelt's physical condition seems to have helped him to attract mass support.*

Can we describe Schumacher's mental condition as pathological? I think not. The concept of mental health, ill-defined as it is, is always relative to external social conditions. The person who is judged a psychotic in one setting may be considered not only sane, but unusually perceptive, in another. Behavior that is regarded by some observers as pathologically "aggressive" and "antisocial" because "it is not called for by the objective situation" may strike others as properly "self-assertive" because it appears to be "socially beneficial."[6] To Schumacher, Adolf Hitler was "a sick person, a mentally deranged person obsessed with his own self; to make this self powerful he regarded any means as justified." But, significantly, Schumacher said that if he was politically successful, it was because he was "a sick man in sick times. . . . In periods of turbulent, restless searching, sick men have a sinister influence on desperate, simple people who no longer know how to deal with the problems of their times."[7] In contrast, he apparently saw himself—and was perceived by his admirers—as an eminently sane person who conscientiously and altruistically served an impersonal higher cause. Insofar as he sought to play roles that incorporated some of Hitler's behavioral traits, he apparently did so deliberately in the belief that the postwar climate of German mass opinion was not so very different from that which brought Hitler to power. He was mistaken, as we have seen. The lesson he preached about Hitler had been learned better than he suspected, to his own detriment. His analysis of the Nazi leader, however, calls attention to the fact that personality traits that may be dysfunctional in some political situations may be highly functional in others, and vice versa. This phenomenon seems particularly pertinent in Schumacher's own case.

A person is said to be mentally healthy "if his behavior is 'adequate' in every situation."[8] In this sense Schumacher was certainly not a pathological case. On the basis of a strong sense of identity and competence as a "political man," he evidently maintained his psychic equilibrium, even under conditions of intense strain. As a prominent psychiatrist informs us, "the 'must' and the 'inability-to-do-otherwise' are not always unequivocally criteria of pathology. . . . Healthy people, too, obey 'musts'. . . . Luther's 'Here I stand—I cannot do otherwise' is not pathological behavior."[9] But in another context, a Luther or any other "deviant" responding to compulsive "inner voices" could have been

---

* "His legs became actually something of a political asset. They won him sympathy. Millions of Americans were electrified in later years by Roosevelt's physical appearance." Burns, p. 91. See also p. 89.

judged insane.[10] Traits that in a Charles de Gaulle might seem pathological to a Franklin Roosevelt or a Winston Churchill, and in a Gamal Nasser to a General Naguib, might at the same time, or at some later time, be associated by others with courage and tenacity, and regarded as evidence of "great leadership."*

Had Schumacher been in command of the S.P.D. before Hitler came to power, or had the conditions when he finally obtained control been more like those of the Weimar period, the power drive and the obsessive-compulsive characteristics that we have detected in his personality might have had different results. In other words, I submit as a general proposition that a strong power drive and obsessive-compulsive traits need not necessarily lead to goal-denying behavior in a political actor, but may in fact help him to obtain and exercise leadership. Furthermore, under certain circumstances such personality characteristics may bring about the satisfaction not only of the latent and manifest aspirations of the individual actor, but of *group goals*. Historical illustrations, as well as a few psychological studies, suggest that this generalization may hold true in other sectors of society besides the political one. For example, some military organizations may be most effectively promoted under the leadership of such personality types;[11] and a determined power drive and a certain amount of compulsiveness may give a pioneer or an innovator the inner strength to persevere in the face of a hostile climate of opinion, just as it permits a statesman to rise above particularistic, conflicting demands when making policy decisions. Such psychological equipment, by providing the means to withstand external conformist pressures, may allow today's deviant to become tomorrow's hero. If such persons were excluded from public life on the basis of psychiatric examinations testing their "fitness," a course of action that has lately been suggested, a community might assure itself "normal" leaders, but deprive itself of the potential services of the "abnormal" men who sometimes become great leaders and innovators.

In conclusion, we come to the question of whether or not Schumacher was a "great" man. By what standards, though, are we to measure him? The "judgment of history" is capricious, as we have seen, and may well be reversed when times and values change. Judged by standards that equate greatness with political victories and success, Schumacher was in the last analysis a "failure,"

---

* Roosevelt complained in 1943 that de Gaulle, then an aspiring leader in exile, saw himself as a messiah, and Churchill pictured him as a strutting combination of Joan of Arc and Georges Clemenceau. Naguib, displaced by Nasser after the 1952 Egyptian revolution, claimed that Nasser's determination "to alienate every segment of Egyptian public opinion, if necessary, to achieve our goals" might "in the long run serve pathology better than policy," since "to compensate the fantasy life for damages inflicted in a no longer relevant past obscures the lines to a realistic political future." Quoted from his memoirs in Daniel Lerner, "Politics and Psyche in the Vicious Circle," reprinted in David E. Apter and Harry Eckstein, eds., *Comparative Politics* (New York, 1963), pp. 541–46.

though posterity may credit him with considerable achievements as a party leader. Judged in terms of his creative accomplishment, whether he was a great innovator or an "event-making" man, he seems again to fail the test, though some have called him the creator of the postwar S.P.D. Finally, we come to the standards that measure a man's stature by his individual moral accomplishments and his personal fulfillment—an area in which we have to rely on purely personal values and can no longer claim to speak as objective observers. It is in this respect that we may perhaps call Schumacher great. His courage and firm convictions, his personal sacrifice, and his dedication to the moral mission he had assigned himself may not have made him a great politician or a great innovating leader, but they do possibly allow us to see him as a figure of heroic proportions. There was nobility and grandeur in the essentially tragic life of Kurt Schumacher, and a moral virtue rare in his own time and perhaps in any time.

Appendixes

Schumacher's Political Associates, 1947-52

1. KEY PARTY ASSOCIATES*

AGARTZ, VIKTOR. Born 1897. Minor S.P.D. functionary before 1933. S.P.D. Exec. Comm. 1946–48 and economic adviser.

ARNDT, ADOLF. Born 1904. Bizonal Eco. Council 1947–49, Bundestag 1949– .

BAADE, FRITZ. Born 1893. S.P.D. member of Reichstag 1930–33. In exile during Nazi era. Exec. Comm. Bundestags Fraktion 1949– .

BÖGLER, FRANZ. Born 1902. Bezirk secretary for Pfalz and member of Bavarian diet before 1933. Employee of S.P.D. Exec. Comm. in exile and member of socialist resistance group "Neu Beginnen" during Nazi era. Bezirk chairman for Pfalz 1946– , S.P.D. Exec. Comm. 1946– .

EICHLER, WILLI. Born 1896. Leader of dissident socialist group I.S.K. before 1933 and during Nazi era. Bezirk secretary for Köln-Aachen 1945– , member S.P.D. Exec. Comm. 1946– , Exec. Comm. Bundestags Fraktion 1949– .

ERLER, FRITZ. Born 1913. Imprisonment as member of socialist resistance group "Neu Beginnen" during Nazi era. Member of Württemberg diet 1946–49, member of Bundestag 1949– .

FRANKE, EGON. Born 1913. Minor S.P.D. functionary in Hannover before 1933. Imprisonment for resistance during Nazi era. Bezirk secretary for Hannover 1945– , salaried member S.P.D. Exec. Comm. 1947– .

GAYK, ANDREAS. Born 1893. S.P.D. functionary before 1933. Minor imprisonment during Nazi era. Lord Mayor of Kiel 1946– , member of Parl. Council 1948–49, member S.P.D. Exec. Comm. 1946– .

GOTTHELF, HERTA. Born 1902. S.P.D. member before 1933. Active in S.P.D. exile movement during Nazi era. Employee of S.P.D. Exec. Comm. 1946, salaried member (Women's Affairs) 1947– .

HEINE, FRITZ. Born 1904. Minor S.P.D. functionary in Berlin before 1933. Employee of S.P.D. Exec. Comm. in exile during Nazi era. Salaried member S.P.D. Exec. Comm. 1946– .

HENSSLER, FRITZ. Born 1886. S.P.D. member of Reichstag 1930–33. Imprisonment 1935–45. S.P.D. chairman for Dortmund and member S.P.D. Exec. Comm. 1946– , Exec. Comm. Bundestags Fraktion 1949– .

* Where terminal dates for positions held are not indicated, the incumbent continued in office beyond Schumacher's death.

KNOERINGEN, WALDEMAR VON. Born 1906. Minor S.P.D. functionary in Bavaria before 1933. Émigré member of socialist resistance group "Neu Beginnen" during Nazi era. State chairman for Bavaria 1947– , member S.P.D. Exec. Comm. 1948– , Exec. Comm. Bundestags Fraktion 1949– .

KOPF, HINRICH. Born 1893. S.P.D. functionary before 1933. Minister-president for Lower Saxony 1946– .

KRIEDEMANN, HERBERT. Born 1903. Minor S.P.D. functionary in Berlin before 1933. Exile 1935–40, imprisonment 1940–43. Salaried member S.P.D. Exec. Comm. 1946–50, member of Lower Saxony diet 1947–49, member of Bizonal Eco. Council 1947–48, member of Bundestag 1949– .

LÜTKENS, GERHARD. Born 1893. Member S.P.D. before 1933. In exile during Nazi era. Later employee of S.P.D. Exec. Comm., member of Bundestag 1949– .

MARX, FRANZ. Born 1903. Member of S.P.D. before 1933. Concentration camp prisoner during Nazi era. Member of Bavarian diet 1946–49, chairman of S.P.D. in Munich 1949– , member of Bundestag 1949– .

MELLIES, WILHELM. Born 1899. Member S.P.D. before 1933. Bezirk secretary for East Westphalia and member of Bundestag 1949– .

MENZEL, WALTER. Born 1901. Member S.P.D. before 1933. Member S.P.D. Exec. Comm. 1946– , Parl. Council 1948–49, Exec. Comm. Bundestags Fraktion 1949– , Minister of the Interior for North Rhine–Westphalia 1946–50.

NAU, ALFRED. Born 1906. Minor S.P.D. functionary in Berlin before 1933. Minor resistance, but no imprisonment or exile during Nazi era. Salaried member S.P.D. Exec. Comm. 1946– .

NEUMANN, FRANZ. Born 1904. Minor S.P.D. functionary in Berlin before 1933. Imprisonment for resistance during Nazi era. Bezirk chairman for Berlin 1945– , S.P.D. Exec. Comm. 1947– , Exec. Comm. Bundestags Fraktion 1949– .

NEUMANN, SIGMUND ("Siggi"). Born 1907. K.P.D. member before 1933. In exile during Nazi era. Employee of S.P.D. Exec. Comm. (Soviet zone, Trade Unions) 1946– .

NÖLTING, ERIC. Born 1892. S.P.D. member Prussian diet before 1933. Imprisonment during Nazi era. Minister of Economic Affairs for North Rhine–Westphalia 1947– , Exec. Comm. Bundestags Fraktion 1949– .

OLLENHAUER, ERICH. Born 1901. Major S.P.D. functionary in Berlin before 1933. Member of S.P.D. Exec. Comm. in exile during Nazi era. Deputy party chairman 1946– , assistant Fraktion leader 1949– .

SCHMID, CARLO. Born 1896. Member S.P.D. Exec. Comm. 1947– , member Parl. Council 1948–49, assistant Fraktion leader 1949– .

SCHOETTLE, ERWIN. Born 1899. Minor S.P.D. functionary in Stuttgart before 1933. Émigré member of socialist resistance group "Neu Beginnen" during Nazi era. State chairman for Württ.-Baden, member S.P.D. Exec. Comm. 1948– , member of Bizonal Eco. Council 1947–49, assistant Fraktion leader 1949– .

SCHOLZ, ARNO. Born 1904. Minor S.P.D. functionary before 1933. After 1945 publisher and editor of Der Telegraf (Berlin).

THOMAS, STEFAN. Born 1910. S.P.D. member before 1933. Resistance during Nazi era. Employee of S.P.D. Exec. Comm. (Soviet zone) 1947– .

WEHNER, HERBERT. Born 1906. K.P.D. functionary before 1933. Member of K.P.D. exiled leadership 1933–42. Member of Bundestag 1949– .

ZINN, AUGUST. Born 1901. Minor S.P.D. functionary before 1933. Minor imprisonment during Nazi era. Minister of Justice in Hesse 1947–51, minister-president 1951– , Exec. Comm. Bundestags Fraktion 1949–50.

2. KEY PARTY ASSOCIATES BY YEAR*

(Numbers 30 and over in italics)

Name	Recorded contacts with Schumacher				
	1947	1948	1949	1950	1951
Ollenhauer	36	44	133	132	Almost daily
Heine	44	44	104	Almost daily	Almost daily
Mellies	–	–	12	74	130
Schmid	8	10	49	47	92
Wehner	–	–	16	54	110
Kopf	16	20	41	31	57
Scholz	12	7	27	44	70
Lütkens	–	2	22	64	60
Thomas	4	2	38	28	72
Franke	13	8	40	14	68
Arndt	–	–	10	48	81
Neumann, F.	13	3	13	36	56
Nau	18	7	29	20	28
Neumann, S.	29	7	12	9	24
Henssler	7	4	11	19	39
Zinn	3	5	16	51	–
Menzel	5	1	19	25	24
Schoettle	8	3	6	22	30
Agartz	3	–	–	20	38
Erler	–	–	1	10	46
Baade	–	–	22	18	15
Knoeringen	5	1	14	20	12
Gayk	2	–	22	12	14
Kriedemann	11	10	8	16	4
Eichler	4	9	7	18	8
Gotthelf	4	4	18	2	11
Marx	2	–	2	12	20
Nölting	2	–	12	13	9
Bögler	3	–	10	2	13

* All data in this and the following two sections are from Schumacher's appointments calendar. A dash means "No information."

3. Associates Contacted Immediately Before
and After Key Events

July 25, 1947. *Event:* Unable to get key positions demanded, S.P.D. becomes the principal opposition party in Bizonal Economic Council.

K.S. APPOINTMENTS. *Before event:* July 21, Ollenhauer, Heine, von Knoeringen; July 22, Ollenhauer; July 23, Ollenhauer; July 24, Kriedemann, Franke. *After event:* July 26, Heine; July 27, Agartz, Kriedemann, Heine; July 29, Ollenhauer; July 30, Ollenhauer, Franke, Kriedemann, Henssler.

June 1, 1948. *Event:* London Tripartite Agreement for international control of Ruhr and economic integration of Western occupation zones.

K.S. APPOINTMENTS. *Before event:* May 27, Ollenhauer; May 29, Ollenhauer, Kopf, Henssler, Schmid; May 30, Kriedemann, Gotthelf; May 31, Heine. *After event:* June 2, Heine, Nau, Ollenhauer; June 3, Ollenhauer, Heine; June 5, Heine; June 6, Nau.

June 20, 1948. *Event:* Currency reform in three Western zones, leading to Berlin blockade four days later.

K.S. APPOINTMENTS. *Before event:* None. *After event:* June 21, Ollenhauer; June 22, Heine; June 23, Ollenhauer; June 26, Ollenhauer; June 27, Ollenhauer, Schmid, Kriedemann.

July 7, 1948. *Event:* Meeting of S.P.D. Executive Committee and heads of state governments with Western military governors on Berlin blockade and German reunification.

K.S. APPOINTMENTS. *Before event:* July 5, Ollenhauer; July 6, Ollenhauer, Heine. *After event:* July 9, Nau; July 10, Heine.

April 20, 1949. *Event:* Meeting of S.P.D. leaders votes, 63 to 4, to support K.S. veto of Allied-endorsed draft of Basic Law for West Germany.

K.S. APPOINTMENTS. *Before event:* April 16, Kopf, Menzel; April 17, Zinn; April 18, Ollenhauer; April 19, Ollenhauer, Heine, Henssler, Gayk, Zinn, Schmid, Menzel, Kopf. *After event:* April 22, Ollenhauer, Heine, Kopf, Scholz, Schmid; April 23, Ollenhauer, Heine; April 24, Ollenhauer, Scholz.

August 14, 1949. *Event:* Election of Bundestag produces 29.2 per cent S.P.D. votes. K.S. decides to go into opposition.

K.S. APPOINTMENTS. *Before event:* None. *After event:* August 16, Ollenhauer, Heine, Scholz, Kopf, Franke, Henssler, Nölting, Baade; August 17, Ollenhauer, Heine, Nau; August 19, Ollenhauer, Heine, Nau, Thomas, Gayk.

August 29–30, 1949. *Event:* Meeting of S.P.D. Executive Committee at Bad Dürkheim accepts K.S.'s 16-point opposition program.

K.S. APPOINTMENTS. *Before event:* August 23, Heine; August 24, Heine; August 25, Bögler; August 26, Bögler, Menael, Gayk, Ollenhauer; August 27, Ollenhauer, Schmid, Eichler, Bögler; August 28, Eichler, Schmid, Kriedemann, Nölting, Gayk. *After event:* August 30, Ollenhauer, Heine, Schmid, Henssler, Baade, Nölting, Zinn.

September 12, 1949. *Event:* K.S. insists on opposing Heuss for election of federal president, and gains support of majority of S.P.D. delegation to Federal Assembly.

K.S. APPOINTMENTS. *Before event:* September 9, Ollenhauer, Schmid, Kopf;

September 10, Schmid, Kopf; September 11, Schmid, Kopf. *After event:* September 13, Nau, Ollenhauer, Schmid, Nölting, Baade.

SEPTEMBER 15, 1949. *Event:* Adenauer is elected Chancellor.

K.S. APPOINTMENTS. *Before event:* None. *After event:* September 15, Arndt, Ollenhauer; September 16, Ollenhauer, Schmid.

NOVEMBER 21, 1949. *Event:* Adenauer signs Petersberg Agreement with Western powers, providing for German participation in Ruhr authority.

K.S. APPOINTMENTS. *Before event:* November 17, Heine, von Knoeringen, Thomas; November 18, Mellies, Eichler; November 19, Ollenhauer, von Knoeringen, Baade. *After event:* November 22, Ollenhauer, Schmid, Baade, Mellies, Arndt, Lütkens; November 23, Heine, Franke; November 24, Ollenhauer, Schmid, Arndt, Henssler, Lütkens, Baade, Bögler.

NOVEMBER 25, 1949. *Event:* In heated debate in Bundestag, K.S. calls Adenauer "Chancellor of the Allies" and is barred from attending parliament.

K.S. APPOINTMENTS. *Before event:* None. *After event:* November 25, Ollenhauer, Schoettle; November 26, Arndt, Mellies; November 27, Eichler; November 28, Ollenhauer, Mellies, Lütkens.

APRIL 11, 1951. *Event:* S.P.D. decides to join C.D.U. to pass Codetermination Law in Bundestag.

K.S. APPOINTMENTS. *Before event:* April 9, Ollenhauer, Arndt, Marx, Heine, Lütkens, Agartz, Scholz; April 10, Heine, Agartz, Arndt, Wehner. *After event:* April 11, Ollenhauer, Wehner, Schmid, Schoettle, Arndt, Henssler, Agartz, Franke; April 12, Heine, Wehner, Schmid, Arndt, Kopf, Erler, Lütkens, Baade, Thomas; April 13, Kopf, Arndt, Schmid, Heine, Wehner.

SEPTEMBER 14, 1951. *Event:* Washington Foreign Ministers Conference decides to replace occupation statute with contractual agreement providing for greater sovereignty and German rearmament.

K.S. APPOINTMENTS. *Before event:* September 13, Franke, Henssler, Eichler, Schoettle, Wehner, Schmid. *After event:* September 18, Lütkens, Ollenhauer, Schmid, Henssler, Schoettle, F. Neumann, Eichler.

4. S.P.D. STATE GOVERNMENT LEADERS

BRAUER, MAX. Born 1887. Lord Mayor, city-state of Hamburg, 1946–51 (coalition 1946–49). Not on S.P.D. Exec. Comm. *Recorded contacts with K.S.:* 1947, 6; 1949, 6; 1950, 1; 1951, 6.

HOEGNER, WILHELM. Born 1887. Deputy minister-president, Bavaria, 1946–47; Minister of the Interior 1950–51 (coalition). Not on S.P.D. Exec. Comm. *Recorded contacts with K.S.:* 1947, 1.

KAISEN, WILHELM. Born 1887. Lord Mayor, city-state of Bremen, 1945–51 (coalition). Member of S.P.D. Exec. Comm. 1946–50. *Recorded contacts with K.S.:* 1947, 2; 1949, 1; 1950, 2; 1951, 4.

KOPF, HINRICH. Born 1894. Minister-president, Lower Saxony, 1946–51 (coalition). Not on S.P.D. Exec. Comm. *Recorded contacts with K.S.:* 1947, 16; 1948, 20; 1949, 41; 1950, 31; 1951, 57.

LÜDEMANN, HERMANN. Born 1880. Minister-president, Schleswig-Holstein, 1947–49. Not on S.P.D. Exec. Comm. *Recorded contacts with K.S.:* 1947, 4; 1949, 3; 1950, 1.

REUTER, ERNST. Born 1889. Lord Mayor, city-state of Berlin, 1947–51 (coalition). Member of S.P.D. Exec. Comm. 1948–52. *Recorded contacts with K.S.:* 1947, 9; 1948, 2; 1949, 4; 1950, 14; 1951, 12.

STOCK, CHRISTIAN. Born 1884. Minister-president, Hesse, 1947–50 (coalition). Not on S.P.D. Exec. Comm. *Recorded contacts with K.S.:* None.

5. PERCENTAGE OF VOTES CAST FOR MEMBERS OF S.P.D. EXECUTIVE COMMITTEE AT PARTY CONGRESSES OF 1946, 1947, 1948, 1950, 1952, and 1958

(Schumacher's key associates in italics)

Name	Party congress					
	1946	*1947*	*1948*	*1950*	*1952*	*1958*
Schumacher	99	99	99	98	–	–
Agartz	99	94	–	–	–	–
Ollenhauer	93	99	96	99	98	84
Nau	93	95	94	90	93	71
Heine	93	95	93	88	88	n.r.[a]
Henssler	87	98	94	93	93	–
Kriedemann	83	70	68	–	–	–
Nölting	83	–	–	–	–	–
Helmstaedter	83	89	–	–	–	–
Lossmann	80	95	–	–	–	–
Menzel	79	90	89	90	93	96
Grimme	79	92	66	–	–	–
Gnoss	78	89	92	–	–	–
Knothe	77	92	82	n.r.	–	–
Bögler	77	95	95	86	74	–
Gayk	76	94	95	87	89	–
Metzger	76	–	–	–	–	77
Kaisen	74	95	90	n.r.	–	–
Eichler	73	92	90	90	84	79
Baur	70	91	68	n.r.	–	–
Selbert	70	74	82	83	80	–
Gross	68	89	77	74	79	68
Beyer	66	n.r.	–	–	–	–
Görlinger	66	75	75	n.r.	–	–
Veit	62	85	n.r.	96	75	78
Gotthelf	–	97	96	83	–	–

SOURCE: S.P.D., *Protokoll, Parteitag,* 1946, 1947, 1948, 1950, 1952, 1958.
  [a] Not re-elected; i.e., sought re-election but lost.

APPENDIX A, SECTION 5 (*continued*)

Name	Party congress					
	1946	*1947*	*1948*	*1950*	*1952*	*1958*
Schmid	–	98	92	94	91	92
Schröder	–	97	98	93	85	–
Neumann, F.	–	97	98	88	80	–
Meitmann	–	95	83	78	63	–
Albrecht	–	89	91	79	67	–
Franke	–	65	86	83	n.r.	63
Knoeringen	–	–	95	99	97	90
Reuter	–	–	93	84	95	–
Fischer	–	–	86	70	–	–
Krahnstöver	–	–	86	90	74	–
Schoettle	–	–	86	93	88	87
Jaksch	–	–	–	88	85	–
Albertz	–	–	–	86	88	79
Steinhoff	–	–	–	68	74	94
Dobbert	–	–	–	66	n.r.	–
Alberts	–	–	–	64	89	85
Zinn	–	–	–	–	91	97
Kukil	–	–	–	–	90	64
Mellies	–	–	–	–	87	–
Wehner	–	–	–	–	87	78
Haas	–	–	–	–	67	–

Social Democratic Participation in Appointed and Elected State Governments, 1945–52

(Key ministries in italics)

State and dates of governments	Ministries held by Social Democrats	Other parties in government[a]
BADEN		
v.45–xi.46	*Economics,* Education, Culture	CDU, FDP
xii.46–vii.47	*Economics, Interior*	CDU, FDP, KPD
vii.47–i.48	Justice, Economics, Labor	CDU
State dissolved iv.52		
SÜDWÜRTTEMBERG-HOHENZOLLERN (after vii.47 Württemberg-Hohenzollern)		
x.45–xii.46	*Minister-president, Justice,* Culture, Education & Art, *Interior*	CDU
xii.46–vii.47	*Minister-president, Justice,* Culture, Education & Art, *Interior*	CDU, FDP
WÜRTTEMBERG-BADEN		
ix.45–xii.46	*Interior,* Transport	FDP, CDU
xii.46–i.51	*Interior, Economics,* Transport, Labor (vii.48–i.51), Polit. Liberation (to xii.48)	FDP, CDU, KPD (to vii.48)
i.51–iv.52	Deputy minister-president, *Economics, Interior,* Culture	FDP
State dissolved iv.52		
BADEN-WÜRTTEMBERG		
iv.52–x.53	Deputy minister-president, *Economics, Interior, Justice,* Labor, Culture	FDP, BHE

SOURCE: Albrecht Schultz and Martin Virchow, in Lange, ed., pp. 521–44.

[a] Though initially some of the parties operated under different names, they are here identified by their appellation in 1952, as follows: CDU Christlich Demokratische Union, CSU Christlich Soziale Union, FDP Freie Deutsche Partei, DP Deutsche Partei, KPD Kommunistische Partei Deutschlands, SED Sozialistische Einheitspartei (SPD-KPD amalgamation in Soviet zone), Z Zentrum, BHE Bund der Heimatlosen und Entrechteten.

APPENDIX B (*continued*)

State and dates of governments	Ministries held by Social Democrats	Other parties in government[a]
BAVARIA		
v.45–ix.45	Labor	CSU
x.45–xii.46	*Minister-president, Justice,* deputy minister-president, Labor, *Interior,* Culture, Education	CSU, KPD (to i.46)
xii.46–ix.47	Deputy minister-president, *Interior, Justice, Economics,* Social Welfare	CSU
xii.50–	Deputy minister-president, *Interior,* Finance, Labor, Social Welfare	CSU, BHE
BERLIN		
xii.46–i.49	Lord Mayor, Mayor, *Administration, Economics & Trade,* Housing, Education & Culture, Youth Affairs, Transport, Food, Banks & Insurance	SED (until xii.48), CDU, FDP
i.49–i.51	Lord Mayor, Mayor, *Administration, Economics,* Food, Housing, Education, Transport, Labor, without portfolio	CDU, FDP
i.51–x.53	*Lord Mayor,* Transport, Labor, Social Affairs, *Economics,* without portfolio	CDU, FDP
BREMEN		
viii.45–xi.46	*Lord Mayor,* Housing, Food & Labor, Transport, Education, Social Welfare	FDP, KPD
xi.46–i.48	*Lord Mayor, Economics & Labor,* Food & Agriculture, Housing, Construction, Education, Health & Social Welfare	FDP, KPD
i.48–xi.51	*Lord Mayor, Interior, Economics,* Education, Labor, Social Welfare, Housing, Construction, Food & Agriculture	FDP
xi.51–	*Lord Mayor, Interior, Economics,* Construction, Labor, Youth Affairs	FDP, CDU
HAMBURG		
v.45–xi.46	Deputy Lord Mayor, *Economics,* Food, Education, Social Welfare	CDU, FDP, KPD
xi.46–xi.49	*Lord Mayor,* Food, Agriculture, Education, Housing, Justice, Finance, *Economics,* Social Welfare, Labor, Youth & Sports, Health	FDP, KPD (to vii.48)
xi.49–xii.53	*Entire government*	None
HESSE		
xi.45–i.47	*Interior, Justice,* Food, Agriculture, Reconstruction & Polit. Liberation	CDU, KPD
i.47–x.49	*Minister-president, Interior,* Reconstruction, *Justice, Economics,* Transport, Polit. Liberation	CDU
xi.49–i.51	*Minister-president, Interior, Economics,* Labor, Agriculture	CDU
i.51–	*Entire government*	None

Appendix B (*continued*)

State and dates of governments	Ministries held by Social Democrats	Other parties in government[a]
LOWER SAXONY		
xii.46–xi.47	*Minister-president, Economics, Justice,* Education, Refugee Affairs	FDP, CDU, DP, KPD
vi.47–vi.48	*Minister-president, Economics,* Transport, Culture, without portfolio	CDU, DP, FDP, KPD (to ii.48), Z
vi.48–vi.51	*Minister-president, Interior,* Transport (from viii.50), *Economics* (from viii.50), Labor, Reconstruction, Health, Culture, Refugees	Z, CDU (until viii.50)
vi.51–	*Minister-president, Interior,* Culture, Finance	BHE, Z
NORTH RHINE–WESTPHALIA		
viii.46–xii.46	Deputy minister-president, *Interior, Economics*	FDP, Z, KPD
xii.46–vi.47	*Interior, Economics*	CDU, FDP, Z, KPD
vi.47–vii.50	Deputy minister-president, *Interior, Economics,* Labor, Reconstruction	CDU, Z, KPD (to iv.48)
RHINELAND-PFALZ		
xii.46–vi.47	*Interior,* Labor	CDU, KPD
vii.47–vi.51	Deputy minister-president (to x.49), Labor (to x.49), Finance, Reconstruction, Social Welfare (from xii.49)	CDU, FDP, KPD (to iv.48)
SCHLESWIG-HOLSTEIN		
xii.46–v.47	Deputy minister-president, *Interior, Economics,* Education, Health, Reconstruction	CDU
v.47–viii.49	*Entire government*	None
viii.49–ix.50	*Entire government*	None

Main Themes of 129 Schumacher Speeches, 1945-52

(Roman numerals in the column heads indicate the successive quarters of the year)

Theme	1945 IV	1946 I	1946 II	1946 III	1946 IV	1947 I	1947 II	1947 III	1947 IV	1948 I	1948 II	1948 III	1948 IV	1949 I	1949 II	1949 III	1949 IV	1950 I	1950 II	1950 III	1950 IV	1951 I	1951 II	1951 III	1951 IV	1952 I	1952 II	1952 III	1952 IV	Total themes
Policies and actions of all four occupation powers	8	6	4	1	5	1	7	3	3	—	—	2	—	—	2	1	—	1	3	—	—	1	2	—	—	—	1	1	—	*52*
Opp. to punitive economic measures (e.g. dismanting)	3	2	2	1	3	1	6	3	2	—	—	1	—	—	1	—	—	1	2	—	—	—	—	—	—	—	—	—	—	28
Opp. to "collective guilt" thesis	—	—	—	1	—	—	—	—	—	—	1	1	1	—	1	1	1	—	—	—	—	1	1	—	—	—	1	—	—	8
Demand for reunification	3	1	2	—	1	1	1	—	1	—	1	1	—	—	1	1	1	—	1	—	—	1	1	—	—	—	1	1	—	16
Relationship with USSR; anti-Communism; opp. to merger with Communist party; criticism of conditions in Soviet zone	—	—	3	1	1	5	4	1	3	1	1	—	1	2	4	1	2	1	1	1	2	7	3	—	—	2	1	—	—	*43*
Relationship with Western Allies	1	1	1	2	3	2	2	—	1	3	1	1	—	5	1	1	1	5	1	2	4	3	20	5	3	2	1	—	—	*65*
Qualified or absolute opp. to German rearmament	—	—	—	—	—	—	—	—	—	—	—	—	—	—	1	—	—	—	—	2	4	3	—	1	3	2	1	—	—	16
Opp. to annexation or alienation of German territory, particularly Saar and Ruhr	—	—	—	1	3	—	2	—	—	1	1	—	1	—	1	—	1	5	1	—	—	—	20	1	—	—	1	—	—	37
For independent, sovereign German state: opp. to dominance of Western Allies	1	1	1	1	—	2	—	—	1	2	—	1	1	—	1	—	—	1	1	1	1	—	—	4	1	1	—	—	—	12
Germany and European unity	1	—	1	—	2	4	1	2	1	5	—	1	1	1	—	1	7	1	1	1	1	5	18	1	1	1	2	2	—	*39*
General desirability of international amity and European unity	—	—	1	—	—	2	1	—	—	1	—	1	—	—	—	—	—	—	—	—	1	—	1	—	—	—	—	—	—	7
German problems before European or international problems	—	—	—	—	2	2	—	—	—	—	—	—	—	—	—	—	—	1	—	1	—	—	—	1	1	—	—	—	—	5
Opp. to ECSC (Schuman Plan)	—	—	—	—	2	2	—	—	1	—	—	—	—	—	—	—	1	—	1	1	2	5	17	1	1	1	2	2	—	27
Domestic issues	5	12	13	3	21	2	1	2	1	5	—	2	—	1	2	7	2	4	10	2	2	4	2	1	3	1	2	2	—	*112*
Attacks on Adenauer, CDU, alleged intervention of RCC in politics	3	3	5	—	3	2	—	2	1	1	—	1	—	1	1	5	2	3	5	—	1	2	—	1	3	1	1	1	—	43
Class struggle against large capitalists and property owners and big-business interests; reactionaries, ex-Nazis	2	4	3	—	1	1	1	—	—	3	—	1	—	—	1	—	—	—	2	—	—	—	1	—	—	—	1	1	—	16
For planned economy, socialization of key industries	2	2	1	1	11	1	—	2	1	3	—	1	—	—	1	1	1	—	—	—	2	2	1	—	—	—	1	1	—	33
Social justice through currency reform and equalization of war burden	2	1	3	1	6	—	—	—	—	1	—	—	—	1	—	1	—	—	2	—	—	—	—	—	—	—	—	—	—	14
For land reform and other aid for farmers	1	2	1	1	6	—	—	—	—	1	—	—	—	1	—	—	—	—	2	—	—	—	—	—	—	—	—	—	—	6
Total themes	13	19	22	7	32	14	15	6	7	9	1	7	0	3	10	9	5	12	16	6	9	20	42	10	7	3	4	3	—	*311*
Total speeches	4	7	9	3	7	6	7	4	2	6	0	1	0	0	3	3	2	7	6	4	6	9	20	6	3	2	1	1	—	*129*

A Sampling of Schumacher's Public Image

1. In the Foreign Press

VERY NEGATIVE

1. K.S. a chauvinist demagogue who might be the forerunner of a new Hitler; recalls the demagogic intelligence of Goebbels.—British journalist Geoffrey Frazer in *Servir* (Switzerland), 14.xi.46.

2. K.S. an imperialist like Hitler.—Anonymous article in *Dziennik Zachodi* (Poland), 1.ii.47.

3. K.S. a new Hitler.—Anonymous article in *Concorde,* a French journal of unknown political orientation, 13.ii.47.

4. K.S. a Nazi demagogue and nationalist who hates the French and refuses to acknowledge German war guilt; a cynical man.—Florimont Bontré in the Communist newspaper *L'Humanité* (France), 3.ii.47.

5. K.S. an arrogant enemy of the Soviet Union, and an unprincipled demagogue who wants a disunited working class, American rule, and war.—Grigorjew, Tass (U.S.S.R.), 10.ii.51.

NEGATIVE

1. K.S. has no sense of German guilt, and spends his time criticizing and demanding concessions.—Dutch historian Jan Romein in *De Nieuwe Stem* (Netherlands), 14.ii.47.

2. K.S. has no understanding of the security needs of the Western powers.— British radio commentator Thompson, 16.vi.49.

NEUTRAL

1. K.S. the leading German politician, but unfit to be chancellor because a fighter and no diplomat.—Gosta Ollen in the Swedish liberal journal *Expressen,* 18.vi.50.

NEUTRAL-POSITIVE

1. K.S. too radical, but has makings of a great democratic leader.—Charles Roesmer in the Belgian liberal journal *Dernière Heure,* 20.ix.47.

2. K.S. a patriot who is the only real German leader, but overzealous and prone to overlook German war guilt and anti-German sentiments abroad; bold and brave, but it is difficult to know whether he is always honest in his statements.—M. Bedont in the French liberal Catholic paper *La France Catholique,* 7.xi.47.

POSITIVE

1. K.S. the coming leader of the new Germany who believes in Western democracy.—British journalist J. Reynolds in the Swiss nonpartisan journal *Die Tat*, 11.vii.47.

2. K.S. a German patriot first, a socialist only second, and a passionate anti-Communist.—Bud Kane in *The Philadelphia Inquirer* (U.S.), 20.ii.49.

3. K.S. a forward-looking realist, a party activist rather than an ideologist; a man of fantastic energy.—Anonymous article in *The British Zone Review* (Germany), 27.iv.46.

VERY POSITIVE

1. K.S. a tough fighter for democracy and a defender of individual liberty; a human wreck who symbolizes devastated Germany, and a man of great intellect.—Rolf Gerhardsen in the Norwegian socialist journal *Arbeiderbladet*, 18.vii.47.

2. K.S. a pro-Western democrat; an enthusiastic and inspiring leader.—Sandro Volta in *Corriere della Sera* (Italy), 20.iii.48.

3. K.S. a man who thinks only of others, never of himself, is ready to die for human rights, and deserves to be supported as a great hero.—Karl Berchtold in the Swiss socialist paper *Volksrecht*, 14.vi.47.

4. K.S. the champion of the "little man"; a brave fighter.—Carl F. Jaeger in *The Lutheran* (U.S.), 25.ii.48.

5. K.S. a political leader of great intellect and fiery temperament.—Karl von Wiegand in *The San Francisco Examiner* (U.S.), 23.iv.50.

2. AMONG NON-SOCIALIST GERMAN OPINION LEADERS

VERY NEGATIVE

1. K.S. a betrayer of true socialism.—Willi Eildermann, Communist news agency P.D., 25.vi.47.

2. K.S. a demagogue like Hitler.—Emil Frenzel in the Christian Democratic newspaper *Deutsche Tagespost*, 21.xi.50.

3. K.S. a warmonger and pseudo-oppositionist.—Otto Winzer in the Communist newspaper *Neues Deutschland* (D.D.R.), 5.iv.51.

4. K.S. represents the powers of evil, and there can be no compromise with him.—Father Demian, a Christian Democrat, in a sermon given at Wirtheim, Bavaria, 23.iii.52.

5. K.S. the leader of the Trojan forces of Communism.—Martin Euler, leader of the Free Democratic party, at a mass meeting in Frankfurt, 1.vi.52.

NEGATIVE

1. K.S. is just as reactionary as Adenauer, but he lacks the ability to get the votes.—W. K. Gerst, own press service, 27.x.49.

2. K.S.'s view does not extend beyond Germany.—A. Winbauer in the *Heidelberger Tageblatt*, 24.v.52.

3. K.S. pursues opposition for its own sake, without offering alternatives to government policies.—Helmut Lindemann in the independent newspaper *Stuttgarter Zeitung*, 18.iii.52.

4. K.S. an unrealistic dreamer; intolerant.—Rudolf Spitz in the independent newspaper *Main Echo*, 20.vii.50.

5. K.S. an obstructionist Don Quixote.—Heinrich von Brentano, leader of the C.D.U., at a C.D.U. state convention, 15.vii.51.

NEUTRAL

1. K.S. an acute thinker and impressive orator, but also a fanatic whose irritating behavior loses votes.—Walter Henkels in the newspaper *Essener Tageblatt*, 4.iii.50.

2. K.S.'s militancy is both his strength and his weakness, his weakness because with it he wounds himself.—Heinrich Vogt in the independent newspaper *Westdeutsche Allgemeine*, 17.xi.49.

POSITIVE

1. K.S. a good opposition leader whom Germany needs as much as it needs Chancellor Adenauer.—Karl Silex in the independent newspaper *Neues Tageblatt*, 17.xi.50.

2. K.S. the productive dissenter, the Luther of German politics.—Ernst Glaser in the independent newspaper *Stuttgarter Zeitung*, 24.xi.51.

Chronology of Schumacher's Career, 1945-52

1945

April
10. Hannover occupied by American troops.
30. Hitler commits suicide.

19. Reorganizes Hannover S.P.D.

May
7. German surrender.

6. Announces postwar program in address to organization meeting, Hannover S.P.D.

June
15. Grotewohl leads establishment of S.P.D. Central Committee in Berlin.

July

"Büro Dr. Schumacher" becomes unofficial center of West German S.P.D. K.S. visits major cities in British and U.S. zones.

August
2. Potsdam Agreement.

20. Asks British M.G. for permission to re-establish S.P.D. in Hannover. Contacts S.P.D. exiles in London. Receives authorization from 14 districts of West German S.P.D. to summon meeting to Hannover.

September
15. Western occupation authorities permit local organization of licensed parties.

5. Leads meeting of new executive, Hannover S.P.D.
10. In Hamburg to stem sentiment for collaboration with Communists.
15. Leads meeting of Hannover S.P.D.

October
5–7. Meeting of S.P.D. delegates from all occupation zones, Hannover. K.S. authorized to speak for S.P.D. in Western zones, Berlin Central Committee in Soviet zone.

13. First major public speech, Hannover.
23–29. Confers with S.P.D. leaders in Hesse, Kiel, Hamburg.

The Setting	*The Actor*

November

20. S.P.D.-K.P.D. conference, Berlin, on amalgamation.

25. S.P.D. state convention meets in Berlin under Grotewohl's leadership.

15–18. Public appearances and speeches in Ruhr.

20. Speaks at mass meeting, Hannover-Badenstedt.

29. Prevails upon meeting of S.P.D. functionaries in Frankfurt to oppose Central Committee's unity proposals.

December

21. Allied conference in Paris sets German reparations payments.

9. First broadcast, British zone. Continues to oppose proposals to amalgamate with K.P.D.

1946

January

15. Berlin S.P.D. Central Committee opts for amalgamation with K.P.D.

26–27. S.P.D. and K.P.D. leaders in Berlin announce intention to amalgamate.

3–4. Confers with S.P.D. functionaries of U.S. and British zones about opposing amalgamation with K.P.D. British zone S.P.D. Conf. opts against amalgamation.

February

6–8. French government demands internationalization of Ruhr and Rhineland.

1–5. Tours cities in Ruhr and Rhineland to speak against amalgamation and denounce Western "collective guilt thesis."

6–8. In Brunswick for conference with Grotewohl.

19–22. Final break with Grotewohl and his Central Committee during visit to Berlin.

March

1. Several S.P.D. leaders in Berlin revolt against Central Committee. Demand referendum on fusion issue.

26–27. Allied Control Council sets goals for German industry at 50–55% of 1938 production. Excess capacity to be dismantled or destroyed.

31. Referendum of S.P.D. in West Berlin: 82% oppose amalgamation with K.P.D., but 62% for close collaboration.

15–20. First trip to Bavaria (U.S. zone) to rally support for a West German S.P.D. reorganization. Meeting with Hoegner, opponent of plan.

26–27. Attends first meeting of British zone Advisory Council, Hamburg. (Adenauer heads C.D.U. group.)

29–30. Attends trade union conference, Hannover.

April

7. West Berlin S.P.D. severs relations with Grotewohl's Central Committee.

9. Socialist Unity party established in Soviet zone; Grotewohl becomes its cochairman.

16–23. In Berlin to lead mass meetings against establishment of Socialist Unity party.

25–30. Confers with S.P.D. leaders in Hannover and Frankfurt.

The Setting	*The Actor*

May

9–11. First postwar S.P.D. congress, Hannover, elects K.S. chairman (99% of votes cast). S.P.D. becomes interzonal party.

9–11. Major programmatic speech to delegates from Western zones at Hannover congress.

June

5. Foreign Ministers Conference, Paris, opens (continues until July 15). U.S. proposes 25-year occupation and demilitarization of Germany. U.S.S.R. vetoes unification of occupation zones. Western powers propose inter-Allied office to coordinate occupation policies.

30. Election of constituent assemblies in states of U.S. zone (44.3% S.P.D. in Hesse, 28.9% in Bavaria, 32.3% in Württemberg-Baden).

2. First visit to French zone for S.P.D. conference in Saarbrücken.

12–18. Confers with S.P.D. leaders in Stuttgart, Rhineland, northern Germany.

19–20. Visits Berlin, demands unification of zones.

23–30. Campaigns in U.S. zone for election of state constituent assemblies.

July

2, 10–13. Attends meetings of British zone Advisory Council, Hamburg.

15–16. In Berlin for conference with S.P.D. leaders.

August

During entire month intensive campaigning throughout West Germany.

17. First major attack on Adenauer.

September

5. U.S. and Britain agree to economic merger of zones.

6. U.S. Sec. of State Byrnes announces new U.S. policy for German economic recovery.

Intensive campaigning for municipal and rural county elections in British zone.

8. Welcomes Byrnes's speech.

22. Protests French "annexation" of Saar.

26. Presides over meeting of S.P.D. Executive Comm., which calls upon S.P.D. ministers in the states to resign unless Western powers move toward unitary state (Cologne Resolution).

October

4. Minister-presidents and mayors of U.S. and British zones call for an all-German Council of State.

13. Municipal and rural council elections in British zone (S.P.D. 33.4% in North Rhine–Westphalia, 41% in Schleswig-Holstein, 41.9% in Lower Saxony, 47.6% in Bremen, 43.2% in Hamburg). S.P.D. strongest party in zone.

7–12. Campaigns in British zone for municipal council elections.

13–22. In Berlin to campaign for city assembly elections.

The Setting   *The Actor*

20. City assembly elections, Berlin, give S.P.D. plurality with 48.7% of votes in all sectors as against 19.8% for the new Unity party.

November
24. State diet elections in Württemberg-Baden (S.P.D. 31.9% as against 38.4% C.D.U., 19.5% D.V.P., and 10.2% K.P.D.)

18–27. Campaigns in U.S. zone, esp. Bavaria, for state diet elections.
29. Visits London on invitation of British Labour party (until Dec. 12).

December
1. State diet elections in Bavaria (S.P.D. 28.6%, C.S.U. 58.3%) and Hesse (S.P.D. 42.7%, C.D.U. 30.9%, F.D.P. 15.7%, K.P.D. 10.7%).

1947

January
1. Economic merger of British and U.S. zones (Bizonia).

21–24. In Berlin for conferences with U.S. Gen. Clay, British Gen. Robertson, and S.P.D. leaders.

March
4. Adenauer opposes S.P.D. efforts to socialize basic industry in Lower Saxony.
12. Pres. Truman announces program of U.S. aid to countries threatened by internal or external Soviet pressure.

17–22. In Berlin for conferences with S.P.D. leaders.

April
3–24. Foreign Ministers Conference, Moscow, fails to agree on government for all Germany. Western powers decide to proceed with revival of economy.
20. State diet elections in Lower Saxony (S.P.D. 43.3%, C.D.U. 19.9%, N.L.P. 19.4%), North Rhine–Westphalia (S.P.D. 32.0%, C.D.U. 37.4%, K.P.D. 14.0%), and Schleswig-Holstein (S.P.D. 44.4%, C.D.U. 34.5%). S.P.D. strongest party in British zone.

During entire month campaigns in British zone for state diet elections. Campaign speeches criticize reported Allied plans for German reparations, particularly dismantling of industry. Demands return of POWs still in Soviet Union.

May
31. S.P.D. minister-presidents decide to participate in all-German ministerial conference in Munich in spite of K.S.'s objections.

1–18. Illness forces cancellation of all public engagements.

| *The Setting* | *The Actor* |

June

5. U.S. proposes U.S. aid program to European nations (Marshall Plan).

6–8. All-German ministerial conference ends in failure to agree.

10. Establishment of Bizonal Economic Council for U.S. and British zones.

29. Second postwar S.P.D. congress, Nuremberg (to July 2).

6–8. Fails to get S.P.D. admitted to International Socialist Consultative Conference in Zurich.

29. Major policy speech at S.P.D. congress.

July

25. Having failed to get economic directorate in new Bizonal Eco. Council, S.P.D. goes into opposition to "bourgeois" coalition.

8–13. In Berlin for conferences with U.S. and British officers and S.P.D. leaders.

17. Confers with leaders of Evangelical Church.

August

28. Western powers announce plans to raise German industrial production to 90–95% of 1936 level (cf. March 27, 1946, Control Council directive).

9–17. In Berlin for conferences with Western officials and S.P.D. functionaries.

23. In Hannover, demands end to dismantling of industrial plants, increase in production.

September

20. Leaves for visit to U.S. on invitation of A.F.L. (until Oct. 29).

November

21. S.P.D. admitted to International Consultative Conference in Antwerp.

17–25. Visits Denmark, Norway, and Sweden.

December

11–15. Foreign Ministers Conference, London, fails to reach agreement on Germany. U.S. refuses to deliver further reparations from West German production to Soviets.

1948

January

7. U.S. and British M.G.'s confer with minister-presidents about expansion of bizonal economic institutions.

6. Confers with S.P.D. minister-presidents on Western plans for expansion of Bizonia.

February

2–9. Reorganization and expansion of Bizonal Economic Council.

18–25. Communists seize control of Czechoslovakia.

2–9. In Frankfurt to instruct S.P.D. delegation to Bizonal Eco. Council.

14–21. Confers with S.P.D. leaders in U.S. zone.

The Setting	*The Actor*

March

6. Conference of six Western powers, London, calls for creation of a West German federal state and German participation in an international Ruhr authority.

15. Western occupation powers represent West Germans at planning conference of O.E.E.C.

17. Brussels Pact for Western European Union.

19. Soviets leave Allied Control Council. End of four-power rule for Germany.

April

3. U.S. Congress passes Eco. Cooperation Act for aid to Western Europe.

16. Allied occupation officials sign aid agreement on behalf of West Germans.

June

1. Six-power conference, in London, agrees on establishment of International Ruhr Authority and creation of West German federal state.

12. U.S. Senate passes Vandenberg Resolution calling for Western collective security arrangements.

16. Soviets leave Berlin Kommandatura. End of four-power rule in Berlin.

18–21. Currency reform in West Germany.

23. Currency reform in Soviet zone.

24. Beginning of Berlin blockade.

30. Start of Berlin airlift.

July

1–26. Western occupation authorities and West German minister-presidents agree on convening a West German Parliamentary Council to draft a Basic Law for "provisional" West German state.

August

8–23. Meeting of Preparatory Committee to draft Basic Law.

18. *De facto* merger of three Western zones.

September

1. Convening of Parliamentary Council in Bonn. Adenauer elected president.

---

20. In London for conference of socialist leaders of Marshall Plan countries. Severe pains in left foot compel premature departure.

From March 1948 to April 1949 K.S. is confined to sickroom in Hannover (leg amputated Sept. 25, 1948), and direction of party is exercised through a few key aides.

The Setting	*The Actor*

6. Separate governments set up for Soviet and Western parts of Berlin.

11–14. Third postwar S.P.D. congress, Düsseldorf, re-elects K.S. chairman in his absence.

December

5. West Berlin city council elections give S.P.D. absolute majority with 64.5% as against 19.4% for C.D.U. and 16.1% for F.D.P.

7. Reuter elected lord mayor of West Berlin.

12. Beginning of Western negotiations for creation of N.A.T.O.

28. Final six-power agreement on creation of Int'l Ruhr Authority.

1949

April

4. N.A.T.O. agreement is signed.

10. Three Western powers, meeting in Washington, announce plan to establish West German state and end military government.

23. Western occupation powers agree to K.S.'s demands on Basic Law.

20. In first major action since illness, announces S.P.D. refusal to accept draft of Basic Law unless demands for more centralized state are met.

May

8. Parliamentary Council adopts Basic Law.

10. Parl. Council chooses Bonn for "temporary" capital over S.P.D. opposition.

12. End of Berlin blockade.

20–23. Establishment of West German Federal Republic and Allied High Commission.

9. Confers with British Foreign Secretary Bevin in Cologne.

June and July

Opening of campaign for Bundestag elections.

Campaigns for Bundestag elections.

August

14. Election of first Bundestag (S.P.D. 29.2%, C.D.U. 31.0%, F.D.P. 11.9%).

27–30. S.P.D. leaders, meeting in Bad Dürkheim, issue 16-point opposition program.

19. In post-election statement declares that S.P.D. will become opposition party in new Bundestag.

The Setting	*The Actor*

September
7. Opening session of Bundestag.
12. Heuss elected federal president by 416 votes against 312 for K.S.
15. Adenauer chosen chancellor by majority of one. Forms coalition.

6. At meeting of S.P.D. leaders, wins narrow approval for his candidacy for federal presidency.
21. First major speech in Bundestag as leader of opposition.
28. First conference with Chancellor Adenauer.

October
7. Establishment of German Democratic Republic (D.D.R.) in Soviet zone. Grotewohl prime minister.

21. Conference with Adenauer.

November
10. Western foreign ministers in Paris call for greater independence for Federal Republic and its gradual integration into a European community.
22. Adenauer and three Western Powers sign Petersberg Agreement for participation of Fed. Rep. in Council of Europe.

11. Attacks proposed Int'l Ruhr Authority.
13. Meeting with U.S. Sec. of State Acheson.
15. First major foreign policy speech in Bundestag.
24. Calls Adenauer "Chancellor of Allies" for signing Petersberg Agreement, and is excluded from Bundestag.

December
15. U.S. agreement with Fed. Rep. for Marshall Plan aid.

1. Readmitted to Bundestag following three meetings with Adenauer.

1950

January
26. Western powers grant Fed. Rep. right to appoint diplomatic representatives in their capitals.

14. Confers with Robert Schuman, French foreign minister.
16. Attacks French policy in Saar.
24. Confers with Dutch socialists, who urge consent for membership in Council of Europe.

February
14. French socialists criticize K.S.'s opposition to Saar policy and Council of Europe membership.

25. Demands new Bundestag elections because political situation radically altered.

March
4. France and Saar government sign agreement for Saar autonomy under French protection. Adenauer government protests.
7. Adenauer proposes Franco-German union.

10. Attacks Adenauer's Saar policy in major Bundestag speech.
30. Confers with Adenauer; also with British High Commissioner Gen. Robertson.

The Setting	*The Actor*

30. Council of Europe invites Fed. Rep. and Saar to become associate members.

April
19. S.P.D. Exec. Comm. endorses K.S.'s opposition to assoc. membership in Council of Europe.

21. Demands new federal elections.

May
9. French Foreign Minister Schuman proposes European Coal and Steel Community.
21–25. Fourth S.P.D. congress, Hamburg, endorses K.S.'s opposition to assoc. membership in Council of Europe. K.S. reelected chairman.

14. Attacks Schuman plan.
26–30. Mass meetings and group discussions in Berlin with members of East German Free German Youth.

June
6. East German leader Ulbricht accepts Oder-Neisse border with Poland as permanent.
15. Bundestag majority votes assoc. membership in Council of Europe. S.P.D. opposes.
18. Legislature elections in North Rhine–Westphalia (S.P.D. 32.3%, C.D.U.–F.D.P.–D.P., "German Electoral Bloc," 50.7%). "Bonn Coalition" forms gov't. S.P.D. in opposition.
25. North Korean troops invade S. Korea.

Entire month: Campaigns for state legislature elections in North Rhine–Westphalia and Schleswig-Holstein. Themes: Class struggle, German sovereignty, opposition to Schuman Plan.
13. Major Bundestag speech opposing assoc. membership in Council of Europe.

July
9. Legislature elections in Schleswig-Holstein: S.P.D. drops to 27.5%, C.D.U. to 19.7%. New Refugee party (B.H.E.) get 23.4%. S.P.D. leaves gov't and becomes opposition.
26. S.P.D. delegates Bundestag deputies to participate in C. of Europe despite previous opposition.

1–8. Campaigns for legislature elections in Schleswig-Holstein. Attacks R.C. clergy and industrialists for supporting Adenauer.
11. Conferences with Adenauer and with Norwegian socialist leaders.
19. Meeting with new British High Comm. Kirkpatrick.

August
7. Fed. Rep. and Saar become assoc. members C. of Europe (Strasbourg).
11. C. of Europe adopts Churchill's proposal for European Army. Adenauer proposes a German defense contribution, and appoints ex-General Schwerin military adviser.

22, 23. Confers with Adenauer about rearmament; advances conditional armament thesis: equal risks call for equal opportunities.

The Setting	*The Actor*

September

16–26. Foreign Ministers Conference, New York, calls for 30,000 German soldiers to aid Western defense.

2, 4, 14. Confers with Schwerin about rearmament.
21. Confers with ex-Generals Gehlen, Heusinger, Grolman about rearmament.
28–30. In Berlin demands assurances that Western forces can win first battle in case of Soviet attack. Wants Berlin to join Fed. Rep.

October

10. Interior Minister Heinemann resigns over rearmament.
21. Soviet bloc calls for declaration outlawing German rearmament, and providing for an all-German gov't and the withdrawal of all foreign troops.
24. French Defense Minister Pleven introduces plan for European Army including West German units.

3. Demands new elections in view of rearmament.
4, 10. Conferences with Schwerin, Adenauer, and ex - Generals Speidel and Foertsch on rearmament.
19, 30. Confers with leaders of Evangelical Church.
24. Demands new elections in view of rearm. question.
28. Confers with ex-General Heusinger, Adenauer's new military adviser.

November

8. Adenauer declares West Germany willing to contribute to European defense if guaranteed equality and protection.
19. S.P.D. gains in state legislature elections in Hesse (S.P.D. 44.4%, C.D.U. 18.8%, F.D.P.-B.H.E. alliance 31.8%) and Württ.-Baden (S.P.D. 30.2%, C.D.U. 29.2%). S.P.D. continues coalition gov'ts in both states.
26. State legislature elections in Bavaria give S.P.D. plurality first time in history (S.P.D. 28.0%, C.S.U. 27.4%). S.P.D. forms coalition government with C.S.U. and minor party. Hoegner becomes deputy minister-president.
30. Grotewohl proposes All-German Constituent Council, with equal represent. of both German states, to prepare nationwide elections for Constituent Assembly.

Entire month: Campaigns for state legislatures in Hesse, Bavaria, Württ.-Baden. Theme: Conditional rearm. only.
2. Discussion with former Hitler Youth leaders.
7. Conference with Adenauer.
8. Responding to Adenauer, stresses need for massive Western build-up before armament can get under way.
27. In Berlin (to Dec. 2) to campaign for city assembly of new West Berlin citystate.

December

3. West Berlin assembly elections bring major drop in S.P.D. vote over 1948 (S.P.D. 44.7%, C.D.U. 24.6%, F.D.P. 23.0%). Over K.S.'s apparent opposition, Reuter re-forms coalition with C.D.U. and F.D.P.

3. Condemns Grotewohl proposal of Nov. 30.
16. Criticizes Spofford Plan for German N.A.T.O. units as denying Fed. Rep. full equality. Again calls for new elections.

The Setting	*The Actor*

19. N.A.T.O. ministers meeting, Brussels, calls for German partic. in European defense.

30. Soviet Union declares readiness to discuss German unific. and demilit. with West.

1951

January

26. France invites Fed. Rep. to participate in conference of six European powers on formation of European Army.

6. Confers with Böckler, D.G.B. chairman, about cooperation between S.P.D. and Trade Union Confed.

26. Criticizes categorical pacifism of some Germans on rearm. Rejects any negotiation with Grotewohl gov't or Communists about rearm. Objects to Pleven Plan for European Army as denying Germany equality.

February

15. Fed. Rep. joins Paris conf. on European Army.

16. Böckler, chairman of D.G.B., dies.

3. Confers with Heusinger and Speidel about rearmament.

27. First of series of conferences with trade union leaders directed at influencing choice of new chairman of D.G.B.

28. In Berlin to confer with S.P.D. functionaries during Reuter's trip to U.S.

March

5. Big Four meet in Paris to discuss Germany.

6. Western powers modify Occupation Statute of 1949.

2. Confers with Heusinger and Speidel.

6. Confers with Adenauer.

11. Conference with U.S. High Comm. McCloy.

17–22. At series of meetings in Hannover, Kiel, Hamburg, attacks Schuman Plan and agrees to rearm. under conditions of "equality."

April

10. Codetermination Law passes with S.P.D. and C.D.U. joining forces.

18. Treaty on E.C.S.C. (Schuman Plan) signed in Paris.

29. State legislature election, Rhineland-Palatinate, causes fall of coalition. (S.P.D. 34.0%, C.D.U. 39.2%, F.D.P. 16.7%). S.P.D. becomes opposition to "Bonn Coalition" gov't.

7. Confers with Heusinger and Speidel about contemplated milit. intelligence office.

13–16. Campaigns in Rhineland-Palatinate for legislature elections. Theme: Opposition to Schuman Plan.

The Setting	*The Actor*

May

2. Fed. Rep. accepted as regular instead of associate member of Council of Europe.

6. Elections in Lower Saxony result in major setback for S.P.D. and gain for Refugee and neo-Nazi parties. (S.P.D. 33.7%, C.D.U.-D.P. 23.7%, B.H.E. 14.9%, S.R.P. 11.0%). S.P.D. forms new coalition with B.H.E.

1–5. In Lower Saxony to campaign for state legislature elections.

June

13. Appointment of West German diplomatic representatives in Washington, London, and Paris.

21. Fed. Rep. becomes member of U.N.E.S.C.O.

4–6. In conferences with trade union leaders, opposes Fette and favors Freitag for new D.G.B. chairman.

Confers with French socialist leaders who have criticized his position on European integration.

30. Delivers keynote address at International Socialist Conference, Frankfurt.

July

7. Britain ends state of war with Germany (France, July 13; U.S., Oct. 19).

1–2. More conferences with European socialist leaders about opposition to Schuman Plan, European Army.

12. Confers with Adenauer's military advisers.

15. Vacation in Austria (until Aug. 6). Meets Austrian socialist and trade union leaders.

August

15–18. Communist-sponsored World Youth Festival in East Berlin.

15–18. Meetings with members of East German Free German Youth in West Berlin.

Confers with Heusinger and Speidel about future defense establishment.

September

14. Big Three agree to give Fed. Rep. sovereignty within a European Defense Community (E.D.C.).

27. Bundestag, incl. S.P.D., calls for reunification of Berlin.

October

7. City council elections in Bremen bring major defeat for C.D.U. (S.P.D. 39.1%, C.D.U. 9.1%, F.D.P. 11.8%, D.P. 14.7%). Kaisen continues to head coalition, and includes C.D.U. despite K.S.'s stand.

Entire month: Intensive activity. Conferences and public appearances throughout Fed. Rep.

|| *The Setting* | *The Actor* |

November
22. Adenauer and three Western powers agree on treaty to give Fed. Rep. sovereignty upon entrance into E.D.C.

14. Confers with Heusinger about rearmament.

December
3. Adenauer pays first official visit to Great Britain.

17. Confers with Adenauer on foreign policy.
21. Suffers paralytic stroke.

1952

January
11. Bundestag approves E.C.S.C. treaty over S.P.D. opposition.

April

10. Limited resumption of polit. activities through a few key deputies.

May
26–27. Adenauer signs Contractual Agreement for West German sovereignty and E.D.C. treaty.

31. In interview refuses to accept Contractual Agreement and E.D.C. because they endanger reunification of Germany.

June

11. Radio broadcast, first public activity since stroke.
24. Confers with Heusinger.

July
25. E.C.S.C. goes into effect.

15–16. In interview and broadcast (R.I.A.S.) insists on modification of E.D.C. and Contractual Agreement. Reunification primary goal.

August

8. Last radio broadcast.
20. Dies.

September
29. Fifth S.P.D. congress adopts Dortmund Program, and elects Ollenhauer party chairman to succeed K.S.

Notes

Notes

Complete authors' names, titles, and publication data for works cited in short form are given in the Bibliography.

Chapter One

1. Karl Lowenstein, *Political Reconstruction* (New York, 1946), p. 233.
2. Prittie, "Dr. Schumacher's Role in Post-War Germany," p. 5.
3. See Wesemann, *Kurt Schumacher,* and Scholz and Oschilewski, eds., *Turmwächter der Demokratie* (hereafter cited as *Turm.*), Vol. I. Ritter, *Kurt Schumacher,* was not yet available when this book was in preparation.
4. For a fuller discussion of this topic, as well as the general methodologies that underlie this study, see Lewis J. Edinger, "Political Science and Political Biography: Reflections on the Study of Leadership," *Journal of Politics,* Vol. XXVI (1964), Nos. 2 and 3.
5. David Easton, in Charlesworth, ed., p. 19.
6. Robert A. Dahl, "The Behavioral Approach in Political Science: Epitaph for a Monument to a Successful Protest," *American Political Science Review,* LV (1961), 767.
7. The following discussion of the role of a political leader and that of his counterplayers relies on the terminology and concepts developed by Gross *et al.,* in *Explorations in Role Analysis,* on the basis of earlier work by Herbert Mead, Theodore Newcomb, and Talcott Parsons. I have also found useful Biddle, "Roles, Goals, and Value Structures in Organizations," and Theodore R. Sarbin, in Lindzey, ed., pp. 223–58.
8. Levinson, p. 177. See also Hartmann, *Ego Psychology.*
9. Gross *et al.,* pp. 65f. See also Parsons and Shils, eds., pp. 47–158.

Chapter Two

This chapter is based on interviews with and communications from Lotte Trinkwalter and Elizabeth Müller (sisters), Dorothea and Hedwig Kollmorgen (cousins), and Annemarie Renger and Maria Seibert; and on an unpublished tape of a long interview that Schumacher gave a German journalist named Kaufmann shortly before his death (hereafter cited as Kaufmann Int.), which is in the possession of the S.P.D. Parteivorstand in Bonn (hereafter referred to as S.P.D., P.V.). See also Wesemann, pp. 8–13, and *Turm.,* I, 9–11, 14.

1. Kaufmann Int.
2. On "political socialization," see Gabriel A. Almond, in Almond and Coleman, eds., pp. 26–33, Almond and Verba, *Civic Culture,* and Hyman, *Political Socialization.*
3. See *Meyers Lexikon,* VII, 298, and *Der Grosse Brockhaus,* IV, 295–96.
4. Personal statement in Personal Archiv, S.P.D., P.V., *Kurt Schumacher Band Biographie* (hereafter cited as Pers. Archiv, S.P.D., K.S. Bd. Bio.).
5. Arendt, *Origins of Totalitarianism,* p. 50.

6. Kaufmann Int.

7. *Ibid.*

8. A letter to Willi Klinowski, Archiv Renger, Nov. 7, 1945.

9. Quoted in Mann, p. 574.

10. Professor Willy Andreas of the Technische Hochschule, Karlsruhe, in *Süddeutsche Monatshefte,* quoted in Pritzlokeit, p. 228.

11. Most valuable for this analysis was Schumacher's own account in the taped interview with Kaufmann. Additional information comes from interviews with his relatives and information in Pers. Archiv, S.P.D., K.S. Bd. Bio. See also "Die militärische Laufbahn Dr. Kurt Schumachers," *Die Deutsche Soldatenzeitung,* Sept. 10, 1952.

12. Both Scholz and Wesemann, Schumacher's biographers, omit most of this period entirely, and several of Schumacher's associates (from various periods in his life) mentioned his evident reluctance to speak of this time.

13. Fenichel, p. 258, and Roger G. Barker and Beatrice A. Wright, in Wittkower and Cleghorn, eds., pp. 419–29.

14. According to one observer, to a large extent "an individual's 'narcissistic' feelings are invested in the limbs," a fact that accounts for the "almost universal reaction of loss of self-esteem following amputation of limbs. This is probably an important factor in the large proportion of so-called 'social' maladjustment in amputees." Victor H. Rosen, in Bellak, ed., p. 67. This problem was observed frequently in American amputees after World War II and the Korean War, and it was effectively dramatized in the motion picture "The Men." See Rosen, in *ibid.,* and Douglas Noble *et. al.,* "Psychiatric Disturbances Following Amputation."

15. Erikson, pp. 14f; also pp. 41, 102–4, 253–54.

16. Fenichel, p. 63.

17. See esp. Lasswell, pp. 58, 98; Alexander and Juliet George, *Woodrow Wilson and Colonel House*; Horney, pp. 162–72; Murphy, pp. 557–92, 743; Fenichel, pp. 40, 258–59, 387; Gerth and Mills, pp. 40f; and Von der Heydte and Sacherl, p. 227.

18. See Murphy, p. 557.

19. Kaufmann Int.

20. *Ibid.*

21. *Protokoll der Verhandlungen des Landtages des freien Volkstaates Württemberg* (hereafter cited as *Protokoll, Landtag*), Jan. 25, 1928, p. 184.

22. Letter, Lotte Trinkwalter, Jan. 19, 1960; Johann Plenge, "Die Doktorarbeit Kurt Schumachers."

Chapter Three

The statements in this chapter about Schumacher's activities in Stuttgart are based on personal interviews with his former associates there.

1. See Edinger, *German Exile Politics,* pp. 3–5, Edinger, "German Social Democracy," and Bracher, pp. 71–77, 265f.

2. See *Meyers Lexikon,* II, 1079–82, *Der Grosse Brockhaus,* XVIII, 297–99, and S.P.D. Württemberg-Hohenzollern, Bericht, pp. 98–100.

3. *Schwäbische Tagwacht,* June 8 and 9, 1920 (hereafter cited as *Tagwacht*), and Keil, II, 67.

4. See Keil, pp. 208, 213.

5. Wilhelm Keil, in *Turm.,* I, 478; see also *ibid.,* pp. 476–77, and Wesemann, p. 16.

6. See, e.g., *Tagwacht,* Jan. 12, 18, Feb. 8, 15, 23, and March 7, 16, 1921.

7. See report in *Tagwacht,* Aug. 17 and 30, Sept. 3, 1921.

8. See Keil in *Turm.,* I, 478. Also Wesemann, p. 19.

9. This clash between S.P.D. party leaders and Arbeiterjugend members was a national phenomenon. See Else Frobenius, *Mit uns zieht die neue Zeit* (Berlin, 1927), and Theodora Huber, *Die soziologische Seite der Jugendbewegung* (Munich, 1929).

10. Murphy, p. 152.

11. "Indolence and inaction and lack of courage" on the part of the supporters of the Weimar Republic, he wrote in 1924, were a far greater threat to the political system than all the weapons of the opponents. "Der Tag der Republik," *Esslinger Volkszeitung* (hereafter cited as *Volkszeitung*), Aug. 9, 1924.

12. "The difference between God and a Stuttgart ... weekly is that God knows everything, but this journal knows it even better," was one of the milder Schumacherisms. ("Politische Glossen," *Tagwacht,* May 29, 1929.) Or, again commenting on a speech by Theodor Heuss, then leader of the Democratic party in Württemberg and the Reichstag (and later the first president of the postwar Federal Republic), Schumacher said that the Democrats seemed to have achieved their ambition of being more Christian than the Roman Catholic Center, for "when somebody strikes them on one cheek, they immediately offer all four." ("Allzu Demokratisch," published anonymously in *Tagwacht,* April 9, 1930.) In an aside on the celebration in Fascist Italy of the wedding of the Italian crown prince, Schumacher wondered why there should be so much fuss "just because two young people go to bed together." ("Umschau im Ausland," *Volkszeitung,* Jan. 18, 1930.)

13. This was evident from Schumacher's curt reference to Keil in the interview with Kaufmann, as well as from Keil's comments about Schumacher in conversations with me. Schumacher is barely mentioned in Keil's highly detailed two-volume memoirs, and then not in the friendly tone used for other figures in the Württemberg party organization.

14. See Keil, Vols. I and II *passim.*

15. "Wenn ich einmal so einem alten Bonzen eins gefeuert habe, so in der Diskussion— der Eine hat gesagt, da hört nur dieses Studentenbürsch'l. Da haben sie mich so angekuckt. ... Das kam aus meinem ganzen Habitus und meinem ganzen Lebensverhältnis." Kaufmann Int.

16. Election returns from *Stuttgarter Nachrichten,* May 5, 1924.

17. See *Handbuch für den Württembergischen Landtag,* 1924–28, and *Protokoll, Landtag.*

18. See S.P.D. Württ.-Hohenzollern, *Protokoll,* 1928.

19. For details, see Wacker, esp. pp. 13, 24, 83–110.

20. See, for example, his speech in *Protokoll, Landtag,* Jan. 24, 1928.

21. See *Tagwacht,* Aug. 16, 17, 20, 28, and Sept. 10, 1928, for Schumacher's most important editorials and speeches on this issue. See also Keil, II, 342, and in *Turm.,* I, 490; Wesemann, p. 21; Wacker, pp. 101–10.

22. *Tagwacht,* July 4, 1930. The fact that over one-third of the members of the Stuttgart organization had joined only in the previous three years undoubtedly weakened such opposition as the old-timers may have offered to Schumacher's election. For the membership figures see S.P.D. Württ.-Hohenzollern, *Bericht,* 1929, p. 62.

23. See *Tagwacht,* Aug. 1 and 11, 1930; and Keil, II, 394, 542, 637f.

24. Löbe's epithets, quoted in "Tiger, Burning Bright," *Time,* June 9, 1952, p. 33.

25. Keil, II, 394, 403.

26. In the Landtag election of April 1932, the party lost seven seats, but the Stuttgart organization retained its four, and lost only 300 out of 57,105 votes. (See *Volkszeitung,*

April 25, 1932.) In the Reichstag election of July 1932, the S.P.D. vote in Stuttgart increased 11 per cent over the 1930 election, while that in the state dropped 12 per cent, and that in the nation 7 per cent. (See *Neues Stuttgarter Tageblatt,* Aug. 1, 1932.)

27. Keil, II, 463f.

28. At the same time, Keil's old friend and associate Karl Hildenbrand, like Alexander Schlicke two years earlier, was involuntarily retired from the Reichstag by the party organization. (See *Tagwacht,* Sept. 11, 1932.)

29. See *Protokoll, Landtag,* June 6, 1924, Beilage 31.

30. See Besson, p. 37, and Keil, II, 258f, 261.

31. See, for example, "Franzose bleibt Franzose," *Volkszeitung,* Dec. 4, 1924. Also *Protokoll, Landtag,* Dec. 16, 1924, and Jan. 28, 1928.

32. *Protokoll, Landtag,* Dec. 18, 1924.

33. See *ibid.,* April 29, 1927, and *Tagwacht,* Sept. 19, 1930, on this specific issue. For examples of Schumacher's anti-particularistic position in general, see *Protokoll, Landtag,* Dec. 16, 1928, April 29, 1927, and Jan. 28, 1928, and a report of a speech in *Tagwacht,* May 16, 1928. See also the section "Political Behavior and Political Values," p. 42 below.

34. In an article in *Tagwacht,* March 11, 1929, six months before the election, Schumacher had called the enemies of the Weimar Republic extremely feeble, and spoke of "this silly talk about a crisis of the democratic state."

35. See, "Betrachtungen zu den Einzelwahlerergebnissen in Württemberg," *Volkszeitung,* May 16, 1924. Also "Hilfstruppen der Kommunisten," *Tagwacht,* Sept. 14, 1924.

36. *Protokoll, Landtag,* July 10, 1925; also *ibid.,* March 2, 1925, and numerous articles and reports of speeches by Schumacher in *Tagwacht,* and *Volkszeitung,* 1920-33.

37. Report of a speech at the *Gaukonferenz* of the *Reichsbanner,* Esslingen, in *Tagwacht,* April 1, 1930.

38. See, reports of speeches in Stuttgart and Esslingen, *Volkszeitung,* Oct. 10 and 21, 1932.

39. "Denn wen halt man denn für so blöd, dass er sich vielleicht abschlachten lässt und zusehen wird wie der Gegner die Formationen aufzieht, mit denen er nachher beseitigt wird." *Protokoll, Landtag,* Jan. 28, 1928.

40. See *Tagwacht,* esp. July–Nov. 1923. My task in tracing Schumacher's early anti-Nazi activities was facilitated by the inadvertent assistance of an official of the Nazi party in Stuttgart who had been the last person before me to examine this particular file of the newspaper (sometime after the Hitler take-over in 1933), and had carefully marked every article and report on the subject. Schumacher also discussed these activities briefly in the Kaufmann interview, and with his biographer Wesemann. See Wesemann, p. 271.

41. "Rigid discipline, large numbers, and a mass of black-red-gold flags [the Republic colors] did not fail to have a strong suggestive impact on the onlookers," Schumacher reported after a series of such demonstrations in 1925. "Undertakings of this sort ... inspire confidence in the republican organization, strongly impress the onlookers, and encourage the participants to work more intensively for the cause of the Republic." *Volkszeitung,* May 26, 1925. Also "Ein Wort zum Esslinger Gautag," *ibid.,* March 28, 1930; and "Reichsbanner und Partei," *ibid.,* March 29, 1930.

42. "Die Prügel haben gesessen. Die Hunde heulen." *Ibid.,* May 25, 1925, p. 3. Also Kaufmann Int. and sundry articles in *Tagwacht,* and *Volkszeitung.*

43. See, e.g., *Protokoll, Landtag,* Dec. 16 and 18, 1924, and Jan. 28, 1928.

44. For Schumacher's famous ad hoc attack on Goebbels in the Reichstag, see *Protokoll, Reichstag,* Feb. 25, 1932 (reprinted in *Turm.,* II, 23-24). Also "Ein Skandal im Reichstag," *Frankfurter Zeitung,* Feb. 24, 1932.

45. Speech at rally in Stuttgart Stadthalle, reported in *Volkszeitung,* July 29, 1932.

46. See Keil, II, 476.

47. Kaufmann Int.

48. Personal communication from Keil, Feb. 22, 1960.

49. "Ich duck mich nicht vor den intoleranten Pfaffen des Freidenkertums ... genau so wenig wie ich mich vor jemanden Anderen sonst duck." Kaufmann Int.

50. Schumacher, "Der Kampf um den Staatsgedanken in der deutschen Sozialdemokratie." A photocopy in the archives of the S.P.D. in Bonn was used for this study. For postwar comments on the importance of the dissertation, see Plenge, "Die Doktorarbeit Kurt Schumachers," in which the work is described as a significant contribution to socialist thought, and Oschilewski, "Am Hebelwerk der Geschichte," in *Turm.*, I, 544ff.

51. See Ferdinand Lassalle, *Offenes Antwortschreiben* (Zurich, 1868), and *The Working Men's Programme* (London, 1884).

52. See S.P.D., *Das Heidelberger Programm*.

53. See, for example, Schumacher's speech celebrating the third anniversary of the Republic, reported in *Tagwacht*, Sept. 10, 1921.

54. See, for example, speeches in *Protokoll, Landtag,* Dec. 19, 1925, and Jan. 26, 1928.

55. *Ibid.*, Jan. 28, 1928.

56. "We reject the support of the German Nationalists; we know we have the support of the German patriots." *Ibid.*

57. "Der Tag der Republik: Ein Jahrfünft Weimar Verfassung," *Volkszeitung,* Aug. 9, 1925.

58. Speech before Stuttgart Reichstagbanner, reported in *ibid.*, March 16, 1925. Also "Reichsbanner und Klassenkampf," *Tagwacht,* March 26, 1929.

59. Schumacher wrote a column "Umschau im Ausland" for his paper, but this usually consisted of little more than a summary of foreign affairs, and at times it included rather absurd prognostications.

60. "Tag der Republik," *Volkszeitung,* Aug. 9, 1924. Also "Sozialistische Aussenpolitik," *ibid.*, Aug. 22, 1925.

61. Thus "Umschau im Ausland," *Tagwacht,* Jan. 28, Feb. 2, 1929, and Dec. 19, 1930.

62. Quoted in Wesemann, p. 23; see also, *ibid.*, p. 24.

63. See S.P.D., *Protokoll der Verhandlungen des Parteitages Magdeburg, 1929,* pp. 150–52. "Um das Wehrprogramm," *Tagwacht,* Jan. 23–24, 1929; speech before S.P.D. Verein Gross-Stuttgart, reported in *Tagwacht,* Jan. 30, 1929. Also articles on army and politics in *ibid.*, March 17 and 18, and report from Magdeburg congress, *ibid.*, June 5, 1929. See also Wesemann, pp. 22ff., and Scholz, in *Turm.*, I, 22f.

64. Richard Petry, p. 670.

65. "I remember the Doctor in those years as a pragmatic politician trained in Marxist theory," one of Schumacher's lieutenants in Stuttgart said later, a judgment fully confirmed by other former associates. See Erwin Schoettle, "Der Parteifuhrer in Stuttgart," *Turm.*, I, 470.

66. See, for example, *Protokoll, Landtag,* speeches April 29, 1927, Jan. 17 and 26, 1928, and March 6, 1930.

67. In this connection see Harold D. Lasswell's observations on the relationship between Marxism and personal insecurity in *World Politics and Personal Insecurity* (New York, 1935), p. 130.

68. For example, Benedict Kautsky, both in "Kurt Schumacher," pp. 245–51, and in conversations with me at Bad Godesberg, October 1959.

69. S.P.D., *Protokoll, Magdeburg*; see also "Der Kampf um den Staatsgedanken," esp. pp. 128–32, 138f, 145.

70. See S.P.D., *Das Heidelberger Programm*.

71. "Der Tag der Republik," *Volkszeitung*, Aug. 9, 1924. See also Schumacher's speech in *Protokoll, Landtag*, Jan. 28, 1928.

72. See, for example, Carl Mierendorff, "Der Sozialistische Weg," *Sozialistische Monatshefte*, LXXVI (1930), 989–93, and Leber, *passim*.

73. Thus Scholz, in *Turm.*, I, 15, 25; Oschilewski, "Am Hebelwerk der Geschichte," *Turm.*, I, 557; and Siemann, pp. 182f.

74. As one of Schumacher's closest collaborators in this period wrote later: "Kurt Schumacher undoubtedly shared . . . the illusions of many German politicians who could not believe that the democratic system might collapse in Germany." Schoettle, *Turm.*, I, 475.

75. To what extent the Iron Front was an effective fighting organization for a domestic conflict has been the subject of considerable controversy. A rather favorable judgment, based on the testimony of participants in the Iron Front, is rendered by Erich Matthias (in Matthias and Morsey, eds., pp. 122–27), but many others have credited it with being very little more than a morale booster for the dispirited Social Democratic masses.

76. Speech in Stuttgart Stadthalle, reported in *Volkszeitung*, July 29, 1932.

77. Stampfer, p. 579.

78. "Schlagt die Gegenrevolution," *Volkszeitung*, Nov. 4, 1932. See also Schumacher's keynote address to the S.P.D. state convention, Oct. 9, 1932, printed in *Volkszeitung*, Oct. 10, 1932. I could find no evidence to support Wilhelm Keil's contentions (see Matthias and Morsey, eds., p. 164, n. 10) that Schumacher nourished any particular hopes about von Papen either before or after the November 1932 election.

79. For an account of this, see my *German Exile Politics*, pp. 7–33; Matthias and Morsey, eds., pp. 151–87; and Bracher *et al.*, pp. 31–199.

80. Besson, p. 351.

81. See Schumacher's remarks at the meeting of the Reichstag Fraktion of the S.P.D. on June 10, 1933; Matthias and Morsey, eds., p. 263; Brandt and Lowenthal, p. 278. See also *ibid.*, pp. 186 and 191, n.16.

82. See Keil, II, 493–94, 497–98; also Besson. Some of my informants claim that for this endorsement of Hitler, Keil and Erich Rossmann (the state chairman) were read out of the party by a secret assemblage of Württemberg party leaders led by Schumacher.

83. The general tenor of this document, which the exiled executive of the S.P.D. published soon after under the title "Revolution Against Hitler," was strongly influenced by Schumacher and his fellow "national socialist" deputy Carlo Mierendorff. This was especially true of those sections that repudiated a class struggle against Hitler in favor of a national struggle of liberation by a popular revolutionary movement of "all of society." My information is based on an interview with Fritz Geyer, final author of the pamphlet. See also Edinger, *German Exile Politics*, pp. 43–48, and Matthias, *Sozialdemokratie und Nation, passim*.

84. *Stuttgarter Zeitung*, July 12, 1933.

Chapter Four

1. *L'Univers concentrationnaire*. Schumacher was arrested on July 6, 1933, and remained imprisoned until March 16, 1943, most of this time being spent in the concentration camp at Dachau in Bavaria. On August 24, 1944, he was arrested again and sent to the notorious camp at Neuengamme, where he remained until September 20, 1944.

2. Wesemann's biography, as well as the relevant sections in *Turm.*, I, provide only the scantiest information, portions of which have proved to be inaccurate upon further investigation.

3. The general analysis of the concentration camps in this section, which has been pre-

pared with the invaluable help of Hanni Edinger, is based on the large number of memoirs and accounts published by participant observers. Particularly valuable were the studies of three psychiatrists who had been prisoners, Bruno Bettelheim, Victor Frankl, and Elie Cohen, along with the perceptive studies of Benedict Kautsky and Egon Kogon. In addition to these published sources, I have utilized information provided in lengthy personal interviews with a number of long-term prisoners, including several of Schumacher's fellow inmates at Dachau (see the list at the end of the Bibliography). A study by Walter Ritter von Bayer et al., Psychiatrie der Verfolgten (Berlin, 1964), appeared too late to be used here.

Naturally, this composite picture is objective only to the extent of the participant observers' ability to maintain relative detachment from the horrors they had seen and experienced, and the accuracy of their memory. Where mistakes or contradictions in the accounts were obvious, I have eliminated passages or sought to arrive at a balanced picture. Also, on the whole, my description disregards the variations between various camps, within the same camps over time, and in the experiences and outlook of the individual observers.

4. Gerth and Mills, p. 76.

5. Frankl (pp. 44f) describes the relief of prisoners in a transport from another camp when they discovered they were going "only" to Dachau. Bettelheim (The Informed Heart, pp. 134f) claims that the treatment of prisoners was better than at Buchenwald.

6. See Edgard Kupfer-Koberwitz, "Als Häftling in Dachau," in Aus Politik und Zeitgeschichte: Beilage zur Wochenzeitung Das Parliament, Feb. 15 and 29, March 7, 1956, and, by the same author, Die Mächtigen und die Hilflosen: Als Häftling in Dachau.

7. Letter to F. Wulfert (Hannover), Dec. 29, 1950. Archiv Renger, Bonn.

8. Kogon, p. 62.

9. For a good discussion of this social structure, see Glicksman, p. 139.

10. The discussion in this section is based on interviews with former concentration camp inmates who knew and observed Schumacher closely during this period, on letters from other former associates in the camp, on interviews with two of his sisters, his former girl friend, and his cousin (all of whom corresponded with him during his imprisonment), and on his letters to his girl friend and cousin. I also found useful the short contribution by Alois Ullmann, another former inmate, entitled "Kurt Schumacher in Dachau," in Turm., I, 506-9, as well as the relevant passages in the essay by Arno Scholz in ibid., pp. 32-36, and in Wesemann, pp. 40-48.

11. On this point, see esp. the works of Cohen, Bettelheim, Frankl, Kogon, and Kautsky. Also Gordon W. Allport et al., in Kluckhohn and Murray, eds., pp. 353f, and H. A. Bloch, "The Personality of Inmates of Concentration Camps," American Journal of Sociology, LII (1946-47), 338.

12. Kautsky, Teufel und Verdammte, p. 182.

13. Rossmann, p. 75.

14. Wesemann, p. 44; Scholz, in Turm., I, 33.

15. On this point, see Bettelheim, The Informed Heart, p. 188, and Kautsky, Teufel und Verdammte, pp. 184-86.

16. Bettelheim, The Informed Heart, p. 157.

17. Secret directive from the Kanzlei des Führers der NSDAP Parteipolitisches Amt to the Auswärtige Amt, Aug. 19, 1937. Photocopy in Pers. Archiv, S.P.D., K.S., Bd. Bio.

18. Schumacher probably suffered from an atrophy of the epithelial tissue (xerophthalmia), a complaint also common among American prisoners of the Japanese in World War II. See Russell L. Cecil et al., A Textbook of Medicine, 9th ed. (Philadelphia, Pa., 1955), p. 599.

19. The visit of the commission was described in the testimony of Dr. Muthig, a former physician at Dachau, at the trial of Nazi doctors at Nuremberg in 1947. Doc. No. 2799, cited in Hansjakob Stehle, "Die Euthanasie im Hitlerstaat," *Frankfurter Allgemeine Zeitung,* Dec. 16, 1959, p. 9.

20. Charles de Werkmann, an Austrian monarchist, quoted in a radio broadcast of the Northwest German broadcasting network (N.W.D.R.), Oct. 5, 1948. (Script in Pers. Archiv, S.P.D., K.S. Bd. Bio.) See also Joos, pp. 58f.

21. Letter to Otto Steinmayer, July 19, 1945 (Archiv Renger, Bonn); extracts from various articles, letters, and statements on this subject were summarized in an unpublished and undated press release, entitled "Verleumdungen gegen Dr. Schumacher," put out by the S.P.D. Parteivorstand in 1946. Original letters, copies of articles, and other material are in Pers. Archiv, S.P.D., P.V. See also Joesten, p. 80.

22. Bettelheim, *The Informed Heart,* p. 147; Arendt, "The Concentration Camp," p. 241.

23. Quoted in Otto Herr, "Um die Seele der Deutschen," obituary broadcast, Hessian Radio Network, Aug. 21, 1952, reprinted in *Turm.,* III, 118.

24. Kautksy, *Teufel und Verdammte,* pp. 191f.

25. Bettelheim, *The Informed Heart,* p. 150.

26. As Gardner Murphy has pointed out (pp. 139f), the strength of a drive, including presumably a compensatory drive, depends to a large extent on the amount of deprivation involved; the greater the deprivation (and the lack of tension reducers), the stronger the drive for satisfaction.

27. Letter to Otto Steinmayer, July 19, 1945.

28. For similar criticisms of the Weimar S.P.D. leaders, see the bitter indictment that the former Social Democratic militant Julius Leber wrote in prison after his arrest in 1933, and that was reprinted, in part, in Leber, pp. 187–247. See also the reflections of Werner Blumberg, a leader of the anti-Nazi underground, written in 1936, and published, in part, in Matthias and Morsey, eds., pp. 269–78, and the discussion in various émigré publications summarized in Edinger, *German Exile Politics,* and in Matthias, *Sozialdemokratie und Nation.*

29. "Die politische Konzeption die ich heute vertrete, habe ich schon damals gehabt," Schumacher wrote on June 18, 1946, in a letter to Philippe Brandt, a Belgian imprisoned with him in Dachau. Pers. Archiv, S.P.D., K.S. Bd., IIIa.

30. Frankl, pp. 69–71.

31. *Ibid.,* pp. 72, 74, 76; also Cohen, pp. 149–50.

32. Frankl, p. 80.

33. See, e.g., Wesemann, p. 46.

34. Letter to Otto Steinmayer, July 19, 1945. Admittedly this claim was made after the event, but fellow prisoners confirmed its accuracy.

35. Frankl, pp. 67, 69.

36. "Dr. Schumacher stand auf der Todesliste," *Lubecker Freie Presse,* Oct. 14, 1948.

Chapter Five

1. Data from U.S. Strategic Bombing Survey, *Over-All Report, European War* (Washington, 1945), *passim,* and Presse- und Informationsamt der Bundesregierung, *10 Jahr Bundesrepublik Deutschland,* 5th ed. (Wiesbaden, 1959), pp. 30–39. On the whole, these figures are conservative. In the case of the widows, orphans, and cripples, they are based on pension claims allowed by German authorities as of 1958.

2. As reported in the *New York Times,* Feb. 28 and March 24, 1947, and cited in Davidson, p. 158.

3. McInnis *et al.*, p. 31.

4. See Wellmann, pp. 591ff.

5. See Böttcher, pp. 331ff.

6. Official Military Government for Germany (hereafter cited as O.M.G.U.S.), *Opinion Survey Reports,* Series I, No. 3, March 15, 1946, No. 88, Jan. 20, 1948, and No. 191, Dec. 6, 1949.

7. Noelle and Neumann, p. 249.

8. O.M.G.U.S., *Opinion Survey Reports,* Series I, No. 68, Oct. 10, 1947, and Noelle and Neumann, p. 134.

9. An O.M.G.U.S. survey found in the fall of 1947 that six out of ten respondents in the U.S. zone expressed this preference. O.M.G.U.S., *Opinion Survey Reports,* Series I, No. 74, Dec. 17, 1947.

10. *Ibid.,* Series I, No. 90, Jan. 23, 1948.

11. See *ibid.,* Series II, No. 27, July 27, 1950, and No. 147 (n.d. but survey of April 1952). See also Noelle and Neumann, p. 241.

12. "Vor Geistesarbeitern," Berlin, Oct. 18, 1946, reprinted in *Turm.,* II, 307.

13. "Für eine Erinnerungsgabe des Karl-Marx Hauses in Trier," *ibid.,* pp. 299f.

14. *Ibid.,* p. 77.

15. This lecture (hereafter cited as "Referat") was delivered in Hannover on May 6, 1945, and has never been published in its entirety. I am indebted for a copy of the original manuscript (now in the possession of Frau Annemarie Renger, Bonn) to Dr. Albrecht Kaden, Falkenstein/Ts. For a selective summary, see Wesemann, pp. 61–75.

16. In a speech entitled "Sozialismus: Eine Gegenwartsaufgabe," which Schumacher delivered at the S.P.D. congress at Hannover in May 1946, he said that 40 per cent of the German people had no longer any property whatever, and 25 per cent had next to none. The remaining 35 per cent, according to him, not only had retained what they once had, but had actually become richer.

17. "Man sieht wie die Klassen auseinanderstreben, wie die Armen immer ärmer und die Reichen immer reicher werden." Speech, Nuremberg, June 28, 1947, in *Turm.,* II, 118.

18. "Warum Sozialdemokratische Partei" (n.d. but probably 1947), Pers. Archiv, S.P.D., K.S., Bd. IV. I have no evidence that this manuscript was ever published.

19. "Referat," p. 23.

20. "Each of us in the course of our development has lived through times that have decisively influenced our view of politics and our formulation of goals [die Äusserungen seiner Gestaltungskraft]," he once told a group of Social Democrats who had applauded his statement that it was false to see the present in terms of the past. Sixth S.P.D. *Landesparteitag,* Berlin, Jan. 8, 1950, in *Turm.,* II, 189.

21. Speech, S.P.D. congress, Nuremberg, June 29, 1947, in *ibid.,* p. 136.

22. See "Referat," pp. 39f.

23. For a selection of Schumacher's postwar writings, see *Turm.,* II, *passim.* Also see the Schumacher entry in the Bibliography.

24. "Sozialismus," p. 8; *Turm.,* II, 80. Also see article in *Die Zeit,* April 4, 1946.

25. Brandt, pp. 157f.

26. *Turm.,* II, 31.

27. *Ibid.,* p. 419.

28. See "Referat," pp. 15–16.

29. Letter to Bernhard Thurow, Heidelberg, Dec. 15, 1950. Archiv Renger, Bonn.

30. Kaufmann Int. The word "advantages" is blurred on the tape.

31. Karl Jaspers, "The Political Vacuum in Germany," *Foreign Affairs,* July 1954, p. 599.

32. Leber, p. 192.

33. S.P.D., *Protokoll, Parteitag,* Nuremberg 1947, p. 37.

34. *Turm.,* II, 205–6.

35. "Neuorientierung oder sicherer Standpunkt," undated ms., Pers. Archiv, S.P.D., K.S., Bd. IV.

36. "Aufruf 1945," *Turm.,* II, 38.

37. *Ibid.,* p. 243.

38. Nazi officials who had been disqualified previously by Allied or German denazification tribunals, who owed their original appointments to their close connection with National Socialism, or whose only appointment had been to the Gestapo were exempted. For a summary, see Hiscock, p. 203.

39. In this connection I am indebted to Mr. Fritz Erler for a copy of a most enlightening letter that Schumacher wrote about his contacts with former members of the Waffen S.S. to Professor L. Hersch of Geneva.

40. Preface to the Dortmund *Aktionsprogramm,* written shortly before Schumacher's death. See n. 13, Chap. 7.

41. "Mit einem Handtuch Deutschland kannst Du nicht Politik machen."

Chapter Six

1. Severing, II, 452, 485.

2. See Keil, II, 677–81.

3. Letter from Schumacher to Oechsle, June 13, 1945.

4. Ebsworth, p. 26.

5. Litchfield, p. 20.

6. "Politische Richtlinien für die S.P.D. in ihrem Verhältnis zu den anderen politischen Faktoren," Pers. Archiv, S.P.D., K.S. Bd. IV. For a summary of this very rare document, see Wesemann, pp. 80–88, and Kaden, pp. 61–65.

7. The membership of the East-zone S.P.D. at the time of amalgamation has been estimated at between 619,000 and 631,000. About 65,000 of these members were in West Berlin and joined the re-established S.P.D. in the Western zones. See Office of the U.S. High Commissioner for Germany, *The Socialist Unity Party as the Soviet Instrument of Power in Eastern Germany,* n.p., Nov. 15, 1950. See also Wesemann, p. 104; Klaus Schütz, "Die Sozialdemokratie im Nachkriegsdeutschland," in Lange, ed., p. 196; and S.P.D., *Protokoll, Parteitag,* Nuremberg 1947, pp. 95f.

8. Wesemann, p. 104.

9. For the 1946 proportion of old members, see Kaden, p. 247. See also Schütz, in Lange, ed., pp. 174–81, 198–215, on the organizational structure of the postwar S.P.D. and the nature of its local leadership and membership.

10. In comparison, almost 47 per cent of the membership of the S.P.D. had been under forty in 1931, and less than 27 per cent over fifty. See Hans Gerth, "The Nazi Party: Its Leadership and Composition," *American Journal of Sociology,* XIV (1940), 530. The 1952 figures are derived from a representative sampling of party members, reported at the Dortmund congress of 1952. See S.P.D., *Protokoll, Parteitag,* Dortmund 1952, p. 170.

11. Mehnert and Schulte, eds., *Deutschland-Jahrbuch 1953,* p. 95.

12. On this point, see Schütz, in Lange, ed., p. 206.

13. See *Protokoll, Sonderausschuss, "Neuaufbau der Länder,"* Sept. 6, 1946. Schumacher was chairman of this special committee on the political reorganization of the German states.

14. See Erich Klabund, "Neuorganisation des Parteilebens?," *Sozialistisches Jahrhundert,* IX (1950), 19.

15. Remarks at a press conference, quoted in S.P.D., "Schumacher-Kurs," *Mitteilungsblatt der Sozialdemokratischen Partei Hessen*, II, 49, Dec. 5, 1947.

16. Oscar Pollack, in *Turm.*, III, 139. See also *ibid.*, pp. 92, 141f, for other descriptions.

17. The discussion that follows derives its inspiration from Fritz Redl's article "Group Emotions and Leadership."

18. Schulz, *Sorge um die deutsche Linke*, p. 26.

19. On this point, see the interview with the Munich psychiatrist P. Matussek, in Theo Lobsack, "Im tiefsten Schatten der Vergangenheit," *Die Zeit*, Aug. 25, 1961, p. 19.

20. Petry, p. 669.

21. Marcus, p. 236. See also Hook, p. 22.

22. Letter to Peter Blachstein, MdB, Nov. 26, 1949. Archiv Renger, Bonn.

23. Kaufmann Int.

24. I am greatly indebted to Wilhelm Kaisen, Annemarie Renger, and the S.P.D. in Bonn for access to the files containing this correspondence.

25. The following account of the Schumacher-Reuter relationship is based on numerous personal interviews with people who were closely associated with either or both men during the period in question; on the accounts of observers, such as Allied occupation officials in Berlin and West Germany; on unpublished sources, such as Schumacher's notes in his appointments diary; and on published material, particularly Brandt and Löwenthal, pp. 358–656.

26. See Ernst Reuter, "Aufgaben und Funktionen der S.P.D.," *Das Sozialistische Jahrhundert*, April 1947, pp. 163–65.

27. *Ibid.*, p. 180.

28. "Wer wie ein Säulenheiliger nur von seiner politischen Leidenschaft lebt und keine Berührung zum Leben hat, der ist nicht immer der allergeeigneste Politiker. Schliesslich soll ja auch der Politiker ein Ausdruck der Kräfte und Vorstellungen sein, die in dem normalen Menschen verkörpert sind." Quoted in Brandt and Löwenthal, p. 576.

29. Quoted in Brandt and Löwenthal, p. 650.

30. For data on Neumann and Scholz, see Appendix A, Secs. 1, 2, and 3.

31. See S.P.D., *Protokoll, Parteitag*, Nuremberg 1947, pp. 55ff, 91, 222.

32. See Lewis J. Edinger and Douglas A. Chalmers, "Overture or Swan Song: German Democracy Prepares for a New Decade," *Antioch Review*, XX (1960), 163–75.

33. See Schütz, pp. 199–205, for relevant data and analysis. Also Egon Franke's report at the Dortmund congress, in S.P.D., *Protokoll, Parteitag*, Dortmund 1952, pp. 170ff.

Chapter Seven

1. Acheson, pp. 171–72.

2. Kirkpatrick, pp. 230–33.

3. "Tiger, Burning Bright," pp. 30–35.

4. *Dzieunik Zachordni*, Feb. 1, 1947; *Pravda*, May 24, 1951; Tass dispatch, Feb. 10, 1951. Also *Pravda*, Oct. 21, 1947.

5. *Turm.*, II, 88, 426.

6. Quoted by Jack Raymond in the *New York Times*, Feb. 7, 1948.

7. "Referat," p. 18.

8. Letter to Dr. Robert Haerdter, Jan. 18, 1949, Pers. Archiv, S.P.D., K.S., Bd. IIIa.

9. S.P.D., *Protokoll, Parteitag*, Nuremberg 1947, p. 54. See also Wesemann, p. 159.

10. See, for example, "Referat," *passim*.

11. Appendix C gives a breakdown of the main themes of Schumacher's speeches.

12. See *Turm.*, II, 470.

13. See Schumacher's Preface to S.P.D., *Aktionsprogramm 1952,* which is considered his political testament, and was adopted by the party conference at Dortmund in September 1952, shortly after his death. The quotations are from the English translation, *Action Program,* published by the S.P.D. in 1952.

14. "Grundlagen einer deutschen Demokratie," *Rheinische Zeitung,* March 6, 1946.

15. Speech at the reorganization meeting of the Socialist International in Frankfurt, quoted in Wesemann, p. 238.

16. Schumacher, "Preface," in S.P.D., *Action Program,* p. 7.

17. "Die deutsche Sozialdemokratie heute und morgen: Vorwort für das Jahrbuch der S.P.D., 1947," ms. Pers. Archiv, S.P.D., Bonn. See also "Von Hannover nach Nürnberg," ms. 1947, Pers. Archiv, S.P.D., Bonn.

18. *Turm.,* II, 427.

19. "Aufruf 1945," quoted in *ibid.,* p. 33.

20. See *ibid.,* p. 77.

21. *Ibid.,* p. 134 (speech, S.P.D. Nuremberg congress, June 29, 1947).

22. See also Chapter 5 above.   23. See *Turm.,* II, 141.

24. *Ibid.,* p. 112.   25. *Ibid.,* p. 173.

26. *Ibid.,* p. 48.   27. *Ibid.,* p. 239.

28. Quoted in Wesemann, p. 115.

29. Ernest O. Hauser, "The German Russia Hates Most," *Saturday Evening Post,* Nov. 15, 1947, p. 25.

30. *Turm.,* II, 67. In this section I am paraphrasing speeches of Schumacher's existing in manuscript or printed form in Pers. Archiv, S.P.D., Bonn, reported in the press, or included in *Turm.,* Vol. II, *passim.*

31. *Turm.,* II, 473.

32. Speech in Bundestag, Nov. 15, 1949. Reprinted in *Turm.,* II, 351.

33. *Ibid.,* p. 152.

34. Bundestag, Sept. 21, 1949, in *Turm.,* II, 172f.

35. See, for example, Grotewohl, *Im Kampf um Deutschland,* and *Zur politischen Lage Deutschlands.*

36. Press opinion extracted from the manuscript collection "Verleumdungen gegen Dr. Kurt Schumacher," Archives of *Der Telegraf,* Berlin.

37. "Facing New Tasks," *News from Germany,* January 1951.

38. Quoted in Wesemann, p. 136.

39. Speech, S.P.D. Nuremberg congress, June 29, 1947, in *Turm.,* II, 112.

40. *Turm.,* II, 161.

41. See, in particular, Schumacher's speech before the Convention of the American Federation of Labor in October 1947, published under the title "A German Democrat Speaks" in the *American Federationist,* LV (1948), 14–16, and his remarks in the Bundestag on Nov. 8, 1950 (reprinted in *Turm.,* II, 457), and on March 9, 1951 (reprinted in the pamphlet *Freie Wahlen,* p. 9). See also Schumacher, *Macht Europa Stark,* which contains Schumacher's speech to S.P.D. leaders on March 31, 1951 (also reprinted in *Turm.,* II, 249ff).

42. Kaufmann Int.

43. "Der Marshall Plan und die Deutschen," ms. May 12, 1948, Pers. Archiv, S.P.D., Bonn.

44. Speech presented before the sixth S.P.D. Landesparteitag, Berlin, reprinted in *Turm.,* II, 216.

45. S.P.D., *Protokoll, Parteitag,* Nuremberg 1947, p. 49.

46. "Der Marshall Plan und die Deutschen."

47. *Turm.,* II, 156. See also *ibid.,* pp. 36, 79, 82, 307.

48. *News from Germany,* English-language newsletter of the S.P.D. executive committee, December 1949, quoted in Sidney Lens, "Social Democracy and Labor in Germany," *Foreign Policy Reports,* XXVI (1950), 148.

49. "Aufruf 1945," in *Turm.,* II, 46f.

50. *Turm.,* II, 90.

51. Minutes of the Second Session, Special Committee "Reorganisation der Länder," Aug. 18, 1946 (Bundestag Archives, Bonn). Schumacher was chairman of this committee.

52. Cited in Kaden, p. 65, n. 410.

53. "Donauföderation," *Die Neue Zeitung,* Dec. 20, 1946.

54. Speech to a group of students in Hamburg, reprinted in *Turm.,* II, 331.

55. "... dass uns mit dieser Kampagne einfach die Schneid abgekauft werden sollte. Man wünscht uns in eine Zerknirschungsstimmung zu versetzen." Letter to Haerdter, Jan. 18, 1949.

56. The chief political adviser to the American Military Governor, Ambassador Robert Murphy, was a Roman Catholic, as were the three Allied High Commissioners in the Federal Republic, John J. McCloy, Ivon Kirkpatrick, and André François-Poncet.

57. Zink, p. 163.

58. See Edward Litchfield, "Emergence of German Government," in Litchfield, ed., pp. 39f.

59. Litchfield, ed., p. 40, and Brandt and Löwenthal, pp. 471–72.

60. See *Turm.,* II, 161–63.

61. See Hans Simons, "The Bonn Constitution and Its Government," in Morgenthau, ed., p. 124.

62. Comments at a press conference, March 10, 1961, reported in "Das Urteil im Fernsehstreit," *Bulletin der Bundesgierung,* March 14, 1961, p. 459.

63. Schumacher, in S.P.D., *Action Program,* p. 7.

64. See S.P.D. Exec. Comm., *News from Germany,* May 1952.

65. Schumacher, in S.P.D., *Action Program,* p. 7.

66. New Year's Eve message, 1951, in S.P.D. Exec. Comm., *News from Germany,* January 1952.

67. *Turm.,* II, 257. See also the report of Schumacher's speech at a meeting of the S.P.D. executive committee in January 1951, reported in the party's paper *Der Neue Vorwärts,* Jan. 26, 1951.

68. See "Tiger, Burning Bright," p. 30.

69. Jack Raymond, "German Socialist Attacks Accords," *New York Times,* June 3, 1952.

70. Quoted in Powell (pseud.), p. 5.

71. See Wesemann, p. 193, and Willis, pp. 191–92.

72. See *Le Populaire,* April 9, 1951.

73. See *Schwäbische Landeszeitung,* Aug. 16, 1951, Pers. Archiv, S.P.D., K.S., Bd. IX.

74. Quoted in Wesemann, p. 124.

75. *Ibid.*

76. See *Rhein-Ruhr Zeitung,* Aug. 6, 1946; also *Fränkische Presse,* Aug. 16, 1946, and related press clippings in Pers. Archiv, S.P.D., K.S., Bd. IV.

77. Golay, p. 100.

78. Kirkpatrick, p. 205.

79. Quoted in Lewis, "The Hard-Bitten Herr Schumacher."

80. Quoted in Middleton, p. 249.

81. See Vorrink's article in *De Volkskrant,* June 17, 1952.

82. Hill, *Struggle for Germany,* pp. 210f.

83. Clark, p. 113.

84. Gabriel A. Almond, in Morgenthau, ed., p. 98.

85. Hirsch, "Adenauer or Schumacher?"

86. "Tiger, Burning Bright," p. 34.

87. "Schumacher: Violent Martyr," *United Nations World,* May 1952, pp. 13–15.

88. *New York Herald Tribune,* Aug. 24, 1952.

89. Drew Middleton, "German Socialists Eye Nationalism," *New York Times,* Feb. 16, 1949.

90. Clay, *passim.*

91. Quoted in Lewis, "The Hard-Bitten Herr Schumacher."

92. Middleton, *The Struggle for Germany,* pp. 130f, 151.

93. Obituary article, *New York Herald Tribune,* Aug. 21, 1952.

94. "Der Marshall Plan und die Deutschen," ms. May 12, 1948, Pers. Archiv, S.P.D., K.S., Bd. IV.

95. Lewis, "The Hard-Bitten Herr Schumacher."

96. Walter Dirks, "Sozialistische Alternativen," *Frankfurter Hefte,* April 1953, p. 249.

97. R. Henri, in *L'Intransigeant,* March 11, 1948.

Chapter Eight

1. *News Chronicle* (London), May 25, 1947.

2. See O.M.G.U.S., *Opinion Survey Reports,* No. 72, November 1947.

3. Klaus Schütz, in Lange, ed., p. 241.

4. See O.M.G.U.S., "Present Level of West German Political and Economic Satisfaction, with Current Standing of Major Political Parties," *Opinion Survey Reports,* Series 2, No. 155, Sept. 22, 1952.

5. See *Turm.,* II, 99, 420.

6. See Schütz, in Lange, ed., p. 242. I find myself in close agreement with the analysis of Schumacher's position in this excellent study.

7. For good studies of the C.D.U. between 1945 and 1950, see Heidenheimer, *passim;* Gerhard Schulz, "Die C.D.U.–Markmale Ihres Aufbaus," in Lange, ed., pp. 3–156; and Wieck, *passim.*

8. "Politische Richtlinien," cited in Wesemann, p. 85.

9. *Turm.,* II, 99. See also *ibid.,* pp. 80–309, 419f.

10. See the summary of his speeches in Appendix C.

11. *Turm.,* II, 148, 156, 160, 165.

12. *Ibid.,* p. 312. See also *ibid.,* pp. 99, 308, 311; Schumacher, *Für Frieden, Freiheit und Sozialismus,* pp. 11f; and Wesemann, p. 235.

13. Quoted in Heidenheimer, p. 133.

14. See Chapters 6 and 7 above.

15. Quoted in Heidenheimer, p. 135, which gives an excellent account of the situation; Schütz, in Lange, ed., pp. 224f, 243, is also good in this connection.

16. Quoted by Schütz, in Lange, ed., p. 243.

17. Heidenheimer, p. 136.

18. "Klare Fronten: Die C.D.U. als Unternehmerpartei," *Sozialdemokratischer Presse-dienst,* July 27, 1947.

19. *Turm.,* II, 148.

20. Heidenheimer, p. 140. See also Bergsträsser, p. 329.

21. Heidenheimer, p. 146, quoting data from Henry C. Wallich, *Mainsprings of the German Revival* (New Haven, Conn., 1955), p. 47.

22. Figures from Davison, p. 228.

23. *Ibid.*

24. My information is based on interviews with a number of people who were close to Schumacher at this time. See also Scholz, "Kurt Schumacher—Leben und Leistung," *Turm.,* I, 256.

25. See Schumacher's address to the S.P.D. national congress in Düsseldorf on Sept. 12, 1948, reprinted in *Turm.,* II, 139–65. Also Schumacher, *Zweimal Deutschland,* Aug. 1, 1948, and *Die Grossverdiener auf Kosten des Volkes,* Feb. 7, 1949, the former a pamphlet, the latter a manuscript, in Pers. Archiv, S.P.D., K.S., Bd. IV.

26. See p. 169 above.

27. Scholz, "Leben und Leistung," *Turm.,* I, 244.

28. To support this statement, Schumacher claimed that Winston Churchill had made the following remark to Ernest Bevin, foreign minister in the Labour government: "Your foreign policy has had one good result: it has cost the German Social Democrats one million votes." *Turm.,* II, 211.

29. Schumacher, *Die Sozialdemokratie in der Bundesrepublik.* Also *Turm.,* II, 195, 209. For a postmortem that Schumacher presented before the sixth Landesparteitag of the Berlin S.P.D. in January 1950, see *Turm.,* II, 195–212.

30. *Turm.,* II, 213. Also *Die Sozialdemokratie in der Bundesrepublik.*

31. See Wesemann, p. 168. For confirmation, see Schumacher's post-election analysis *Die Sozialdemokratie in der Bundesrepublik,* written four days after the election.

32. Heidenheimer, p. 179, n. 1, citing a report from the S.P.D. newsletter *Sopade,* September 1949.

33. See Schütz, in Lange, ed., pp. 237f. The 16 points of the so-called Dürkheim Resolutions, which were made public by the S.P.D. executive committee on August 30, are listed by Scholz in his essay "Leben und Leistung," *Turm.,* I, 258f. Schumacher restated his position in opposition to a "grand coalition" on various later occasions. For example, see his article "Was Bedeutet Heute die Grosse Koalition?," in *Düsseldorfer Nachrichten,* Dec. 30, 1950.

34. See p. 120 above.

35. See Wolfgang Stolper, *Germany Between East and West* (Washington, D.C., 1960), p. 9. See also p. 236 below.

36. *Turm.,* II, 167–85. See also Schumacher's remarks before the sixth Landesparteitag of the Berlin S.P.D. in January 1950, in *ibid.,* p. 217, and to the fourth national congress of the S.P.D., in Hamburg in May 1950, in *ibid.,* pp. 245f.

37. *Turm.,* II, 196, 217. See also Schumacher's speech in the Bundestag on Nov. 15, 1949, reprinted in *ibid.,* pp. 341–54.

38. *Ibid.,* p. 280.

39. He is reported to have said that when as a member of the Reichsrat in the Weimar days he had to make an occasional trip to Berlin, he would cross the Elbe with the thought that he was now in Asia.

40. O.M.G.U.S., *Opinion Survey Reports,* Series 1, No. 191, Dec. 6, 1949.

41. Weymar, pp. 445f.

42. *Ibid.,* p. 120.

43. See Max Gustav Lange, "Die F.D.P.–Versuch einer Erneuerung des Liberalismus," in Lange, ed., p. 397.

44. My information here, as in other parts of this chapter, is based on extensive interviews with people who were closely associated with Schumacher in these years.

45. Paul Otto, as quoted in Weymar, p. 316. I am indebted to Heidenheimer, p. 149, for this reference.

46. Thus he declared in April 1946: "No party in Germany, even if it should get a majority—and that applies to us, the C.D.U., as well—can assume responsibility by itself,

because Germany can only rise again if the large parties agree on a middle line and hold together." Weymar, quoted in Heidenheimer, p. 13.

47. Heidenheimer, p. 149.

48. This is particularly evident in the letters that Adenauer and Schumacher wrote to each other in 1950–51, which I was allowed to see through the courtesy of several of Schumacher's former deputies.

49. *Turm.*, II, 448.

50. According to one analysis, 84.3 per cent of all laws passed by the first Bundestag had the approval of the S.P.D. See Lowenberg, p. 95, citing *Die Gegenwart*, XII (1957), 657–59.

51. Thus Carl J. Friedrich and Herbert Spiro wrote: "On the whole this trend of relationships between the government and a distinct and articulate opposition is a wholesome one and should contribute to strengthening constitutional democracy in Germany. It provides more clear-cut responsibility and enables the voter to exercise a genuine choice." "Constitution of the Federal Republic," in Litchfield, ed., pp. 141f.

52. S.P.D. Exec. Comm., *News from Germany*, May 1952.

53. "Bedenkt eins! Politik besteht nicht nur aus dem Heute, Politik besteht auch aus dem Morgen und dem Übermorgen, und die innere Entwicklung erteilt uns viele bittere Lehren." *Turm.*, II, 201.

54. See *Sopade*, newsletter of the S.P.D., September 1951. See also the excellent discussion by Schütz, in Lange, ed., pp. 254–59.

55. Quoted by Scholz, in *Turm.*, I, 446.

56. Paul Sethe in *Frankfurter Allgemeine Zeitung*, Nov. 13, 1950.

57. Schumacher had made some earlier efforts to make it an issue. For example, in a pamphlet, *Kampf in und um Deutschland*, he had claimed in August 1948 that the Western powers and some Christian Democrats had launched "trial balloons" suggesting some sort of rearmament.

58. See O.M.G.U.S., "German Views on the Remilitarization Issue," *Opinion Survey Reports*, Series 2, No. 58, Jan. 1, 1951; also Noelle and Neumann, eds., pp. 360f.

59. Noelle and Neumann, pp. 172f, 252f.

60. Office of the U.S. High Commissioner for Germany, Historical Division, Office of the Executive Secretary, *The West German Federal Government* (n.p., 1952), pp. 138f.

61. Ms., dated January 1951, Pers. Archiv, S.P.D., Bonn.

62. Schumacher, *Für Frieden*, p. 7. See also *Sozialismus: Eine Gegenwartsaufgabe*, p. 10.

63. See, for example, the S.P.D. Executive Committee's resolution "The Problem of West German Security" of December 1948, reported in S.P.D. Exec. Comm., *Jahrbuch*, 1948–49.

64. *Turm.*, II, 230.

65. See the reports of Schumacher's press conferences of Aug. 15 and 24, 1951, reported in *Sopade*, September 1951, p. 3.

66. Paul Sethe in *Frankfurter Allgemeine Zeitung*, Nov. 23, 1951.

67. Schumacher's appointments calendar lists 12 such meetings with former General Speidel and 17 with ex-General Heusinger between September 1950 and December 1951 (when he had his stroke).

68. Lania, p. 13.

69. For a brilliant discussion of these developments, see Dahrendorf, pp. 293–98, 302ff.

70. Lens, p. 142.

71. Otto Kirchheimer, "Notes on the Political Scene in Western Germany," *World Politics*, April 1954, pp. 300–321.

72. O.M.G.U.S., "The Basic Economic Orientation of the West German People," *Opinion Survey Reports*, Series 2, No. 147.

73. In this connection, see Karl O. Freiherr von Aretin, "Widerstand und Wiederauf-stieg," *Bulletin des Presse und Informationsamt der Bundesregierung,* July 18, 1962.

74. Werner Müller, "Verständnis für die Jugend," letter to the Berlin socialist journal *Das Sozialistische Jahrhundert,* I (1947), 189. See also Alfred Andersch, "Die Sozialis-tische Situation," *Der Ruf,* March 15, 1947.

75. See O.M.G.U.S., "Present Level of West German Political and Economic Satisfac-tion, with Current Standing of the Major Political Parties," *Opinion Survey Reports,* Series 2, No. 155, which contains an excellent analysis of the S.P.D. supporters at the time of Schumacher's death, based on a representative survey of West German opinion. Also Ernst Tillich, "Quo-Usque Tandem?," *Das Sozialistische Jahrhundert,* III, 355, and *Sopade,* October 1953.

76. Heidenheimer, p. 34.

77. O.M.G.U.S., *Opinion Survey Reports,* Series 2, No. 56.

78. Noelle and Neumann, p. 192.

79. In this connection, see Schütz, in Lange, ed., pp. 246f, and Erbe (pseud.), pp. 82f.

80. See, for example, his remarks at a state convention of the Berlin S.P.D. in January 1950, reprinted in *Turm.,* II, 209.

81. Josef Müller, quoted in Heidenheimer, p. 155.

82. This was the phrase he used in a letter to Pfarrektor Dresen, Jan. 30, 1950 (S.P.D. Pers. Archiv, K.S. File).

83. See Hans Speier, "German Rearmament and the Old Military Elite," *World Politics,* VI (1954), 147–68.

84. For good discussions of the evolution of the postwar labor movement, see Grosser, *Die Bonner Demokratie,* pp. 224–42; Taylor Cole, "Labor Relations," in Litchfield, ed., pp. 365ff; Lens, pp. 143–52; Office of the U.S. High Commissioner for Germany, *Labor Problems in West Germany* (Bad Godesberg–Mehlem, 1952); Wolfgang Hirsch-Weber, *Gewerkschaften in der Politik.*

85. "Ich sage den guten Gewerkschaftern und den sozialdemokratischen Funktionären in den Gewerkschaften: Ihr könnt das Ziel der politischen Neutralität der Gewerkschaf-ten, das wir ja bejahen, nicht dadurch erreichen, dass ihr den Gegnern der Sozialdemo-kratie innerhalb der Gewerkschaften Narrenfreiheit gebt. Jetzt müssen die Sozialdemo-kraten in den Gewerkschaften und in den Betrieben die Genossen um die Fahne der Sozialdemokratie sammeln." *Turm.,* II, 127.

86. S.P.D. Pers. Archiv, K.S. File.

87. See Ernst Haas, *The Uniting of Europe* (Stanford, 1958), pp. 219f.

88. Schumacher's notes in his appointments calendar for a meeting of the Wirtschafts-politischer Ausschuss of the S.P.D. on Oct. 26, 1951, read as follows: "Chr. Fette Angst vor eigener Courage. Der eigentliche Vorsitzende Hans vom Hoff. Inspirator und Beichtvater. Brennender Ehrgeiz." Vom Hoff was the leader of the trade union representatives on the German delegation negotiating the E.C.S.C. treaty in 1950, and he subsequently became one of the directors of the E.C.S.C. High Commission.

89. This point is well brought out in Juan Linz, "The Social Basis of German Politics," unpublished Ph.D. dissertation, Columbia University, 1959, p. 140.

Chapter Nine

1. Arno Scholz, "Der Letzte Weg," in *Turm.,* III, 16.

2. *Ibid.,* p. 29.

3. *Ibid.,* p. 15. See also the remainder of *Turm.,* Vol. III, for a collection of excerpts from funeral orations and obituary articles.

4. See *Turm.,* Vols. I–III, and Wesemann, *passim.*

5. Scholz, in *Turm.*, III, 16.

6. *New York Herald Tribune,* Aug. 22 and 24, 1952.

7. *Frankfurter Hefte,* VII (1952), 651.

8. Personal communication, April 12, 1961.

9. Personal communication, May 27, 1963.

10. Hans Habe, *Our Love Affair with Germany* (New York, 1953), p. 62.

11. Prittie, *Germany Divided,* p. 15.

12. Lania, p. 15; Laski, p. 11.

13. Thus Werner Friedmann, "Eine Flamme ist erloschen," *Süddeutsche Zeitung,* Aug. 22, 1952; reprinted in *Turm.*, II, 65–67.

14. Schulz, "Seid männlich und seid stark."

15. *Frankfurter Hefte,* VII (1952), 651.

16. Quoted in S.P.D. Exec. Comm., *Kurt Schumacher,* p. 23.

17. Rudolf Kircher, "Der Unerbitterliche," *Deutsche Zeitung und Wirtschaftszeitung,* Aug. 23, 1952; reprinted in *Turm.*, III, 72–73.

18. *Der Kampf um den Staatsgedanken,* p. 32.

19. I am indebted for this very apt quotation to Heidenheimer, p. 152.

20. For an elaboration of the categories of orientation I have employed here, see Keller, pp. 156f, and the sources cited in n. 8, p. 168; Parsons and Shils, eds., pp. 53–109. See also Verba, *Small Groups and Political Behavior,* pp. 155, 171–75, and Chapter 1 above.

21. Heuss made this statement in his funeral oration. *Turm.*, III, 28.

22. "Carolus" (pseud.), p. 330.

23. See, e.g., Schulz, "Seid männlich und seid stark," and *Sorge um die deutsche Linke,* pp. 56–57. Also Elmer Plischke, *Contemporary Government of Germany* (Boston, 1961), p. 147, as well as various obituary articles reprinted in *Turm.*, Vol. III, *passim.*

24. The discussion to follow and the interviews upon which it is based (see the Bibliography, p. 370, for a listing) owe much to an unpublished paper by Alexander L. George and Juliette L. George, "Woodrow Wilson: Personality and Political Behavior," prepared for the 1956 meeting of the American Political Science Association in Washington, D.C. Although I do not accept the psychoanalytic framework of this paper or its conclusions, I found it of considerable help in structuring my interviews and in searching for certain characteristics of behavior in Schumacher's life history. In the following sections, as elsewhere in this study, the confidential nature of these semi-structured interviews, and the manner in which they had to be conducted and recorded to make for maximum rapport with informants, precludes the use of direct quotations or specific identification of informants.

25. S.P.D. Exec. Comm., *Kurt Schumacher,* p. 3.

26. See a manuscript copy of a news release entitled "Schumachers privates Testament geöffnet," in Pers. Archiv, S.P.D., K.S., Bd. Bio.

27. *Deutschlands Forderung,* p. 12.

28. "Vertagte Krisen . . . sind in ihren Folgen immer zerstörender als durchgestandene und damit überwundene Krisen." "Referat," p. 13.

29. Es is eine Illusion, zu meinen, dass aus dem Tatbestand des Siegerseins eine höhere Quelle der Erkenntnis resultiert." *Macht Europa Stark,* p. 3.

30. Quoted in Wesemann, p. 183.

31. Walter Dirks, "Ein Politiker grossen Stils," *Turm.*, III, 116.

32. Funeral oration in the Bundestag, Aug. 23, 1952, in *ibid.,* p. 23.

33. *My Road to Berlin,* p. 159.

34. F. H. George and J. H. Handlon, "A Language for Perceptual Analysis," *Psychological Review,* LXIV (1957), 14, quoted in Rokeach, pp. 402f. For a fascinating report

on neurological studies relating memories of past experiences to the interpretation of present events, see William L. Laurence, "Mechanism Discovered in the Brain Which Unlocks Streams of Consciousness Record," *The New York Times,* Nov. 24, 1963, p. 8.

35. See Rokeach, *passim*; Leon Festinger, *A Theory of Cognitive Dissonance* (Evanston, Ill., 1957); F. Heider, *The Psychology of Interpersonal Relations* (New York, 1958); Charles Osgood *et al., The Measurement of Meaning* (Urbana, 1957); Parsons, *The Social System,* pp. 201–383; Parsons and Shils, eds., pp. 53–109.

36. Parsons and Shils, eds., pp. 57, 110–58.

37. Speech, S.P.D. congress, Hannover, May 1946, *Turm.,* II, 75.

38. I have quoted here from Rudolf Kircher, "Der Unerbitterliche," *Deutsche Zeitung,* Aug. 23, 1952 (reprinted in *Turm.,* III, 72).

39. Rokeach, pp. 14f.

40. Theodore H. White, *Fire in the Ashes* (New York, 1953), p. 149.

41. *Turm.,* III, 23.

42. Wesemann, p. 242.

43. Rokeach, p. 45. See also Stewart E. Perry, "Notes on the Role of the National," reprinted from *The Journal of Conflict Resolution* (1957), in James N. Rosenau, ed., *International Politics and Foreign Policy* (New York, 1961), pp. 87–97, and references cited in n. 37 above.

44. Scholz, "Leben und Leistung," *Turm.,* I, 464.

45. See Rokeach, *passim,* and esp. pp. 36ff, 55f, 73ff, 172, 181–84, 396, 398. Rokeach lists the following among the qualities indicating a "closed belief system": (1) the compartmentalization of logically contradictory beliefs; (2) the accentuation of differences and minimization of similarities; (3) the perception as irrelevant of what may be relevant by objective standards; (4) the denial of contradictory facts; (5) comparative ignorance about the sources of what is disbelieved (e.g., the statements of foreign leaders and non-German press reports in Schumacher's case); (6) the perception of similarities between various disbeliefs (e.g., in Schumacher's case similarities between "red" and "black" reactionaries); (7) extreme rejection of what is disbelieved (e.g., the indifference of the postwar German masses to patriotic appeals); (8) the interpretation of the external environment as threatening; (9) a strong propensity toward absolutes; (10) affective judgment of others in terms of their acceptance or rejection of the actor's own belief system; and (11) a strong inclination to view the events of the present in terms of future developments (i.e., the present, perceived as full of injustice and suffering, is seen only in terms of future developments that the actor believes he can predict better than other people).

46. "Mein persönlicher Ergeiz hat mir in meinem Leben noch nicht viel zu schaffen gemacht." Letter to Willi Klinowski, Nov. 1, 1945, Pers. Archiv., S.P.D., K.S. Bd. Briefe von K.S.

47. *My Road to Berlin,* p. 157.

48. Marck, p. 81.

49. Before arriving at this hypothesis, I carefully considered a number of alternative theories, but was forced to dismiss them in the light of the evidence and various analogous studies. First, I considered physiological factors, which were put forward by many of Schumacher's contemporaries as the principal explanation of his postwar behavior, particularly after the amputation of his left leg in 1948. The irritability and impatience of the multiple amputee, his temperamental outbursts and his lack of finesse, were attributed to nervous tensions caused by the physical suffering that preceded his death. His appearance as well as his behavior—the pinched face, the painfully limping figure, his heavy dependence on drugs, coffee, and tobacco—seemed to confirm the impression that "the burden of illness was becoming too heavy for a once brilliant mind," and that as his "judgment

began to falter," he was no longer "as coherent nor as charitable as he would have wished to have been." Prittie, p. 5.

Indeed, illness and pain probably influenced his state of mind and behavior. But if somatic factors produced psychic effects, it seems also that latent, tension-producing personality factors contributed significantly to his physiological complaints, not only after the war but in the concentration camp and earlier. As is commonly the case in such psychosomatic and somatic-psychic syndromes, it is virtually impossible to separate physiological from psychological factors; however, for reasons to be explored more thoroughly later, it does seem that some of Schumacher's somatic ailments were at least partially attributable to earlier psychic problems.

Second, I considered the possibility that subconscious guilt feelings may have led Schumacher to invite frustration, sanctions, and defeat as a form of masochistic punishment. This hypothesis, suggested by Theodore Reich as applicable to "great men" (*The Need to Be Loved*, New York, 1963), seems unsupportable in this instance. Schumacher apparently externalized rather than internalized, projected rather than incorporated, his aggressive need dispositions.

Finally, I considered the possibility that Schumacher's behavior suggested a megalomanic syndrome, but I came to the conclusion that his distorted sense of reality characterized obsessive-compulsive rather than delusional symptoms.

50. David Shapiro, "Aspects of Obsessive-Compulsive Style," *Psychiatry*, XV (1962), 52–55. See also Horney, pp. 167–70. For helping me to formulate the thoughts presented here, I am particularly indebted to these two works and to the unpublished paper by Alexander and Juliette George cited in n. 24 of this chapter.

51. Parsons, p. 255. See also pp. 254–62.

52. Hartmann, p. 25.

53. "Kurt Schumacher war ein Mann von überragender Intelligenz, leidenschaftlich, willensstark, der gegebene Führer; und doch trug er von Beginnen an das Zeichen tragisches Missgelingens auf seiner Stirne. . . . Aufmerksamen Beobachtern entging . . . nicht wie schwer die Hypothek war, die auf dieser ungewöhnlichen Begabung lastete. Seine hohe Geistigkeit, seine Fähigkeit, blitzschnell zu reagieren, seine Begabung für geistreiche und ätzend spöttische Bemerkungen waren in einem Zeitalter der Massendemokratie nicht immer eine Empfehlung für ihn. . . . Schlimmer noch als die Ueberfrachtung mit Ironie und Geist wirkte seine oft hemmungslose Besessenheit und seine tiefe Bitterkeit. Sie müssen wohl in seiner Natur gelegen haben und hatten sich im Konzentrationslager noch verschärft." Paul Sethe, "Die Ära Adenauer: Der Kanzler und sein Werk," *Die Welt,* Sept. 28, 1963, p. 3.

54. See Hartmann, pp. 49–54.

55. "Frustration is the blockage of a path to a goal . . . tension is kept high, permitted no reduction. From this follows a series of struggling movements more or less directed toward removal of the interference or destruction of the obstacle. If, however, the motive system is itself complex and fluid, the very failure of tensions to spread is itself frustration. . . . We . . . encounter the problem of *degree* of frustration, as well as its locus, quality, and form. The tension system that is 'frustrated' may initiate a wider tension leading to struggling movements, and these, depending on the cultural conditions of development, may either lead to diffuse kicking or directed assault. The investigation of the relation of frustration to aggression becomes in large measure an investigation of the locus, degree, the quality, and the form of the frustration, and similarly of the "aggressive" behavior, the complex inner pattern of tension which may . . . follow. The past and the present relations of the organism and environment, not the fixed relations between 'frustration' and 'aggression,' will be involved." Murphy, p. 145.

56. See esp. Schaffner, pp. 44–60.

57. In this connection, see Robert W. White, pp. 297–333.

58. On this point see Murphy, p. 576, and Parsons, pp. 255f.

Chapter Ten

1. "Personal Identity and Political Ideology," p. 307.

2. *The Ruling Class* (New York, 1939), p. 429.

3. "Es war tragisch, dass er nicht an die Macht und damit an die spezifische Verantwortung des Regierens herankam." Marck, p. 84.

4. "Bei der Beurteilung seiner Persönlichkeit gewinnt die Unterscheidung von Beruf und Berufung ihren vollen Sinn. Kurt Schumacher war Politiker von Berufung." *Turm.,* III, 25.

5. Frankl, p. 92.

6. According to Clifford J. Sager, "Aggressive behavior ... can be defined as behavior that is not called for by the objective situation—that is directed against others and one's self and is essentially anti-social in nature"; it is "evidence of some damage to the psychological organization of the individual." In contrast, "self-assertiveness" is for him "socially beneficial" behavior. "It is the self-assertive tendency that makes us defend ourselves against attack," he claims, "that gives us the stimulus to further ourselves in our work, to earn a position of respect ... and to set up and work for a goal in life." Sager, p. 211.

7. "Seine Gaben sind die eines Mannes der den Mangel an Geist durch die Ekstase der Worte überkomponierte. Seine Gaben sind die eines Kranken, eines Defekten, der von seinem eigene Ich besessen ist. Um dieses Ich geltend zu machen war ihm jedes Mittel recht." "Adolf Hitler war ein Kranker zu einer kranken Zeit ... Kranke aber haben in aufgeregten, unruhig suchenden Epochen eine unheimliche Suggestivkraft auf verzweifelte Primitive, die mit den Erscheinungen ihrer Zeit nicht mehr fertig werden können." "Referat," p. 38.

8. Hartmann, p. 94.

9. *Ibid.,* p. 81.

10. See Milton Rokeach, *The Three Christs of Ypsilanti* (New York, 1964).

11. In this connection, see Gerhard Cotts, "A Socially Constructive Type of Psychopathologically Determined Activity," *Psychiatry,* XVII (1954), 97–99, which suggests several interesting hypotheses relevant for this subject derived from the observed role behavior of leaders in community action at the local level.

Bibliography

The Bibliography is divided into two parts, "Interviews" and "Works Consulted." In addition to the sources listed in the Bibliography proper, I have relied heavily on the following:

Schumacher's annotated appointments calendar, 1945–52. This invaluable document was transcribed shortly after Schumacher's death by his secretary, Frau Annemarie Renger. I am much indebted to Frau Renger for permission to use her copy of the typescript for this study.

Schumacher Papers, S.P.D. Parteivorstand (Bonn). This material consists of three items. (1) A lengthy taped interview, apparently never published, which a German journalist named Kaufmann had with Schumacher in late July 1952. It includes valuable references to his early life as well as comments about his career shortly before his death. (2) Published and unpublished material in the central personnel office (Personalkartei) of the S.P.D. in Bonn, particularly 19 binders containing letters, newspaper clippings, draft manuscripts, and other important documents relating to Schumacher. The material in Binders IIIa and IIIb, which contain much of his postwar official correspondence, proved especially useful. (3) Material in the central party library and archives, including a copy of Schumacher's doctoral dissertation and two folders of notes and manuscripts for the period 1945–52.

Schumacher File, Der Telegraf (Berlin). This material consists of 54 binders of newspaper clippings relating to Schumacher's postwar activities. It was collected for Arno Scholz, the editor of *Der Telegraf,* for his study of Schumacher, "Leben und Leistung," published in Vol. II of *Turmwächter der Demokratie* (listed below under Scholz and Oschilewski).

Schwäbische Tagwacht, 1920–33. I found an incomplete set of this newspaper in the Württembergische Landesbibliothek (Stuttgart-Ludwigsburg), which happily I was able to complete with material from the *Esslinger Volkszeitung, 1918–33,* in the Stadtarchiv of Esslingen am Neckar.

Letters and documents in private hands. In most cases these were made available to me on the understanding that the source would be kept confidential. Where this was not stipulated, the source has been identified in the Notes.

Interviews

Dates in parentheses are those of the informant's principal period of association with Schumacher. All interviews were carried out between October 1959 and August 1960.

Arndt, Adolf (1949–52). Close political associate.

Aschauer, Anton (1936–38). Fellow inmate of Dachau.

Bauer, Fritz (1925–30). Close personal friend and political associate.

Bazille, Helmut (1946–52). Political associate.

Biel, Ulrich (1945–49). Chief, Polit. Div., U.S. Office of Milit. Govt., Berlin.

Boulton, Seymour (1946–51). Staff, U.S. Milit. Govt.

Brandt, Willy (1948–50). Political associate.

Dehler, Thomas (1949–52). Free Democratic leader.

Denker, Emma (1925–33). Friend and political associate.

Dercum, Adolf (1946–49). Personal physician.

Erler, Fritz (1949–52). Close political associate.

Felder, Josef (1932–38; 1946–52). Reichstag, 1932–33; Dachau, 1933–38; political associate, 1946–52.

Fliess, Walter (1947–50). Official, British Milit. Govt.

Franke, Egon (1945–52). Very close political associate.

Gerstenmaier, Eugen (1949–51). Christian Democratic leader.

Geyer, Curt (1932–33). Political associate.

Grotz, Cläre (1921–33). Secretary.

Hasselbring, Hermann (1945–49). Close political associate.

Hausmann, Heinrich (1943–45). Friend and employer.

Heine, Fritz (1946–52). Very close political associate.

Helmstädter, Fritz (1928–33). Close political associate.

Herz, Oscar (1924–33). Political associate, 1924–33; fellow inmate of Dachau, 1938–43.

Heuer, Albert (1945–49). Political associate.

Heuss, Theodor (1949–52). Federal President.

Hoegner, Wilhelm (1930–33; 1946–50). Reichstag, 1930–33; S.P.D. associate 1946–52.

Hofstetter, Paul (1920–30). Political associate.

Höhne, Franz (1936–38; 1946–52). Fellow inmate of Dachau, 1936–38; S.P.D. associate, 1946–52.

Holweg, August (1944–52). Political associate.

Kaisen, Wilhelm (1945–52). S.P.D. leader.

Kautzky, Benedikt (1938–50). Austrian socialist in Dachau, 1938; postwar association.

Keil, Wilhelm (1920–33). Close political associate.

Kimmisch, Hans-Jörg (1949–51). Political association.

Kleinknecht, Wilhelm (1920–33). Close political associate.

Klingelhofer, Gustav (1945–52). Political associate.

Knoeringen, Waldemar von (1947–52). Political associate.
Kollmorgen, Dorothea (1915–33; 1943–45). Cousin and friend.
Kriedemann, Herbert (1945–49). Close political associate.
Leber, Annedore (1930–33). Political associate.
Löbe, Paul (1930–33). Political associate; major S.P.D. leader, 1930–33.
Maier, Reinhold (1924–33; 1947–49). Friend; political associate as leader of Free
    Democratic party, 1947–49.
Menzel, Walter (1946–52). Close political associate.
Mielcke, Helmuth (1928–33). Close political associate.
Molt, Karl (1920–33). Political associate.
Müller, Elisabeth (1895–1952). Sister.
Nau, Alfred (1946–52). Very close political associate.
Neumann, Franz (1945–52). Close political associate.
Neumann, Sigmund ("Siggi") (1946–49). Close political associate.
Ollenhauer, Erich (1946–52). Very close political associate.
Oster, Fritz (1925–36). Close political associate.
Peters, Hermann (1935–43). Close friend in Dachau.
Pope, Lance (1945–48). Official, British Milit. Govt., Hannover.
Renger, Annemarie (1945–52). Secretary and assistant; very close associate.
Rössle, Ernst (1920–33). Political associate.
Sauter, Willy (1925–33; 1936–38). Political associate; fellow inmate of Dachau
Schmid, Carlo (1947–52). Very close political associate.
Schmidt, Albert (1928–30). Political associate.
Schoettle, Erwin (1925–33; 1946–52). Very close political associate.
Scholz, Arno (1945–52). Very close political associate, editor of Der Telegraf, and
    biographer.
Schreiber, Fritz (1945–46). Assistant to Otto Grotewohl.
Schulz, Klaus Peter (1945–49). Political associate.
Seibert, Maria (1925–35). Close friend.
Staff, Curt (1935–36). Fellow inmate of Dachau.
Swolinski, Kurt (1945–50). Political associate.
Thiele, Franz (1946–52). Political associate.
Thomas, Stefan (1947–52). Political associate.
Tiemann, Friedrich (1950–52). Personal physician.
Trinkwalter, Lotte (1895–1952). Sister.
Ulrich, Fritz (1920–33). Political associate.
Vogel, Friedrich (1938–43). Dachau; close associate.
Wahrhaftig, Samuel (1945–51). Official, U.S. Office of Milit. Govt.
Wehner, Herbert (1949–52). Very close political associate.
Wesemann, Fried (1950–52). Personal biographer.
Wirkner, Roman (1940–43). Fellow inmate of Dachau.
Wulfert, Fritz (1945–49). Political associate.
Wurm, Frieder (1920–33). Close political associate.
Zimmermann, Karl (1937–43). Fellow inmate of Dachau.

Works Consulted

Acheson, Dean. "Konrad Adenauer," in Sketches from Life of Men I Have Known. New York, 1961.

Adler, A. G. "Selbstverwaltung und Widerstand in den Konzentrationslagern der S.S.," *Vierteljahreshefte für Zeitgeschichte,* VIII (1960), 221–36.

Alexander, Edgar. Adenauer und das neue Deutschland: Einführung in das Wesen und Wirken des Staatsmannes. Rechlinghausen, 1956.

Allemann, F. R. "Das deutsche Parteiensystem," *Der Monat,* January 1953, pp. 365–88.

———. "Die Krise der deutschen Aussenpolitik," *Der Monat,* March 1955, pp. 5–6.

Allport, Gordon W. The Use of Personal Documents in Psychological Science. Social Science Research Council Bulletin No. 49, 1942.

Allport, Gordon W., J. S. Bruner, and E. M. Jandorf. "Personality under Social Catastrophe," in Kluckhohn and Murray, eds., Personality in Nature, Society, and Culture.

Almond, Gabriel A., and James S. Coleman, eds. The Politics of Developing Areas. Princeton, 1960.

Almond, Gabriel A., and Sidney Verba. The Civic Culture. Princeton, 1963.

Arendt, Hannah. "The Concentration Camp," in The New Partisan Reader. New York, 1953.

———. Origins of Totalitarianism. New York, 1958.

———. "Social Science Techniques and the Study of Concentration Camps," *Jewish Social Studies,* XII (1950), 49–64.

Barker, Roger G., *et al.* Adjustment to Physical Handicap and Illness: A Survey of the Social Psychology of Physique and Disability. 2d ed. New York, 1953.

Barker, Roger G., and Beatrice A. Wright. "Disablement: The Somato-Psychological Problem," in Wittkower and Cleghorn, eds., Recent Developments in Psychosomatic Medicine.

Bass, Bernard M. Leadership, Psychology, and Organizational Behavior. New York, 1960.

Bellak, Leopold, ed. Psychology of Physical Illness. New York, 1952.

Bergsträsser, Ludwig. Geschichte der politischen Parteien in Deutschland. Munich, 1960.

Besson, Waldemar. Württemberg und die deutsche Staatskrise, 1928–1933. Stuttgart, 1959.

Bettelheim, Bruno. The Informed Heart. Glencoe, Ill., 1960.

———. "Individual and Mass Behavior in Extreme Situations," *Journal of Abnormal and Social Psychology,* XXXVIII, 417–50.

Biddle, Bruce J. The Present Status of Role Theory. Columbia, Mo., 1961.

———. "Roles, Goals, and Value Structures in Organizations." Unpublished manuscript prepared for presentation to the Conference on Organization Research at the Carnegie Institute of Technology on June 22, 1962.

Blum, Gerald S. Psychoanalytic Theories of Personality. New York, 1953.

Bornemann, Ernst. "Sozialpsychologische Probleme der Führung," *Kölner Zeitschrift für Soziologie und Sozial-Psychologie,* XIV, 105–23.

Böttcher, Karl Wilhelm. "Die Neuen Reichen und die Neureichen in Deutschland," *Frankfurter Hefte,* VI (1951), 331–38.

Bracher, Karl Dietrich. Die Auflösung der Weimarer Republik. Stuttgart, 1955.

Bracher, Karl Dietrich, Gerhard Schulz, and Wolfgang Sauer. Die Nationalsozialistische Machtergreifung. Cologne, 1960.

Brandt, Albert A. "Germany's Toughest Democrat," *This Month,* February 1947.

Brandt, Willy. My Road to Berlin. As told to Leo Lania. New York, 1960.

Brandt, Willy, and Richard Löwenthal. Ernst Reuter: Ein Leben für die Freiheit. Munich, 1957.

Bretton, Henry L. "The German Social Democratic Party and the International Situation," *American Political Science Review,* XLVII (1953), 980–96.

Brown, C. G., and T. S. Cohn, eds. The Study of Leadership. Danville, Ill., 1958.

Buber, Margarete. Under Two Dictators. New York, n.d.

Burns, James M. Roosevelt: The Lion and the Fox. New York, 1956.

Carolus (pseud.). "Kurt Schumacher," *The Nation,* October 11, 1952, p. 329.

Charlesworth, James C., ed. The Limits of Behavioralism in Political Science. Philadelphia, 1962.

Christie, Richard, and Marie Jahoda, eds. Studies in the Scope and Method of the Authoritarian Personality. Glencoe, Ill., 1954.

Clark, Delbert. Again the Goose Step: The Lost Fruits of Victory. New York, 1949.

Clay, Lucius D. Decision in Germany. New York, 1950.

Cohen, Elie A. Human Behavior in the Concentration Camp. New York, 1953.

Dahrendorf, Ralf. Gesellschaft und Freiheit: Zur Soziologischen Analyse der Gegenwart. Munich, 1961.

Davidson, Eugene. The Death and Life of Germany: An Account of the American Occupation. New York, 1959.

Davison, W. Phillips. The Berlin Blockade. Princeton, 1958.

Dethleffsen, Erich. "The Chimera of German Neutrality," *Foreign Affairs,* XXX (1952), 361–75.

Dirks, Walter. "Sozialisten ausserhalb der Parteien," *Das Sozialistische Jahrhundert,* II (1949), 5–12.

Easton, David. The Political System. New York, 1953.

Ebsworth, Raymond. Restoring Democracy in Germany: The British Contribution. London and New York, 1960.

Edelman, Murray. "Symbols and Political Quiescence," *American Political Science Review,* LIV (1960), 695–704.

Edinger, Lewis J. "German Social Democracy and Hitler's 'National Revolution' of 1933: A Study in Democratic Leadership," *World Politics,* V (1953), 330–67.

———. German Exile Politics: The Social Democratic Executive Committee in the Nazi Era. Berkeley, Calif., 1956.

———. "Post-Totalitarian Leader: Elites in the German Federal Republic," *American Political Science Review,* LIV (1960), 58–82.

Eissler, K. R. Goethe: A Psychoanalytic Study. 2 vols. Detroit, 1963.

Erbe, Friedrich (pseud.). "Vierzehn Jahre Wahlen in Westdeutschland," in Erwin Faul, Ed., Wahlen und Wähler in Westdeutschland. Villingen, 1960.

Erikson, Erik H. Young Man Luther: A Study in Psychoanalysis and History. New York, 1958.

———. "Wholeness and Totality: A Psychiatric Contribution," in Carl J. Friedrich, ed., Totalitarianism. Cambridge, Mass., 1954.

Eulau, Heinz, Samuel Eldersveld, and Morris Janowitz, eds. Political Behavior: A Reader in Theory and Research. Glencoe, Ill., 1956.

Eysenck, Hans Jurgen. The Psychology of Politics. New York, 1955.

Fenichel, Otto. The Psychoanalytic Theory of Neurosis. New York, 1945.

Frankl, Victor E. From Death Camp to Existentialism. Boston, 1959.

Freud, Sigmund. "Eine Kindheitserinnerung des Leonardo da Vinci," in Gesammelte Werke, Vol. VII. London, 1943.

George, Alexander, and Juliette George. Woodrow Wilson and Colonel House. New York, 1956.

Germany. Handbuch des deutschen Reichstag, 1932. Bundestag archives, Bonn.

———. Handbuch für den Württembergischen Landtag, 1924–28. 7 vols. Bundestag archives, Bonn.

———. Materialen des Zonenbeirates der Britischen Besatzungszone—Ausschussprotokolle 1946, Sonderausschuss "Neuaufbau der Länder." Bundestag archives, Bonn.

———. Protokoll der Verhandlungen des deutschen Reichstag, 1932. Bundestag archives, Bonn.

———. Protokoll der Verhandlungen des Landtages des freien Volkstaates Württemberg, 1924–28, 1928–31. 11 vols. plus supplements. Bundestag archives, Bonn.

———. Verhandlungen des deutschen Bundestages, 1. Wahlperiode, 1949–53.

Gerth, Hans, and C. Wright Mills. Character and Social Structure. New York, 1953.

Gleissberg, Gerhard. "Die Aussenpolitik der deutschen Sozialdemokraten," Die Zukunft, September 1952, pp. 251–56.

Glicksman, W. "Social Differentiation in the German Concentration Camp," Yivo Annual of Jewish Social Science, Vol. XIII. New York, 1953.

Golay, John. The Founding of the Federal Republic of Germany. Chicago, 1957.

Gottfried, Alex. Boss Cermak of Chicago. Seattle, 1961.

Gouldner, Alvin W., ed. Studies in Leadership. New York, 1950.

Gross, Neal, Ward S. Mason, and Alexander W. McEachern. Explorations in Role Analysis: Studies of the School Superintendency Role. New York, 1958.

Grosser, Alfred. Die Bonner Demokratie. Düsseldorf, 1960.

———. "La Structure du parti social-democrat d'Allemagne," Occident, 1955, pp. 58–81.

Grotewohl, Otto. Im Kampf um Deutschland. Berlin, 1947.

———. Zur politischen Lage Deutschlands. Berlin, 1947.

Grygier, Tadeuz. Oppression: A Study in Social and Criminal Psychology. London, 1954.

Haerdter, Robert. "Ein Mann, eine Partei, und Deutschland," Die Gegenwart, August 30, 1952, pp. 549–50.

————. "Eine deutsche Partei: Die Chance und das Risiko der S.P.D.," *Die Gegenwart,* December 1, 1948, pp. 5–7.

Hall, Calvin S., and Gardner Lindzey. Theories of Personality. New York, 1957.

Hammer, Walter. Hohes Haus in Henkers Hand. Frankfurt, 1956.

————, ed. Theodor Haubach zum Gedächtnis. Frankfurt, 1955.

Hartmann, Heinz. Ego Psychology and the Problem of Adaptation. New York, 1958.

Heidenheimer, Arnold J. Adenauer and the C.D.U.: The Rise of the Leader and the Integration of the Party. The Hague, 1960.

Hill, Russell. The Struggle for Germany. New York, 1947.

————. "This Guy Schumacher," *New York Herald Tribune,* July 14, 1952, p. 26.

Hirsch, Felix. "Adenauer or Schumacher?" *Current History,* February 1952.

Hirsch-Weber, Wolfgang. Gewerkschaften in der Politik. Cologne, 1959.

Hiscocks, Richard. Democracy in Western Germany. London, 1957.

Hoegner, Wilhelm. Der schwierige Aussenseiter. Munich, 1959.

Holsti, Ole R. "The Belief System and National Images," *Journal of Conflict Resolution,* VI (1962), 244–52.

Hook, Sidney. The Hero in History: A Study in Limitations and Possibility. New York, 1943.

Horney, Karen. The Neurotic Personality of Our Time. New York, 1937.

Hyman, Herbert. Political Socialization. Glencoe, Ill., 1959.

Joesten, Joachim. Germany: What Now? New York, 1948.

————. "Kurt Schumacher: Politician on a Tightrope," *Tomorrow Magazine,* July 1947, pp. 25–28.

Joos, Joseph. So Sah ich Sie: Menschen und Geschehnisse. Augsburg, 1958.

Kaden, Albrecht. "Die Wiedergründung der S.P.D., 1945–1946." Unpublished dissertation. Hamburg, 1960. Published in Hannover under same title in 1964.

Kautsky, Benedict. "Kurt Schumacher: Der Wiederwecker der deutschen Arbeiterklasse," *Die Zukunft,* September 1952, pp. 245–51.

————. Teufel und Verdammte. Zurich, 1946.

Keil, Wilhelm. Erlebnisse eines Sozialdemokraten. 2 vols. Stuttgart, 1947–48.

Keller, Suzanne. Beyond the Ruling Class: Strategic Elites in Modern Society. New York, 1963.

Kirkpatrick, Ivon. The Inner Circle. London, 1959.

Kluckhohn, Clyde, and Henry A. Murray, eds. Personality in Nature, Society, and Culture. New York, 1948.

Kogon, Eugen. The Theory and Practice of Hell. New York, n.d.

Kupfer-Koberwitz, Edgar. Die Mächtigen und die Hilflosen, Vol. I. Stuttgart, 1957.

Lane, Robert E. "Political Personality and Electoral Choice," *American Political Science Review,* XLIX (1955), 173–90.

Lange, Max Gustav, ed. Parteien in der Bundesrepublik. Stuttgart, 1955.

Lania, Leo. "Schumacher: Violent Martyr," *United Nations World,* VI (1952), 13–15.

Lasky, Melvin J. "Preparing the Post-Adenauer Era," *The New Leader,* June 18, 1956, p. 11.

Lasswell, Harold D. Power and Personality. Compass ed. New York, 1948.

Leber, Julius. Ein Mann geht seinen Weg. Frankfurt and Berlin, 1952.

Lens, Sidney. "Social Democracy and Labor in Germany," *Foreign Policy Reports,* XXVI (1950), 142–52.

Levinson, Daniel J. "Role, Personality, and Organizational Structure in the Organizational Setting," *Journal of Abnormal and Social Psychology,* Vol. LXIII (1959).

Lewis, Flora. "The Hard-Bitten Herr Schumacher," *New York Times Magazine,* July 31, 1949.

Lindzey, Gardner, ed. Handbook of Social Psychology, Vols. I and II. Cambridge, Mass., 1954.

Litchfield, Edward H., ed. Governing Postwar Germany. Ithaca, N.Y., 1953.

Lorenz, Franz. Die Persönlichkeit in der Volksmeinung. Constance, 1949.

Lowenberg, Gerhard. "Parliamentarism in Western Germany: The Functioning of the Bundestag," *American Political Science Review,* Vol. LV (1961), No. 1.

Luthy, Herbert. "Behind the Reawakened German Nationalism: Which Path, Schumacher or Adenauer's?," *Commentary,* XIII (1952), 115–23.

McInnis, Edgar, Richard Hiscocks, and Robert Spencer. The Shaping of Postwar Germany. New York, 1960.

McIver, Robert. Social Causation. Boston, 1942.

Mahler, Karl. Die Programme der politischen Parteien im neuen Deutschland. Berlin, 1945.

Mann, Golo. Deutsche Geschichte des neunzehnten und zwanzigsten Jahrhunderts. Frankfurt, 1959.

Marck, Siegfried. Grosse Menschen unserer Zeit: Portraits aus drei Kulturkreisen. Meisenheim, 1954.

Marcus, John T. "Transcendence and Charisma," *Western Political Quarterly,* XVI (1961), 236–40.

Matthias, Erich. Sozialdemokratie und Nation. Stuttgart, 1952.

Matthias, Erich, and Rudolf Morsey, eds. Das Ende der Parteien, 1933. Düsseldorf, 1960.

Mead, George Herbert. Mind, Self, and Society. Chicago, 1934.

Mehnert, Klaus, and Heinrich Schulte, eds. Deutschland-Jahrbuch 1949. Essen, 1949.

———. Deutschland-Jahrbuch 1953. Essen, 1953.

Merkl, Peter. "Equilibrium, Structure of Interest, and Leadership: Adenauer's Survival as Chancellor," *American Political Science Review,* LVI (1962), 334–50.

Merton, Robert K. Social Theory and Social Structure. Rev. ed. Glencoe, Ill., 1957.

Meyer, Ernest Wilhelm. Political Parties in Western Germany. Washington, D.C., 1951.

Meyer, Heinz. "Zur Struktur der deutschen Sozialdemokraten," *Zeitschrift für Politik,* December 1955, pp. 356ff.

Middleton, Drew. The Struggle for Germany. Indianapolis, 1949.

———. "The Hitler Youth Eight Years After," *New York Times Magazine,* May 3, 1953, pp. 17, 60–66.

Miller, Daniel R., and Guy E. Swanson. Inner Conflict and Defense. New York, 1960.

Mommer, Karl. "The German Socialists' Dilemma," *New Republic,* May 30, 1949.

Money-Kyrle, R. E. Psychoanalysis and Politics. London, 1951.

Morgenthau, Hans, ed. Germany and the Future of Europe. Chicago, 1951.

Muhlen, Norbert. The Return of Germany. Chicago, 1953.

Murphy, Gardner. Personality: A Biosocial Approach to Origins and Structure. New York, 1947.

Nardini, J. E. "Survival Factors in American Prisoners of War of the Japanese," *American Journal of Psychiatry,* CIX (1952), 241–48.

Nettl, Peter. "Economic Checks on German Unity," *Foreign Affairs,* XXX (1952), 554–63.

Neumann, Sigmund. Germany: Promise and Perils. New York, 1950.

Newcomb, Theodore M., and Eugene L. Hartley. Readings in Social Psychology. New York, 1949.

Noble, Douglas, *et al.* "Psychiatric Disturbances Following Amputation," *American Journal of Psychiatry,* CX (1954), 609–13.

Noelle, Elisabeth, and Peter Neumann. Jahrbuch der öffentlichen Meinung, 1947–1955. Allensbach, 1956.

[O.M.G.U.S.] Office of Military Government for Germany, U.S. Opinion Survey Reports. March 1, 1946–January 25, 1951. (After 1949 published by the Office of the U.S. High Commissioner for Germany.)

———. Political Parties in Western Germany. Berlin, 1949.

———. Reports of the Military Governor. Frankfurt-Berlin-Bad Godesberg, 1946–49.

Office of the U.S. High Commissioner for Germany. Elections and Political Parties in Germany, 1945–1952. N.p., June 1952.

———, Historical Division. Labor Problems in West Germany. Bad Godesberg, 1952.

Office of the U.S. Secretary, Allied General Secretariat, Liaison/Interpreters Section. "The First Year of the Legislature of the Federal Republic of Germany." N.p., 1950. Hectographed.

Olmsted, Donald W. Social Groups, Roles, and Leadership. East Lansing, Mich., 1961.

Parsons, Talcott. "Psychoanalysis and the Social Structure," *Psychoanalytical Quarterly,* Vol. XIX (1950), No. 3.

———. The Social System. Glencoe, Ill., 1951.

———. "Some Highlights of the General Theory of Action," in Roland Young, ed., Approaches to the Study of Politics. Evanston, Ill., 1958.

Parsons, Talcott, and Edward A. Shils, eds. Toward a General Theory of Action. Cambridge, Mass., 1951. Harper Torchbooks, 1962.

Pear, T. H. "The Psychological Study of Tension and Conflict," in *The Nature of Conflict.* Paris, Unesco, 1957.

Petrullo, Luigi, and Bernard Bass, eds. Leadership and Interpersonal Behavior. New York, 1961.

Petry, Richard. "Die S.P.D. und der Sozialismus," *Frankfurter Hefte,* October 1954, pp. 663–76.

Pieck, Wilhelm. Probleme der Vereinigung von K.P.D. und S.P.D. Berlin, 1946.

Plenge, Johann M. "Die Doktorarbeit Kurt Schumachers," *Westfälische Rundschau,* June 28, 1947.

Powell, Robert (pseud.). "Germany After Schumacher," *New Republic,* September 15, 1952, p. 12.

Prittie, Terence. Germany Divided. Boston, 1960.

———. "Dr. Schumacher's Role in Post-War Germany," *Manchester Guardian Weekly,* LXVII (1952), 5.

Pritzlokeit, Kurt. Das kommandierte Wunder: Deutschlands Weg im zwanzigsten Jahrhundert. Vienna-Munich-Basel, 1959.

Protokoll, Landtag. *See* Germany.

"Psychiatrische KZ-Nachwirkungen," *Aufbau* (New York), December 27, 1963.

Pye, Lucien W. "Personal Identity and Political Ideology," in Dwaine Marvick, ed., Political Decision-Makers: Recruitment and Performance. Glencoe, Ill., 1961.

Redl, Fritz. "Group Emotions and Leadership," *Psychiatry,* V (1942), 573–96.

Ritter, Waldemar. Kurt Schumacher: Eine Untersuchung seiner politischen Konzeption und seiner Gesellschafts- und Staatsauffassung. Hannover, 1964.

Rogow, Arnold A. James Forrestal. New York, 1963.

Rokeach, Milton, *et al.* The Open and the Closed Mind. New York, 1961.

Rommetveit, Ragner. Social Norms and Roles. Oslo and Minneapolis, 1955.

Rossmann, Erich. Ein Leben für Sozialismus und Demokratie. Tübingen, n.d.

Rousset, David. L'Univers concentrationnaire. Paris, 1946.

Sager, Clifford J. "The Concept of Aggression in Modern Psychiatry," *Mental Hygiene,* XXXVI (1952), 210–19.

Sänger, Fritz, ed. Die Volksvertretung: Handbuch des deutschen Bundestags. Stuttgart, 1949, 1952.

Schaffner, Bertram. Fatherland. New York, 1948.

Schmid, Carlo. "Germany and Europe: The German Social Democratic Program," *Foreign Affairs,* XXX (1952), 531–44.

Scholz, Arno, and Walther G. Oschilewski, eds. Turmwächter der Demokratie: Ein Lebensbild von Kurt Schumacher. 3 vols. Berlin, 1952–54. Cited as *Turm.*

Schuetz, Otto. "Das Konzentrationslager Syndrom," *Aufbau* (New York), June 9, 1961.

Schulz, Klaus Peter. Sorge um die deutsche Linke. Cologne, 1954.

———. "Seid männlich und seid stark: Erinnerungen an Kurt Schumacher," *Deutscher Rundschau,* October 1952, pp. 1046–53.

Schumacher, Kurt. Deutschlands Forderung. Hannover, n.d.

———. Durch freie Wahlen zur Einheit Deutschlands. Bonn, 1951.

———. Ein Winter der Entscheidungen. Bonn, 1951.

———. Für Frieden, Freiheit, und Sozialismus. N.p., 1946.

———. Kampf in und um Deutschland. Hannover, 1948.

———. "Der Kampf um den Staatsgedanken in der deutschen Sozialdemokratie." Unpublished doctoral dissertation. Münster, 1926.

———. Macht Europa stark. Bonn, 1951.

————. Nach dem Zusammenbruch: Gedanken über Demokratie und Sozialismus. Hamburg, 1948.

————. "Reden und Schriften." Vol. II of Arno Scholz and Walther G. Oschilewski, eds., Turmwächter der Demokratie. Berlin, 1953.

————. "Referat." Lecture delivered in Hannover on May 6, 1945. Unpublished. Summarized in Wesemann, pp. 61–75.

————. Die Sozialdemokratie im neuen Deutschland. Hamburg, 1946.

————. "Die Sozialdemokratie in der Bundesrepublik." August 18, 1949. Manuscript in Pers. Archiv, S.P.D., Bonn.

————. Was wollen die Sozialdemokraten. N.p., 1946.

————. Zweimal Deutschland. N.p., 1948.

Severing, Carl. Mein Lebensweg. 2 vols. Cologne, 1950.

Shapiro, David. "Aspects of Obsessive-Compulsive Style," Psychiatry, XV (1962), 46–59.

Siemann, Joachim. "Der sozialdemokratische Arbeiterführer in der Zeit der Weimarer Republik." Unpublished dissertation, Göttingen, 1955.

Smith, Brewster, Jerome S. Brunner, and Robert W. White. Opinions and Personality. New York, 1956.

[S.P.D.] Sozialdemokratische Partei Deutschlands. Aktionsprogramm 1952. Bonn, 1952. An English translation, Action Program of the Social Democratic Party of Germany, was published by the S.P.D. in 1952.

————. Das Heidelberger Programm. Printed in Protokoll des Sozialdemokratischen Parteitages, 1925, in Heidelberg. Berlin, 1925.

————. Protokoll der Verhandlungen des Parteitages. Magdeburg 1929, Hannover 1946, Nuremberg 1947, Düsseldorf 1948, Hamburg 1950, Dortmund 1952.

————. Sopade. Informationsdienst, 1947–52.

————. 8 Jahre sozialdemokratischer Kampf um Einheit, Frieden, und Freiheit. Bonn, 1954.

————, Executive Committee [Vorstand der S.P.D.]. Jahrbuch der Sozialdemokratischen Partei Deutschlands, 1946, 1947, 1948–49, 1950–51, 1952–53.

————, ————. Kurt Schumacher. Bonn, 1952.

————, ————. "Material zu den Verhandlungen zwischen dem Zentralausschuss und den Vertretern der K.P.D. über die Einheit der deutschen Arbeiterbewegung." London, 1946. Hectograph.

————, ————. News from Germany. English-language newsletter.

————, ————. "Die Wiedergeburt der deutschen Sozialdemokratie." London, 1945. Hectograph.

————, Württemberg-Hohenzollern. Bericht des Landesvorstandes für die Zeit vom 1. Januar bis 31. Dezember 1929.

————, ————. Protokoll über die Verhandlungen des Bezirksparteitages, 1928.

Stampfer, Friedrich. Die ersten vierzehn Jahre der deutschen Republik. Carlsbad, 1936.

Stanton, Alfred H., and Stewart E. Perry, eds. Personality and Political Crisis. Glencoe, Ill., 1951.

Stemmler, Johannes. "Führertypen," Kölner Zeitschrift für Soziologie, VI (1953/54), 333–62.

Thayer, Charles W. The Unquiet Germans. New York, 1957.
"Tiger, Burning Bright," *Time,* June 9, 1952, pp. 30–35.
Turm. See Scholz, Arno, and Walther G. Oschilewski, eds.
Uhlig, A. W. Hat die S.P.D. noch eine Chance? Munich, 1956.
United States, Department of State. Germany 1947–1949: The Story in Documents. Washington, D.C., 1950.
———, Department of State. Office of Intelligence Research. West German Attitudes on Selected National and International Issues, Series 3, No. 96 (July 15, 1952).
———, Office of Military Government for Germany. *See* O.M.G.U.S
———, Office of the High Commissioner for Germany. *See* Office.
———, Office of the U.S. Secretary. *See* Office.
Vaughn, Elizabeth H. Community under Stress. Princeton, 1949.
Verba, Sidney. Small Groups and Political Behavior. Princeton, 1961.
———. "Assumptions of Rationality and Non-Rationality in Models of the International System," *World Politics,* XIV (1961), 93–117.
Von der Heydte, Friedrich August, and Karl Sacherl. Soziologie der deutschen Parteien. Munich, 1955.
Vorstand der Sozialdemokratischen Partei Deutschlands. *See* S.P.D., Executive Committee.
Wacker, Wolfgang. Der Bau des Panzerschiffes 'A' und der Reichstag. Tübingen, 1959.
Wagner, Klaus. "Der Cincinnatus von Bremen: Kleinsiedler und Senatspräsident Wilhelm Kaisen," *Frankfurter Allgemeine Zeitung,* January 23, 1960, p. 19.
Wahlke, John, *et al.* The Legislative System. New York and London, 1962.
Wahrhaftig, Samuel L. "Der Weg der Sozialdemokraten," *Frankfurter Hefte,* November 1952.
Weber, Max. Politik als Beruf. Munich and Leipzig, 1919.
———. The Theory of Social and Economic Organization. New York, 1947.
Wellmann, Thomas. "Die soziologische Lage der Bundesrepublik," *Deutsche Rundschau,* LXXIX (1953), 591–600.
Werth, Alexander. "German Social Democracy," *The Nation,* October 18, 1952, p. 354.
———. "German Report," *New Statesman and Nation,* October 11, 1952, p. 412.
———. "Schumacher Lives On," *New Statesman and Nation,* October 4, 1952, p. 370.
Wesemann, Fried. Kurt Schumacher: Ein Leben für Deutschland. Frankfurt, 1952.
Weymar, Paul. Adenauer: His Authorized Biography. New York, 1957.
White, Robert W. "Motivation Reconsidered: The Concept of Competence," *Psychological Review,* LXVI (1959), 297–333.
White, Theodore H. "Kurt Schumacher: The Will to Power," *The Reporter,* December 11, 1951, pp. 12–16.
Wieck, Georg. Die Entstehung der C.D.U. und die Wiedergründung des Zentrums in Jahre 1945. Düsseldorf, 1953.
Wildenmann, Rudolf. Partei und Fraktion: Ein Beitrag zur Analyse der politischen

Willensbildung und des Parteiensystems in der Bundesrepublik. Meisenheim, 1954.

Willis, F. Roy. The French in Germany, 1945–1949. Stanford, Calif., 1962.

Wirtschaftswissenschaftliches Institut der Gewerkschaften. Deutschland in Zahlen 1959. Cologne, 1951.

Wittkower, Eric D., and R. A. Cleghorn, eds. Recent Developments in Psychosomatic Medicine. Philadelphia, n.d.

Zink, Harold. The United States in Germany, 1944–1956. Princeton, 1957.

Index